Justin against Marcion

Justin against Marcion

Defining the Christian Philosophy

Andrew Hayes

Fortress Press
Minneapolis

JUSTIN AGAINST MARCION

Defining the Christian Philosophy

Copyright © 2017 Fortress Press. All rights reserved. Except for brief quotations in critical articles or reviews, no part of this book may be reproduced in any manner without prior written permission from the publisher. Email copyright@1517.media or write to Permissions, Fortress Press, PO Box 1209, Minneapolis, MN 55440-1209.

Cover design: Alisha Lofgren

Hardcover ISBN: 978-1-5064-2344-9

Paperback ISBN: 978-1-5064-2039-4

eBook ISBN: 978-1-5064-2040-0

The paper used in this publication meets the minimum requirements of American National Standard for Information Sciences — Permanence of Paper for Printed Library Materials, ANSI Z329.48-1984.

Manufactured in the U.S.A.

This book was produced using Pressbooks.com, and PDF rendering was done by PrinceXML.

Contents

	Preface	vii
	Abbreviations for Justin's Works	ix
	Introduction	xi
1.	Who Are the "Christians"?	1
	Persecution	*11*
	Greco-Roman Perspectives	*40*
	Teacher and Pupils	*60*
2.	Reading between the Lines: The Conspicuousness of Marcion in the *Dialogue*	89
	The Dialogue: Introduction and Commentary	*92*
	Repetition of Themes in the Dialogue	*141*
	Philosophies and "Christians"	*155*
	Conclusion	*161*
3.	Case by Case	163
	Introduction	*163*
	Politics	*164*
	Who Are the Atheists?	*177*
	Evidence of True Worship	*189*
	Different Teacher, Different Confession	*199*
	Conclusion	*216*
	Bibliography	*221*

Ancient Literature Index	*233*
Author Index	*235*

Preface

This book arose out my doctoral work at King's College, London, and there are a considerable number of people and groups to whom I owe my thanks for their help and support in its production. Financially, I owe much thanks to a number of trusts who supported my research in the form of grants: the Leverhulme Trust, the Hope Trust, the William Honeyman Gillespie Trust, the St Matthias Trust, and the King's College London Theological Trust. Without the generous support of these bodies this work would not have come to fruition. My gratitude must also go to my colleagues at the Queens Foundation, Birmingham, for their support and, in particular, the support of Librarian Michael Gale for his assistance over a number of years and his commitment to sustaining an excellent theological library resource in the West Midlands. I am grateful too for the support of staff at New College Library, University of Edinburgh, and those of the Institute of Classical Studies, University of London, the Maugham Library, King's College London, and the University of Birmingham's main library. I am grateful for my relationships with each of these institutions which have assisted my research greatly.

Thanks are also due to friends and advisors in the Rev. Matthew Tomlinson, the Rev. Dr. Sam Ewell, Emma Worthington, Helen Stanton, and Joan Cape for their encouragement and assistance at various stages of this work. I am indebted also to those who have taught me as an undergraduate and as a graduate and inspired my path to become a theological educator. Such people represent a number of theological disciplines but each have contributed a great deal to me and deserve special thanks: Paul Parvis, Sara Parvis, Paul Foster, Nicholas Adams, John McDowell, David Fergusson, and Fergus Kerr, O.P. I also owe a considerable debt of gratitude to Markus Vinzent for supervising the doctoral dissertation on which this work is based and who encouraged, praised, and critiqued it in constructive ways. In regard to publication I am very grateful for the patience and hard work of Neil Elliott of Fortress Press and all those at 1517 Media who have helped to make this book a reality.

Finally, a great debt of thanks is due to close friends who have helped and supported in many ways. The support of all these people and institutions has been essential to bringing this book to fruition.

A word about the text that follows. Throughout these pages, I have not capitalized the word *god*. This is in order to avoid confusion when Marcion's god and the god of the Jews are under discussion and to avoid prejudicing the nature of their debate about who and what the latter god is.

Andrew David Robin Hayes
The Queen's Foundation, Birmingham

Abbreviations for Justin's Works

1 Apology   The First Apology
2 Apology   The Second Apology
Dialogue   The Dialogue with Trypho the Jew

The English and Greek presented for the *Apologies* come from the Minns and Parvis edition (2009) unless otherwise stated as my own. The Greek for the *Dialogue* comes from the Bobichon (2003) edition and the English from Slusser's edition of the Falls translation (2003) unless otherwise stated as my own.

Introduction

As far back as 1977, Jon Nilson wrote:

> Increasing awareness of these contacts [between Jews and Christians] has prompted a new appreciation of Judaism as a forceful influence upon the evolution of early Christianity. Despite the disappointing paucity of certitudes, a more accurate grasp of the Sitz im Leben of much early Christian literature is emerging. This creates the possibility that hitherto familiar documents might be read in a new light and so take on a renewed utility in the effort to understand the historical and theological dimensions of the development of early Christianity.[1]

Forty years on, new and revealing ways of reading the familiar documents of early Christianity are still being found. The most recent development has been the confluence of early Judaism, New Testament, and Patristic scholarship working together to learn from one another and better map the emergence of both Christianity and Judaism. Even the terms are unhelpfully polarising in this period, as we have come to know them. In this context this work cannot help but be influenced by some of the key scholars and works within the relevant body of literature. It shares the aim for a clearer understanding of the early Christian period. It does this by considering Justin Martyr's relationship with or to the arch-heretic Marcion.

Why Justin? Because Justin is one of our earliest witnesses, the first to attempt to advise the rulers as to the merits of Christianity, and the first to deal explicitly with Marcion. As Sara Parvis and Paul Foster

---

1. Jon Nilson, "To Whom is Justin's *Dialogue with Trypho* Addressed?," *TS* 38 (1977), 538.

note, Justin "is a veritable mine of information about mid-second century Christian and even Jewish and Roman theology, attitudes and practices."[2] It is well known that Justin commented on Marcion in his *First Apology*, but it is my contention that Marcion is relevant to a great deal more of Justin's work than the few mentions that are obvious. I will argue that Justin is concerned in a great deal of what he says with the spectre of Marcion, and that much of what he says makes more sense against the background of an influential Marcionite theology. The core thesis is that Justin's approach to theology is deeply, although not wholly, motivated by an effort to distinguish true "Christianity" from the Marcionite tradition, at a time when the two are not easily distinguishable. Many of the distinctions that come to be recognised are the fruits of Justin's labor.

I will not argue for any greater achievements on Marcion's part than the traditional claims. The relationship of Marcion to the canon is not a topic Justin discusses, and neither will I do so. Justin is my primary concern, and so, I assume, the portrayal of Marcion as told by Justin and Irenaeus, the other witness in close proximity to him, is relatively accurate, although always in need of careful critical analysis. Below I will sketch the picture of Marcion that will provide the background for my argumentation throughout. The main aim is to explore what Christian identity is for Justin and the way in his views are to some extent a response to the crisis Marcion represents. Justin's Christian identity takes a more definitive shape because of the threat Marcion presents. As Reed has put it:

> When we examine these works together [the *Dialogue* and the *Apologies*], the contours of a wider project begin to emerge. Polemical and apologetic concerns may occasion each of his works, but in the process Justin begins to articulate a distinctly Christian identity, the borders of which are defined against three different categories of "others": pagans, Jews, and heretics.[3]

---

2. S. Parvis and P. Foster, "Introduction: Justin Martyr and His Worlds," in *Justin Martyr and His Worlds*, ed. Sara Parvis and Paul Foster (Minneapolis: Fortress, 2007), 1.
3. Annette Yoshiko Reed, "The Trickery of the Fallen Angels and Demonic Mimesis of the Divine: Aetiology, Demonology, and Polemics in the Writings of Justin Martyr," *JECS* 12 (2004): 154.

Nilson, quoted above, saw clearly that new insights and understandings concerning Jewish–Christian relations transformed familiar texts, opened much to question, making the texts new again in a sense. This process has only accelerated in the forty years since he wrote. It is the development of deeper understanding of the *Sitz im Leben* of Justin's writings that makes possible my demonstration here: that it is Justin in the mid-second century who rises to the political challenge of being on the fringes of the Jewish community, but not obviously or necessarily part of it and its protections, while at the same time being linked with Christians who follow Marcion and seek to drag other Christians away from this same community. The way Justin attempts to deal with these challenges is to define and make known what it is to be Christian. Specifically, he addresses the relationship between Christians and Israel and its god and considers the ways Christianity is both within and without that community. In doing so, prompted by the attempts of Marcion to pull Christians out of the Jewish community, Justin forms a distinctive and clear Christian identity for the first time. It goes without saying that this process does not end with Justin, and nor does engagement and argument with Marcionism: both continue for many centuries. Nonetheless, Justin takes the first steps, and those who contribute to the task after him (Irenaeus and Tertullian initially) are in his debt.

Chapter 1 will introduce Justin's texts as intimately bound to the question of Christian identity. Specifically, they are exercises in defining what it is to follow Jesus when there was no clear answer to this question. Marcion represents the strongest, although not the only, alternative proposal for what it is to follow Christ. Before progressing to the relevance of Marcion, however, the first chapter will set the scene for the simultaneously Jewish and Greco-Roman "religio-political" world they both inhabit.

On this last point, chapter 1 will proceed to demonstrate how there is no way of explaining what a Christian is at this stage without some reference to Judaism; even Marcion's theology is definitively shaped by the Jewish tradition. It is not clear if Christians are distinguished from

Jews by the Romans, nor is it clear that they seek to transcend ethno-racial Jewish ties. The Jewish story is an essential one for the Christian story. Justin's tales of Jewish persecution of Christians, which we can assume hold some truth, nonetheless rhetorically recast Christians as the genuine exponents of the Jewish tradition, as the true Israel.

Once we have established the irreducible relevance and complexity of the Christian relation to Judaism, chapter 2 will go on to consider the particular use of the term "Christian" in Justin's texts and what it reveals about who or what Christians are. At this time, Christian is a shame name, mainly used by others to describe the followers of Jesus. The application of this term is itself evidence of perceived dishonor. This is slowly changing as Christians like Justin claim the term for themselves, in a similar manner to which members of ethnic minority groups sometimes adopt and invert the meaning of derogatory names for their group. Furthermore, beyond the derogatory tone of this term, it is largely devoid of meaning when used by non-Christians, as precisely who and what Christians are and do is not clear to them. What is most important, however, is that this usage indicates the dynamic that motivates Justin's text: to clarify and define what it means to be Christian. The nature of this project entails that there can be only one, or only one centrally agreed, understanding of this and thus we find the beginnings of the making of Orthodoxy. In defining and clarifying what a Christian is, Justin cannot allow beliefs that contradict the true understanding of who Christ is, such as those of Marcion, to stand.

In order to make this clear, chapter 2 will draw attention to how Justin defines what it is to follow Christ, that is, what it is to be a pupil of his philosophy, as opposed to other philosophies, doctrines, and teachers. Only those who follow Christ and his own teaching directly can be thought of as Christians. This entails some central Christian dogma, which Marcion would find repugnant. By framing the debate thus, Justin is able to expose Marcion as a follower of his own doctrines, rather than those of Christ, whatever he and his followers claim. The central question then is one of Christian identity: who has the right to be called Christian and what does this mean? This is what Justin is trying to deal with in the *Dialogue with Trypho the Jew* (*Dialogue*) and the *First Apology* (*1 Apology*). This endeavour necessarily involves Marcion and does so beyond the few places Marcion is specifically mentioned in these texts. Rather, the whole structure of Justin's project is designed to rule out Marcion and others like him. Philosophy is an immensely powerful analogy for Justin because it is readily understood by all in the Greco-Roman world and draws attention to the lineage of teaching, which is precisely what Justin wants to secure for his group and expose its lack as a failing in others. The conclusion drawn in this section is that Justin displays evidence for a highly disputed and emerging "Christianity" that, being so diverse, cannot be understood by Romans. This is the heart of Justin's philosophy, to define and establish the true Christianity and rule out pretenders, rather than to mollify or convert the Greco-Roman authorities.

Chapter 2 continues to examine this theme, this time with detailed examination of the *Dialogue*. This chapter focuses on the *Dialogue* and draws out the significance of Justin's presentation of the following of Christ as philosophy. The first half of chapter 2 builds on van Winden, who successfully challenged the notion that the early, "philosophical" part of the *Dialogue* is at odds with the rest of the piece. The eleven chapters are taken to constitute an introduction to the whole piece, establishing the major themes that will occur in the rest of the discussion. These themes, it will be argued, which are presented by Justin in the form of a philosophical debate with a great Christian teacher, are noticeably contra-Marcionite. The opening section lays down a series of markers for what Justin, and Christians, deny or do not deny. The crucial point about this section is that Trypho and his friends do not know Justin is a Christian until late in this section. They think of him as a philosopher and listen without prejudice. Only once they have discovered he is a Christian can the piece segue into the rest of the discussion about the claims of Christians and the interpretation of Scripture. Yet Justin never ceases to see himself as philosopher; he sees himself as a representative of the teaching of Christ. This understanding was outlined initially in the philosophical introduction, and the themes and teachings outlined there continue to run through the whole course of the debate between Justin and Trypho. The second half of the chapter traces these themes (particularly the number of gods, providence, justice, and righteousness, and prophecy) as they reappear at various points in the text and considers the ways they are suggestive of a contra-Marcionite agenda. The second part of chapter 3 concludes with analyses of two sections of the *Dialogue* with clear relevance to Marcion: 35 and 80. These two sections are where Justin draws out the function of philosophy established in his introduction and uses it to rule out those who claim to be Christians, but do not share the true Christian teaching that he has from Christ. Marcion or Marcionites cannot be considered the only group to whom this material is germane, but it will be argued that several features suggest that Marcion is foremost in Justin's mind. Chapter 2 concludes that philosophy is central for Justin because it upholds standards and regulates dissemination of teaching, which is precisely what Justin is trying to achieve in clarifying what it is to be Christian and who can be considered Christian.

Chapter 3 turns attention to the *Apologies* (mainly *1 Apology*). Justin's *1 Apology* is ostensibly an appeal to the rulers to end the persecution of Christians. Jews and Judaism feature much less in this text and the tone is more judicious and political. This chapter will argue that while *1 Apology* appears to be an appeal to the rulers to stop the persecution of Christians, it is not a stable form of apologetics from a settled Christian position but is rather, as with the *Dialogue*, a claim for what and who is Christian. It is only a slight exaggeration to say that Justin is not looking to stop persecution from the rulers in this piece, but only to clarify who ought to be punished as a Christian and who ought to be punished as something else. Despite the different form of the piece, *1 Apology* is no less than the *Dialogue* a part of an attempt to define and clarify what it means to follow Christ (and to exclude Marcion from this).[4] To this end, Justin is appealing to the rulers to put Christians

---

4. The relationship of *2 Apol* to *1 Apol* is longstanding vexation. There are numerous advantages

under more scrutiny not less, for them to be subject to more probing investigation rather than to be left alone to worship their god in peace. The reason for this is that the probing investigation, which will examine who is Christian on the grounds Justin himself suggests, will vindicate Justin's Christianity at the expense of the also popular Marcionite movement. For example, the criteria Justin lays down for the authentic way of Christ is defended against atheism and demonology. This exposes Marcionites to these charges because the defence Justin adopts would be untenable within a Marcionite theology. Furthermore, Justin presents Christians as reliable and dutiful citizens. His predicates for this are assuredly Judeo-Christian, mainly adherence to and worship of the omnipotent and just one true god. By implication, this excludes Marcionites since they do not worship this god, and thereby suggests they are less than good citizens.

The final third of Chapter 3 returns to the theme of recognised teaching. No less in *1 Apology* than in the *Dialogue* does Justin emphasize the importance of the source of one's doctrines, which for him must be Christ and the prophets. It will be shown that he expends a great amount of energy in *1 Apology* to demonstrate this. In doing so, he aims to expose Marcion and his followers as teaching something other than the way of Christ or divine philosophy, and thus demonstrate that they

---

to seeing them as comprising one text, two texts and one and half texts. Recently Minns and Parvis proposed a hypotheses which envisages *2 Apol* as closely related to *1 Apol* but distinct in the form of working notes which came to be separated, they call this the *"cutting-room floor"* theory. This, one of two theories they present, though by no means faultless has the advantage of accounting for intertextuality (including the contextually incongruous appearances of the prophets, who foretold Christ, who are thoroughly introduced in Justin's other texts leaving nothing to the readers' prior knowledge) whilst granting difference of tone and style on account of their different literary reality of each. Thorsteinsson has responded to this with a renewed case for the two-text solution. His position more directly accounts for tonal differences and the absence of scriptural referents in *2 Apol*. However the *"cutting-room floor"* theory accounts for the later by in effect suggesting these references were too important to be left out whilst qualifying the references to the prophets in *2 Apol*, since scripture and the prophets cannot be separated for Justin. Ultimately neither explanation enjoys total supremacy but the *"cutting-room floor"* theory accounts for both difference and similarity better in my view. I will move from *1 Apol* to *2 Apol* relatively freely considering them as part of common project if not precisely the same text. See Denis Minns and Paul Parvis, *Justin, Philosopher and Martyr: Apologies, Introduction, Translation and Commentary* (OECT; Oxford: Oxford University Press, 2009), 26. And R. M. Thorsteinsson, "The Literary Genre and Purpose of Justin's Second Apology: A Critical Review with Insights from Ancient Epistolography," *HThR* 105 (2012). Also for a recent defense of the one-text position see Lorraine Buck, "Justin Martyr's Apologies: Their Number, Destination and Form," *JTS* 54 (2003): 45-59.

are not Christians and should be punished as non-Christians. Chapter 3 makes clear that Justin places Marcion not only outside of the Christian philosophy, but into the tutelage or possession of the demons. The demons offer a metanarrative for all that conceals truth and is evil, and Justin places Marcion right in the centre of this. By doing so, he identifies Marcion as the clear and present contemporary danger: not only not Christian, but in fact anti-Christian. In this way, Marcion is part of the wider story which includes earlier "heretics" (as they would come to be known) and future ones.

Marcion is not the overt subject of Justin's work, but clarification of what is genuinely Christian is one of the main thrusts and it is this which pushes contra-Marcionite claims to the fore. Therefore, before proceeding to chapter 1 and the main argument, it is necessary to offer an account of Marcion's beliefs as recent scholarship has defined them so as they can be identified accurately in Justin's text. Therefore the following section will offer a prelude by way of a short sketch of the Marcion to whom Justin was reacting.

Whose Marcion?

Before we begin an investigation into the influence or relevance of Marcion as background to much of what Justin had to say about defining a "true Christian," we must pay attention to the question of whose Marcion we are talking about. That is, we have a number of witnesses to him whose claims are not always transparent or in agreement. Furthermore, we have a series of early fathers with a polemical purpose, whose testimonies must be taken seriously, but critically. These include famous figures such as Clement of Alexandria and Origen as well as Hippolytus, Epiphanius of Salamis, and anonymous writers such as the author of the *Refutation of All Heresies*. These accounts build on earlier accounts, glossing, generalizing, and sometimes augmenting them. Together such accounts come to represent a more or less agreed tradition of what is "known" about Marcion.[5] The main exponents for our Marcionite background will be Justin himself, Irenaeus as another early commentator and potential pupil of Justin, and Tertullian who gives the fullest account within relatively close proximity of time. These also need to be viewed critically yet will help us to establish some basic early claims about Marcion that are pertinent to his wider project and writings.[6]

In the field of modern scholarship, the name of Adolf von Harnack stands above all others for defining who Marcion was. His strong claim was that "Marcion, in all probability, was the first to conceive and, and in great measure to realise the idea of placing Christendom on the firm foundation of a definite theory of what is Christian."[7] In recent years (as well as at the time of his own writing), however, von Harnack's Marcion has attracted criticism and review. Sebastian Moll has presented an important recent portrait, and Markus Vinzent has also been engaged with understanding who Marcion was.[8] Most recently, Judith Lieu has provided a comprehensive account which closely examines the variations and sources of the "constructed Marcions" from within the apologetic and polemical tradition of the early church. In addition to these, Dieter Roth's reconstruction of Marcion's gospel attempts to correct certain methodological weaknesses in Harnack's interaction which condition his picture of Marcion with his own bias.[9]

This book aims to demonstrate that Marcion features in Justin's texts as more than an occasional heretical nuisance character. Rather in a subtle manner, he helps to shape much of Justin's project as a whole. I will not offer a comprehensive representation of Marcion and his work since that work has been effectively done by others. Rather this chapter will lay out a sufficient working understanding of Marcion's beliefs that seems reasonable from the primary source material and recent secondary engagement with the subject. It is not exhaustive, but sufficient for understanding the context and theology of a man who

---

5. Judith Lieu, *Marcion and the Marking of a Heretic: God and Scripture in the Second Century* (Cambridge, UK: Cambridge University Press, 2015), 9.
6. The work of thoroughly reassessing the various traditions and accretions about Marcion over time has recently been executed by Judith Lieu. Her recent *Marcion and the Marking of a Heretic* sets out in detail the relationships between earlier and later claims and the agendas in play.
7. Adolf Von Harnack, *History of Dogma*, vol. 1, trans. Neil Buchanan (Boston: Roberts, 1895), 279.
8. Sebastian Moll, *The Arch-Heretic Marcion* (Tübingen: Mohr Siebeck, 2010); Markus Vinzent, *Marcion and the Dating of the Synoptic Gospels*, Studia Patristica Supplements 2 (Leuven: Peeters, 2014).
9. Dieter T. Roth, *The Text of Marcion's Gospel* (Leiden: Brill, 2015), 25-28.

was a successful evangelist, whose theology was considered the most dangerous of contemporary theologies as it continued to be engaged with by church fathers for centuries after his death. The number of engagements, as well as their length, is testament itself to his importance in the early patristic period.[10] Adolf von Harnack took Marcion very seriously and sought to show the true Marcion behind all the polemical renderings.

Understanding what Marcion believed, as much as the sources allow us to, is essential to this attempt. That said, there are issues relating to Marcion that I will not attempt to elucidate. Sebastian Moll, at the beginning of his excellent book on Marcion, identifies two levels of portrait about Marcion. The first of these is Marcion himself and his relation to his world and time. The second is his relationship to the development of the New Testament, as we know it. My argument requires an interest in the first of these but not the second. It matters greatly what Marcion believed, because traces of this are what I believe motivated and drove much of what Justin says in his texts as a form of indirect refutation. His relationship to the formation of the New Testament is not an irrelevant question, but represents a separate project, which is outside the bounds of my work here.[11] My argument can proceed quite normally, simply on the understanding that Marcion had a distinctive understanding of the New Testament Scriptures without pushing this question any further.[12]

Why Marcion, then, and not Valentinus or Basilides? After all, the followers of Valentinus and Basilides, both of whose teachings are harder to reconstruct than Marcion's, are mentioned along with Marcionites in *Dial.* 35.6. There is therefore a question over the extent

---

10. Dieter T. Roth, "Marcion and Marcionites," in *The Encyclopedia of Ancient History*, ed. Roger S. Bagnall et al. (Oxford: Wiley-Blackwell, 2012), n.p., online at http://onlinelibrary.wiley.com/doi/10.1002/9781444338386.wbeah05110/pdf.
11. Questions in this area have recently come to the fore once more and are being intensely debated by contemporary scholars, yet no firm consensus has emerged hitherto. See Dieter T. Roth, "Marcion's Gospel and Luke: The History of Research in Current Debate," *JBL* (2008): 513–27; Roth, "Marcion's Gospel: Relevance, Contested Issues, Reconstruction," *ExpTim* (2010): 287–94; and Markus Vinzent, *Dating of the Synoptic Gospels* (Leuven: Peeters, 2014), 15.
12. To explore this issue in its own right and in detail, Roth's recent reconstruction of Marcion's gospel examines the major issues and presents the text. See Roth, *Marcion's Gospel*.

INTRODUCTION

to which the arguments Justin makes have particular reference to Marcion and his followers as opposed to other heretical groups. However, even if some of his arguments can be applied to other groups, my argument will be that Justin's texts nonetheless read as if the danger presented by Marcionite theology has particular import that other "heresies" do not.[13] Relating to this kind of difficulty, Moll has said: "When Origen explains the allegorical meaning of the battles of Joshua for instance, he explicitly addresses Marcion, Valentinus and Basilides. Thus, these other heretics could also be envisaged in the elder's preaching."[14] Moll here is pointing out the difficulty of isolating theological views at this time, although here he is particularly concerned with the case of entirely unnamed heresies in an Irenaean text. Although I will argue that points made by Justin, which have not usually been discussed as part of a wider contra-Marcionite project by Justin, are evocative of Marcion, I acknowledge the possibility that other heretical groups named by Justin may share in parts.

Though their followers are mentioned in *Dial.* 35.6 (as are Marcionites), these two Gnostics do not feature personally in *1 Apol.* 26 or 58, where Marcion himself appears as the successor to previous heretical leaders (Simon Magus and Menander). Marcion not only appears more often, but as a contemporary of Justin;[15] he is a real and present danger. Furthermore, we know Justin wrote a text specifically to Marcion (πρὸς Μαρκίωνα). All of these points are suggestive of his particular relevance to Justin.[16] Furthermore, Marcion is also said by Justin to have influenced all peoples; there is no province where his teaching is not known,[17] and Marcionite "Christians" are known to

---

13. Charles E. Hill has argued similarly that the central arguments of the letter to Florinus, although not solely anti-Marcionite in argument, reveal an anti-Marcionite agenda. The thesis here is the same in relation to Justin. Although not all of his arguments can be specifically tied to Marcion, many are suggestive of Marcion and, more importantly, Marcion seems to form the background picture that provokes the response, which goes on to include other related heresies. See Charles E. Hill, *From the Lost Teaching of Polycarp: Identifying Irenaeus' Apostolic Presbyter and the Author of* Ad Diognetum (WUNT 186; Tübingen: Mohr Siebeck, 2006).
14. Moll, *Arch-Heretic*, 18.
15. Valentinus (100–160) would have also been a contemporary of Justin's but Justin does not name him as such as he does pointedly on two occasions concerning Marcion, but only his followers. Basilides could have been a contemporary but was probably dead (138 CE) by the time of Justin's conversion.
16. Vinzent, *Dating of the Gospels*, 29–34.

have formed the majority of "Christians" in Syria in the time of Justin and his student Tatian.[18] This is therefore a power and influence reserved only for Marcion among the heretics Justin mentions. As Lampe bluntly puts it: "One can conclude that Marcion in his lifetime undoubtedly surpassed all other heretics in effectiveness."[19] Also, it is salient to point out that the knowledge of, or of the primary engagement with, Valentinus and Basilides is dwarfed by that of Marcion. Marcion simply seems to be a bigger deal, and many of the particular arguments Justin makes to distinguish his group, the Christians, from the Marcionites, which I aim to present, do not seem to pertain to followers of Valentinus and Basilides as easily. That said, the influence of these other heretics cannot be discounted completely, and nor can Simon Magus, Menander (who appears for a quite particular reason which I demonstrate in chapter 3), and Cerdo (who does not appear, but the tradition closely associates him with Marcion as his teacher). However, in order to make this argument, it is important to be clear about what Marcion believed, so there can be clarity about issues that are particularly redolent of Marcion's specter and those who may be more widely applicable among heresies insofar as Justin knew them.

To begin this short but necessary explication, Sebastian Moll has a concise and helpful list concerning what Justin reports about Marcion:

1. He has many followers all around the world;
2. His followers revere him;
3. He believes in a god who did not create the universe and who is superior to the Demiurge;
4. He believes in a son of this superior god, who is not the Christ predicted by the prophets; and
5. His teaching is ἄλογος (irrational) and without ἀπόδειξις (proof).[20]

---

17. Peter Lampe, *From Paul to Valentinus* (Minneapolis: Fortress, 2003), 250.
18. Han Drijvers, "Syrian Christianity and Judaism," in *The Jews Among Pagans and Christians: In the Roman Empire*, ed. Judith Lieu, John North, and Tessa Rajak (London: Routledge, 1992), 130.
19. Lampe, *Paul*, 251.
20. Sebastian Moll, "Justin and the Pontic Wolf," in Parvis and Foster, eds., *Justin Martyr*, 149.

INTRODUCTION

Obviously this list concerns not only what Marcion believed as such, but also what Justin believed about Marcion's project. For current purposes, the most relevant of Moll's five points are points three, four, and five, because they identify key differences between Justin's and Marcion's theologies. Point three establishes Marcion's belief in another, hitherto unknown god. Point four's reference to the prophets should alert the reader to the distance between Justin and Marcion on the issue of prophecy and the god it comes from: the god of the Jews. This might seem obvious but it ought to be explicitly stated. Marcion's demiurge could in fact have been Platonic, or of almost any tradition other than Judaism. That he is not is significant. Just why Marcion is so opposed to this god has not been easy to establish. Bauer postulated that a hatred of the Jews was in part a motivating factor, but Moll has shown that there is no evidence for this.[21] "But what else could have made him believe that this evil deity, which he detests so much, was the god of the Jews? The answer is almost anticlimactic: because the Old Testament[22] says so."[23] Moll has correctly identified that Marcion had a strong aversion to the created order as such, and that he believed that the creator was the god of the Jews because this was what the Scriptures told him.[24] Marcion was an avowed biblicist and was probably brought up in a tradition that valued the Scriptures highly so it ought to be no surprise that this is the god he rejects.[25] If he came from an entirely different pagan tradition, it would certainly

---

21. Moll, *Arch-Heretic*, 60. Moll's argument is that while Marcion did not hate the Jews and respected the integrity of their tradition and the expectation of a messiah to come on the basis of prophecy, he was not positive about, or an advocate of, Judaism. For Marcion, their god is a deceiver and they are a trapped people. There is evidence to suggest that the Jews understandably responded to this by defending their traditions against Marcion. This suggests that his threat was not just to Christians, like Justin, but extended to non-Christian Jews also. See Judith Lieu, *Image and Reality: The Jews in the World of the Christians in the Second Century* (Edinburgh: T&T Clark, 1996), 265–70.
22. I call these texts the Old Testament because it is important to those who became the orthodox to defend the continuity and complementarity of the two 'testaments'. For Marcion they would be more like the Hebrew Scriptures in being part of another, quite separate, tradition from the revelation of Christ.
23. Moll, *Arch-Heretic*, 61.
24. J. B. Tyson has also come to the same conclusion. Joseph B. Tyson, "Anti-Judaism in Marcion and His Opponents," *SCJR* 1 (2005–2006): 201.
25. Moll believes it likely that Marcion was raised in a Christian home and carried over Christian patterns into his new Church. See S Moll, *Arch-Heretic*, 27. Harnack believed he was more likely to have been raised in a consciously Jewish community. See Adolf Von Harnack, *Marcion: The Gospel of the Alien God*, trans. J. E. Steely and L. D. Bierma (Durham, NC: Labyrinth, 1990), 15. Either way

seem arbitrary to pick on the god of the Jews. Marcion does not deny the existence of the god of the Jews, then, nor does he hate the Jews. Rather he believes in a superior god to whom Christ belongs rather than the creator god of the Scriptures. For him, the god of the Jews is the god of the Jews alone, and Christians are those who follow the Christ of the superior god.[26]

Point five is particularly important; For Justin, Marcion's teaching is without proof because prophecy is the criterion for evidence. Justin dedicates vast stretches of text to the prophets. Justification for this does not necessarily require attention to Marcion, but if the notion that one of Justin's main aims in his texts is to clarify and distinguish his theology and practice from the Marcionite alternatives, then the volume of this material takes on another dimension; so his project comes to be seen as careful exposition of the evidence from prophecy for the true theology over against the indemonstrable claims of Marcion.

Witnesses to Marcion after Justin are numerous and say a great deal more; but it would be unreasonable to assume that the above table represents all Justin knew of Marcion, at least because they lived in the same city where the population of "Christians" of any kind would not have been huge at the time and were known to dispute among themselves.[27] Philosophical disputes were a popular phenomenon in Greco-Roman cultural life at Rome and in other major imperial centres. Christian teachers such as Justin and Marcion are to be located within this wider Greco-Roman social context. The disputant context of this cultural form frames the projects of both men and eventually became a common pattern of Christian *paideia*.[28] Furthermore, they were educated Christians, hardly a common breed, and Marcion was at least a prominent leader, as Justin himself attests.[29] Even if Justin had not

---

the Old Testament Scriptures would have been central to his experience. Vinzent has recently revisited this issue. See Markus Vinzent, "Marcion the Jew," *JAAJ* 1 (2013): 159–201.

26. In *Marc.* 4.33,4, Tertullian asks how the Creator could be alien to the Pharisees when, as Marcion says, this god is "the particular god of the Jewish nation": *proprius deus Iudaicae gentis*.

27. Markus Vinzent, "Give and Take amongst Second Century Authors: The Ascension of Isaiah, the Epistle of the Apostles and Marcion of Sinope," *StPatr* 50 (2011): 126–29.

28. Lieu, *The Marking of a Heretic*, 303–4.

met Marcion personally, he would, however, surely have met quite a few first-phase Marcionites in a Christian community as small as Rome's in the early second century. We also know of at least one text, and potentially two, that Justin wrote where Marcion was the main topic. Furthermore, Irenaeus, who reveals a great deal about what Marcion believed, is well attested to have been familiar with Justin's texts and perhaps even a young member of Justin's own school.[30] This being the case, much of what Irenaeus knew of Marcion was most likely taught to him by Justin as well as his own experience, which would have been contemporary with Justin's also. Irenaeus is therefore also an important source in establishing what Marcion believed; as all who comment on Marcion will agree. The next nearest contemporary who wrote greatly on Marcion is Tertullian, without whose witness most studies on Marcion would prove impossible to sustain. By the time of Tertullian's *Against Marcion*, it is increasingly less certain what refers to Marcion himself and what refers to Marcionites. Nonetheless, Tertullian clearly had Marcion's writings[31] and thus has to be taken seriously, always remembering his polemical purpose, as a witness to what the man and his school believed.

The beliefs of Marcion that inform this reading of Marcion in Justin from Irenaeus and Tertullian include:

1. That the other son in whom Justin asserts Marcion believes is Jesus Christ; this is obviously what Justin has in mind when he speaks of those who claim to be Christians but are not, a group that at least includes Marcionites.[32]

---

29. Moll makes this point in relation to Ptolemy and Marcion's common acquaintance, but the same can be thought to apply here. See Moll, *Arch-Heretic*, 48.
30. Michael Slusser has argued for this directly and has support in this from John Behr. See Michael Slusser, "How Much Did Irenaeus Learn from Justin?," *Studia Patristica* 40 (2006): 515–20; and John Behr, trans., *St Irenaeus of Lyons, On the Apostolic Preaching* (PPS; Crestwood, NY: St. Vladimir's Seminary Press, 1997), 1–11.
31. However, it is an important qualification that there is some doubt as to when precisely in his career Tertullian gained direct access to Marcion's texts. It may well be that he did not possess these texts until quite late in his writing. See Lieu, *The Marking of a Heretic*, 53. Further to this it is important to remember that Tertullian, and other fathers who interacted with Marcion's texts, did so not to catalogue and preserve them for posterity but to refute them so what they present is they felt they need to make their case. Their witness therefore are not simply witnesses to his texts but to a tradition of interpretation. See Roth, *Marcion's Gospel*, 7.

2. That Marcion sees a radical separation between the Scriptures of the Jews and the New Testament; namely that they come from different gods and do not interact any way other than antithetically.[33]
3. That Marcion understands the god of the Jews to be a tyrannical judge in contrast to the welcoming superior god.[34]

The final point is particularly important to us because this is a topic upon which Justin expends a lot of time and energy. The precise nature of Marcion's view of the god of the Jews as a judge is not straightforward. Winrich Löhr has recently challenged the received (Harnackian) wisdom on this and his views must be taken into account, albeit briefly. The central issue here is that both Justin and Marcion agree that the god of the Jews is a judge, but disagree on how this is understood and the extent to which he can care for his creation while being a judge.[35] For Justin, the one god, providence, justice, and righteousness all go together in the only divine being. For Marcion, these characteristics are not virtues and his new divinity does not partake in them. The second issue, which is not isolated from the first, is Scripture or prophecy. This concerns the demonstration of the character of the one true god and who Jesus is. These are the main spheres of engagement, and they are by no means limited to the two chapters of *1 Apology* where Marcion is named, nor the appearance of Marcionites at *Dial.* 35.6. These topics divide Justin and Marcion and dominate much of the discussion Justin's *1 Apology* and the *Dialogue*.

The task of the rest of this chapter then is to explicate what we can know of Marcion's views on these two issues. In particular, it considers his understanding of the cruel, judgmental, uncaring god of the Jews, the relationship between his own higher god and Christ, and his approach to the Jewish Scriptures as antithetical material to the testimony of his *other* god.

---

32. See Irenaeus, *Haer.* 1.27.2.
33. Irenaeus, *Haer.* 1.27.2.
34. Irenaeus, *Haer.* 3.25.2-3, Tertullian, *Marc.* 1.25.2, 2.11.1.
35. Moll, *Arch-Heretic*, 62.

Marcion's Dualism

Although the earliest contemporary sources[36] describe Marcion's theology as dualistic, the precise nature of this dualism has come to be disputed.[37] It had been generally accepted, following the testimony of Harnack, that Marcion distinguished between a just god (the god of the Jews) and a good god (his supreme non-creator god). Löhr's engagement with the topic challenges this view. Specifically, Löhr believes that Marcion is more likely to have distinguished between a good god and an evil god rather than a good god and a just god, a designation that does not appear precisely until the work of Tertullian.[38]

Moll takes Ptolemy's *Letter to Flora* to identify and target a Marcionite position. The key quotation says: "For some say that it [the Law] was given by God the Father, while others turn the opposite way and insist that it was given by the adversary, the devil who causes perdition, just as they attribute to him the fashioning of the world, saying that he is the father and maker of the universe" (Epiphanes, *Pan.* 33.3.2 [P. R. Amidon]). Moll notes that a reference to the justice of the creator is conspicuous by its absence; the creator is plainly identified as evil alone in terms of characterization. More directly, Löhr brings forth from Irenaeus explicit evidence for Marcion's belief in the evil nature of the creator: "He [Marcion] uttered the impudent blasphemy that the God who was proclaimed by the law and the prophets was the author of evil, and desirous of war" (Irenaeus, *Haer.* 1.27.2 [D. J. Unger]). In 3.12.12 Irenaeus also calls him bad (*malus*) although in 3.25.2 the picture is complicated somewhat by the ascription of the distinction between the good and the judge: "Again, in order that they might take away from the Father the power of reproving and of judging, thinking that it is

---

36. These can be taken to include Ptolemy as well as Justin in Moll's scheme alongside Irenaeus and Rhodo as closest non-contemporary sources.
37. A tripartite system emerges later in the tradition but is not attested in the relevant period. See Moll, *Arch-Heretic*, 54.
38. Winrich Löhr, "Did Marcion Distinguish between a Just God and a Good God?," in *Marcion und seine kirchengeschichtliche Wirkung: Marcion and His Impact on Church History*, ed. Gerhard May, Katharina Greschat, and Martin Meiser (TU 150; Berlin: de Gruyter, 2002), 131–46.

unworthy of God, and believing they have found a god who is good and free from anger, they asserted that one god judges and the other saves" (Irenaeus, *Haer.* 3.25.2 [Rousseau 482]). This begins to sound again a little like the classic distinction between the just and the good god.

In *Haer.* 3.25.3, Irenaeus describes the former god mentioned above as judicial by saying there is one good god and one of the court (*alterum bonum et alterum iudicalem dicens*). Moll, however, points out that *iudicalem* not *iustum* is employed by Irenaeus here, and that in Greek judge (κρίτης) and just (δίκαιος) are not etymologically related.[39] Irenaeus could call this god a judge without implying he is a just or righteous judge. This description can mean more prosaically that there is a good god and a lower god who handles legal matters without the dense moral overtones of righteousness. Judgment itself, rather than judgment qualified by the adjective *righteous* or *just*, is the problem for Marcion that Irenaeus can be seen to describe. This is in fact exactly what Löhr thinks Irenaeus is trying to demonstrate: "A judge reprehends and shows anger—but not the true God. Marcion therefore allotted these characteristics of a judge to a different, lower god. If Irenaeus is right, Marcion did not so much distinguish between a just god and a good god as rather between a god who is a severe and angry judge and a good god."[40] So, rather than there being degrees or qualities of judgment, the concept itself is out of the question for Marcion when it comes to his supreme god; any god who practices judgment must be therefore a lower sort of god, and not the father of Jesus. As Harnack said, "Marcion proclaimed with a splendid assurance that the loving will of Jesus (and, that is, of God) does not judge, but comes to our aid, and he intends that nothing else at all be said of him."[41] In Irenaeus, then, we do not find convincing evidence that Marcion distinguished between a good god and just god but rather an angry or bad judge and a good god. If Ptolemy is accepted as witness, this is consistent with his view of Marcion having an evil god and a good god in mind. Tertullian ostensibly presents counterevidence that

---

39. Moll, *Arch-Heretic*, 50n13.
40. Ibid., 137.
41. Harnack, *Marcion*, 143.

Marcion believed in a good god and a just god when he appears to argue against interlocutors who confidently assert a good and a just god in book two of *Adversus Marcionem;* however, Löhr argues that things are not as they seem here either.

Löhr understands that Tertullian can be seen to have developed Irenaeus's critique, according to which Marcion was mistaken in his view that judicial emotions in the creator god were unpalatable and so to be denied in the father of Jesus Christ.[42] *Marc.* 1.25.2 is a key text here: "So our next subject of discussion rightly is whether a god is to be accounted such by virtue of goodness alone, to the exclusion of those other adjuncts, those feelings and affections, which the Marcionites deny to their god and attach to the Creator, but which we recognize in the Creator as no dishonour to God" (Tertullian, *Marc.* 1.25.2 [Evans]).[43] Tertullian introduces the discussion about what is proper to god and what is not, in contrast to Marcionites. As Löhr presents it, however, what Tertullian does not deny is that *justice* is an attribute of god; rather he denies that his god is not good in contrast to the Marcionite god. His main objection is to deny the attribution of cruel judgment to god:

> In II.11.1 Tertullian starts his argument by reminding his readers that for the Marcionites the creator is a severe and cruel judge. Tertullian first argues that the saevitia [severity] of the divine judge is something essentially secondary, a reaction to the Fall. God is primarily the good and benevolent creator. Then, as a second step, Tertullian wishes to demonstrate that justice and goodness belong together. God the creator is good and just right from the beginning: 'His goodness constructed the world, his justice regulated it'.... As a third step, Tertullian demonstrates that the justice and goodness of the one God do not only cooperate in creating the world but also in punishing evil men afterwards. Severity is not a problem for Tertullian then.... If one analyses Tertullian's argument more closely, it becomes quite clear that in this section of Book II he argues against a Marcionite position that wishes to distinguish the patient goodness of the highest god and father from the severity and cruelty of the second god, the creator, legislator and punishing judge.

---

42. Ibid., 138.
43. *Iam enim et hoc discuti par est, an deus de sola bonitate censendus sit, negates ceteris appendicibus, sensibus et affectibus, quos Marcionitae quidem a deo suo abigunt in creatorem, nos vero et agnoscimus in creatore ut deo dignos.*

> There is no indication whatsoever that Tertullian argues against a Marcionite distinction between a good god and a just god.... Even if Marcion had indeed designated the god of the Old Testament as 'just', it would have been only an abbreviation for his being a severe and cruel judge, a petty-minded and self-contradictory legislator ... not merely an invention but a later development in the school.[44]

All this being the case, Moll sums up the most important aspect quite succinctly:

> For even although it must be doubted that Marcion ever thought of the God of the Old Testament as just, he certainly saw him as a judge, and from what has been said about his role as Creator and Lawgiver so far, it can hardly be surprising that Marcion considered him to be a particularly cruel one. The Old Testament God created man as a compulsive transgressor, gave him the Law which he was too feeble to obey, and now judges him for his transgressions. Obviously this God is playing a very cruel game with his subjects.[45]

Marcion saw the god of the Jews as cruel and against his people; as limited and petulant. This is a stark contrast to the position of Justin and those like him in the claims they are compelled to make from Scripture about the universality of the creator god and agency of humankind.

Still it is important that we have carefully established that it is likely that Marcion distinguished between a good god and a god who was an evil and angry judge because this governs how we read the specter of Marcion in Justin's texts. The old distinction (between a good god and a just god) would have drawn attention to those moments where Justin calls god just, and seen these as indicative of a deliberate or necessary distinction from Marcion. Enrico Norelli makes a subtle argument that can preserve something of the former distinction between just and good, while at the same time acknowledging the evil nature of the creator god. Norelli does this by arguing that, for Marcion, the creator god is as much a victim of the law as his human subjects.[46] He is angry

---

44. Löhr, "Just God," 139, 144.
45. Moll, *Arch-Heretic*, 62.
46. Enrico Norelli, "Marcion: ein christlicher Philosoph oder ein Christ gegen die Philosophie?," in May, Greschat, and Meiser, eds., *Marcion and His Impact*, 118.

but not primarily so. Primarily, he is a rational god locked into a logic of transgression and repayment, which necessitates formal justice. To Marcion, however, formal justice can been seen as nothing but injustice and injustice as nothing but evil:[47]

> It is not possible for evil to be repaid, without at the same time repaying this justice, moreover: one must eliminate all justice grounded on the repayment principle, for all who repay evil with evil cannot escape the devilish logic of evil. Therefore Marcion rejects justice and judgement by the good God. This God is not only fully indifferent to any violation of the law of the creator, he sets absolutely no new law at all.[48]

This creator god has created and perpetuates evil by giving a law, which he himself cannot escape, that causes evil and suffering. Noting that Marcion saw the god of the Jews as the cause of evil and as involved in judgment means that where Justin argues contrary to this, especially to Trypho who should not need convincing that this is not so, there is potential to see Justin's points as constitutive of a counterargument against Marcion concerning god's mercy, providence, and sovereignty, even where Marcion is not directly under discussion in the text. Below, in chapter 2 chiefly, attention will be paid to the instances and overall flow of Justin's claims for god's goodness and judgment to assess the footprint of Marcion as an interlocutor.

Before moving on, we must also consider Marcion's distinctive perspective on the Jewish Scriptures, because only then can we understand just how much Justin's use is contrary to Marcion's.

Biblicism

Marcion was a biblicist. That is, his theology was informed by a very literal reading of the Old Testament texts.[49] Consequently, Marcion is not considered a philosopher or systematic theologian, rather more a

---
47. Norelli, "Marcion," 117.
48. Ibid., 119 (my translation): *Das Böse läßt sich unmöglich tilgen, ohne diese Gerechtigkeit zugleich zu tilgen, noch mehr: man muß jede auf dem Entlohnungsprinzip begründete Gerechtigkeit beseitigen, denn alles, was Böses mit Bösem vergilt, kann der teuflischen Logik der Bosheit nicht entfliehen. Deswegen schließt Marcion beim guten gott Gerechtigkeit und Gericht einfach aus, Diesem Gott ist nicht nur jegliche Übertretung des Gesetzes des Schöpfers völlig gleichgültig, er setzt überhaupt kein neues Gesetz.*
49. Moll, *Arch-Heretic*, 78.

"biblical theologian," who took for granted what the text reported.[50] In this regard, his attitude was uncritical and accepting. Marcion did not employ allegory in his interpretations and was suspicious of those who did. His approach in this regard drew the attention of Tertullian, who criticises him for it.[51] For the time, such a suspicion was very unusual, at least among Christians. That said, his contemporary and countryman Aquila,[52] took a similar literal approach to the Scriptures in his translation.[53] If Marcion's background were Jewish then a close relationship between the two might be relatively likely; but the fact of Marcion's attitude, in seeing the god of the Jews as a cruel tyrant, casts doubt that he could have a close relationship to an otherwise orthodox Jewish exegete. Therefore, it seems unlikely that the views of one man shaped the views of the other. Furthermore it does not seem to be the case that Marcion's opponents objected as such to his literal methodology. Moll has pointed out that although Marcion was very literal in his interpretations, this only seems to cause conflict with regards to the messianic prophecies with reference to Christ who has come. Tertullian, when countering Marcion's views on the creator, does not employ allegorical interpretation but argues that Marcion has misread what the text means in a simple sense. Neither does Justin argue allegorically for anything other than the messianic prophecies.[54] The rest, including the creator's character, he simply states in a way that is contrary to Marcion's understanding without exegeting it. The balance of understanding about the character of the god of the Jews is different between Justin and Marcion, but it is only with relevance to Christ's relationship to this god that the former is allegorical and the later introduces a new antithetical tradition.

It is important to note that Marcion does not reject or discredit the Old Testament as such. He does not assume or suggest interpolations or

---

50. Heikki Raisanen, *Marcion, Muhammad and the Mahatma: Exegetical Perspectives on the Encounter of Cultures and Faiths* (London: SCM, 1997), 65.
51. Tertullian, *Marc.* 2.21.2; 3.5:4; 3.12.1. In 3.6.2 and 7.1 Tertullian associates Marcion with Jews on account of the lack of willingness of both to understand the manner in which the prophecies speak of Christ. Origen also has strong words concerning Marcion's literalism in *Princ.* 2.5.2.
52. Indeed, they were from the same city.
53. Harnack, *Marcion*, 15.
54. Moll, *Arch-Heretic*, 81.

corruptions in the text but rather regards it as a trustworthy historical account of and for the Jews.[55] Indeed, far from rejecting it, the Old Testament is vital to Marcion's theological position as the antithesis of his other, good, god. It is for him "the book of the less-worthy Jewish god."[56] Despite what past scholars have maintained, it is neither the Old Testament nor the Jewish people that are rejected, but rather their god. He takes Scripture to be divinely inspired, accurate, and authoritative, and at the same time irrelevant for Christians.[57] This contrasts with his contemporary pagan philosopher Celsus who considered the entire tradition to be an invention and saw Christians and Jews as foolish.

The understanding Marcion had of the Old Testament is completely consistent with his theological position of two gods. Put simply, he believes the Old Testament to be a document, record, and prophecy of and for the Jews.[58] This is to be contrasted with the new covenant of Christ, which is from a different god and does not include the Jews. As Harnack has argued:

> Marcion wanted to free Christianity from the Old Testament, but the church preserved it. He did not forbid his followers to pick up the book but even recognized that it contained material that was useful for reading. But he saw in it a spirit different from that of the gospel, and he wanted nothing to do with two different spirits in religion.[59]

These spirits were so antithetical that one did not know the other; the prophets of the creator god did not and could not know and predict the Christ from Marcion's god.[60] It was essential to Marcion that the god of this covenant was completely unknown and hidden before Jesus appeared and revealed him.[61] In fact, not only was this Jesus unknown in the world; he, and his father the second god, were unknown to the creator god. Therefore, he was unable to prophesy about him in the

---

55. Raisanen, *Mahatma*, 67.
56. Harnack, *Marcion*, 138.
57. Tyson, "Anti-Judaism," 207.
58. Irenaeus, *Haer.* 4.34.1; 4.35.15.
59. Harnack, *Marcion*, 133.
60. Ibid., 67.
61. Tertullian, *Marc.* 1.2.3; 1.9.2.

Scriptures of his people. In this way, Marcion did not believe the Old Testament to predict Jesus.[62] Consequently, the Church for Marcion does not, and cannot, have any notion of being Israel or of being in relation to the god of the Jews, and cannot expect the prophecy of the Old Testament to have anything to do with them or their Christ.

To recap, Marcion believes:

1. In a god who did not create the universe and who is superior to the Demiurge;
2. That the god of the Jews is a cruel judge who toys with his own people;
3. In a son of the superior god, who is not the Christ predicted by the prophets;
4. That the Old Testament is accurate and complete for the Jews but that it does not concern Christians.

Anything in Justin's texts that denies any of these claims has the potential to be part of a project of differentiation and clarification concerning what is and is not Christian. Thus, when we find Justin's heavy insistences that there is only one god, the creator, that the Church is Israel, and that the prophets announce Jesus Christ Lord of all, we have to ask the question whether this is likely to have a particular relation to Marcion. The argument that follows will demonstrate that instances such as these coalesce to suggest Justin has Marcion in mind throughout far more of his work than has previously been noticed: not that he is targeting or attacking Marcion as such, but that he is trying to rule out positions that would count as Marcionite in the definition of what counts as Christian.

---

62. Harnack, *Marcion*, 79. See Tertullian, *Marc.* 3.1.2–3. Later in 4.36.11 Tertullian says that Marcion's Jesus was intent on destroying the law and the prophets; and Irenaeus had earlier confirmed Marcion's opposition to the prophets by reporting that the law and the prophets are null and void for Marcion (see Irenaeus, *Haer.* 1.27.2).

1

Who Are the "Christians"?

This chapter will demonstrate the provisional nature of Christian identity and argue that Justin attempts to usurp and correct the contemporary use of "Christian" as a shame name employed by non-Christians:

> A Christian? What's that? I can do no more than attempt to describe some phenomena; some of them may appeal to us, others may not. A quick glance at the early church, even if we break off very suddenly and very artificially in Theodosian times, will reveal that our question about "the Christian" is a question about diversity. . . . Let us confuse things still more: In addition to that kaleidoscope of perspectives—I do not call them objective perspectives because they are only internal to Christian historiography—there are further perspectives quite different from these internal ones. We can also meet a variety of external views, where the contemporaries of antiquity, whether they were Jews or so-called pagans, knew that certain individuals were Christians. I think they simply knew it from living in the same city or village, in the same street or insula-block. They knew it even though it did not normally interest them too much. . . . Diversity prevails even if the nomen Christianum and the unitas ecclesiae are not unknown but (as I would like to think) a common term for the surrounding world, at least if we follow the records of Roman administration and the fiction of Lucian.[1]

Although Wischmeyer ignores Justin and starts his study with Tertullian, this characterization of the challenge of early Christianity is extremely pertinent to this project. Specifically, "what" a Christian is, rather than simply who (and by extension who are Christians), is of paramount importance to Justin beyond a superficial reading of him as an apologist for apologetics' sake. Before one can know who counts as Christian one needs to know what a Christian is. Even if the name "Christian" is known and used, which Justin's presentation suggests it is, it is by no means clear that what a "Christian" is is understood either by non-Christians or indeed by the claimants of the term themselves.[2] This is Justin's challenge: to make it known, definitively, what a Christian is and to demonstrate the true Christianity, which he believes comes from Christ, the apostles, and the spirit of prophecy. This was, as mentioned above, the task that Harnack attributed to Marcion.[3] Both men were involved with and related to one another in the task of Christian identity-making and definition. The task of the historian and theologian is to reconstruct Justin's questions, the motivations that led him to shape his account of what it is to follow Christ in the ways in which he did. As R. M. Grant has noted, this cannot be done without giving due attention to the political and social struggles of the time. Justin's and other ancient texts are not theological vacuums but the products of precise circumstances, and it is these circumstances that require attention if the texts are to speak as intended.[4]

The political and social struggles of the time shape how and what Justin says. The social struggle is one of identity: who the Christians are (or who is Christian) is one of the central questions of all of Justin's

---

1. Wolfgang Wischmeyer, "A Christian? What's That?," *StPatr* 34 (2001): 270–72.
2. The term is uncommon in Christian usage before Justin. Grant surveys its use: It can be found in two New Testament texts (Acts 11:26; 26:28 and 1 Pet 4:16) and five times in the works of Ignatius, once in the *Didache* (12.4) and four times in the *Martyrdom of Polycarp*. However, Justin claims that there are many who claim the name "Christian," and in contrast to rare Christian textual usage, the term occurs frequently in Roman usage in those such as Pliny, Tacitus, Suetonius, and Lucian, suggesting that this was indeed so. See R. M. Grant, "A Woman of Rome: The Matron in Justin, *Apology* 2.1-9," *CH* (1985): 469.
3. Harnack, *History of Dogma*, 279.
4. R. M. Grant, *The Greek Apologists of the Second Century* (London: SCM, 1988), 10.

texts. In particular, are they "Jews,"⁵ or are they something else? Boyarin has also drawn attention to the issue of self-definition as a central plank of the *Dialogue* with particular reference to "Jews." However he has also noted that many of arguments Justin deploys against "Jews" and the identity claim can also be applied to heretics, as two sides of one coin, so a much wider debate about who the people of god are is discernible in the text.⁶ There is a political struggle that follows from this. If they are "Jews" then they are due a certain tolerance. However, "Jews" were particularly unpopular with the Roman rulers following the latest revolt lead by Simon Bar Kokhba, so very close association with the "Jewish" body politic may not have been desirable. This is a multi-dimensional question. The argument of this chapter will be that "Christian" identity has no fixed form in Justin's period and that this is one of the key issues that motivates and drives his addresses to non-"Christians." This involves the origins of "Christians" and their relationship to "Judaism." As Buell has argued, the distinction between these two groups was by no means obvious in this period and identity is always negotiable and open to revision according to particular needs:

> "The complex dynamism within and overlap between Christianness and Jewishness in Justin's rhetoric make sense if we think of the mid-second century as a time when these identities are neither uniform nor wholly distinct. Justin is staking out a distinct domain and meaning for Christianness when these are murky and contested."⁷

Staking a claim for "Christian" identity is indeed exactly what Justin is doing, but not only in relation to "Jews." His claims concern the

---

5. For reasons of good style and sense, the term "Jew" will be presented in quotation marks to highlight its provisional and ambiguous nature. The same will follow for the term "Christian," which we shall see below is also a less stable term than we might expect. This is done in order to make the word strange to ourselves and help us to keep in mind the disputed identity of "Christians," which we shall see is a central feature of the debate. "Jew" will be taken as referring to circumcised Hebrews like Trypho and his teachers. However, in chapter 2, where the *Dialogue* is the main focus, "interlocutors" or "Trypho's nation/people" will be preferred to reflect the specific ambiguity within that text.
6. Daniel Boyarin, *Border Lines: The Partition of Judaeo-Christianity* (Philadelphia: University of Pennsylvania Press, 2004), 38.
7. Denise Kimber Buell, *Why This New Race: Ethnic Reasoning in Early Christianity* (New York: Columbia University Press, 2005), 96.

wider Greco-Roman population also. The political implications of being "Jewish" or not, or being some other group in categories recognisable to Greco-Romans or not, were great. How one presented oneself and was understood could mean the difference between life and death. Presentation of identity is a subtle art, and one at which Justin was a master. Indeed, it was not just "Jews" and "Christians" who were engaged in deliberate, and unavoidable, self-presentation; Greeks and Romans were just as invested in this phenomenon:

> Most identifiable perceptions of ethnicity were not passive, erudite, or antiquarian but self-aware and aimed at being meaningful and convincing. In attempting a response to the question "Who is a Greek" [most ancient writers] would play with acceptable conventions, choosing to emphasize particular aspects or even invent new ones. Greek ethnicity appears to have been something that was always both traditional and negotiable.[8]

Something similar can be said of Romans, Egyptians, Lydians, and Aphrodisians: each has to "invent" themselves, or give an account of themselves, that reflects and creates, how they see themselves. Justin is presenting an account of what a "Christian" is but his account is not the only one. Consequently, he has to do so in such a way that is most credible to his audience and that undermines the credibility of alternative visions, particularly that of Marcion. That there are disputed claimants to Christ is the root of all the problems Justin is trying to address.

Central to my argument is the claim that the term "Christian" in the early to mid-second century is not an obvious marker of identity as we would take it to be in modern times, or as it became at least as early as the legalisation of "Christianity" after Constantine. K. H. Rengstorf in the *New International Dictionary of New Testament Theology* characterizes the term thus:

> The identification of the messiah with Jesus of Nazareth brought the disciples the name Christianoi. Compared with other names for the

---

8. Irad Malkin, *Ancient Perceptions of Greek Ethnicity* (Washington, DC: Centre for Hellenic Studies; Cambridge, MA: Harvard University Press, 2001), 6.

followers of Jesus, like disciple or believer, the word is quite rare in the NT. By its whole formation it is a word which defines the one to whom it is applied as belonging to the party of a certain Christos, very much as Herodianos is a technical term for the followers of Herod (Mk 3:6; 12:13; Matt 22:16). Its use also presupposes that for the Greek environment of developing Christianity Christos had taken on the meaning of a proper name, a process which would have been facilitated by the resemblance to the name of Chrestos, pronounced Christos. According to Acts 11:26, Christianos was first used for Christians in Syrian Antioch. This passage, like the two others in which the word occurs in the NT (Acts 26:28; 1 Pet 4:16), leads us to suppose that, being applied to Christians by outsiders, it contained an element of ridicule and that in this it did not differ from the description Nazarenos or Nazoraios. Like it and like many other names formed in the same way, it soon clearly became a name which those called by it felt honoured to bear.[9]

This definition, short as it necessarily is for its context, matches to some extent what we will find in Justin.[10] In agreement with Rengstorf, I argue that for Justin, the term "Christian" (Χριστιανός) functions very much like "Herodian" and that this is indeed the beginning of bearing this name as an honor. Beyond this, I argue that Justin has very particular motivations, both theological and political, for doing so.

The New Testament usage is, as Rengstorf states, extremely rare (two of three attestations coming from the same book) and should not be taken as representative of the experience of "Christians" everywhere within the empire. I agree that it functions as a term of ridicule primarily employed by outsiders. I will show that both Justin's texts and external Greco-Roman sources support this view and suggest that it has become, or is becoming, more widely known and used.

Comparison with the attribtution of the name Jesuit is instructive here. Jesuit, an anglicized version of the Latin *Jesuita*, originated as a pejorative term for members of the Society of Jesus and later came to be adopted by those members as a term that makes sense apart from the derogatory overtones. This is similar to the development of the term "Christian". However, difference can be seen in the fact that the

---

9. Karl Heinrich Rengstorf, "Χριστιανός (Christianos), Christian," in *The New International Dictionary of New Testament Theology*, ed. Colin Brown (Grand Rapids: Zondervan; Exeter, UK: Paternoster, 1975), 2:343.
10. In *2 Apology* Justin makes a pun precisely on the similarity between Christos and Chrestos.

Jesuits were not more or less loosely connected groups of Jesuits with different understandings of Ignatius Loyola's vision. The application of the term Jesuit, albeit as reproach, was to a clearly identifiable and self-organized society.[11] "Christians" in Justin's period have yet to fully become such an organization and the adoption of the term, transitioning from pejorative to honorific, is part of this slow and contested transformation.[12] That is, Justin is staking a claim for the identity of followers of Christ, staking a claim against alternative positions (of which Marcion's is the most significant for Justin's purposes), and taking this term along with it. Sebastian Moll has said, "His [Justin's] mission is to clear the Christian name."[13] Consequently apologetics in this period needs to be thought of as an attempt to create clarity and definition as much as, and probably more so than, defense and presentation of a defined faith.[14]

The "Christian" name that Justin is trying to clear is first and foremost the name of Jesus, the Christ, and only by extension is it the title of those who follow him. It is only becoming a proper title internally, and many who claim to follow Jesus and are considered "Christians" (not by Justin but by Romans and probably "Jews," and some other "Christians") abuse the name of Christ by their association with it. Buell points out that:

> Other texts studied as early Christian do not use the name "Christian," however, opting instead for other collective terms of self-identification

---

11. J. C. H. Aveling shows that the term Jesuit was that of an outsider's world view which the society usually rejected but gradually tolerated. For this, "their motive was partly practical convenience, and partly a sense that it would be fitting if they wore 'a badge of shame' as a 'badge of glory.'" Furthermore, the term predates the society and originated in the Netherlands and Rhineland for people who were overly zealous in their devotions in the name of Jesus and set themselves against the religious authorities and ordinary Catholics. The term "Jesuit" thus came to be applied to members of the Society of Jesus because this is how they behaved also. Both of these features present a striking similarity to the phenomenon I observe in Justin in relation to the name "Christian." See J. C. H. Aveling, *The Jesuits* (London: Blond & Briggs, 1981), 20.
12. The technical term for such transformation in linguistics is "semantic amelioration." See Rodica Calciu-Hanga, "Semantic change in the age of corpus Linguistics," *JHSS* 1 (2012): 50–52.
13. Moll, "Justin and the Pontic Wolf," 149.
14. A scholarly consensus has emerged on the provisional and rhetorical nature of all claims to Christian truth in this period: perspectives in general concert on this include the of voices Judith Lieu, Denise Kimber Buell, Laura Nasrallah, Karen L. King, Rebecca Lyman, and Shelly Matthews. However we should not forget that figures like Justin really believe they are presenting the faith of the apostles and see themselves as defending this faith.

(for example, the elect, Hebrews, etc.). This is worth noting since it suggests that the importance of the name "Christian" does not apply to every individual or group in the second and third centuries that might now be classified by scholars as "early Christian."[15]

Justin is right in the middle of this diversity of purpose and understanding. We shall see that Justin uses the term "Christian" in different ways at different points in his argument. We shall see examples of Justin speaking of "us Christians" (*Dial.* 78.10; 110.2) where he is claiming the identity in order to define it, but we shall also see that he often prefers to talk about Christ directly and about those taught by him or who follow his teaching. Furthermore, often Justin's use seems to reflect a pejorative label used by outsiders (such as Romans) or potential insiders who do not wish to be associated with this group (such as other "Jews"). In this way, the comparsion made with the term Jesuit is apt. Peter Tomson's work on the development of the term the term "Jew" (Ἰουδαῖος) in the Greco-Roman period is also instructive here. He sees it is a designation belonging primarily to non-"Jews."[16] He qualifies this saying:

> In every language, albeit to varying degrees, particular speech forms are used when addressing persons of either sex, of a specific age or of other social distinction. Speech differs according to the relative social status of speaker and listener. More specifically: such speech differentiation signals social identity. Naturally, group names such as ethnic appellations are strong signifiers of social identity. Speaking in these terms, "Jew" and "Israel" signal different social identities: an "outside" identity as a Jew in regard to the ancient world of nations, or alternatively, an "inside" identity as one belonging to the "people of Israel." ... An even closer parallel [than the distinction between "Dutch" and "Hollander" and similar] is found in the Gypsies. While their "outside" appellations are Gypsy, Bohemien, Gitano or Zigeuner, they call themselves Rom, and their "inside" language Romany.[17]

For Tomson, the term "Israel," as an internal designation, is to be

---

15. Buell, *New Race*, 195–96n94.
16. Peter J. Tomson, *If this be from Heaven: Jesus and the New Testament Authors in their Relationship to Judaism* (Sheffield: Sheffield Academic, 2001), 110.
17. Peter J. Tomson, "The Names Israel and Jew in Ancient Judaism and in the New Testament," *Bijdr* 47 (1986): 120–21.

contrasted with "Jew": the two names have distinct social functions. A "Jewish" speaker refers to "Jews" in speech addressing or quoting non-"Jews," but when communicating with fellow "Jews" calls them "Israel." It will be argued below that this is precisely what Justin is doing when he uses the term "Israel" to refer to "Christians" rather than to the ethnically uniform claimants to the title whom he calls "Jews."[18] Tomson argues that this distinction is well established and observable across all three of the major languages spoken by "Jews" in the Greco-Roman period and is thus not just a geo-linguistic variant.[19] In the context of an argument for the anachronistic nature of the scholarly term "Christian Judaism," Boyarin suggests something similar when he says "non-Christian Jews rarely (at best) called themselves Ioudaioi, and ... Christian Jews seemed to have used the term for someone other than themselves."[20] Boyarin does not draw out the specific parameters of what he means by "rarely, whereas Tomason goes further citing numerous examples of the term "Jew" as a term that projects an external objectivity onto the community across five categories in the Greco-Roman period, including influential figures close in time to Justin, for example in Philo and Josephus.[21] Margaret Williams, however, has argued that Tomson overstates the case because counterexamples can be found. Nonetheless, she recognises that Tomson has identified one of the legitimate "range of connotations" of a term not easily defined in the period.[22] Something

18. Ibid., 21. Naturally there is need to note that "inside" and "outside" speech always has a degree of rhetoric and intentional definition about it. With this proviso, however, Tomson's thesis, that "Jew" ceases to have territorial or linguistic association and comes to define an *ethnos* from an external perspective, makes much sense of what Justin, and other early "Christians", are doing in claiming the term "Israel" for Christ and arguing against the inheritance of Abraham κατα σάρκα.
19. Ibid., 127.
20. Daniel Boyarin, "Rethinking Jewish Christianity: An Argument for Dismantling a Dubious Category (to which is Appended a Correction of my *Border Lines*)," *JQR* 99 (2009): 32.
21. Further examples are taken from papyri, coins, inscriptions; hagiographa, apocrypha, and pseudepigrapha; Qumran, rabbinic literature, and the New Testament. Tomson, "Names," 129–39.
22. Margaret H. Williams, *Jews in a Graeco-Roman Environment* (Tübingen: Mohr Siebeck, 2013), 267–79. In fact one such counterexample might be detectable in *Dial.* 80.4, where Justin speaks of sects that Trypho would not recognize as genuinely "Jewish," so "Jew" functions as normative to sectarian *hairesis*. As far as Tomson's thesis is concerned however it would be noteworthy that Justin here is an outsider offering this term. Furthermore there is a doublespeak in the *Dialogue*, to which Boyarin draws attention, where Justin sometimes highlights not to a distinction between "Jew" and "Christian," but between "Jew" and "Jew" and "Christian" and "Christian." This may be one such instance where the analogy of *hairesis*/authenticity is more relevant than the

similar can be said of "Christian" in Justin's time: He does use the name in a way that suggest internal "Christian" identification but also in ways which suggest that it is a term whose meaning is supplied by outsiders and is primarily general and pejorative. Tacitus, in his report on Nero's fire (Annals 15.44.4), identifies "Christians" as "called Christians by the populace" (*vulgus Christianos appellabat*) rather than as "Christians," so the emphasis is on external application of the title.[23] Furthermore, we shall see that this pejorative usage frequently lacks any specific content concerning the practices and beliefs of these so-called "Christians"; that it can function as a criminal charge apart from any seemingly obvious criminal content is a scandalous facet of the messy identity confusion that Justin is trying to address. Buell, using the example of a contemporary of Justin engaged in a similar struggle in another part of the Empire, clearly and succinctly summarizes the issues:

> Athenagoras and other apologists give the appearance that accusations using the name "Christian" are scandalous and not sparked by anything but the name. Yet even if Christians might have been called to public attention for illegal deeds rather than by (or for) their name alone, Athenagoras and many other early Christian writers seek to gain recognition and rights as "Christians"; that is, the name is actually central to their aims.[24]

Regardless of how the name, and they themselves, come to be known, the task is, as Lieu says, to "reject the power of others to determine the meaning of the name."[25] Justin, and other like him such as Aristides, Athenagoras, and Theophilus of Antioch, mean to take control of this

---

"Jewish"/"Christian" identity debate. The present example occurs at a point in the *Dialogue* where Justin is reprising the arguments made in his philosophical introduction and again at *Dial.* 35 which have a particular and limited point to make (namely the difference between true teaching and sectarian imitations), whereas the *Verus Israel* language (of which Justin is the first attested source) is much more relevant to the later portions of the *Dialogue* where kinship and ancestry are brought to the fore. See Boyarin, *Border Lines*, 71.

23. H. Furneaux notes that the implication is strongly that "Christians" had not yet begun to call themselves such but were know as such popularly in Rome. H. Furneaux, *Annals of Tacitus* (Oxford: Clarendon, 1907), 374.
24. Buell, *New Race*, 55.
25. Judith Lieu, *Christian Identity in the Jewish and Graeco-Roman World* (Oxford: Oxford University Press, 2004), 267.

name in order to redefine it without changing its meaning entirely.[26] The aim is to gain rights and recognition: aims which can only be achieved where their identity can be seen to function, within tolerable limits, with coherent practices and beliefs. This is the beginning of the formal recognition of heresy and orthodoxy, where what really counts as genuinely "Christian" is being claimed and tested. Before moving the discussion on another important proviso is required. Having already noted that "Jew" ('Ιουδαίοις) is a complicated and loaded term when focusing on late antiquity, it is important to mark how Justin uses this term and how we shall employ it.

In the *Dialogue* Justin seldom uses the term at all. It occurs only six times in the space of four chapters.[27] This is perhaps because in the *Dialogue* Justin is articulating an internal debate and wishes to promote the idea that he is not discussing a group completely separate from his own. His argument in the *Dialogue* centres on the common project of the Hebrews and the "Christians" and so Israel ('Ισραήλ) is the preferred (and the more scriptural) term. Though Justin is highly critical of the customs practiced by "Jews" and their lack of recognition of Jesus, in his eyes the responsibility for these faults usually rests at the feet of their teachers, who form a category that we shall see is very important for Justin.[28] In this way, "Jews" are understood as erring brethren under the influence of the wrong teachers rather than a separate people, religion, or ethnicity.

In *1 Apology* Justin refers to "Jews" in a more external fashion with far greater frequency than he does in the *Dialogue*.[29] In *1 Apology* Justin is, ostensibly at least, addressing Greco-Roman pagans. As Tomson noted, "Jew" is in many ways their term, so Justin's use of it reflects to whom he is speaking and their understanding of whom he speaks about. Furthermore, perhaps because of this Justin mainly avoids the

---

26. Lieu, *Christian Identity*, 267.
27. *Dial.* 72.3 (twice); 77.3; 80.4 (twice); 103.3.
28. Timothy J. Horner, *Listening to Trypho: Justin Martyr's Dialogue Reconsidered* (Leuven: Peeters, 2001), 104.
29. There are thirty-four references to "Jews" or "Jewish" things in *1 Apology*: 31.1 (twice), 2, 5, 6 (twice); 32.2 (twice), 3 (thrice), 4, 6, 14; 34.2; 35.6; 36.3; 38.7; 40.6 (twice); 47.1, 6; 49.1, 5; 52.10; 53.2, 3, 4, 5, 6; 63.1, 3, 10, 14. Unsurprisingly these all occur in the dense middle part of *1 Apology* which takes prophecy as its main topic.

term in the *Dialogue*, where he is addressing a "Jew," because his primary target in that text is the teachers who pull the strings and control what "Judaism" is and who constitutes it rather than ordinary "Jews" like Trypho.[30] In this regard, Horner goes as far to say that Justin views the "Jewish" people as victims rather than as his main competition, and though this is not always obvious in the text, it does appear to be the general pattern.[31] Therefore, in *1 Apology* it is more than possible that the frequent naming and criticising of "Jews" functions in the same way as the treatment of the teachers in the *Dialogue*; namely, at the level of summary for outsiders.

Persecution

An important feature of Justin's claiming of "Christian" identity is the story he tells of its misrepresentation and persecution. This, as Justin describes it, proceeds in stages. In the first stage is persecution at the hands of the/fellow "Jews" in which "Christians" come to be labeled as different. Often this is connected with the Bar Kokhba revolt, but this is not always explicit. The second step, as we shall see in the Greco-Roman treatment of "Christians," is that by virtue of this process, this identity has become more widely known and, because of the political threat it might pose to "Judaism's" already fragile position in the aftermath of the Bar Kokhba revolt, opposed by the "Jewish" teachers beyond the time of Bar Kokhba. The third step is that "Christians" like Justin adopt this identity as their own and beginning to understand themselves as a new genos, leading them to take control of this identity and attempt to define and police it—with similar intentions to the "Jewish" treatment of themselves. This first section will deal with the persecution by "Jews," and the other two points will be taken in turn thereafter in the sections which follow.

---

30. Ibid., 130–36.
31. Ibid., 186. This also brings to mind a loose commonality between Justin and Marcion. On this analysis both see the "Jewish" people as victims; Marcion as the victim of the evil god they do not choose but who takes them as his own and Justin as the victim of teachers who do not understand their god, which is parallel to his thinking on Marcion also. Neither hate the "Jewish" people as such.

Justin presents the persecution of "Christians" by "Jews" first and foremost as a misrepresentation, a recasting, of who "Christians" are. In the *Dialogue*, "Christians" are a class of people hated by the "Jews" (e.g. Trypho's teachers).[32] These people have singled "Christians" out and publicized their opinions about them. In doing so they have attempted to define "Christians" in pejorative terms. The significance of this presentation is that it suggests a close relationship between "Jews" and "Christians" at this time that non-"Christian" "Jews" wish to end or distinguish themselves from. *Dial.* 17.1-2 offers us an introduction to this theme:

> The other nations have not inflicted on us and on Christ injustice to such an extent as you have, who in very deed are the instigators of the evil prejudice against the Just One, and us who hold by Him. After that you had crucified Him, the only blameless and righteous Man,—through whose wounds those who approach the Father through Him are healed, and when you understood that He had risen from the dead and ascended to heaven, as the prophets foretold He would, you not only did not repent of the evilness, but you selected and sent out from Jerusalem to all lands, certain men to tell that the godless heresy of the Christians had sprung up, and to publish those things which all they who do not know us say against us. So that you cause not only of your own unrighteousness, but in fact of that of all others. And Isaiah cries justly: "By reason of you, My name is blasphemed among the Gentiles."[33]

We should note straight away that Justin does not say that other nations have not inflicted as much on "Christians," but rather that they have not inflicted as much *"on us and Christ."* Justin does not use the term "Christian" (Χριστιανῶν) here but refers to the person of

---

32. Though Justin does not call them "Jews" in the *Dialogue*, he does mean the same body of people he calls "Jews" in *1 Apology*.
33. My translation. Οὐχ οὕτως γάρ ἄλλα ἔθνη εἰς ταύτην τὴν ἀδικίαν τὴν εἰς ἡμᾶς καὶ τὸν Χριστὸν ἐνέχονται, ὅσον ὑμεῖς, οἳ κἀκείνοις τῆς κατὰ τοῦ δικαίου καὶ ἡμῶν τῶν ἀπ' ἐκείνου κακῆς προλήψεως αἴτιοι τοι ὑπάρχετε· μετὰ γὰρ τὸ σταυρῶσαι ὑμᾶς ἐκεῖνον τὸν μόνον ἄμωμον καὶ δίκαιον ἄνθρωπον, δι' οὗ τῶν μωλώπων ἴασις γίνεται τοῖς δι' αὐτοῦ ἐπὶ τὸν πατέρα προσχωροῦσιν, ἐπειδὴ ἐγνώκατε αὐτὸν ἀναστάντα ἐκ νεκρῶν καὶ ἀναβάντα εἰς τὸν οὐρανόν, ὡς αἱ προφητεῖαι προεμήνυον γενησόμενον, οὐ μόνον οὐ μετενοήσατε ἐφ' οἷς ἐπάξατε κακοῖς, ἀλλὰ ἄνδρας ἐκλεκτοὺς ἀπὸ Ἰερουσαλὴμ ἐκλεξάμενοι τότε ἐξεπέμψατε εἰς πᾶσαν τὴν γῆν, λέγοντας αἵρεσιν ἄθεον Χριστιανῶν πεφηνέναι, καταλέγοντάς τε ταῦτα ἅπερ καθ' ἡμῶν οἱ ἀγνοοῦντες ἡμᾶς πάντες λέγουσιν· ὥστε οὐ μόνον ἑαυτοῖς ἀδικίας αἴτιοι ὑπάρχετε, ἀλλὰ καὶ τοῖς ἄλλοις ἅπασιν ἁπλῶς ἀνθρώποις. Καὶ δικαίως βοᾷ Ἠσαΐας. Δι' ὑμᾶς τὸ ὄνομά μου βλασφημεῖται ἐν τοῖς ἔθνεσι.

Christ and his own group. The first time the word "Christian" appears in the *Dialogue* it is present in reported speech from the mouths of non-"Christians" where it is paired with the word *heresy* (αἵρεσιν) and used in propaganda against followers of Christ. The very first time the word "Christian" appears it is therefore to be understood as the shame name attributed to followers of Christ by a group of people external to, or rather who wish to be considered as external to, that group. The term "Christian" is not a given here, nor is the group identity. Instead, the term is a pointer, synonymous with shame and depravity, and it is Justin's task to capture and redefine it. Before inviestigating how this term operates further it is necessary to consider more closely the content of Justin's claims that "Jews," more than other nations, are shaming followers of Christ and are the originators of this prejudice.

"Christians" here are introduced as a "godless heresy." Bearing in mind that heresy can mean just school or opinion at this time, having not yet taken on its later formal meaning,[34] it is the term "godlessness" (ἄθεος) that is truly the operative word.[35] The god(s) that one worships, and the manner in which one worships, are fundamental factors affecting one's standing at this time. As godlessness would certainly limit their authentic "Jewishness," portraying "Christians" as a "godless heresy" has to be taken as casting them as "non-Jewish."[36] "Christians" must have been difficult to distinguish from "Jews" (if it occurred to one to try do so), but according to Justin, "Jews" embarked

---

34. Lieu notes that though early attestations of the term in Justin and Hegesippus are too inconsistent to suggest new coinage by them into a settled new sense for the term, even Irenaeus's more extensive usage is not sufficiently consistent to reflect confidently an established "concept of heresy" by the late second century. See Lieu, *Making of a Heretic*, 86.
35. A. le Boulluec's *La Notion d'hérésie* is still the most important text on this. Here he argues that the formation of the category of heresy is modeled after philosophical schools transformed from modes of thought into institutions with a pejorative meaning. Le Boulluec understands that "Christian" writers like Justin are influenced by rabbinic world (questioned by Boyarin), but the thesis that in the mid-second century hairesis moves from describing a philosophical school to a wrong opinion is salutary. See Alain le Boulluec, *La Notion d'hérésiedans la littérature grecqueIIe-IIe siècles*(Paris: Etudes Augustiniennes, 1985), 82–91.
36. This is a serious claim for Justin and he repeats it at *Dial.* 108.2: "I said before, you have sent chosen and ordained men throughout all the world to proclaim that a godless and lawless heresy had sprung from one Jesus, a Galilean deceiver" (ὡς προεῖπον, ἄνδρας χειροτονήσαντες ἐκλεκτοὺς εἰς πᾶσαν τὴν οἰκουμένην ἐπέμψατε, κηρύσσοντας ὅτι αἵρεσίς τις ἄθεος καὶ ἄνομος ἐξήγερται ἀπὸ Ἰησοῦ τινος Γαλιλαίου πλάνου).

on their clarification mission to achieve just this by casting the ones they called "Christians" as atheists.

Boyarin has convincingly built on le Boulluec's classic monograph to argue that the nascent nature of heresy is not only emerging at this time, but is being created dialectically by "Christians" and "Jews" ruling each other in and out and forming new standards of belonging in the process. Boyarin's thesis is not that these two groups witness to one another's existence, but rather that, in the course of their conversation, they invent one another. They are not two religions, or obvious diametric poles of one, but differing strands, wide and varied, with different points of overlap in different places.[37] Rhetorical recastings and claims for identity become rarefied and separate bodies form. This is a process that he sees as beginning in approximately the mid-second century.[38] Nina E. Livesey has put this even more starkly by saying: "What we see in the Dialogue, then, is not just the beginning of orthodoxy and heresy—a theological enterprise that determines who is in and who is out—but also the advent of understanding Jews and Christians as split selves, as theological beings in distinction from social ones."[39]

The relationship between "Christians" and "Jews" at this time is very much a complicated and socially negotiated one. There is much evidence that "Christians" and "Jews" have a lot to do with one another for a long time to come after Justin, with many "Christian" texts preserving fears about interaction and confusion of the groups.[40] But even this evidence can be construed in overly deterministic ways. As Andrew Jacobs has argued, it is important we avoid insouciant claims for boundaries and difference. Getting away from assumptions about

---

37. Indeed Boyarin rejects the notion of "religion" as an internal Jewish category until modern times and understands the invention of the category to be a Christian achievement taking definitive shape around the fourth century. See Boyarin, "Rethinking," 7–36.
38. Daniel Boyarin. "Justin Martyr Invents Judaism," *CH* 70 (2001): 438.
39. N. E. Livesey, "Theological Identity Making: Justin's Use of Circumcision to Create Jews and Christians," *JECS* 18 (2010): 79.
40. Blanchetière points to the Council of Elvira in its prohibitions against mixed "Christian"–"Jewish" marriage, blessing "Jewish" owned fields, or eating with "Jews" as evidence of just those things as well as the presence of "Christians" in synagogues. See François Blanchetière, "The Threefold Christian Anti-Judaism," in *Tolerance and Intolerance in Early Judaism and Christianity*, ed. Graham Stanton and Guy B. Stroumsa (Cambridge, UK: Cambridge University Press, 1998), 194.

boundaries means recognizing their provisional and rhetorically negotiated nature: "The textualization of religious difference may lie not in logical resolution, but in dialogical irresolution: the problems of difference (and similarity) are not resolved, but rather enacted, creating the sense of a boundary (between speaker and interlocutor) without finite closure."[41]

This is to say that not only "heresy," but "Christianity" and "Judaism" are coming into existence in this period, and coming into existence by mutual and multifaceted exclusion. Indeed, it is not until a number of centuries later that it becomes possible firmly to identify a "Christianity" which is uniformly not "Jewish" or a "Judaism" which hierarchically excludes all "Christians" from its orthodoxy. Many voices, agreeing and differing, at different points and places, but not different sides make this distinction over time. Justin is part of this process, of which his interaction with Marcion is an exemplary element as well as his explicit debate with Trypho.

Justin reiterates the point that the "Jews" are the cause of "Christians" being maligned at *Dial.* 108.2:

> As I stated, you chose certain men by vote and sent them throughout the whole civilized world, proclaiming that a godless and lawless sect has been started by a deceiver, one Jesus of Galilee, whom we nailed to the cross, but whose body, after it was taken down from the cross, was stolen at night from the tomb by his disciples, who now try to deceive men by affirming that he has arisen from the dead and has ascended into heaven. And you accuse him of having taught those irreverent, riotous, and wicked things, of which you everywhere accuse all those who look up to and acknowledge him as their Christ, their Teacher, and Son of God.[42]

Here the "Jews" have sent certain men appointed for a task. This was a particular and specially planned mission, not just a knee-jerk reaction.

---

41. Andrew S. Jacobs, "Dialogical Differences: (De-)Judaizing Jesus' Circumcision," *JECS* 15 (2007): 298.
42. Καὶ οὐ μόνον οὐ μετενοήσατε, μαθόντες αὐτὸν ἀναστάντα ἐκ νεκρῶν, ἀλλ', ὡς προεῖπον, ἄνδρας χειροτονήσαντες ἐκλεκτοὺς εἰς πᾶσαν τὴν οἰκουμένην ἐπέμψατε, κηρύσσοντας ὅτι αἵρεσίς τις ἄθεος καὶ ἄνομος ἐξήγερται ἀπὸ Ἰησοῦ τινος Γαλιλαίου πλάνου, ὃν σταυρωσάντων ἡμῶν, οἱ μαθηταὶ αὐτοῦ κλέψαντες αὐτὸν ἀπὸ τοῦ μνήματος νυκτός, ὁπόθεν κατετέθη ἀφηλωθεὶς ἀπὸ τοῦ σταυροῦ, πλανῶσι τοὺς ἀνθρώπους λέγοντες ἐξηγέρθαι αὐτὸν ἐκ νεκρῶν καὶ εἰς οὐρανὸν ἀνεληλυθέναι κατειπόντες δεδιδαχέναι καὶ ταῦτα ἅπερ κατὰ τῶν ὁμολογούντων Χριστὸν καὶ διδάσκαλον καὶ υἱὸν θεοῦ εἶναι παντὶ γένει ἀνθρώπων ἄθεα καὶ ἄνομα καὶ ἀνόσια λέγετε.

Here the "Jews" are displayed as taking full responsibility for the death of Jesus, "whom we crucified," and as countering the claims of Jesus's followers and slandering Jesus himself in order to cut them off from "Jewishness." Atheism, deception,[43] and lawlessness are on the agenda. All of these are socially and politically sensitive charges: To move somebody from being "Jewish" to being an atheist is pushing the person outside the legal realm, set by the Romans for "Jews," and to oppose Roman society; deception suggests hidden agendas and threatening behavior; and lawlessness intimates apostasy from "Judaism," and rebellion towards Romans.

Bar Kokhba

1 Apol. 31.5–6 further develops our understanding of the manner in which, for Justin, the "Jews" distinguish between themselves and the followers of Christ by demonising them. For Justin "Christians" are to be understood as abiding by the prophets while the "Jews" kill them (as they killed the prophets of old):

> And after this [the legend of the origins of the Septuagint] the rolls remained among the Egyptians until now, and are also present everywhere to all the Jews, who, even though they read them, do not understand what has been said, but consider us to be enemies and adversaries. And, like you, they destroy and punish us whenever they are able, as you are able to learn. For even in the recent Jewish war, Bar Kokhba, the leader of the rebellion of the Jews, ordered only Christians to be led away to fearsome torments, if they would not deny Jesus as the Christ and blaspheme him.[44]

Why did Bar Kokhba target only "Christians" and force them to deny

---

43. In chapter 3 we will note that those who deceive (ἐχαπατήσωσιν) are usually connected with the work of the demons, as Simon, Menander, and Marcion are in *1 Apology*, and that Justin's demonology is of "Jewish" origin. As such, it is possible that this charge of deception has more weight to it than that of a simple liar and represents an unholy trickster who is working actively against god and therefore must be outside of his people.

44. καὶ τούτου γενομένου ἔμειναν αἱ βίβλοι καὶ παρ' Αἰγυπτίοις μέχρι τοῦ δεῦρο, καὶ πανταχοῦ παρὰ πᾶσίν εἰσιν Ἰουδαίοις, οἳ καὶ ἀναγινώσκοντες οὐ συνιᾶσι τὰ εἰρημένα, ἀλλ' ἐχθροὺς ἡμᾶς καὶ πολεμίους ἡγοῦνται, ὁμοίως ὑμῖν ἀναιροῦντες καὶ κολάζοντες ἡμᾶς ὁπόταν δύνωνται, ὡς καὶ πεισθῆναι δύνασθε. καὶ γὰρ ἐν τῷ νῦν γεγενημένῳ Ἰουδαϊκῷ πολέμῳ, Βαρχωχέβας, ὁ τῆς Ἰουδαίων ἀποστάσεως ἀρχηγέτης, Χριστιανοὺς μόνους εἰς τιμωρίας δεινὰς εἰ μὴ ἀρνοῖντο Ἰησοῦν τὸν Χριστὸν καὶ βλασφημοῖεν ἐκέλευεν ἀπάγεσθαι.

and blaspheme Jesus as Messiah? This may have been because he himself was seen either by himself or at least by some as a Messiah-figure. The title "Christians" here again is used by Justin, in order to make "Jews" (here Bar Kokhba) distinguish followers of Christ from themselves.[45] According to him, Bar Kokhba had separated these "Christians" who did not deny Jesus as the Christ and did not blaspheme him from the body of "Jewish" people, a claim that is supported by Eusebius.[46] It is interesting that this claim occurs only in *1 Apology*. The war or its affects are alluded to six times in the *Dialogue* and three times in *1 Apology*,[47] but this is the only point at which Justin suggests any strong or direct link between the campaign of Bar Kokhba and the slander of those who follow Christ. This singling out strongly suggests that "Christians" at this time were sufficiently part of "Jewish" society in Palestine such that they could be meaningfully targeted and separated from it by Bar Kokhba. Singling out "Christians" in this way identifies them as disloyal and not truly belonging. As Justin does not seem to fabricate this account the plausibility of such a development must be investigated.

Peter Schäfer notes that "shirkers" are recorded in the letter from Bar Kokhba to Yehonatan Bar Ba'ayan and Masabala Bar Shimon, military commanders at Ein Gedi, found in the Judean desert.[48] These are the men of Tekoa. Punishment for these and any harbouring them was severe.[49] We see here that the rebels were more than prepared to enforce their authority on the "Jewish" people and make examples of them. Schäfer puts the coarse tone of much the Bar Kokhba letters down to his character and the increasingly desperate situation towards

---

45. Justin's use of this event to create an interpretive narrative is striking because, as Lieu notes, contemporary reactions are sparse. Key to Justin is that the failure of the revolt constitutes punishment, but most sources would give the decisive significance to the fall of Jerusalem in 70 CE. Justin is unusual in making so much of Bar Kokhba. See Lieu, *Making of a Heretic*, 317.
46. Eusebius, *Chron.* 660, 18. "Barchochebas, the only son whose name was interpreted as star, was the cause of the revolt of the Jews. This [Barchochebas] punished in many ways the 'Christians' for desiring not to be in alliance against the Romans" (my translation: Τῆς Ἰουδαίων ἀποστάσεως Χοχεβᾶς τις ὁ μονογενὴς ἡγεῖτο, ὃς ἑρμηνεύετο ἀστήρ· οὗτος Χριστιανοὺς ποιχίλως ἐτιμωρήσατο μὴ βουλομένους κατὰ Ῥωμαίων συμμαχεῖν).
47. *Dial.* 1.3; 9.3; 16.4; 24.3; 92.2; 110.6; *1 Apol.* 31.6; 47.4–6; 52.11.
48. Peter Schäfer, "Bar Kokhba and the Rabbis," in *The Bar Kokhba War Reconsidered*, ed. P. Schäfer (Tübingen: Mohr Siebeck, 2003): 8.
49. Ibid., 8.

the end of the revolt. Bar Kokhba presumably was not successful in asserting his authority if such letters were necessary.[50] This further suggests that not all "Jews" were supporters of Bar Kokhba and those who did not ally themselves with the war effort could expect to be attacked. We know then that Justin's comment has the air of plausibility even if this singling out was not necessarily exclusively reserved for "Christians," and even then only those who maintained their allegiance to Jesus as Christ. This restriction is perhaps the reason why Justin reserves this claim for *1 Apology* rather than presenting it in the *Dialogue* since in the latter he speaks to Trypho and "Jews" who were certainly not singled out by Bar Kokhba, but still might have known the situation and known that "Christians" did not necessarily suffer alone.

Further evidence that Bar Kokhba singled out "Christians" can be found in Richard Bauckham's reading of the *Apocalypse of Peter* as an early "Jewish" "Christian" text contemporary with the second revolt that warns "Christians" to avoid the false messiah.[51] As he claims many scholars agree, Bauckham takes this "false messiah" to be Bar Kokhba, which again displays persecution of "Christians."[52] Justin does not tell us why Bar Kokhba singled "Christians" out during the revolt. He is, however, clear that this happened *during* the revolt. This suggests that resources would have been diverted away from fighting the true enemy in order to target "Christians," and that there must, therefore, have been a compelling reason for doing so. Bauckham posits such a reason by holding that the aim of rebuilding the temple was not shared by "Jewish" "Christians" who understood Jesus to be the spiritual and final temple. This comes out in the narrative of Peter declaring who Jesus is.[53] This being the case, "Christians" may be denying the messianic ambitions of the regime, the extent of whose existence as

---

50. Ibid., 9.
51. Richard Bauckham, "The Two Fig Tree Parables in the Apocalypse of Peter," *JBL* 104 (1985): 286–87.
52. Independently Skarsaune came to the same, albeit brief, conclusion concerning this text and the impact of the Bar Kokhba revolt on "Christians." See Oskar Skarsaune, *The Proof from Prophecy* (Leiden: Brill, 1987), 272.
53. Ibid., 233.

an explicit mythos is unclear,⁵⁴ but also standing in opposition to an imminent and nationally important practical agenda which causes "Christians" to become conscientious objectors and vulnerable to attack as disloyal and cowardly. Furthermore, Cassius Dio's testimony that "many outside nations, too, were joining them [the 'Jews'] through eagerness for gain" only sharpens the contrast between loyal participant and disloyal nonconformist.⁵⁵ For Hannah Cotton, this explains the supposed Nabatean involvement suggested by *P. Yadin* 52.⁵⁶ Cotton believes that the revolt may have spread into other regions, such as Syria and Arabia, and been successfully put down there earlier.⁵⁷ Further, she argues that the Nabateans involved may have been refugees from the revolutionaries' activities in neighbouring provinces.⁵⁸ If this were so, and if "Christians" really abstained from the revolt, then "Christians" would have looked strikingly aloof at a time when even non-"Jews" were prepared to join in to challenge the Romans, and the evidence suggests that Bar Kokhba did not look kindly on those who did not follow the party line. This being the case it seems that we must take Justin seriously in this claim that "Christian" persecution by "Jews" was rooted in the Bar Kokhba war.

Though Justin does not assert that "Christians" were singled out by Bar Kokhba in the *Dialogue,* he does repeat the claim that Bar Kokhba suppressed them in *Dial.* 9.1, 3:

> If you will agree to hear our account of him, how we have not been deceived by false teachings, and how we shall not cease to profess our faith in him (even though men thereby persecute us, and the most cruel tyrant tries to force us to deny him) ... two of his friends, joking and making fun of our earnestness, went their way. When we came to that part of the stadium where there were stone seats on both sides, Trypho's other

---

54. Schäfer claims that apart from Aqiva it is only "Christian" sources that apply the name Bar Kokhba with messianic overtones to Simon. Schäfer does not believe this was a self-designation nor one by his close followers. See Schäfer, "Bar Kokhba," 17.
55. πολλοί τε ἄλλοι καὶ τῶν ἀλλοφύλων ἐπιθυμίᾳ κέρδους σφίσι συνελαμβάνοντο (Cassius Dio, *Rom. Hist.* 69.13.2).
56. Hannah M. Cotton, "The Bar Kokhba Revolt and the Documents from the Judaean Desert: Nabataean Participation in the Revolt," in Schäfer, *War Reconsidered*, 148.
57. Ibid., 149.
58. Ibid., 151.

companions went to sit on the one side and after one of them had made a remark about the war waged in Judea, they spoke of it.[59]

This passages comes at the conclusion of Justin's long account of his conversion, just after the point that Trypho and his followers have discovered that he is a follower of Christ. At this point Trypho's friends become indignant and laugh at Justin, casting a seemingly throw-away and incongruous comment about the Bar Kokhba revolt, after he had spoken of a "terrible tyrant" who compelled them to deny (ὁ δεινότατος ἀπιοπεῖν ἀναγκάζῃ τύραννος) Jesus. As this description is close to what we have read before in *1 Apol.* 31.6, where Bar Kokhba used fearsome torments to attempt to force "Christians" to deny Christ, it seems Justin has in mind Bar Kokhba here also. This sense is increased by the fact that the war is mentioned in the same passage. Why do the friends make this comment? This is hard to establish. What it does suggest, though, is that the link between the revolt and "Christians" seems to reflect fresh and real experience.[60]

Justin's speech immediately following this gives us a further clue as to meaning of this comment: "My friends, is there any accusation you have against us other than this, that we do not observe the Law, nor circumcise the flesh as your forefathers did, nor observe the Sabbath as you do? Or do you condemn our customs and morals?"[61] (*Dial.* 10.1).

The reply comes back in the negative. There is no suspicion of corruption from Trypho but only incredulity at Justin's claim to be one of god's children and yet not to keep his commandments. Justin's "Jewish" friends are not necessarily questioning his non-"Jewishness" here, but the non-"Jewish" behavior of people who they supposed were

---

59. Εἰ δὲ βούλοιο τούτου πέρι δέξασθαι λόγον, ὡς οὐ πεπλανήμεθα οὐδὲ παυσόμεθα ὁμολογοῦντες τοῦτον, κἂν τὰ ἐξ ἀνθρώπων ἡμῖν ἐπιφέρωνται ὀνείδη, κἂν ὁ δεινότατος ἀπειπεῖν ἀναγκάζῃ τύραννος . . . τῶν δὲ σὺν αὐτῷ δύο, χλευάσαντες καὶ τὴν σπουδὴν ἡμῶν ἐπισκώψαντες, ἀπηλλάγησαν. Ἡμεῖς δὲ ὡς ἐγενόμεθα ἐν ἐκείνῳ τῷ τόπῳ, ἔνθα ἑκατέρωθεν λίθινοί εἰσι θῶκοι, ἐν τῷ ἑτέρῳ καθεσθέντες οἱ μετὰ τοῦ Τρύφωνος, ἐμβαλόντος τινὸς αὐτῶν λόγον περὶ τοῦ κατὰ τὴν Ἰουδαίαν γενομένου πολέμου, διελάλουν.
60. A plausible conjecture as to the specific significance is that the comment comes just at the point Justin tries to flee the conversation at their cruelty. It could be that they are commenting on a typical pattern among "Christians" of fleeing when the going gets tough and of not being prepared to meet a challenge.
61. Μὴ ἄλλο τί ἐστιν ὃ ἐπιμέμφεσθε ἡμᾶς, ἄνδρες φίλοι, ἢ τοῦτο ὅτι οὐ κατὰ τὸν νόμον βιοῦμεν, οὐδὲ ὁμοίως τοῖς προγόνοις ὑμῶν περιτεμνόμεθα τὴν σάρκα, οὐδὲ ὡς ὑμεῖς σαββατίζομεν; Ἢ καὶ ὁ βίος ἡμῶν καὶ τὸ ἦθος διαβέβληται παρ' ὑμῖν;

bound by or ought to be bound to the same standards and practices as they themselves were. That is, it is possible that they see themselves as talking to fellow "Jews" who had been persecuted as "Christian" by Bar Kokhba. That this is what they were supposing makes good sense in light of Trypho's demand that "Christians" should follow the law and be circumcised. Nonetheless, Trypho is aware of their claim to follow their own god, and he is also familiar with their alternative commandments, which suggests close proximity, but also a form of distinction. A further point of connection and simultaneous distinction comes at Trypho's friends' remark about the war as they depart. Though it is only conjecture that Trypho's friends snigger at "Christian" non-participation in the war, it is clear that the war is an issue between "Jews" and followers of Christ or else it would be strange that Justin chose to record this detail. This furthers suggests close links between "Christians" and "Jews," and lends credibility to Justin's claims for the singling out of "Christians" by "Jews."

Further evidence, as far as Justin is concerned, of the singling out of "Christians" can be found in *Dial.* 110.5–6:

> For the words, her that is afflicted and cast out (that is, from the world), indicate that, whenever you and all other men have the power, you cast out every Christian, not only from his own property but even from the whole world, for you allow no Christian to live. You object that this same fate has befallen your people. But since you have been cast out after defeat in battle, such sufferings are your just desserts, as all the Scriptures testify. We, on the contrary, who are guilty of no such crime after we knew the divine truth, are assured by God that we are to be taken from the earth together with the most just and immaculate and sinless Christ.[62]

In this example, those who follow Christ are being singled out and forcibly separated from their own property and their "whole world." Here we have an explicit claim that "Christians" are not permitted to

---

62. Τὴν γὰρ ἐκτεθλιμμένην καὶ ἐξωσμένην, τουτέστιν ἀπὸ τοῦ κόσμου, ὅσον ἐφ᾽ ὑμῖν καὶ τοῖς ἄλλοις ἅπασιν ἀνθρώποις, οὐ μόνον ἀπὸ τῶν κτημάτων τῶν ἰδίων ἕκαστος τῶν Χριστιανῶν ἐκνέβληται ἀλλὰ καὶ τοῦ κόσμου παντός, ζῆν μηδενὶ Χριστιανῷ συγχωροῦντες. Ὑμεῖς δὲ ἐπὶ τὸν λαὸν ὑμῶν συμβεβηκέναι τοῦτό φατε. Εἰ δὲ ἐξεβλήθητε πολεμηθέντες, δικαίως μὲν ὑμεῖς ταῦτα πεπόνθατε, ὡς αἱ γραφαὶ πᾶσαι μαρτυροῦσιν· ἡμεῖς δέ, οὐδὲν τοιοῦτον πράξαντες μετὰ τὸ ἐπιγνῶναι τὴν ἀλήθειαν τοῦ θεοῦ, μαρτυρούμεθα ὑπὸ τοῦ θεοῦ, σὺν τῷ δικαιοτάτῳ καὶ μόνῳ ἀσπίλῳ καὶ ἀναμαρτήτῳ Χριστῷ ὅτι ἀπὸ γῆς αἰρόμεθα.

live, which can be seen as an extension of the killing of the righteous Christ, spotless and sinless, and it seems as if "Jews" are seen as the perpetrators of such killing. With the proviso that Justin has a rhetorical axe to grind when it comes to the position of "Jews" as a rebellious people who persecute their prophets and the followers of Christ as heirs to that prophetic tradition through Christ, it seems that Justin believes he is accurately reporting the singling out of followers of Christ by "Jews." However the claim that the same "has befallen" Trypho's "own nation" complicates the matter. This being the case, it must be either that Bar Kokhba also attacked and killed "Jews" other than "Christians" or that this is referred to the Romans driving the "Jews" out of Jerusalem after the revolt. This is confirmed by Justin's claim that the suffering visited upon Trypho's kind is the just and legitimate result of defeat "in battle" but that "Christians," having taken no part in such evil acts, have suffered them unjustly. Justin then is claiming that the main thrust of persecution towards "Christians" has come, at least primarily, from other "Jews." The suffering of "Christians" under the Romans during the war was a result of their being caught in the crossfire and presumably not noted as different from other "Jews" by the Romans. And this was the case despite "Christians" distinguishing themselves by not rebelling, and also being singled out as separate by other "Jews," Bar Kokhba's sympathizers, because of it.

Contemporary Relations in the Time of Justin

This story of the singling out of "Christians" is, according to Justin, not only a historical one. He also presents contemporary "Jewish" leaders as persisting with the isolation of "Christians." This suggests that even during the time of his writing "Christians" were in close relationship to "Judaism." For example, in *Dial.* 38.1 Trypho reveals that "Jewish" leaders have banned "Jews" from speaking with "Christians."

> And Trypho said, "sir, it were good for us if we obeyed our teachers, who laid down a law that we should not discuss these subjects nor converse with any of you for you made many blasphemies, in seeking to persuade

us that this crucified man was with Moses and Aaron, and spoke to them in the pillar of the cloud; then became man, was crucified, and ascended up to heaven, and comes again to earth, and ought to be worshipped."⁶³

"Christians," then, are presently and actively isolated from "Jews." Trypho mentions that their teachers had prescribed them neither to mix with nor to have any communication with "Christians" on these questions, which implies that even on such controversial dogmatic issues "Christians" and "Jews" were in fact talking when the "Jewish" leaders wished them to be separate. Yet, such an exchange suggests that "Christians" still were not entirely separated from "Jews" and that they were having discussions like the one that is reported in Justin's *Dialogue*, here with the point of disagreement being the equation of the "crucified" with the Lord. However formally one takes this proscription, as a decreed ban or a less centralized informal recommendation, it reads as an act of self-defense on the part of Trypho's teachers, a move of self-isolation designed to remove a threat.⁶⁴

It is not only that "Christians" may have been singled out during the Bar Kokhba revolt and that "Jews" may have come out of Jerusalem on propaganda missions against them. Up to the time of Justin's writing, followers of Christ were being shunned by "Jewish" brothers and sisters.⁶⁵ This is seen as an act of "Jewish" teachers, rather than as a longstanding policy or attitude typical of people like Trypho and his companions. As such, Justin believes that all that is necessary for Trypho and other "Jews" like him to come to recognize Christ is that they abandon these "Jewish" teachers.⁶⁶ Justin also encourages Trypho

---

63. My translation. Καὶ ὁ Τρύφων εἶπεν. Ὦ ἄνθρωπε, καλὸν ἦν πεισθέντας ἡμᾶς τοῖς διδασκάλοις, νομοθετήσασι μηδενὶ, ἐξ ὑμῶν ὁμιλεῖν, μηδέ σοι τούτων κοινωνῆσαι τῶν λόγων· βλάσφημα γὰρ πολλὰ λέγεις, τὸν σταυρωθέντα τοῦτον ἀξιῶν πείθειν ἡμᾶς γεγενῆσθαι μετὰ Μωϋσέως καὶ Ἀαρὼν καὶ λελαληκέναι αὐτοῖς ἐν στύλῳ νεφέλης, εἶτα ἄπθρωπον γενόμενον σταυρωθῆναι, καὶ ἀναβεβηκέναι εἰς τὸν οὐρανόν, καὶ πάλιν παραγίνεσθαι ἐπὶ τῆς γῆς, καὶ προσκυνητὸν εἶναι.
64. Steven T. Katz, "The Rabbinic Response to Christianity," in *The Cambridge History of Judaism: Volume Four the Late Roman-Rabbinic Period*, ed. S. T. Katz (Cambridge, UK: Cambridge University Press, 2006), 275.
65. Justin does indeed call and think of them as brothers (ἀδελφοί). See *Dial.* 134.6; 137.1.
66. Horner, *Listening*, 133.

and his friends to ignore their teachers, who are consistently portrayed as foolish, ignorant, and malicious on numerous matters:

> Unless, therefore, you detest the doctrines of those proud teachers who aspire to be called Rabbi, and apply yourself with such persistence and intelligence to the words of the prophets that you suffer the same indignities from the hands of your people as the prophets did, you cannot derive any benefit from the prophetic writings.⁶⁷ (*Dial.* 112.5)

Further on, in *Dial.* 137.2, Justin urges the group to give their assent to (συμφάμενοι) and not to rail against or slander (λοιδορῆτε) the Son of god and instead to "ignore your Pharisaic teachers, and do not scorn the King of Israel, (as the chiefs of your synagogues instruct you to do after prayers)."⁶⁸ In such passages, Justin is warning Trypho as a concerned brother because it is Trypho's particular teachers, who are sectarian and lack the wisdom and authority of the *presbutoi* that translated the LXX, who keep them from the truth of Christ.⁶⁹ Trypho himself had apparently not listened too closely to these teachers as he does not obey their segregational laws and does not seem to fear reprisal from them.⁷⁰ Furthermore, these teachers must not have kept their own rules, as they admit to having interrogated the "Jewish" teachers frequently in *Dial.* 94. Regardless, the idea that segregation is plausible and desirable is enough to sow the idea that "Christians" are not to be trusted and that no right-thinking "Jew" should be hospitable to them, indulge their conversation, or interact with them in any way.

According to Justin, followers of Christ therefore appear to have been, at least in recent history and living memory, "Jews" pushed out of the "Jewish" polity by internal slander and violence. Furthermore,

---

67. Ἐὰν οὖν μὴ τῶν διδαγμάτων τῶν ἑαυτοὺς ὑψούντων καὶ θελόντων ῥαββὶ ῥαββὶ καλεῖσθαι καταφρονήσητε, καὶ μετὰ τοιαύτης ἐνστάσεως καὶ νοῦ τοῖς προφητικοῖς λόγοις προσέλθητε, ἵνα τὰ αὐτὰ πάθητε ὑπὸ τῶν ὑμετέρων ἀνθρώπων ἃ καὶ αὐτοὶ οἱ προφῆται ἔπαθον, οὐ δύνασθε ὅλως οὐδὲν ἀπὸ τῶν προφτικῶν ὠφέλιμον λαβεῖν.
68. μηδὲ φαρισαίοις πειθόμενοι διδακάλοις τὸν βασιλέα τοῦ Ἰσραὴλ ἐπισκώψητέ ποτε, ὁποῖα διδάσκουσιν οἱ ἀρχισυνάγωγοι ὑμῶν, μετὰ τὴν προσευχήν.
69. Ibid., 133.
70. Of course Trypho did not know Justin was a "Christian" when he invited him to dialogue with him and his companions. Furthermore, Horner has argued that Trypho has relatively little knowledge of the "Jewish" teachers that Justin establishes as his main target and does not display much personal interest in the things that are thought to characterize them, such as forms of exegesis and scriptural analysis (ibid., 136–46).

this slander has been propagated deliberately by "Jews" in order that "Christians" may be known as shameful and have no peace elsewhere. Justin says that "death is the lot of the Christians" (*Dial.* 44.1). They are, in his eyes, a persecuted minority of true Israelites, worshipers of god, banished by god's own people. This banishment has caused them to become involuntarily labelled as a separate people ("Christians") when they really ought only to be considered followers of the god of Israel via the teaching of Christ. Christ was, in the prophetic mold, calling the "Jews" and gentiles back to god. For Justin "Christians" should not then be seen as separate people but as "true Israel." The difference between Justin and his companions, and Trypho and his, is that the former practice their "Jewishness" (that is, the faith of Israel) spiritually, whereas the latter do so physically.

Justin's "true Israel" is not wholly distinct, then, from the physical practicing of the "Jewish" law at that time. "Christians" are still mixed up with and involved with what appear to be family squabbles with "Jews" who should not be considered a uniform body either. Indeed, Jacobs argues that the unresolved nature of the *Dialogue*, lacking as it does a triumphant conversion like the *Dialogue between Jason and Papiscus the Jew*, can be taken as evidence of the ambiguous give and take of the period.[71] One does not win over or erase the other and the core arguments ultimately fail to force a break where the two cannot share the same space: "In a text whose fundamental purpose would seem to be the articulation of the difference between Judaism and Christianity, absolute difference from the Jew is deferred."[72] This is because Justin's position, the position of "Christians" as he sees it, is nuanced. Justin, unlike Marcion, does not seek a total separation from "Judaism" but rather continuity with it, albeit in a new way.

---

71. However, Horner has made an interesting case that in the ending of the *Dialogue* might be intended to imply Trypho's imminent conversion in parallel to Justin's own which only happened after he had parted company with the *presbutes*. In this case, the end of the debate would be a necessary step towards Trypho's conversion. Horner argues for a series of parallels between Justin's conversion and his attempt to convince Trypho which might lead to this conclusion. Ibid., 103–7.
72. Jacobs, "Dialogical Differences," 304.

The Christian Race

Before moving on to how the name "Christian" functioned as shame name for Greco-Romans as well as "Jews," it is pertinent to pause and consider further the relationship between "Christianity" and "Judaism" that Justin envisions. The break is not clean and simple.

Justin presents "Jews" as exiling "Christians" and rejecting their renewal and reformation of god's way of living, according to god's commands. Consequently, it is clear that what defines one's identity is how one lives, what one practices, the commands and doctrines one follows. "Christian" identity is for Trypho neither recognizably "Jewish" nor clearly distinguishable from the other nations:

> But this is what we are most puzzled about, that you who claim to be pious and believe yourselves to be different from the others do not segregate yourselves from them, nor do you observe a manner of life different from that of the Gentiles, for you do not keep the feasts or Sabbaths, nor do you practice the rite of circumcision. You place your hope in a crucified man, and still expect to receive favours from God when you disregard his commandments.[73] (*Dial.* 10.3)

As Boyarin has pointed out, Trypho's speech here is an articulation of the "Christian" identity crisis. It is this crisis that Justin is trying to settle and it is this that forms the justification for the *Dial* itself as an account of what distinguishes Gentile "Christianity."[74] From a "Jewish" perspective, "Christians" are not recognisably different from other nations. This has frequently been expressed in modern scholarship by view that "Christianity" is a universal phenomenon in contrast to a fixed ethno-racial tradition (such as "Judaism").[75] Yet,

---

73. Ἐκεῖνο δὲ ἀποροῦμεν μάλιστα, εἰ ὑμεῖς, εὐσεβεῖν λέγοντες καὶ τῶν ἄλλων οἰόμενοι διαφέρειν, κατ' οὐδὲν αὐτῶν ἀπολείπεσθε, οὐδὲ διαλλάσσετε ἀπὸ τῶν ἐθνῶν τὸν ὑμέτερον βίον, ἐν τῷ μήτε τὰς ἑορτὰς μήτε τὰ σάββατα τηρεῖν μήτε τὴν περιτομὴν ἔχειν, καὶ ἔπι, ἐπ' ἀνθρώπον σταυρωθέντα τὰς ἐλπίδας ποιούμενοι, ὅμως ἐλπίζετε τεύξεσθαι ἀγαθοῦ τινος παρὰ τοῦ θεοῦ, μὴ ποιοῦντες αὐτοῦ τὰς ἐντολάς.
74. Boyarin, *Border Lines*, 38.
75. As Buell points out, this has usually been because moderns have taken race and ethnicity to be immutable categories. This understanding fails to take account of the complexity of the structural organizations, systems of power, and ordinary interaction of people in the ancient world and the intergenerational transmission of teachings that are necessary to count as a member of a particular group, *ethnos, genos*, or *laos*. See Denise Kimber Buell, "God's Own People: Spectres of Race, Ethnicity, and Gender in Early Christian Studies," in *Prejudice and Christian Beginnings*:

the claim from Trypho still expects obligations for "Christians" before the law and expects that they ought to have a different "mode of living from the nations," and thus remain involved in ethno-religious practices. The discussion about "Christian" identity from Trypho's perspective is not about living in contrast to "Jewish" customs, as free universal people, but about living similarly to gentiles by not obeying god's commandments, while "expecting to obtain some good thing" from this same god.

A further question for Trypho is how people can rest their hopes in the crucified one, if they expect good from the god of the "Jews." From the previous quotation it becomes clear: to Trypho, "Christians" are bound up, or supposed to be bound up, in the same enterprise as "Jews" and they run the danger of becoming indistinguishable from the non-"Jews" by not following god's commandments. "Christians" appear as though they are something different from "Jews," but they should not. For Trypho there is only one way to be a child of god: not to be an ancestor according to the flesh, as Justin presents the "Jewish" position to be, but to keep the commandments. If one can keep the commandments then one is of god and therefore in the *genos* and *ethnos* of the "Jewish" people. This is why followers of Christ who do not keep these commandments are so vexing to Trypho: they simply do not seem to meet the necessary criterion of keeping the commandments. Justin, in contrast, reports this debate in order to reject this criterion by introducing the new Law and route to god through Christ. In doing so, however, he does not go as far as the writer of the *Letter to Diognetus*, which is more succinct on the same point, and self-consciously separates "Christians" from "Jews":

> So I suppose that you have learned enough about the general silliness and deceit, officiousness and arrogance of Jews.... For Christians are not distinguishable from other people either by country, language or custom. For nowhere do they live in their own cities, speak some unusual Dialect, or practice an uncommon lifestyle. This teaching of theirs has not been discovered by the consideration or reflection of inventive people, nor

Investigating Race, Gender, and Ethnicity in Early Christian Studies, ed. L. Nasrallah and E. S. Fiorenza (Minneapolis: Fortress, 2009), 178.

like some people do they endorse a human doctrine. Yet while living in both Greek and barbarian cities according to each one's lot and following local customs with respect to clothing and food and the rest of life, they illustrate the admirable and admittedly unusual character of their own citizenship.[76]

Justin shares with the author of this letter the belief that "Christianity" is not bound by particular ethnic boundaries (unlike the followers of the Law) but open to all, regardless of background. We shall see however that this does not necessarily comit Justin to the view that "Christianity" is post-racial however. Conversion to "Christianity" of this kind, has frequently been interpreted as intending a freeing and transcending of race and ethnicity onto a universal non-ethnoracial "Christian" plane.[77] Even eminent scholars of great subtly are content to make this claim plainly. Laura Nasrallah, in an article arguing the complexities of identity in the second sophists, claims that Justin characterizes "Christians" as transcending the bounds of ethnos.[78] This would be misleading if left unqualified by Justin and many other early "Christian" texts that speak of "Christians" as a people (the new Israel) constituted by practices such as baptism, prayer, abstinence, and martyrdom.[79] As for Trypho, the "Jewish" people are not defined according to an ethnoracial linage that Justin applies to them, but by their religious practices that constitute them as the unified people of god despite their geographical dispersion.[80] "Christians," as far as Trypho is concerned, cannot be successful candidates for followers of

---

76. τῆς μὲν οὖν κοινῆς εἰκαιότητος καὶ ἀπάτης καὶ τῆς Ἰουδαίων πολυπραγμοσύνης καὶ ἀλαζονείας ὡς ὀρθῶς ἀπέχονται Χριστιανοί, ἀρκούντως σε νομίζω μεμαθηκεναι. . . . Χριστιανοὶ γὰρ οὔτε γῇ οὔτε φωνῇ οὔτε ἔθεσι διακεκριμένοι τῶν λοιπῶν εἰσὶν ἀνθρώπων. οὔτε γάρ που πόλεις ἰδίας κατοικοῦσιν οὔτε διαλέκτῳ τινὶ Παρηλλαγμένῃ χρῶνται οὔτε βίον παράσημον ἀσκοῦσιν. οὐ μὴν ἐπινοίᾳ τινὶ καὶ φροντίδι πολυπραγμόνων ἀνθρώπων μάθημα τοῦτ᾽ αὐτοῖς ἐστιν εὑρημένον, οὐδὲ δόγματος ἀνθρωπίνου προεστᾶσιν ὥσπερ ἔνιοι. κατοικοῦντες δὲ πόλεις Ἑλληνίδας τε καὶ Βαρβάρους, ὡς ἕκαστος ἐκληρώθη, καὶ τοῖς ἐγχωρίοις ἔθεσιν ἀκολουθοῦντες ἔν τε ἐσθῆτι καὶ διαίτῃ καὶ τῷ λοιπῷ βίῳ θαυμαστὴν καὶ ὁμολογουμένως παράδοξον ἐνδείκνυνται τὴν κατάστασιν τῆς ἑαυτῶν πολιτείας (*Diogn.* 4.6–5.4).
77. Denise Kimber Buell, "Race and Universalism in Early Christianity," *JECS* 10 (2002): 436.
78. Laura Nasrallah, "Mapping the World: Justin, Tatian, Lucian, and the Second Sophistic," *HThR* 98 (2005): 310.
79. Indeed the fact that it is disagreement over the practices that god commands in daily life that causes Trypho not to recognize "Christians" as part of the people in relation to god undergirds this point.
80. Since ethnicity was usually associated with a nominal geographical placement. See Denise Kimber Buell, "Rethinking the Relevance of Race for Early Christian Self-Identity," *HThR* 94 (2001): 459.

god, unless they follow his ways, the religious practices of the "Jews." The point is not that "Christians" are not or do not claim to be "universal;" they do. Rather, as Buell notes, this does not rule out that they continue to see themselves as a race.[81] This race is the race of Israel, more widely defined but no less specific a people.[82]

That the "Christian" community of this time would not have had a singular ethnic makeup and would have been a diverse mix of peoples mirrors the mixed constitution of "Judaism" at this time. As "Jews" were of different countries, cultures, languages, and traditions, so too were the followers and pupils of Christ. When Arthur J. Droge tries to make a point by differentiating "Christians" from "Jews" with respect to "nation" and "race," he overlooks that "Christians," as seen in Justin, see themselves as the "true Israel" precisely rooted in the grand narrative of the Davidic story.[83] Early "Christians," Justin included, did in fact often write in such a way as to deliberately portray themselves as a *genos* or *ethnos*, as a genuine people comparable to others.[84] Despite claiming "Christians" to be a race, however, Justin does not yet describe "Christians" as a third race. To him "Christians" are a genuine people, not by physical ancestry, as Christians do not follow a physical, but a spiritual law; hence he defines "Christians" rather by faith and its practices.[85] Justin exemplifies this in the later portions of the *Dialogue*

---

81. Ibid., 459.
82. As the audience of his texts varies so does Justin's emphasis on universal or racial "Christian" identity. Nasrallah has noted that the racial identity appears stronger in the *Apologies* through his references to his Samaritan heritage, and that the *Dialogue* seems to pay more attention to the universal aspects of "Christian" identity. There is some truth to this; however, it fails to note that the universal elements in the *Dialogue* serve to allow Justin to present the "true philosophy" to "Jews" in terms they could accept, as philosophical truth. Furthermore in the later portions of the *Dialogue*, when Justin's "Christian" identity has been well and truly revealed and detailed, Justin is far more comfortable using racial language for "Christians," especially when the topics of discussion concern salvation and the place of the "Jews" in this. See Nasrallah, "Mapping the World," 310.
83. "Unlike the Egyptians, Babylonians, Phonenicians, and Jews, the Christians did not comprise a distinct national or racial group whose history could be written. Even so, this did not stop such writers as Aristides, the anonymous author of the Epistle to Diognetus, and Eusebius from describing Christianity as a *triton genos* or 'third race' distinct from Greeks and barbarians." Author J. Droge, *Homer or Moses? Early Christian Interpretations of the History of Culture* (Tübingen: Mohr Siebeck, 1989), 196.
84. Buell, *New Race*, 63–93.
85. Buell points out that this was not the only way to define *ethnos* and that the Romans often had scant regard for genealogy when it came to defining who was Roman. See ibid., 40. Even more obvious, by modern standards, indices of race or ethnicity such as skin color were not a given

where he feels free to speak of "Christians" as a race. Furthermore, "Christians" do not just claim to be any people, they claim to be nothing less than the new and true Israel.[86] As Tomson points out via Josephus, who frequently uses *genos Hebraios* and *Israelitai*, such appeals to language were designed to connote antiquity and respect.[87] By calling themselves Israel, "Christians" are therefore claiming "Jewish" ancestry by a different means than "Jews" (who do so according to the flesh as Justin presents it). As such, they are not claiming to be a new people, but rather the true form of an ancient and venerable people. As discussed above, Tomson believed that "Jews" in the Greco-Roman period used the term Israel as an insider's appellation and "Jew" when giving an outsider's perspective. If Israel is the *bona fide* term for the children of god, then Justin is using the same term as an insider. To say "Christians" are the true Israel can be read as though Justin is claiming an identity that is his own. It is certainly a claim that presents itself from within the Israelite tradition.[88]

A salient point with reference to Justin's claim that Christians are the "true Israel" is his proximity to and his upbringing in Samaria, where he will have been aware of Samaritans who also claim to be the "true Israel." Justin calls himself an uncircumcised gentile, neither a "Jewish" proselyte nor a Samaritan, but he claims the "Abrahamic," and the prophetic, tradition for himself in order to claim to be member of the "true Israel." Furthermore, the question of Justin's relationship to the Samaritan tradition should not be too hastily dismissed. Admittedly, Justin has a father with a Greek name and does not practice Samaritan customs, but this does not necessarily mean he was not intimately aware of the tradition or attached to it in some way.[89]

---

as differential, or prejudicially differential, factors in Roman culture. Shelley P. Haley has argued convincing that the Romans were aware of skin color difference as a factor in the construction of difference, but that it was so in a much less obvious and significant way than today and could only function in concert with many other important differentials. See Shelly P. Haley, "Be Not Afraid of the Dark: Critical Race Theory and Classical Studies," in Nasrallah and Fiorenza, eds., *Prejudice and Christian Beginnings*, 27–49.

86. Justin makes this claim explicitly in *Dial.* 11.5; 35.3, and it is the main topic of chapter 123.
87. Tomson, "Names," 138.
88. That said, it is possible that using the language in this way is something Justin has observed and copied, as "true Israel" would seem to be something of a tautology from Tomson's analysis.
89. P. R. Weis demonstrated over fifty years ago that where Justin has sometimes been thought to

After all, in *Dial.* 120.6 he describes the Samaritans as his own people and claims to be "Israel" despite practicing none of the "Abrahamic" customs. Furthermore, the claim for Justin's distance from the Samaritans is closely related to the view that Justin did not know the Scriptures until the *presbutes* revealed them to him as recorded in introduction to the *Dialogue* and therefore he could not have known the Samaritan traditions prior to this. Revealed is the operative word because it does not seem that the *presbutes* is presenting new information in *Dial.* 7.1. Justin has asked him if it is worth having a teacher and the *presbutes* reveals the prophets as teachers. Further, he presents this as though Justin does not already know it. Grace, as we shall see below, is the gift of right instruction that comes from Christ and his followers. Without this, the Scriptures cannot be understood. This grace is what the *presbutes* has and what Justin and the "Jews" (as Justin casts them) lack. While Justin may not be ignorant of the Scriptures, he is nonetheless coming to see them as they truly are for the first time. This is consistent with the conversion moment that follows which appears as a moment of instant revelation and epiphany rather than interest in new information. It is also commonly thought that Justin's philosophical journey happens outside of Palestine. As Oskar Skarsaune correctly notes, however, at this time this learning could have taken place at any point along the coastline from Palestine to Rome and need not demand removal from the Samaritan culture.[90] It is quite possible, therefore, that Justin's claims to be "true Israel" are not completely innovatively "Christian" but are the product of a wide understanding of, and stake in, an older "Abrahamic" debate about who has the right to be called Israel.

Though "Christians" are not born into their ancestry in becoming "Christians" they join a common ancestry from Abraham, Jacob and Jesus. More than a birth rite, this is an ancestry of faith, the same faith that Abraham had. That Justin describes "Christians" this way in

---

make mistakes about the "Judaism" of his time it could be the case that he is, in fact, referencing contemporary Samaritan traditions. See P. R. Weis, "Some Samaritanisms of Justin Martyr," *JTS* 45 (1944): 199–205.

90. Skarsaune, *Proof from Prophecy*, 245–46.

the *Dialogue* but not in *1 Apology* demonstrates the different agendas that dictate the vocabulary with which Justin operates. The early part of the *Dialogue*, as the following chapter will demonstrate, is chiefly dedicated to marking out what "Christian" faith is in a clandestine manner without Trypho knowing he is talking with a "Christian." This is done in order to circumvent Trypho's prejudices as a "Jew," given that Justin presents the "Jews" as enemies and oppressors of "Christians." Once Justin reveals that he is a "Christian" much of the groundwork is already done. Trypho's questions concerning the status of the "Jews" prompt answers about "Christians" being the true Israelite race and promised people of god.[91] In *Dial.* 135 Justin quotes from assorted passages from Isaiah (42:1-6; 65:9-12; 2:5-6) in order to assert that because they have lived in disobedience and must therefore be unacceptable to god, Trypho's people cannot be the promised seed of Jacob and to reinforce the point that "Christians" are the true Israel. Even so, at the very end of the passage he says: "It is necessary for us here to observe that there are two seeds of Judah, and two races, as there are two houses of Jacob: the one begotten by blood and flesh, the other by faith and the Spirit." (*Dial.* 135.6). In this way, even when claiming to be the true inheritors of the promises of god, Justin is prepared to acknowledge the lineage of Trypho's people. This serves as a way of reconnecting "Jews" with "Christians" and demonstrating that the "Christians" were predicted as god's people from within the "Jews'" own tradition.

The political advantage of reinforcing the relationship between "Christians" and "Jews" is that it counters some "Jewish" factions' desire to attempt to separate "Christians" from the "Jewish" body politic. Further, being more closely associated with "Jews" goes some way to establishing that "Christians" are not a novelty of human opinion (a new *Superstitio* as Pliny saw them) but rather an ancient and venerable people to be tolerated just as the "Jews" are. Indeed, as *1 Apology* argues, "Christians" should be respected even more than

---

91. Justin refers to "Christians" as γενος (genus, which we can translate as race, family or class) on five occasions and once as a tribe (the same term he uses to for the "Jews" in the *Dialogue*). See *Dial.* 119, 123, 135.

"Jews" because they are more trustworthy and less volatile. Justin displays a further advantage to understanding "Christians" as an Israelite people: peoples have borders. A simple collection of different peoples united under Christ may not have been recognizable and interpretable to Romans. Furthermore, speaking of "Christians" as a race allows "Christians" to place reasonable limits on the tradition. "Christians" are united by their trust in Christ but only those who trust truly are genuinely united and constitute Christ's people, who are simultaneously god's people, the new Israel. "Jews" who do not follow Christ obviously do not meet this criteria and nor do many of those called "Christians," as Justin will go on to argue. Nationhood is a key part of "Christian" identity for Justin, then, even if it is not the only formulation of this identity by him.

The language of peoplehood that Justin and other early "Christians" employ is not contradictory with the universal nature of "Christianity," nor are they two poles of an argument. Rather, they aim at the same point: anyone can be called "Christian," but being "Christian" is joining a definitive people:

> Christian Self-definition as a people was not mutually exclusive with universalism. By locating themselves in a historical narrative whose trajectory moved in an arc from one kind of human (either unified or internally composite) to many kinds of humans Christians could claim to represent the future reunification or perfection of the entire human race. This argument sought its authority in the past and was especially elaborated in terms of peoplehood.[92]

"Christians" unite themselves with a history, a single, ancient, and true history, one which builds on "Judaism" while at the same time making claims for Christ that reject this history. We shall see below that the Romans may not have known "Christians" as a people yet, probably because they could not clearly tell them apart from "Jews," despite the efforts of the "Jews" as Justin describes them. Nonetheless in Justin's presentation of "what" "Christians" are, it is inescapable that they are a definitive people, predicated on a "Jewish" history but

---

92. Buell, *New Race*, 84.

not bound by its practices. Compared to those who practice God's law physically, the spiritual law obeyers are a new race. Even if the Romans cannot discern this, Justin wants the true Israelites to be thought of as a people with a history, the "Jewish" history, but not as irascible, dull-minded (his insults for "Jews" can be seen as means of undermining their credibility while rescuing their history, thus making it credible to worship God by dissociating himself from this volatile people) "Jews."

The Motif of the Persecuted Prophet

It is pertinent to ask why "Jews" might want to exile "Christians" or clarify their relationship to them. Why would the "Jews" persecute "Christians" more than any other nation as Justin has claimed them do? This is, in fact, an extremely important question because Paula Fredriksen has argued that claims such as Justin's, not uncommon among early "Christians," for widespread persecution by "Jews" are difficult to sustain in light of evidence of much ordinary social interaction.[93] Livesey has gone even further than Fredriksen to say that the story Justin tells is more or less implausible: "I conclude that Justin's constructions are theological and do not correspond with the contemporary social situation among Christians and Jews. These theological distinctions would serve to create divisions where no such distance between these groups otherwise existed."[94] If Justin is making stronger social distinctions than may have existed, then why? The story of "Jewish" persecution is recurrent in the *Dialogue* and we ought not to think this is something Justin has fabricated on a whim. It seems he really believes this account; but it is also shaped into a powerful rhetoric that repays closer inspection.

First of all it is salient to note that Justin has claimed that the "Jews" persecute "Christians" and that they do so more than any other people. More importantly he says they persecute Christ and his followers. It is not "Christians," in a straightforward sense as a people, who are

---

93. Paula Fredriksen, "What 'Parting of the Ways?'," in *The Ways That Never Parted: Jews and Christians in Late Antiquity and the Early Middle Ages*, ed. Adam H. Becker and Annette Yoshiko Reed (Tübingen: Mohr Siebeck, 2003), 58–60.
94. Livesey, "Theological Identity Making," 57.

persecuted. Rather it is Christ himself who is persecuted and blasphemed and those who stand by him share in this. "Christians" confess to being his followers and suffer the same suffering he did in the present time. In *Dial.* 26.1 we see evidence of this: "And I replied, 'I did not say that [namely that none of Trypho's kind shall inherit from God] but I do say that those who have persecuted Christ in the past and still do, and do not repent, shall not inherit anything on the holy mountain, unless they repent.'"[95]

As in the above-quoted *Dial.* 17, Christ is the one persecuted here and it is the "Jews" who are prejudiced against him and those who hold by him. "Christians" as a persecuted body are secondary to Christ. Why might it be significant for Justin that the "Jews" persecute Christ? Because Christ is Israel, the one against whom Jacob was wrestling, but who overcame Jacob and executed god's will:

> And the name Israel means, a man who overcomes power; for Isra is a man overcoming, and El is power. That Christ would do this when He became man was foretold by the mystery of Jacob's wrestling with Him who appeared to him, in that He ministered to the will of the Father.... But His name from the beginning was Israel, the name which he gave to the blessed Jacob when He blessed him with His own name, proclaiming thereby that all who through Him have fled for refuge to the Father, are blessed Israel. But you have not understood any of this, and not being prepared to attempt to understand, expect assuredly to be saved because you are the children of Jacob according to the flesh. But in such matters you deceive yourselves, I have shown by many words.[96] (*Dial.* 125.3, 5)

Christ being called Israel, having been so forever and foretold in Scripture, demonstrates his credentials as not only a figure genuinely part of this tradition but also its source and fulfillment. Being associated with Christ is to be associated with the true and original

---

95. Κἀγώ· Οὐ τοῦτό φημι, ἀλλ' οἱ τὸν Χριστὸν διώξαντες καὶ διώκοντες καὶ μὴ μεντανοοῦντες οὐ κληρονομήσουσιν ἐν τῷ ὄρει τῷ ἁγίῳ οὐδέν.
96. My translation. Καὶ τὸ οὖν Ἰσραὴλ ὄνομα τοῦτο σημαίνει· ἄνθρωπος νικῶν δύναμιν· τὸ γὰρ ἴσρα ἄνθρωπος νικῶν ἐστι, τὸ δὲ ἢλ δύναμις. Ὅπερ καὶ διὰ τοῦ μυστηρίου τῆς πάλης, ἣν ἐπάλαισεν Ἰακὼβ μετὰ τοῦ φαινομένου, ἀγγέλου μὲν ἐκ τοῦ τῇ τοῦ πατρὸς βουλῇ ὑπηρετεῖν.... Ὁ δὲ Ἰσραὴλ ἦν ὄνομα αὐτῷ ἄνωθεν, ὃν ἐπωνόμασε τὸν μακάριον Ἰακὼβ εὐλογῶν τῷ ἑαυτοῦ ὀνόματι, κηρύσσων καὶ διὰ τούτου ὅτι πάντες οἱ δι' αὐτοῦ τῷ πατρὶ προσφεύγοντες εὐλογημένος Ἰσραήλ ἐστιν. Ὑμεῖς δέ, μηδὲν τούτων νενοηκότες μηδὲ νοεῖν παρασκευαζόμενοι, ἐπειδὴ κατὰ τὸ σαρκικὸν σπέρμα τοῦ Ἰακὼβ τέκνα ἐστέ, πάντως σωθήσεσθαι προσδοκᾶτε. Ἀλλ' ὅτι καὶ ἐν τούτοις ἑαυτοὺς πλανᾶτε, ἀποδέδεικταί μοι ἐν πολλοῖς.

Israel. In *Dial.* 123.9 Justin makes this point clearly: "As therefore from that one Jacob, who was named Israel, your whole race was named Jacob and Israel, so we also because of our being born into Christ are born into God; we are true children of God just like Jacob and Israel and Judah and David, and those who keep the commandments of Christ."[97] Trypho's nation may well have been called Israel, but they are only called so because of Christ; Christ overcame Jacob in the wrestling match and renamed them as his own. So "Christians," for Justin, are the true Israel because they are directly from Christ. If "Christians" are the true Israel, then the persecution of Christ and of "Christians" is the persecution of Israel. Consequently, those who engage in this persecution betray themselves as not Israel, as outside of god's holy people. To further show that "Christians" are truly Israel in contrast to "Jews" Justin utilizes the motif of the persecuted prophets of Israel. Christ is the victim, he is the hated prophet who is murdered in "Jewish" tradition like his prophets before him (*Dial.* 16.4), and "Christians" share in this office; they participate in his name and victimhood. This is significant because Justin continues to employ this strategy frequently in the *Dialogue*. He claims the prophets as witnesses to Christ, and in doing so casts "Christians" as the righteous truth-speaking prophets of the established "Jewish" tradition that addressed the people's disobedience in the hope of bringing them to repentance, but were hated for it. In this model, Christ and his followers are heirs of the prophets in the tradition of Isaiah and Jeremiah calling the people to repentance, while the "Jews" take the role of those who disbelieved the prophets and hated them while continuing in disobedience.[98] Again, at *Dial.* 117.3, Justin casts blame on to the "Jews," this time their leaders specifically, for how "Christians" are treated:

---

97. My translation. Ὡς οὖν ἀπὸ τοῦ ἑνὸς Ἰακὼβ ἐκείνου, τοῦ καὶ Ἰσραὴλ ἐπικληθέντος, τὸ πᾶν γένος ὑμῶν προσηγόρευτο Ἰακὼβ καὶ Ἰσραήλ, οὕτω καὶ ἡμεῖς ἀπὸ τοῦ γεννήσαντος ἡμᾶς εἰς θεὸν Χριστοῦ, ὡς καὶ Ἰακὼβ καὶ Ἰσραὴλ καὶ Ἰούδα καὶ Ἰωσὴφ καὶ Δαυῒδ καὶ θεοῦ τέκνα ἀληθινὰ καλούμεθα καὶ ἐσμέν, οἱ τὰς ἐντολὰς τοῦ Χριστοῦ φυλάσσοντες.
98. Judith Lieu, "Accusations of Jewish persecution in early Christian sources, with particular reference to Justin Martyr and the Martyrdom of Polycarp," in Stanton and Stroumsa, eds., *Tolerance and Intolerance*, 281.

…whereby the passion which the Son of God endured for us is commemorated. But your high priests and teachers have caused his name to be profaned and blasphemed throughout the whole world. But those filthy garments, which you have placed upon on all who have become "Christians" by the name of Jesus, God will show will be taken from us when he raises all up from the dead.[99]

As before, the name "Christians" with reference to Jesus is seen as "filthy garments" which Jesus" his followers have not taken upon themselves but have been put on them by outsiders. The action against Christ is always primary and the action against "Christians" is only by extension. In this way, Christ is an example of the persecuted profit motif that, according to Judith Lieu, Justin relies greatly on in his arguments concerning the "Jews" pointing out that *1 Apol.* 35 clearly fulfils this function through an extended discussion in which *Zechariah* 9:9[100] *Isaiah* 9:6, and *Psalm* 22 are used in combination to prove the culpability of the "Jews" in the death of Jesus:

> The Jews are thus killing their prophets still, Jesus and now his followers, and since they can be demonstrated to be his prophets, words foretold from God, then they are true and of God. The Jewish misunderstanding of prophecy serves as a fulfilment of prophecy as their hostility to Jesus and his followers proves that they have not understood their own tradition and are unrepentant sinners in the face of a true revelation from God.[101]

Justin is clearly convinced of the enmity that "Jews" have towards "Christians" and this ought to be taken seriously.[102] However, as we proceed we must keep in mind that casting the "Jews" in this light also does significant work for his argument by making "Christians" appear as the true Israel, the persecuted truth-speaking children of god.

---

99. My translation. ἐν ᾗ καὶ τοῦ πάθους, ὃ πέπονθε δι' αὐτοὺς ὁ υἱὸς τοῦ θεοῦ, μέμνηνται. οὗ τὸ ὄνομα βεβηλῶθῆαι κατὰ πᾶσαν τὴν γῆν καὶ βλασφημεῖσθαι οἱ ἀρχιερεῖς τοῦ λαοῦ ὑμῶν καὶ διδάσκαλοι εἰργάσαντο, ἃ ῥυπαρὰ καὶ αὐτὰ ἐνδύματα, περιτεθέντα ὑφ' ὑμῶν πᾶσιτ τοῖς ἀπὸ τοῦ ὀνόματος τοῦ Ἰησοῦ γενομένοις Χριστιανοῖς, δείξει αἰρόμενα ἀφ' ἡμῶν ὁ θεός, ὅταν πάντας ἀναστήσῃ.
100. Wrongly attributed by Justin to Zephaniah.
101. Lieu, "Accusations," 284.
102. As noted above, while in the *Dialogue* Justin holds the "Jewish" teachers more specifically responsible for the enmity he still understands it as general problem of persecution by "Jews" at large, albeit stoked by the agenda of the few.

Further evidence that Justin believes the "Jews" persecute and single out "Christians" can be seen in *Dial.* 96.1-2:

> For the statement in the law, "Cursed is every one that hangs on a tree," confirms our hope which depends on the crucified Christ, not because He who has been crucified is cursed by God, but because God foretold that which would be done by you all, and by those like you, who do not know that this is He who existed before all, who is the eternal Priest of God, and King, and Christ. And now you clearly see that this has happened. For you curse in your synagogues all those who are called Christians through Him, and other nations carry out the curse, killing those who only confess themselves to be Christians; to all of whom we say, You are our brothers; recognise the truth of God.[103]

Here again the prophecy of the "Jews" themselves has foretold of the death of Christ which they did not see nor repent of. They curse Christ and his followers, failing to see what their god has done in and through him. Precisely what form and significance this *cursing* took is difficult to tell. Scholarship is littered with examples of those who have seen this as an example of the famous *birkath hamminim*.[104] However, as Boyarin points out, this conclusion is weak since the *birkath hamminim* is not attested from a "Jewish" source until the *Tosefta* dating from the mid-third century, and there are good reasons to doubt the historicity of the council at Yavneh founding such a curse.[105] There is no reason to assume that Justin is fabricating his account, but caution is to be advised before interpreting Justin as referring to an established, uniform, and formalized rabbinic policy rather than reflecting a more general disharmony among "Jews," or their teachers, towards "Christians."

---

103. Καὶ γὰρ τὸ εἰρημένον ἐν τῷ νόμῳ, ὅτι Ἐπικατάρατος πᾶς ὁ κρεμάμενος ἐπὶ ξύλου, οὐχ ὡς τοῦ θεοῦ καταρωμένου τούτου τοῦ ἐσταυρωμένου, ἡμῶν τονοῖ τὴν ἐλπίδα ἐκκρεμαμένην, ἀπὸ τοῦ σταυρωθέντος Χριστοῦ, ἀλλ' ὡς προειπόντος τοῦ θεοῦ τὰ ὑφ' ὑμῶν καὶ πάντων τῶν ὁμοίων ὑμῖν, μὴ ἐπισταμένων τοῦτον εἶναι τὸν πρὸ πάντων ὄντα καὶ αἰώνιον τοῦ θεοῦ ἱερέα καὶ βασιλέα Χριστὸν μέλλοντα γίνεσθαι. Ὅπερ καὶ ὄψει ἰδεῖν ὑμῖν ἔστι γινόμενον· ὑμεῖς γὰρ ἐν ταῖς συναγωγαῖς ὑμῶν καταρᾶσθε πάντων τῶν ἀπ' ἐκείνου γενομένων Χριστιανῶν, καὶ τὰ ἄλλα ἔθνη, ἃ καὶ ἐνεργῆ τὴν κατάραν ἐργάζονται, ἀναιροῦντα τοὺς μόνον ὁμολογοῦντας ἑαυτοὺς εἶναι Χριστιανούς· οἷς ἡμεῖς ἅπασι λέγομεν, ὅτι Ἀδελφοὶ ἡμῶν ἐστε, ἐπίγνωτε μᾶλλον τὴν ἀλήθειαν τοῦ θεοῦ.
104. William Horbury offers a clear summary account of this in William Horbury, *Jews and Christians in Contact and Controversy* (Edinburgh: T&T Clark, 1998), 67-110.
105. See Boyarin, "Justin Martyr Invents Judaism," 434-35, for further reasons why this might not be so.

Beyond this, it is interesting that Justin here refers to his "Jewish" interlocutors as brothers (ἀδελφοί) and appeals that they should recognize the truth of god that is Christ. This suggests Justin considers "Jews" as family, further evidence that they are all part of the Israelite tradition. As family they share the same *genos* to which he himself belongs. Even if "Jews" are erring, they share the same god and, as Justin will go on to claim, common ancestors. In other words, Justin is saying, "The prophets (who are ours as well as yours) were right; recognize this and come back to god." As the boundaries between "Jewish" and "Christian," at least rhetorically, are not fixed,[106] Justin can in this way include "Jews" as part of the same tradition while criticizing them for failing it. This is another instance of the strategy we saw above of portraying followers of Christ as those who follow god and who are god's own people, Israel. As we shall see, this extends to the claim that "Christians" have a correct/inspired understanding of the Scriptures, while the "Jews" choose to remain in rebellion against God and persecute the truth-tellers, the prophets.

In explaining "Jewish" persecution of "Christians" this way, Justin is able to emphasize the rightful status of "Christians" as Israel. Justin makes this claim from a theological conviction to worship this God. "Christian" is a shame name but Israel carries antiquity and honor. "Christians" are to be distinguished from "Jews," however, because they are more truly Israel by virtue of truly keeping god's commandments. "Jews" are presented as a rebellious people, less than Israel, who have been habitually disobedient to their god and whom the rulers will not have forgotten as having been involved in a series of major revolts against Rome. Bar Kokhba, who led only the most recent in a series of failed revolts, had singled out "Christians" as of questionable "Jewishness," and their increasingly gentile composition

---

106. Indeed Justin will later state that "Jews" who observe the law yet follow Christ truly can be saved and be a part of "Christian" communities. Not all "Christians" agree on this, and so Justin alludes to the diversity among "Christians," though this probably does not include heretics, as Justin sometimes prefaces dissenters as pure (καθαρὸς) "Christians," but Justin expects, and states, that pagan converts give up their former ways at conversion. It seems this is not required of Jews entirely which suggests they are already closely bound up in the "Christian" (or Jewish under Christ) way of life. See Buell, *New Race*, 109–15.

could make them vulnerable to appearing as converts from pagan ancestry, in contravention of Roman law, who worship another failed messianic martyr. Given the recent history, any messianic strands within "Judaism" posed a potential threat. The persecution of "Christians" by "Jews" allows Justin to speak of "Christians" as the truly reliable and honest ancient people who are protected by Roman law, while "Jews" are belligerent and rebellious. If this kind of explanation could be in anyway influential, and there is no evidence to suggest any Roman rulers would have been impressed by it, then it would be quite understandable why some fellow "Jews" would want to halt the spread of "Christians," be they gentile or ethnically Hebrew. Justin may be rhetorically spinning the persecution of "Christians," but there is no reason to assume it is complete fiction. Yet, the use he puts it to suits his end to define "what" "Christians" are; in summary not just followers of Christ, but true Israelites, no new thing, no fresh or foreign superstition, but the genealogical heirs of old.

Greco-Roman Perspectives

We have established not only that "Christians" are shamed by and because of "Jews," as Justin presents it, and that they wish to be seen as genuine people, rather than an entity beyond peoplehood as historians and theologians have often explained early Christianity.[107] Furthermore, since we have seen that "Christians" wish to be seen as a truer Israelite race, the ground is laid to consider Justin's testimony regarding how Greco-Romans (and the Roman rulers in particular) seemed to view them. It is clear what Justin thinks "Christians" means but to what extent are the Greco-Romans aware of "Christians" and what do they think they are according to Justin? Understanding the perspectives of those Justin addressees is important because their understanding is part of what Justin is responding to in his attempt to define "Christian" identity. Furthermore the prejudices of his addressees can also provide ammunition for defining and distinguish-

---

107. Ibid., 35–37.

ing true followers of Christ from false ones like the followers of Marcion.

The question of whether Greco-Roman pagans, either rulers or populace, could easily tell the difference between "Christians" and "Jews" is a pertinent and difficult one. There is much evidence to suggest that the both the rulers and the populace had difficulties in neatly distinguishing "Jews" and "Christians." As we will see, the sources testify that Romans knew the name "Christians" and, considered them criminal, but that in itself should not be taken as evidence that they understood them to be a separate entity from "Jews."[108] Benjamin Isaac has suggested that in Roman literature "Christians" were at best called "a sort of men" (*genus hominum*) whereas "Jews" were always called "a people" (*gens*). While this could suggest a clear distinction between the two,[109] Isaac does not make this claim directly. Regardless of what "Christians" called themselves, the Romans would only have called them "a people" if they saw them as distinct from the "Jewish" people. To call them a "kind of men" is to recognize their entity without necessarily removing them from "Jewishness."[110] In the fifth book of Tacitus's lost work, the *Historiae* recorded by Sulpicius Severus, Tacitus reports concerning Titus, who desired that "the religion of the Jews and the Christians be destroyed completely: For although these religions are conflicting, they nevertheless developed from the same origins. The Christians arose from the Jews: With the root removed, the branch is easily killed."[111] Here, Tacitus speaks first of one religion, then of two conflicting religions, and ends by calling "Christians" a branch of "the

---

108. For example, Ronald Mellor has recently argued that even though Tacitus identifies "Christians" as a popular title in *Ann.* 15.44.4, he knew very little about them as a group and did not distinguish them clearly from "Jews," seeing their movement as part of the spread and threat of "Jewish" ideas. See Tacitus, *Annals*, trans. R. Mellor (*OACL*; Oxford: Oxford University Press, 2011), 57–62.
109. Benjamin, Isaac, "Roman Religious Policy and the Bar Kokhba War," in P. Schäfer, ed., *War Reconsidered*, 51.
110. A more effective classification of the difference would be to examine how Romans spoke of other "Jewish" sects and fringe "Jewish" groups (the more diverse the better) close to the time of their inception. However, even this may not yield comparable results because no other group turned into a different religion.
111. *Plenius Iudaeorum et Christianorum religio tolleretur: quippe has religiones, licet contrarias sibi, isdem tamen ab auctoribus profectas; Christianos ex Iudaeis extitisse: radice sublata stirpem facile perituram* (Severus, *Chron.* 2.30.7).

Jews," suggesting both togetherness and separation. As such, this account does not represent clarity and suggests anything but a clean distinction between "Christians" and "Jews." All it does testify is that they are closely related, with "Christians" being in some way part of "Jews." Titus reigned in the late first century, meaning this report would reflect quite an early stage of "Christianity." Tacitus died in 117 CE and recorded his report sometime in the early second century. Crucially, though, this preceded Bar Kokhba by fifteen years (though it was roughly contemporary with the Kitos War), meaning that even if this were a reflection of his time of writing as much as that of Titus it would still predate the time that Justin marks out as the pivotal moment. By Justin's time it seems that "Christianity" is branching out further from "Judaism," or, following Justin's presentation, had been further subject to a program of expulsion begun under Bar Kokhba.

Pliny's letter to Trajan will be discussed in detail in chapter 3, but it is pertinent to note here that it reveals that in his long career in Roman leadership, as an advocate, judge and assessor, he has not come across a problem such as the "Christians." This suggests that if similar trials had occurred previously, they would have been very rare, and, furthermore, that within the empire, up to high levels of governance, there existed confusion as to exactly what kind of thing "Christians" were. An illustration of this is clearly seen in Pliny's words: "For I was in no doubt that, whatever it might be that they were admitting to, their stubbornness and unyielding obstinacy certainly ought to be punished."[112] Putting this into context, Pliny has asked those under investigation if they are "Christians" and they, in the knowledge that the penalty is death, proceed to confess this numerous times, but he does not understand the content of what they are claiming to be. This becomes even clearer when Pliny reports that he tortured[113] two deaconesses (*ministrae*) in order to gain a clearer a picture of what "Christians" are following a series of confusing testimonies.

It is worth bearing in mind that Pliny wrote from Bythinia which

---

112. *Neque enim dubitabam, qualecumque esset quod faterentur. Pertinaciam certe et inflexibilem obstinationem debere puniri* (Pliny, *Ep. Tra.* 10.96.3).
113. Slave evidence being inadmissible without torture.

had a large "Jewish" population, and yet he does not mention "Jews" anywhere in his letters. This could suggest that he, unlike Titus, was not aware (or not concerned) that those charged whom he investigated were not "Jews." In not understanding what "Christians" believe or "are" it is not necessarily the case that Pliny understands them to be a non-"Jewish" or counter-"Jewish" group. Pliny remarks that he observes "depraved and excessive superstition" (*superstitionem pravam, immodicam*) among those he investigated.[114] This might suggest a new, non-traditional, potentially non-"Jewish" group, but this need not necessarily be the case. The term *superstitio* has a shifting history and its usage varies greatly from Cicero, the earliest use of the noun, to Diocletian.[115] As Rives notes, it is a term better defined by what it is not than by what it is, and that can applied in different ways and with different force to the rational religious practices of the Greco-Roman elite.[116] Buell outlines it well:

> In the late republican period, Romans increasingly attempt to differentiate "religion" from nonreligion. "Nonreligion" was a moving target but was most commonly embraced by concepts of superstitio and atheism. Superstitio in particular comes to function both as a term for improper religious worship by Romans and for foreignness. Thus, religion could be used to highlight differences within an ethnos or genos or to locate apparent insiders as outsiders.... The meaning and application of the term superstitio shifted over time. Where the label superstitio had previously connoted improper or excessive religious practices, including Roman cults, by the second century C.E. its primary connotation shifted to participation in non-Roman cults that were deemed improper or excessive in their practice. Thus superstitio, as the converse of religio, shifts from having as its primary meaning something Romans risk doing by improper or excessive religious observances of Roman deities to a characteristic of non-Romans.[117]

The term then refers to internal Roman irrationalities or to external foreign practices. *Superstitio* is what the poor, uneducated, or barbarian

---

114. Pliny, *Ep. Tra.* 10.96.8.
115. Richard Gordon, "Superstitio, Superstition and Religious Repression in the Late Roman Republic and Principate (100 BCE–300 CE)," *Past Present* 199 (2008): 77–78.
116. James B. Rives, *Religion in the Roman Empire* (Oxford: Wiley-Blackwell, 2007), 184.
117. Buell, *New Race*, 49.

practiced in contrast to the Roman elites. Therefore it is clear that when Pliny says he only found superstition it need not mean a new group but could simply mean distasteful or excessive religious practice of a foreign nature.[118] This term, then, does not clearly mark out what he has discovered as non-"Jewish," which would also be foreign, though the term can be used to in connection with non-native or non-ancestral and novel religious ideas which would not be tolerated by Rome. It is not completely clear that Pliny understands "Christians" to be independent superstition rather than another form of "Jewish" excess religion, which could also be foreign superstition.

Being a contemporary of Tacitus, Pliny also predates Bar Kokhba, which as we have seen features in a pivotal fashion in Justin's story of the rejection of Christ by the "Jews." Rejection of followers of Christ by extension would make for more isolated and obvious "Christians," but would not provide absolute clarity as to "what" they are. Justin sees himself as a non-"Jewish," gentile member of Israel, but not a proselyte to "Judaism." This is quite a complicated position to present to the pagans who are familiar with the term "Christian," and its negative implications, but little else.

Another Greco-Roman view about "Christians" that Justin details is that they were considered to be atheists (ἄθεοι). Specifically, In 1 Apol. 6.1 and 46.3 Justin notes "Christians" were described as atheists, and Crescens makes the same accusation in 2 Apol. 3.2. Justin denies the accusation in 1 Apol. 13.1: "What sensible man will not grant that we are not atheists, we who worship the Creator of this world; we who say, as we have been taught, that he does not need blood, and libations, and incense."[119] The accusation of atheism was also commonly made

---

118. Beard, North, and Price make the point that this general shift from *superstitio* towards foreign practice began in the late republic and was well established by the early second century. They note that Tacitus refers to the druidic prophecy of the fall of Rome at the hands of the Gauls as "an empty *superstitio*," as he did for various Jewish and Egyptian rituals (*Histories* 4.54.4). Further, they relate Tacitus's claim that the people of Alexandria are "subject to superstitions" and the Jews are a people "prone to superstition, and opposed to religious [meaning well ordered] practices" (*Histories* 4.81.2; 5.13.1). They elaborate that for Tacitus such an understanding of foreign "religious" practices as *superstitio* also led them to cast those practices as possible routes of political subversion to be feared. See Mary Beard, John North, and Simon Price, eds., *Religions of Rome, Vol. 1: A History* (Cambridge, UK: Cambridge University Press, 1998), 221–22.

against "Jews" in the Roman world.[120] Perhaps "Christians" are not being distinguished from "Jews" here, or from gentile proselytes to "Judaism," since, as Justin claims in 1 Apol. 53.5, the majority of "Christians" by this time are gentiles living in the midst of the pagan empire. In making this denial, Justin has claimed the one true god (that is, the god of the "Jews") as the god worshipped by "Christians" and has also denied the need for cultic practice that gives Roman "religion" its cohesion.[121] Such a denial represents a challenge to any thinking that understands "Christians" to be a rival cult or superstition. Given how important cultic acts were to Roman society pre-Constantine, this move should not be underestimated. Ste. Croix characterizes the issue well:

> By far the most important of these [differences between ancient and modern religion] was that pagan religion was a matter of performing cult acts rather than of belief, or ethics. . . . No compulsion was necessary, because until the advent of Christianity no one ever had any reason for refusing to take part in the ceremonies which others observed—except of course the Jews, and they were a special case, a unique exception. The gods would forgive the inexplicable monotheism of the Jews, who were, so to speak, licensed atheists. The Jews of course would not sacrifice to the emperor or his gods, but they were quite willing, while the Temple still stood, to sacrifice to their own god for the well-being of the emperor; and Augustus, if we may believe Philo, by a happy compromise not only accepted this but himself paid for the sacrifices.[122]

"Jews," though aloof, were not opposed to sacrifice as such, and though they kept their own laws, they were happy, at least before the fall of the temple, to support the empire and pay lip service to its system. In the same way, neither were "Christians" necessarily opposed to the empire and Justin is keen to demonstrate "Christians" have no designs

---

119. Ἄθεοι μὲν οὖν ὡς οὔκ ἐσμεν, τὸν δημιουργὸν τοῦδε τοῦ παντὸς σεβόμενοι, ἀνενδεῆ αἱμάτων καὶ σπονδῶν καὶ θυμιαμάτων, ὡς ἐδιδάχθημεν.
120. As Struoumsa notes, it is hardly surprising that the Jews were seen as atheists by Roman standards given they had a god with an unspeakable name and no images to represent him. Guy B. Stroumsa, *The End of Scrifice: Religious Transformations in Late Antiquity* (Chicago: Univeristy of Chicago Press, 2012), 66.
121. Oskar Skarsaune, "Justin and the Apologists," in *The Routledge Companion to Early Christian Thought*, ed. D. Jeffrey Bingham (Abingdon: Rougtledge, 2010), 126.
122. G. E. M. de Ste. Croix, "Why were the Early Christians Persecuted?," in *Christian, Persecution, Martyrdom, and Orthodoxy*, ed. M. Whitby and J. Streeter (Oxford, 2006), 135.

to be a rival to Rome (*1 Apol.* 11). Though understood by the authorities as atheists, "Jews" were tolerated legally because of the antiquity of their traditions. Following this, there is no reason to assume that "Christians" were necessarily seen as a separate body of atheists rather than as another form of "Jews" who were just as irreligious and just as unwilling to make to sacrifices to the Roman gods. In *1 Apol.* 6.1, Justin is forthright in his confession of atheism insofar as the gods of Rome are concerned: "So that we are called atheists, and we confess that we are atheists of such being considered gods, but not towards the most true God, the Father of righteousness and temperance and the other virtues, who is unalloyed with evil."[123] Justin, therefore, aligns himself with the "Jewish" god, and only admits a noncompliance with the multitude of gods, something he had in common with "Jews." No less than the "Jews," true "Christians" will not acknowledge the pagan gods at all. The same can be seen from *1 Apol.* 16.5–7:

> And about not swearing at all and always speaking the truth he commanded thus: "Do not swear at all, but let your yes be yes and your no be no. More than this is from the evil one." And that one must worship God alone he entreated in these words: "The greatest commandment is: you shall worship the Lord your God, and him alone, the Lord who made you shall you serve with all your heart and all your strength." And when someone approached him and said, "Good teacher," he replied: "No one is good expect God alone, who made all things."[124]

The statement Justin relies on here comes from Jesus concerning the rejection of swearing, in principle the same as the *Shema Israel* that was becoming formalized in the morning prayer of the synagogues of Justin's period.[125] Thus "Christians," Justin's community, openly subscribed to the "Jewish" rejection of worship of the Roman gods. This

---

123. My translation. Greek: "Ἔνθεν δὲ καὶ ἄθεοι κεκλήμεθα, καὶ ὁμολογοῦμεν τῶν τοιούτων νομιζομένων θεῶν ἄθεοι εἶναι, ἀλλ' οὐχὶ τοῦ ἀληθεστάτου καὶ πατρὸς δικαιοσύνης καὶ σωφροσύνης καὶ τῶν ἄλλων ἀρετῶν ἀνεπιμίκτου τε κακίας θεοῦ.
124. περὶ δὲ τοῦ μὴ ὀμνύναι ὅλως τἀληθῆ δὲ λέγειν ἀεί, οὕτως παρεκελεύσατο· "Μὴ ὀμόσητε ὅλως, ἔστω δὲ ὑμῶν τὸ ναὶ ναὶ καὶ τὸ οὒ οὔ. τὸ δὲ περισσὸν τούτων ἐκ τοῦ πονηροῦ." ὡς δὲ καὶ τὸν θεὸν μόνον δεῖ προσκυνεῖν οὕτως ἔπεισεν, εἰπών· "Μεγίστη ἐντολή ἐστι· 'Κύριον τὸν θεόν σου προσκυνήσεις καὶ αὐτῷ μόνῳ λατρεύσεις ἐξ ὅλης τῆς καρδίας σου καὶ ἐξ ὅλης τῆς ἰσχύος σου, κύριον τὸν θεὸν τὸν ποιήσαντά σε.'" καὶ προσελθόντος αὐτῷ τινος καὶ εἰπόντος 'Διδάσκαλε ἀγαθέ,' ἀπεκρίνατο λέγων· "Οὐδεὶς ἀγαθὸς εἰ μὴ μόνος ὁ θεός, ὁ ποιήσας τὰ πάντα."
125. Reuven Kimelman, "Rabbinic Prayer in Late Antiquity," in *The Cambridge History of Judaism*, Vol. 4:

is quite important. Both "Jews" and "Christians" can be considered a non-sacrificial people in this period (though Justin treats Trypho and those like him as if they were still maintaining or seeking the old sacrificial system regardless of their practice), and both develop new ways of being sacrificial which would be unrecognizable or uninterpretable to Romans. The new expressions of sacrifice were the rabbinic interpretation of prayer for the "Jews" and the Eucharist for "Christians"[126] These would mean little to the Romans, to whom both "Christians" and "Jews" would appear recalcitrant non-respecters of the Greco-Roman cults. However, we have already seen that Justin reports that his interlocutors' teachers have spread propaganda against them and that they have been cut off since Bar Kokhba. We know "Christian" is a shame name and that "Christians" are isolatable as a group if not separate from the rest of the "Jewish" body politic. As there has been an internal "Jewish" attempt to separate "Christians" from the rest of the body, the threat to "Christians," whether apparent or real, is that they will be denied the conventional status of "tolerable exceptions" enjoyed by the "Jews," and considered instead as atheists, as outside of the ancient Abrahamic tradition.

It is unclear to what extent the Romans would have seen "Christians" this way, but the "Jewish" propaganda and the theological extremism of a sect like Marcionism (which would have appeared atheist and inventing new deities to Roman eyes) makes the case against "Christians" being atheists an important one for Justin. As part of his strategy to address this, Justin shows that others, within the Greco-Roman tradition itself, reject the gods. Most notably, he finds evidence of this in the works of the venerable philosophers.[127] Justin's argument is that philosophers are not decried as criminal or offensive for having said things that could be deemed atheist. Hence, if "Christians" are no longer seen (and protected) as "Jews," they should

---

The Late Roman-Rabbinic Period, ed. S. T. Katz (Cambridge, UK: Cambridge University Press, 2006), 580.
126. Stroumsa, "Sacrafice," 56–83.
127. Athenagoras has an analogous argument about the foolishness of the unsettlable plural relativity of the worship of gods. See Athenagoras, *Leg.* 7.

instead be treated as philosophers. Consequently, they should have the freedom of speech that philosophers enjoy, or should at least be similarly tolerated on artistic license, rather than being seen as a "nationalistic" enterprise that poses a threat to the Empire. In this way, as we see in *1 Apol.* 4.8–9, Justin is seeking to establish parity with other schools:

> For, indeed, some assume the name and appearance of philosophers who behave in no way worthily of their profession. And you know that among the men of ancient times those who contradicted one another in their thought and teaching are nevertheless called by the one name of philosopher. Some of them in their teaching denied the gods and those of them who were poets proclaimed the promiscuity of Zeus as well as of his sons, and you do not bar performers who take up their teaching. Rather, you give prizes and rewards for those who are in good voice when they offer insult to them.[128]

Of course, as Ste. Croix points out, "the vital difference [between 'Christians' and philosophers] was, of course, that the philosophers, whatever they might believe, and even write down for circulation among educated folk, would have been perfectly willing to perform any cult act required of them and that was what mattered."[129] Bizarre views may well be tolerated from philosophers, but Justin's attempt to cite hypocrisy on these grounds is not likely to work. This is because philosophical speculation is not equal to atheism for the Romans. The philosophers may say and do what they like but, as Ste. Croix points out, they will still make offerings to the gods. "Christians" are nonconformists and threaten the communal spiritual life that sustains Roman society. On these grounds at least, they distinguish themselves a little more even than "Jews" in the ordinary sense, though it is still possible that they might have been seen as an excessive superstition among "Judaism" rather than another tradition entirely.

---

128. Οὐκ ὀρθῶς μὲν οὐδὲ τοῦτο πράττεται. καὶ γάρ τοι φιλοσοφίας ὄνομα καὶ σχῆμα ἐπιγράφονταί τινες οἳ οὐδὲν ἄξιον τὴν ὑποσχέσεως πράττουσι. γινώσκετε δ' ὅτι καὶ οἱ τὰ ἐναντία δοξάσαντες καὶ δογματίσαντες τῶν παλαιῶν τῷ ἑνὶ ὀνόματι προσαγορεύνται φιλόσοφοι. καὶ τούτων τινες0 ἀθεότηατ ἐδίδαξαν, καὶ τὸν Δία ἀσελγῆ ἅμα τοῖς αὐτοῦ παισὶν οἱ γενόμενοι ποιηταὶ καταγγέλλουσι, κἀκείνων τὰ διδάγματα οἱ μετερχόμενοι οὐκ εἴργονται πρὸς ὑμῶν· ἆθλα δὲ καὶ τιμὰς τοῖς εὐφώνως ὑβρίζουσι τούτους τίθετε.

129. Ste. Croix, "Persecuted?," 135.

Another difficulty for "Christians" in their Greco-Roman perception is well documented, to the point that Buell calls it a "modern scholarly cliché":[130] the Romans disparaged novelty and valued tradition, ancient and ancestral. Gibbon encapsulated the common view when he said "The Jews were a people which followed, the Christians a sect which deserted, the religion of their fathers."[131] However this does not seem to fit the evidence of the early apologists. On the contrary Christians, including Theophilus, Athenagoras as well as Justin, defend faith in Christ according to the past with the aim of demonstrating continuity. In this sense, they rejected radical novelty, as proposed by Marcion. The claim that "Christians" are wholly outside of "Judaism" is a risk for "Christians" before the empire, and this is why, as we have seen above, Justin is keen to show this not to be true. Pliny and Tacitus were not necessarily clear about this. Tertullian stated in his *Apologeticus* 18.4 that "Christians" were made not born (*Fiunt, non nascuntur Christiani*), that is, that they are not naturally part of the folk by birthright like "Jews," but join the community by personal choice.[132] By Tertullian's time, the description of Gibbon therefore finds support. In Justin's time, however, "Christians" aren't readily and naturally distinguishable from the "Jews." Yet the composition of the "Christian" community is increasingly non-"Jewish." It is incumbent on Justin, then, to demonstrate the continuity of the "Christian" community with Israel, which of course Marcion actively sought to deny.

As noted, Roman authorities mistrusted novelty and valued tradition. Alongside this was a suspicion of conversion and proselytism, and as such the risk of appearing as a convert to "Judaism" was a real one. The issue of proselytism is one of great significance to Justin's studies. The famous rescript of Hadrian has often been thought to be rescinding a full ban on circumcision. Ra'anan Abusch has convincingly argued, however, that a full ban never existed, rather only a general policy against conversion.[133] Instead, "Jews" could

---

130. Buell, *New Race*, 70.
131. Edward Gibbon, *The History of the Decline and Fall of the Roman Empire*, vol. 2 (London: Dent, 1966), VIII.
132. Tertullian, *Apol.* 18.4.

circumcise their own sons according to custom, but no others. This is to say, "Jews" can be "Jews" but no one else is to be added to the number; no one born a pagan ought to become a "Jew." By this logic, anyone born "Christian" could remain one but no one could convert.[134] However, this would only be the case if "Christianity" was a recognized ancient tradition and afforded the associated privileges (which is of course why Justin and other apologists emphasize so greatly their continuity with Israel).

As we have seen, as far as the Greco-Romans are concerned, "Christians," who are even more atheistic than "Jews," ought not to be "Christians" in the first place but remain pagans as they were born. Justin is quite up-front about this in *Dial.* 63.5:

> They further show that the Word of God speaks to those who believe in him (who are of one soul and one synagogue and one church) as to a daughter, namely, to the church, which has arisen from and participates in his name (for we are all called Christians). That this is the case and that we are taught to forget our ancestral customs is proclaimed in the following words: "Hearken, O daughter, and behold, and incline thine ear; forget thy people and the house of thy father, and the King shall desire thy beauty: because He is thy Lord, and thou shalt worship Him.[135]

---

133. Ra'anan Abusch, "Negotiating Difference: Genital Mutilation in Roman Slave Law and the History of the Bar Kokhba Revolt," in Schäfer, *War Reconsidered*, 73–74.
134. An illustration of the importance of the topic of conversion and continuity can be seen in Graham Stanton's argument that Trypho's friends are probably gentiles seeking to become proselytes to "Judaism." In *Dial.* 23.3, at the end of a long discussion about circumcision, Justin admonishes his audience to "remain as you were at birth" (Μείνατε ὡς γεγένησθε). Stanton takes this to mean that Trypho's companions are gentiles who wish to become proselytes to "Judaism." Furthermore, the friends are carefully distinguished from Trypho and portrayed as more cynical and less likely to convert. This distinction is set out early and is consistently maintained throughout the *Dialogue*. Given their sustained hostility to everything Justin says, it is unlikely that they are "Jews" who wish to become "Christians." Further, given Justin's lack of acceptance of the physical traditions of "Judaism," it is unlikely that they see him as a fellow, but less committed, proselyte to god's ways, a kind of sub-follower. This changes the nature of the debate about the *Dialogue*. Conversion now must be seen as a central feature, and a known political risk as well as a theological divide between two groups claiming to be Israel. Trypho is courting controversy and criminality in entertaining such people just as much as Justin is in attempting to convert them, and Trypho, into followers of Christ. See Graham Stanton, "Justin Martyr's Dialogue with Trypho: Group Boundaries, 'Proselytes' and 'God-fearers,'" in Stanton and Stroumsa, eds., *Tolerance and Intolerance*, 265–68.
135. Καὶ ὅτι τοῖς εἰς αὐτὸν πιστεύουσιν, ὡς οὖσι μιᾷ ψυχῇ καὶ μιᾷ συναγωγῇ καὶ μιᾷ ἐκκλησίᾳ, ὁ Λόγος τοῦ θεοῦ λέγει ὡς θυγατρί, τῇ ἐκκλησίᾳ τῇ ἐξ ὀνόματος αὐτοῦ γενομένῃ καὶ μετασχούσῃ τοῦ ὀνόματος αὐτοῦ (Χριστιανοὶ γάρ πάντες καλούμεθα), ὁμοίως φανερῶς οἱ λόγοι κηρύσσουσι, διδάσκοντες ἡμᾶς καὶ τῶν παλαιῶν πατρῴων ἐθῶν ἐπιλαθέσθαι, οὕτως ἔχοντες· Ἄκουσον, θύγατερ, καὶ ἴδε καὶ κλῖνον τὸ οὖς σου,

Justin is saying here that the church of Christ teaches them to "forget old ancestral customs." This, combined with quoting Psalm 45, may make "Christians" look more like "Jewish" proselytes, and claiming at the same time to be "one church and one synagogue" further confuses matters. In some ways the status of "Christians," increasingly of gentile composition, is similar to the gentile friends of Trypho who wish to become "Jewish" proselytes; we know Justin and his group do not count themselves as one with these people, though a competitive distinction would also perhaps be too strong, as the terms of distinction vary, even within Justin's texts, as well as in other second-century "Christian" literature. Being a converted people must also have been a reason for persecution, then, and as Justin's text makes plain by his approach, "Christians" mostly were exactly this, a people who looked to make converts. There are two ways to see the conversion of "Christians" as illegal. First, it would be illegal if they were understood as pagans who have given up the worship of their ancestral gods and become "Christians," regardless of whether or not "Christians" were considered a kind of "Jew." Secondly, it would be illegal if they were understood as "Jews" who have given up their ancestral practices and worship of god in favor of a new tradition, as is the perspective of Trypho.

In the eyes of "Jews," as far as Justin is concerned, "Christian" is a shame name on account of the "Christian" identifying Jesus as the Christ and their interpretation of the Torah in the light of Christ's own teachings. In the eyes of the Greco-Roman pagans "Christian" also is seen as a shame name, because (according to the logic of Justin's story) the "Jews" have successfully cast them as a new group outside of the traditions of Israel. However, it is not entirely clear how distinct "Christians" appeared from "Jews" to the Greco-Roman pagans. Both are deemed atheists. "Christians" may be considered a new sect at times, which would be illegal, but as Titus, Trajan, and Pliny make obvious, their status as a new superstition and their relationship to

καὶ ἐπιλάθου τοῦ λαοῦ σου καὶ τοῦ οἴκου τοῦ πατρός σου· καὶ ἐπιθυμήσει ὁ βασιλεὺς τοῦ κάλλους σου, ὅτι αὐτός ἐστι κύριός σου, καὶ προσκυνήσεις αὐτῷ (Ps 44:11–13).

"Judaism" was not certain. This ambiguity seems to be a reflection of an inner-"Jewish" and inner-"Christian" uncertainty about the precise status of what exactly constitutes "Christian."

Criminality and Confession

Although Romans may well have had difficulty clearly telling "Christians" and "Jews" apart, by the year 117 CE (as we saw in Pliny) they were clearly were familiar with "Christians" as a name given to people, albeit a concept lacking in much definition. This section will focus on how Justin presents the Roman treatment of this group and what this reveals about the content of the name. In doing so, we shall see that the only content "Christian" seems to have is that of a criminal charge. The consistency of Justin's story that "Christians" are slandered because of "Jews," though this need not imply complete historicity, resides in the fact that being "Christian" is considered an offence by non-"Jews" also. Being "Christian" is a charge to which people confess (ὁμολογίαν) or deny (ἀρνέομαι). It is a shame name. 1 *Apol.* 4.3, 4, 5, 7 introduces this theme neatly:

> For neither condemnation nor punishment could reasonably be based on a name unless actions can show something to be virtuous or wicked. And, in point of fact, you do not punish all who are accused in your court before they are proved to be guilty. But with us you take the name as proof, though, so far as the name goes, you should punish our accusers instead. For we are accused of being Christians, and it is not right to hate kindness of heart. . . . For just as certain people, although they have learnt from Christ the Teacher that they should not deny as some who have been taught by the Master, Christ, not to deny, are knocked off course when questioned, so too, perhaps, by their evil lives they play into the hands of those who are already disposed to accuse all Christians of irreligion and injustice.[136]

---

136. ἐξ ὀνόματος μὲν γὰρ ἢ ἔπαινος ἢ κόλασις οὐκ ἂν εὐλόγως γένοιτο, ἢν μή τι ἐνάρετον ἢ φαῦλον δι' ἔργων ἀποδείκνυσθαι δύνηται. καὶ γὰρ τοὺς κατηγορουμένους ἐφ' ὑμῶν πάντας πρὶν ἐλεγχθῆναι οὐ τιμωρεῖτε· ἐφ' ἡμῶν δὲ τὸ ὄνομα ὡς ἔλεγχον λαμβάνετε, καίπερ ὅσον γε ἐκ τοῦ ὀνόματος τοὺς κατηγοροῦντας μᾶλλον κολάζειν ὀφείλετε. Χριστιανοὶ γὰρ εἶναι κατηγορούμεθα τὸ δὲ χρηστὸν μισεῖσθαι οὐ δίκαιον . . . ὃν γὰρ τρόπον παραλαβόντες τινὲς παρὰ τοῦ διδασκάλου Χριστοῦ μὴ ἀρνεῖσθαι, ἐξεταζόμενοι παρακούονται, τὸν αὐτὸν τρόπον κακῶς ζῶντες ἴσως ἀφορμὰς παρέχουσι τοῖς ἄλλως καταλέγειν τῶν πάντων Χριστιανῶν ἀσέβειαν καὶ ἀδικίαν αἱρουμένοις.

From this we learn that Justin and his brothers and sisters in Christ are accused and convicted of being "Christians." The response of the Romans is neither indifference nor praise but prosecution. Justin's argument that a name means nothing apart from actions is to say that actions speak louder than words. This is a prelude to his argument for differentiation amongst those who should be considered worthy to share in Christ's name, those who can reasonably be said to follow his way, and those who cannot. The salient point at this juncture is that Justin is explicit in claiming that being "Christian" is a recognizable charge, related to the Master, Christ, whom he follows. *1 Apol.* 11.1 expands on the name: ". . . whereas we speak of that which is with God, as appears also from the confession of their faith made by those who are charged with being Christians, though they know that death is the punishment awarded to him who so confesses."[137] Death is the reward for those who confess to the crime of being "Christian." This claim is repeated in *Dial.* 46. *2 Apol.* 2 provides an extended account of this reality:

> A certain woman was living with a husband who was licentious, and she had once been licentious herself. But when she learnt the teachings of Christ she came to her senses, and tried to persuade her husband to come to his, reporting what she had been taught, and telling him of the punishment in eternal fire that will come to those who live senselessly and not according to right reason. He, however, continued in his lascivious ways and did things which alienated his wife. For the woman considered it irreligious to sleep any longer with a man who tried, wrongly and against the law of nature, to make use of every opening for pleasure; and she wanted to withdraw from the marriage. But her advisers prevailed upon her to continue living with him, on the grounds that there was hope that her husband might at some time change, and so she forced herself to stay. But then the woman's husband went to Alexandria, and it was reported that he was behaving in even worse fashion. So, to avoid becoming a partner in his evil and impious behaviours by remaining in the marriage and sharing his table and his bed, she gave him what in your language is called a "divorce," and was separated from him. That perfect gentleman, her husband, should have been glad that she had stopped doing the things she had so readily done in the past with servants and

---

137. My translation. Greek: ἡμῶν τὴν μετὰ θεοῦ λεγόντων, ὡς καὶ ἐκ τοῦ ἀνεταζουένους ὑφ' ὑμῶν ὁμολογεῖν εἶναι Χριστιανούς, γινώσκοντες τῷ ὁμολογοῦντι θάνατον τὴν ζημίαν κεῖσθαι, φαίνεται.

hired workers, delighting in getting drunk and in all kinds of evil, and glad that she wanted to stop doing what he had been doing. Instead, when she had left him because he did not want to stop, he brought a charge against her, saying that she was a Christian. She then submitted a petition to you, the emperor, praying that she be given leave to set her financial affairs in order first and to answer the charge later, after she had arranged her affairs; and this you granted. Her former husband, unable for the time being to proceed against her, then turned against a man called Ptolemy, who had been her instructor in the teachings of the Christians, in the following manner. He persuaded a centurion who was a friend of his to arrest Ptolemy and to ask him if he was a Christian. And when Ptolemy, a lover of truth who would not even think of deceiving or lying, confessed that he was a Christian, the centurion had him put in chains and subjected him to punishment for a long time in prison. Finally, when the man was brought before Urbicus, the same question was put to him again, and this only: whether he was a Christian. And again, because through the teaching of Christ he had come to personal knowledge of the good, he confessed the school of divine virtue. For whenever a person denies something, he does so either because he altogether repudiates what he denies, and so becomes a denier, or he shuns confessing it because he knows that he does not deserve it, and that matter has nothing to do with him. Neither of these is the case with a true Christian. And Urbicus ordered him to be led away. Another Christian, a man called Lucius, on seeing the judgement given in this irrational way, said to Urbicus: "Why did you order this man to be punished when he is not convicted of being either an adulterer or a fornicator or a murderer or a thief or a robber or one who has done any evil at all, but confesses that he is called by the name of Christian? Your judgement does not befit a pious emperor, or a philosophical Caesar—his son—or the holy senate, O Urbicus." His only reply was similarly to say to Lucius: "I think you also are one of them." And when Lucius said, "Certainly," Urbicus ordered that he too be led away. Lucius further confessed that he was thankful to have been set free from evil masters such as these and that he was going to the father and king of all. And still another, a third, came forward and was sentenced to be punished.[138]

---

138. Γυνή τις συνεβίου ἀνδρὶ ἀκολασταίνοντι, ἀκολασταίνουσα καὶ αὐτὴ πρότερον. ἐπεὶ δὲ τὰ τοῦ Χριστοῦ διδάγματα ἔγνω, ἐσωφρονίσθη καὶ τὸν ἄνδρα ὁμοίως σωφρονεῖν πείθειν ἐπειρᾶτο, τὰ διδάγματα ἀναφέρουσα τήν τε μέλλουσαν τοῖς οὐ σωφρόνως καὶ μετὰ λόγου ὀρθοῦ βιοῦσιν ἔσεσθαι ἐν αἰωνίῳ πυρὶ κόλασιν ἀπαγγέλλουσα. ὁ δέ, ταῖς αὐταῖς ἀσελγείαις ἐπιμένων, ἀλλοτρίαν διὰ τῶν πράξεων ἐποιεῖτο τὴν γαμετήν. ἀσεβὲς γὰρ ἡγουμένη τὸ λοιπὸν ἡ γυνὴ συγκαταλίνεσθαι ἀνδρὶ παρὰ τὸν τῆς φύσεως νόμον καὶ παρὰ τὸ δίκαιον πόρους ἡδονῆς ἐκ παντὸς πειρωμένῳ ποιεῖσθαι, τῆς συζυγίας χωρισθῆναι ἐβουλήθη. καὶ ἐπειδὴ ἐξεδυσωπεῖτο ὑπὸ τῶν αὐτῆς ἔτι προσμένειν, συμβουλευόντων ὡς εἰς ἐλπίδα μεταβολῆς ἥξοντός ποτε τοῦ ἀνδρός, βιαζομένη ἑαυτὴν ἐπέμενεν. ἐπειδὴ δὲ ταύτης ἀνήρ, εἰς τὴν Ἀλεξάνδρειαν πορευθείς, χαλεπώτερα πράττειν ἀπηγγέλθη, ὅπως μὴ κοινωνοὺς τῶν ἀδικημάτων καὶ ἀσεβημάτων γένηται μένουσα ἐν τῇ συζυγίᾳ καὶ ὁμοδίαιτος καὶ ὁμόκοιτος γινομένη, τὸ λεγόμενον παρ' ὑμῖν ῥεπούδιον δοῦσα, ἐχωρίσθη. ὁ δὲ καλὸς κἀγαθὸς ταύτης ἀνήρ, δέον αὐτὸν χαίρειν ὅτι ἃ πάλαι μετὰ τῶν ὑπηρετῶν καὶ τῶν μισθοφόρων

Key to understanding this passage is the lack of conception of what a "Christian" is at this time. As Thorsteinsson notes, the charge brought against the woman who converts is nothing more than that she is a "Christian," quite apart from any content.[139] As the others come forward it is obvious that no further charges or evidence are required to secure a conviction. As Justin says at *1 Apol.* 4.1, there is nothing that can be judged from a name alone; evidence of something must be required.[140] In this narrative we find three "Christians" individually charged with "being Christian." Though it is not clear what status such charges and trials had in all places under Roman law, it is clear that this is no casual name-calling. These are serious accusations that can and do result in death for the accused if they fail to deny or recant. Following the accusation, the woman is allowed to put her affairs in order and prepare a defense. Ptolemy and Lucius are not as fortunate and suffer at the hands of the authorities on this charge. Furthermore, Justin says in *2 Apol.* 8.6 that Crescens may understand "Christian" teachings and their truth but conceals and distracts from this out of

εὐχερῶς ἔπραττε, μέθαις χαίρουσα καὶ κακίᾳ πάσῃ, τούτων μὲν πᾶν πρᾶξεθν πέπαυτο, καὶ αὐτὸν τὰ αὐτὰ παύσασθαι πράττοντα ἐβούλετο, μὴ βουλομένου ἀπαλλαγείσης, κατηγορίαν πεποίηται, λέγων αὐτὴν Χριστιανὴν εἶναι. καὶ ἡ μὲν βιβλίδιόν σοι τῷ αὐτοκράτορι ἀνέδωκε, πρότερον συγχωρηθῆναι αὐτῇ διοικήσασθαι τὰ ἑαυτῆς ἀξιοῦσα, ἔπειτα τ' ἀπολογήσασθαι περὶ τοῦ κατηγορήματος μετὰ τὴν τῶν πραγμάτων αὐτῆς διοίκησιν· καὶ συνεχώρησας τοῦτο. ὁ δὲ ταύτης ποτὲ ἀνήρ, πρὸς ἐκείνων μὲν μὴ δυνάμενος τανῦν ἔτι λέγειν, πρὸς Πτολεμαῖόν τινα διδάσκαλον ἐκείνης τῶν Χριστιανῶν μαθημάτων γενόμενον ἐτράπετο διὰ τοῦδε τοῦ τρόπου. ἑλαττόνταρχον φίλον αὐτῷ ὑπάρχοντα ἔπεισε λαβέσθαι τοῦ Πτολεμαίου καὶ ἀνερωτῆσαι εἰ Χριστιανός ἐστι. καὶ τὸν Πτολεμαῖον, φιλαλήθη ἀλλ' οὐκ ἀπατηλὸν οὐδὲ ψευδολόγον τὴν γνώμην ὄντα, ὁμολογήσαντα ἑαυτὸν εἶναι Χριστιανόν, ἐν δεσμοῖς γενέσθαι ὁ ἑκατόνταρχος πεποίηκε, καὶ ἐπὶ πολὺν χρόνον ἐν τῷ δεσμωτηρίῳ ἐκολάσατο. τελευταῖον δὲ ὅτε ἐπὶ Οὔρβικον ἤχθη ὁ ἄνθρωπος ὁμοίως αὐτὸ τοῦτο μόνον ἐξητάσθη, εἰ εἴη Χριστιανός. καὶ πάλιν τὰ καλὰ ἑαυτῷ συνεπιστάμενος διὰ τὴν ἀπὸ τοῦ Χριστοῦ διδαχήν, τὸ διδασκαλεῖον τῆς θείας ἀρετῆς ὡμολόγησεν. ὁ γὰρ ἀρνούμενος ὁτιοῦν ἢ κατεγνωκὼς τοῦ πράγματος ἔξαρνος γίνεται, ἢ ἑαυτὸν ἀνάξιον ἐπιστάμενος καὶ ἀλλότριον τοῦ πράγματος τὴν ὁμολογίαν φεύγει· ὧν οὐδὲν πρόσεστι τῷ ἀληθινῷ Χριστιανῷ. καὶ τοῦ Οὐρβίκου κελεύσαντος αὐτὸν ἀπαχθῆναι, Λούκιός τις, καὶ αὐτὸς ὢν Χριστιανός, ὁρῶν τὴν ἀλόγως οὕτως γενομένην κρίσιν, πρὸς τὸν Οὔρβικον ἔφη·'Τίς ἡ αἰτία τοῦ μήτε μοιχὸν μήτε πόρνον μήτε ἀνδροφόνον μήτε λωποδύτην μήτε ἅρπαγα μήτε ἁπλῶς ἀδίκημά τι πράξαντα ἐλεγχόμενον, ὀνόματος δὲ Χριστιανοῦ προσωνυμίαν ὁμολογοῦντα τὸν ἄνθρωπον τοῦτον ἐκόλασω; Οὐ πρέποντα εὐσεβεῖ αὐτοκράτορι οὐδὲ φιλοσόφῳ Καίσαρι παιδὶ οὐδὲ τῇ ἱερᾷ συγκλήτῳ κρίνεις, ὦ Οὔρβικε.' καὶ ὃς οὐδὲν ἄλλο ἀποκρινάμενος καὶ πρὸς τὸν Λούκιον ἔφη·'Δοκεῖς μοι καὶ σὺ εἶναι τοιοῦτος." καὶ Λουκίου φήσαντος· 'Μάλιστα,' πάλιν καὶ αὐτὸν ἀπαχθῆναι ἐκέλευσεν. ὁ δὲ καὶ χάριν εἰδέναι ὡμολόγει τοῦ πονηρῶν δεσποτῶν τῶν τοιούτων ἀπηλλάχθαι καὶ πρὸς τὸν πατέρα καὶ βασιλέα τῶν ὅλων πορεύεσθαι. καὶ ἄλλος δὲ τρίτος ἐπελθὼν κολασθῆναι προσετιμήθη.

139. Runar M. Thorsteinsson, "The Literary Genre and Purpose of Justin's Second Apology: A Critical Review with Insights Ancient Epistolography," *HThR* 105 (2012): 108.
140. Justin is not alone in highlighting and challenging this situation. Athenagoras makes a point identical to Justin's. See Athenagoras, *Leg.* 1.5.

fear, suggesting that being "Christian" is something with which death and punishment are to be associated and expected. Indeed, in *Dial.* 44.1 Justin says that death belongs to "Christians" and Judith Perkins has argued that suffering is the feature which most defines "Christians" in the minds of non-"Christians":

> What did inhabitants of the Roman empire know about Christianity? Notwithstanding the paucity of sources for the period and their elite bias, it is safe to say that one thing contemporaries knew about Christianity (in fact, the only thing they give any evidence of knowing) is that Christians held death in contempt and were ready to suffer for their beliefs.[141]

Perkins adds Galen, Epictetus, and Marcus Aurelius, along with the aforementioned Pliny and Tacitus, to those pagans who early on discuss "Christians" within the parameters of death and suffering. It is death, like that of other "Christians" at the hands of the rulers, that Crescens fears (or at least Justin implies he fears) if the suspicion of his "Christian" status be confirmed.

That being a "Christian" is something to which one confesses (ὁμολογοῦντα), something one admits, implies that it is something disgraceful that one would be expected to keep hidden. The converse of confession is to deny (ἀρνέομαι) and we shall see below that Justin juxtaposes these terms in just this way in order to expose those he cannot accept as "Christians." As we see here, the confession of Christ is apologetic through and through, long before it comes to mean something declaratory like the confessions of credal type.[142] Justin seemingly uses this term in a positive tone at *1 Apol.* 8.2 when he says "we are eager to confess we are Christians." However, this is only in contrast to the possibility to deny a charge. "Christian" is most definitely a shame name in these texts; clearly the name of Christ was indeed blasphemed among the gentiles.

The fact that "Christians" will not deny this name despite its

---

141. Judith Perkins, *The Suffering Self: Pain and Narrative Representation in Early Christianity* (London: Routledge, 1995), 18.
142. For a definition of the meaning of "confessions" as distinct but related to creeds in the reformed tradition, and following into the modern period, see James K. A. Smith, *Letters to a Young Calvinist* (Grand Rapids: Brazos, 2010), 49–54.

criminal status is revealing about the nature of the name itself and the self-understanding of the "Christian" community. Justin says "Christians" will neither deny Christ's name, nor deny or blaspheme Christ himself. These are interchangeable for Justin. To deny his name is to deny Christ and blaspheme against god. "On the other hand, if any of those accused becomes a denier and simply says that he is not a Christian, you release him, as though you were in no way able to convict him of doing anything wrong.... For just as certain people, although they have learnt from Christ the teacher that they should not deny..." (1 Apol. 4.6–7).[143]

In Dial. 131.2 "Christians" would "endure all torments rather than deny Christ even by word."[144] Again, in Dial. 96.2: "But when neither they nor you will listen to us, but you do all in your power to force us to deny Christ, we resist you and prefer to endure death, confident that God will give us all the blessings which He promised us through Christ."[145]

Add to these the same sentiments in Dial. 9; 30; 121 and 1 Apol. 31, and the pattern is clear: "Christians" will always confess to the criminal charge of being "Christians" because Christ's name is made their name and "the church ... has arisen from and participates in His name (for we are all called Christians)," as Dial. 63.5 proclaims. This makes it clear that the name is neither chosen, nor is it given by god as Israel was, but rather the name is dictated by those who killed Christ and persecute his followers. In this way, "Christians" are like Christ; they share in his fate. Christ himself is the central foreground and "Christians" follow behind him. A claim of belonging and composition is being made here. Rhetorically and subtly Justin is elevating Christ, who he is and his teaching, and arguing that despite their criminal status "Christians" are simply those who follow his ways, which he will demonstrate to

---

143. καὶ πάλιν ἐὰν μέν τις τῶν κατηγορουμένων ἔξαρνος γένηται, τῇ φωνῇ μὴ εἶναι φήσας, ἀφίετε αὐτὸν ὡς μηδὲν ἐλέγχειν ἔχοντες ἁμαρτίνοντα ... ὃν γὰρ τρόπον παραλαβόντες τινὲς παρὰ τοῦ διδασκάλου Χριστοῦ μὴ ἀρνεῖσθαι....
144. πάνθ' ὑπομένομεν ὑπὲρ τοῦ μηδὲ μέχρι φωνῆς ἀρνεῖσθαι τὸν Χριστόν.
145. Καὶ μὴ πειθομένων ἡμῖν μήτε, ἐκείνων μήτε ὑμῶν, ἀλλὰ ἀρνεῖσθαι ἡμᾶς τὸ ὄνομα τοῦ Χριστοῦ ἀγωνιζομένων, θανατοῦσθαι μᾶλλον αἱρούμεθα καὶ ὑπομένομεν, πεπεισμένοι ὅτι πάνθ' ὅσα ὑπέσχηται ὁ θεὸς διὰ τοῦ Χριστοῦ ἀγαθὰ Ἀποδώσει ἡμῖν.

be good ways. At *1 Apol.* 14.4 Justin declares that it is for the rulers to judge for themselves "whether we have been taught (δεδιδάγμεθα) and teach these things." "These things" refers to Christ's teaching, but the crucial, self-referential plural does not refers to Justin's community or true "Christians" only. More precisely it applies to all "Christians" but not to all those who are commonly called, charged, and confess to being "Christians." "Christians" will not deny Christ when they are accused because he is all they have.

There is only one group after and under Christ. Though the Romans consider the title shameful in itself, Justin will argue, by outlining what it is to truly follow Christ, that they have failed to understand "Christians" and persecute them needlessly. Christ is the leader with whom "Christians" identify and the criminal understanding of the name shows that the Romans do not know truly who Christ is or who genuinely follows him.

An Outsider's View

In *2 Apol.* 12.1 Justin further demonstrates that "Christian" is a shame name used by those who do not believe in Christ by recounting his own understanding prior to his conversion: "For I myself, too, when I was delighting in the doctrines of Plato, and heard the Christians slandered, and saw them fearless of death, and of all other things which are counted fearful, perceived that it was impossible that they could be living in wickedness and pleasure."[146] Here Justin describes himself as an outsider, delighting in Plato. He recalls the speech he heard about people accused of being "Christians" as well as their endurance and ethics. Justin presents himself as an outsider in this description and is attempting to report how "Christians" are seen outside of the community in an objective fashion. "Christians" were considered bad news. In observing them objectively[147] Justin finds the opposite to be

---

146. Καὶ γὰρ αὐτὸς ἐγώ, τοῖς Πλάτωνος χαίρων διδάγμασι, διαβαλλομένους ἀκούων Χριστιανοὺς ὁρῶν δὲ ἀφόβους πρὸς θάνατον καὶ πάντα τὰ ἄλλα νομιζόμενα φοβερά, ἐνενόουν ἀδύνατον εἶναι ἐν κακίᾳ καὶ φιληδονίᾳ ὑπάρχειν αὐτούς.
147. That is, as recognizably existing and being pejoratively understood but not necessarily strongly separate from "Judaism."

the case. This, naturally, is supposed to tell the audience that if one truly is a "lover of truth," they too should be able to tell objectively that "Christians" are not, in fact, bad. The key point, is that "Christians" were an observable and distinct group and, despite a lack of understanding of their practices, were nonetheless considered a bad group in the eyes of the populace.

Justin is only reporting his pre-"Christian" view, a Greco-Roman outsider's view, understanding there to be a group, whatever its composition and provenance,[148] to which the maligned name is assigned. *2 Apol.* 13.1–2 provides a similar view: "For I too, learning of the evil cloak placed around the divine teachings of the Christians by the wicked demons to divert other human beings, laughed at those falsely making these accusations and at their cloak and popular opinion. Praying and fighting with all my might to be found a Christian...."[149] Here, Justin states again that to him "Christians" were a recognisable group that he first knew of on account of falsehoods spread by others. The default understanding was one of iniquity from which one has to move out and be re-educated. There is no neutral position. Once the label exists it carries associations. When Justin's view changed, he strove to become a "Christian," which is to say something like "if those whom are commonly known as Christians are characterized by such virtue, contrary to what is said about them, then I want to become one of them." He wants to join their group and, indeed, he confesses to, rather than denies, the charge of *being* a "Christian." We must remember that this is a very bold claim. This is not similar to confessing belief in Christ today, which might, in the Western world, bring about nothing more threatening than mild ridicule or indifference. This was equivalent to declaring oneself to be a serious criminal, which is why it is a confession or admission, albeit one that is morphing into a prideful boast as a subversion of what it

---

148. Justin probably only has "true Christians" in mind here rather than those he is wishes to rule out of the "Christian" name.
149. Καὶ γὰρ ἐγώ, μαθὼν περίβλημα πονηρὸν εἰς ἀποστροφὴν τῶν ἄλλων ἀνθρώπων περιτεθειμένον ὑπὸ τῶν φαύλων δαιμόνων τοῖς Χριστιανῶν θείοις διδάγμασι, καὶ ψευδολογουμένων ταῦτα καὶ τοῦ περιβλήματος κατεγέλασα καὶ τῆς παρὰ τοῖς πολλοῖς δόξης. Χριστιανὸς εὑρεθῆναι καὶ εὐχόμενος καὶ παμμάχως ἀγωνιζόμενος....

means to confess. The term "Christian" is still being defined negatively, as an external reference to a group. The term is still conditioned by the negative definition, but is now adopted and defiantly transformed by Justin.

Teacher and Pupils

As already alluded to, Justin thinks of himself as a philosopher. This is for him a "Christian" vocation; being a philosopher and a "Christian" is no contradiction because his philosophy is that of Christ.[150] Justin frequently describes Christ as a teacher (διδάσκαλος). Skarsaune plays down the significance of Christ's teaching office for Justin, noting that in the *Dialogue* he only calls Christ a teacher twice.[151] It is true that Justin only says this explicitly of Christ twice in the *Dialogue* (76.3; 108.2), but he also says this three times in *1 Apol.* 4.7; 19.6; and 32.2. Many of these references occur in the context of the misunderstandings displayed by human teachers of Trypho.[152] Furthermore, as will be shown below, Justin frequently refers to "Christians" as having been taught (ἐδίδαξαν) and as those who follow Christ's teaching (διδάγμασιν). As far as Justin is concerned, this is the main defining feature of any genuine "Christian" group. This should not be thought of as a competing or contradictory definition to his claim for "Christians" being a race. When Justin makes that claim it is in order to demonstrate continuity with "Jewish" heritage, which he usually perceives as being in contrast to his interlocutors. The claim of the teaching and philosophy of Christ is fundamental for his "Christian" definition. It is the first thing that makes a "Christian," and which can be put to the test by examining the evidence that Christ's teaching is followed.

---

150. Rebecca Lyman has pointed out that the perceived natural distinction between Justin being a "Christian," or churchman, and philosopher represents something of a modern misreading which assumes such a distinction on the basis of a model "Christianity" later adopted, but which did not exist in Justin's time. See Rebecca Lyman, "The Politics of Passing: Justin Martyr's Conversion as a Problem of Hellenization," in *Conversion in Late Antiquity and the Early Middle Ages: Seeing and Believing*, ed. Kenneth Mills and Anthony Grafton (Rochester: University of Rochester Press, 2003), 43.
151. Oskar Skarsaune, "The Conversion of Justin Martyr," *ST* 30 (1976): 62.
152. *Dial.* 9.1; 38.1, 2; 43.6; 48.2; 62.2, 3; 68.7; 71.1; 83.1; 94.4; 102.5; 103.2, 9; 110.1; 112.2, 4; 117.3, 4; 120.5; 134.2; 140.2; 142.2.

WHO ARE THE "CHRISTIANS"?

Christ is another means of reconnecting to antiquity, but the first marker of the "Christian" philosophy is Christ himself, no one and nothing else, neither other teachers (be they "Jewish" or Stoic or Platonist), nor Marcion, nor Valentinus or Simon. Only after this is established can Justin defend the antiquity of the faith, open it to his interlocutors and rule out alternative formulations of "Christianity" that do not adhere, by Justin's standards, to Christ's teaching.

In *2 Apol.* 2.2 it is not said of the woman who converts that she became a "Christian." Rather it is said, "But when she learnt the teachings of Christ she came to her senses, and tried to persuade her husband to come to his."[153] And likewise of Ptolemy in the same chapter when asked whether he was a Christian: And again, because through the teaching of Christ he had come to a personal knowledge of the good, he confessed the school of divine virtue"[154] (*2 Apol.* 2.13). Ptolemy was a disciple, one under the rule of the teachings of Christ. The woman was persuaded and attempted to persuade by virtue of these teachings. Not by ritual, custom or birth rite of an ethnos are these converts made but by becoming disciples and pupils under their one and only master, Christ.

There are numerous occasions in the *Dialogue* and both *Apologies* where Justin refers to Christ as having "taught us" (ἐδίδαχεν ἡμᾶς), and to "Christians" as having been taught by the prophetic Spirit or simply being taught without a subject specified.[155] Justin also frequently refers to Christ being a teacher and references his teaching. For example, in *Dial.* 76.3 he says, "And, in calling him angel of great counsel, did not Isaiah predict that Christ would be teacher of those truths which he expounded when he came upon this earth?"[156] The same is found in *Dial.* 105.5 and 108.2 also. This is not reserved only for the *Dialogue*. In *1 Apol.* 12.9 he says: "That all these things should come to pass,

---

153. ἐπεὶ δὲ τὰ τοῦ Χροστοῦ διδάγματα ἔγνω, ἐσωφρονίσθη καὶ τον ἄνδρα ὁμοίως σωφρονεῖν πείθειν ἐπειρᾶτο.
154. καὶ πάλιν τὰ καλὰ ἑαυτῷ συνεοιστάμενος διὰ τὴν ἀπὸ τοῦ Χριστοῦ διδαχήν, τὸ διδασκαλεῖον τῆς θείας ἀρετῆς ὡμολόγησεν.
155. *Dial.* 18.1; 32.5; 48.4; 53.1; 76.3; 96. 3; *1 Apol.* 4.7; 6.2; 13.5; 14.4; 15.9; 19.6; 23.2; 32.2; 33.5; 46.1; 67.8; and *2 Apol.* 10.8 are all examples of this.
156. Καὶ Ἡσαΐας δὲ μεγάλης βουλῆς ἄγγελον αὐτὸν εἰπών, οὐχὶ τούτων ὧνπερ ἐδίδαξεν ἐλθὼν διδάσκαλον αὐτὸν γεγενῆσθαι προεκήρυσσεν.

I say, our Teacher foretold, He who is both Son and Apostle of God the Father of all and the Ruler, Jesus Christ; from whom also we have the name of Christians."[157] Further examples of this understanding of Christ can be found in *1 Apol.* 8.3; 16.14; and 21.1. Christ as the teacher confers his name to his pupils. We have here a positive adoption of the name "Christians" in the context of school tradition. The description of "Christians" as people who have been taught by Christ is by far the most common Justin employs. In addition to the five examples above, the same concept is extended on three occasions to "Christians" which he describes as being disciples (μαθηταί) in Christ's name and of his doctrines, where "disciple" means somebody who is taught, the pupil of a teacher or apprentice of a master. This occurs in *Dial.* 39.2 and *1 Apol.* 15.6.[158] Further, those who are acquainted with Christ (ἐπιγνώσκω, to come to know, to have knowledge) occurs twice (*Dial.* 8.2; 44.4) and those who are his friends (φίλοι) twice (*Dial.* 8.1; 139.4). Friendship is important, but clearly being someone who is taught by Christ is the primary description and focus. Direct relation to Christ as the teacher of truth is the model and the insider definition of what "Christians" are.

Although what Christ has to offer is gained by following his doctrines not by rituals and sacrifices, composition of the "Christian" group around the teaching of Christ has a parallel with the "Jewish" community on precisely these lines. Justin is keen to draw this out. "Christians" are not the only people who have teachers and teaching and, therefore, Justin has to make a point of who the teacher of true teachings is. In doing so, Justin contrasts his interlocutors' teachers with Christ the teacher. For example: "'I am aware,' I replied, 'that my assertion must seem paradoxical, especially to you of your race, who were never interested in understanding or doing what God requires, but rather what your teachers require, as God himself cries'" (*Dial.*

---

157. γενήσεσθαι ταῦτα πάντα προεῖπε, φημί, ὁ ἡμέτερος διδάσκαλος καὶ τοῦ πατρὸς πάντων καὶ δεσπότου θεοῦ υἱὸς καὶ ἀπόστολος ὢν Ἰησοῦς Χριστός, ἀφ' οὗ καὶ τὸ Χριστιανοὶ ἐπονομάζεσθαι ἐσχήκαμεν.
158. Though his disciples, meaning the twelve who travelled with Jesus, are referred to twelve times: *Dial.* 49.5; 51.2; 53.1, 2, 4, 5 (twice); 99.2; 100.4; 105.6; 107.2; and *1 Apol.* 67.8.

48.2).[159] Here, Christ's teaching is claimed to be consistent with and revealing of the requirements of god.

This is sharply contrasted with his interlocutor's teachers who give only their own teaching, like the founder of any philosophical school. Justin makes claims like this numerously in the *Dialogue*. For example, in *Dial.* 27.4 Justin says: "But you are a hard-hearted people, without understanding, blind and lame, children in whom there is no faith. As he [god] himself says, 'Honouring him only with your lips, but your hearts are far from him, teaching your own doctrines and not his.'"[160] The "Jews" are here accused of teaching their own doctrines, neither those of god nor those of Christ. These teachers and their pupils do not understand what god wants, and offer only the appearance of living in god's ways and according to the commandments. The motif of these teachers being hard-hearted is one that Justin repeats often as a contrast to "Christians" who have a spiritual receptiveness to god through their spiritual circumcision. *Dial.* 38.2 also makes the claim that these teachings and teachers are at odds with god:

> I shall recount to you other doctrines which may seem even more paradoxical to you, but don't be disturbed; instead of leaving me, become more zealous and inquisitive listeners. At the same time, forsake the tradition of your teachers, for they are convicted by the prophetic Spirit of being incapable of understanding the truths spoken by God and of preferring to spread their own opinions.[161]

Justin is warning Trypho against the vainglory of his teachers in contrast to the teachings of god. To him they are godless and bow "the knee to Baal" (*Dial.* 39.1). This is remarkably similar to what Justin says about philosophical truth in the introduction to the *Dialogue*. There,

---

159. My translation. Greek: Κἀγὼ πρὸς ταῦτα ἔφην· Οἶδ' ὅτι παράδοξος ὁ λόγος δοκεῖ εἶναι, καὶ μάλιστα τοῖς ἀπὸ τοῦ γένους ὑμῶν, οἵτινες τὰ τοῦ θεοῦ οὔτε νοῆσαι οὔτε ποιῆσαί ποτε βεβούλησθε, ἀλλὰ τὰ τῶν διδασκάλων ὑμῶν, ὡς αὐτὸς ὁ θεὸς βοᾷ.
160. Ὑμεῖς δὲ λαὸς σκληροκάρδιος, καὶ ἀσύνετος, καὶ τυφλός, καὶ χωλός, καὶ υἱοὶ οἷς οὐκ ἔστι πίστις ἐν αὐτοῖς, ὡς αὐτὸς λέγει, ἐστέ, τοῖς χείλεσιν αὐτὸν μόνον τιμῶντες, τῇ δὲ καρδίᾳ πόρρω αὐτοῦ ὄντες, ἰδίας διδασκαλίας καὶ μὴ τὰ ἐκείνου διδάσκοντες.
161. Ἔτι γὰρ καὶ παραδοξοτέρους δοκοῦντας ἄλλους λόγους ἀκούσετε· μὴ ταράσσεσθε δὲ ἀλλὰ μᾶλλον προθυμότεροι γινόμενοι ἀκροαταὶ καὶ ἐξετασταὶ μένετε, καταφρονοῦντες τῆς παραδόσεως τῶν ὑμετέρων διδασκάλων, ἐπεὶ οὐ τὰ διὰ τοῦ θεοῦ ὑπὸ τοῦ προφητικοῦ πνεύματος ἐλέγχονται νοεῖν δυναμενοι, ἀλλὰ τὰ ἴδια μᾶλλον διδάσκειν προαιρούμενοι.

as will be examined in detail in the following chapter, Justin holds that philosophy was once pure revelation given by god, but has degenerated into a loose collection of half-truths perpetuated by the conceited fancy of the leaders of the philosophical schools and the foolish sycophants who follow them. This, which is a key argument in demonstrating the kind of thing Justin claims following Christ to be, the true philosophy, the way and teaching, is a radical critique of what these teachers suggest. Justin is urging Trypho to take heed of those who can perceive the truths of god with the aid of the Holy Spirit, and to join his own school tradition: the true "Christians" and true Israel. In his words:

> Every day some of you are forsaking your erroneous ways to become disciples in the name of Christ, and this same name of Christ enlightens you to receive all the graces and gifts according to your merits. One receives the spirit of wisdom, another of counsel, another of fortitude, another of healing, another of foreknowledge, another of teaching, and another the fear of God. (*Dial.* 39.2)[162]

Teaching is the key term and there can be only one true teaching for Justin; anyone who demurs from the true way of god and Christ is wrong.

A further contrast is that his interlocutors have teachers with whom they are naturally associated as ancestors by virtue of their ethnicity, yet only κατα σάρκα (according to the flesh, that is, descended from Abraham) whereas the "Christians" only have their "Christian" ethnicity through association with their teacher, just as Platonists or Stoics have association only through the philosophy they follow. Furthermore, association according to the flesh, especially the mark of circumcision in the flesh, is rejected by Justin as a sign of a lack of nationhood. At *Dial.* 19.4 Justin points out that neither Adam, nor Abel, nor Enoch, nor Lot, nor Noah ("the beginning of our race"), nor Melchizedek ("the priest of the Most High") was circumcised. To

---

162. γινώσκων ἔτι καθ' ἡμέραν τινὰς μαθητευομένους εἰς τὸ ὄνομα τοῦ Χριστοῦ αὐτοῦ καὶ ἀπολείποντας τὴν ὁδὸν τῆς πλάνης, οἳ καὶ λαμβάνουσι δόματα ἕκαστος ὡς ἄξιοί εἰσι, φωτιζόμενοι διὰ τοῦ ὀνόματος τοῦ Χριστοῦ τούτου· Ὁ μὲν γὰρ λαμβάνει συνέσεως πνεῦμα, ὁ δὲ βουλῆς, ὁ δὲ ἰσχύος, ὁ δὲ ἰάσεως, ὁ δὲ προγνώσεως, ὁ δὲ διδασκαλίας, ὁ δὲ φόβου θεοῦ.

Melchizedek "Abraham the first who received circumcision after the flesh, gave tithes, and he blessed him: after whose order God declared, by the mouth of David, that He would establish the everlasting priest."[163] Justin concludes: "To you alone this circumcision was necessary, in order that the people may be no people, and the nation no nation" (*Dial.* 19.5).[164] Circumcision, then, in contrast to the everlasting priesthood that "Christians" know through Christ without it, is a sign of a different identity; it does not mark out a special people or nation but the opposite, making them not appear as a nation, to blend in (Justin was aware that Egyptians and others also practiced circumcision, as *Dial.* 28.5 makes clear, where he says circumcision was of no use to the Egyptians or the sons of Moab or Edom). Moreover, according to Justin, circumcision and other commandments, like keeping the Sabbath, are necessary only in order to "retain the memorial of God" (ἵνα μνήμην λαμβάνητε τοῦ θεοῦ), because "Jews" had lost sight of god and were practicing idolatry. Being associated with the patriarchs "according to flesh" (that is, being marked by a fleshly circumcision) was therefore, Justin argues, a sign of disobedience. Rather than signaling honorable identity and nationhood under god, it rather indicated distance from god. This is in contrast to the true Israel, the uncircumcised "Christians," who know him through Christ.

For Justin, the identity of a people or a nation is the result of an identity formed by teaching, the type of teaching philosophical schools shape and deliver. Even what we call "religion" is understood by Justin primarily in the sense of "philosophy," school adherence and tradition, a system of beliefs and practices "voluntarily" adopted and maintained. Indeed, as Boyarin suggests: "We see in both such scholastic Christian writers as Justin and in the equally scholastic producers of the Mishnah the impact of the philosophical schools and their own developing notions of orthodoxy and authority, as well as the coming together of other cultural discourses into the aggregate discourse of orthodoxy."[165] Justin is in the vanguard of identity

---

163. Ἀβραάμ, ὁ πρῶτος τὴν κατὰ σάρκα περιτομὴν λαβών, καὶ εὐλόγησεν αὐτόν· οὗ κατὰ τὴν τάξιν τὸν αἰώνιον ἱερέα ὁ θεὸς καταστήσειν διὰ τοῦ Δαυῒδ μεμήνυκεν.
164. Ὑμῖν οὖν μόνοις ἀναγκαία ἦν ἡ περιτομὴ αὕτη, ἵνα ὁ λαὸς οὐ ᾖ καὶ τὸ ἔθνος οὐκ ἔθνος.

formation and orthodoxy. The definition Justin puts forward as "Christian" philosophy further down the line becomes "Christianity." However, Justin is not himself arguing for an independent voluntary belief system. As we have seen in his understanding of "Christians" as the true race of Israel, he primarily recommends practices (baptism, the Eucharist), interpretation of the prophets, and the Torah, rather than merely intellectual doctrines. Nonetheless, Justin's central stress it that it is through Christ, the one and only teacher and teaching, rather than through the traditions of the law, that true friendship with god is handed down. "Christians" are followers who are led directly to god rather than a pre-existing family that thinks it belongs to god by right or birth. As mentioned before, Tertullian will later say that "Christians" are made not born. For Justin, the tutelage of Christ is the first and most important marker of what makes a "Christian." Now we will examine the shape of this philosophy of Christ for which Justin argues, and how he establishes it.

Christian Philosophy, Christian Student

Being a philosopher under the tutelage of Christ is something of great importance to Justin. Concerning the historicity of Justin's philosophical journey, Skarsaune makes a salient point: "the way a man describes his own conversion may reveal some very essential ideas of his concerning conversion in general, indeed, it may tell us something important about his conception of Christianity."[166] Skarsaune surely is right here. Whether or not Justin's philosophical journey is more or less historically factual, his presentation is noteworthy and is a clue to the fundamental shape of "Christian" faith that Justin proposes. We should not overemphasize the novelty of this presentation. Justin does not portray "Christian" faith as a philosophy in order to impress the Romans. Rather, it is a way of demonstrating fidelity and linage from Christ. Loveday Alexander has said: "To the casual pagan observer the activities of the average synagogue or

165. Boyarin, "Rethinking," 34.
166. Skarsaune "Conversion," 55.

church would look more like the activities of a school than anything else. Teaching or preaching, moral exhortation, and the exegesis of canonical texts are activities associated in the ancient world with philosophy, not religion."[167] There is not a qualitative distinction that we moderns tend to apply to religion and philosophy in the second century, and Greco-Roman philosophy participated in "religion" and would appear often to have a "religious" nature.[168] Nor is there a simple distinction between the theoretical and practical at this stage. Justin is doing "philosophical theology" in contrast to the "simple" theology or believing of the worshiping community.[169] Nonetheless, the claim for a "Christian" philosophy is innovative because it allows Justin to claim the heritage of Abraham and Noah and with Noah the idea of being "a race" despite being of gentile stock. Moreover, it allows Justin to present "Christians" as being gathered from all over the world and every nation. "Christians" are no longer a "no-nation," but the true Israel that can demonstrate its antiquity. As such, it should not be understood as a new superstition that undermines the Roman order (and so runs the risks of being threatened by it), but should be legally tolerated by the Roman authorities.

At the beginning of the *Dialogue*, Trypho recognises Justin as a philosopher (chiefly because he wears a philosopher's cloak) and beckons him over so that he and his friends can learn from him. Justin does not waver from this image at any point; he is seen by Trypho and his friends as a philosopher and he sees himself this way too. Indeed,

---

167. Loveday Alexander, "Paul and the Hellenistic Schools: The Evidence of Galen," in *Paul in his Hellenistic Context*, ed. T. Engberg-Pedersen (Edinburgh: T&T Clark, 1994), 60.
168. George H. van Kooten, "Is Early Christianity a Religion or a Philosophy?," in *Myths, Martyrs and Modernity: Studies in the History of Religions in Honour of Jan N. Bremmer*, ed. Jitse Dijkstra, Justin Kroesen, and Yme Kuiper (Leiden: Brill, 2010), 395. Pierre Hadot is to be credited with bringing home the signifance of ancient philosophy being a way of life rather a vehicle for intellectual development. For Hadot ancient philosophy was a "spiritual exercise." The leaders of schools were like spiritual leaders or masters who guided their disciples through a course of study and practice designed not to stimulate their minds but to form them into Epicurean, Stoic, or Platonist types of people. This indeed sounds as religious as it is inherently practical. The mastery of character in line with the ethical goals of the school in question was the aim. This is true of Justin and the Christian schools too. The aim is to form and transform characters into conformity with the way of Christ. See Piere Hadot, *Philosophy as a Way of Life: Spiritual Exercises from Socrates to Foucault* (Oxford: Blackwell, 1995), 49–70.
169. Lieu, *Marking of a Heretic*, 304.

he continues to wear the cloak and states that he is a philosopher in *Dial.* 8.2. In explaining why he has beckoned Justin over, Trypho reveals some philosophical education of his own and his instruction never to despise philosophers. This is interesting in light of the fact that Trypho later reveals that he has been instructed by his teachers not to speak to "Christians," although Trypho does not recognise Justin to be a "Christian" until Justin spells it out for him in *Dial.* 8.1. Justin asks him why the Law is not enough for him after Trypho introduces himself as a Hebrew of circumcision (Ἑβραῖος ἐκ περιτομῆς) in *Dial.* 1.3, and Trypho admits that philosophy takes god as its object.

The following chapter will examine the claims made about philosophy in the *Dialogue* in detail, but it is sufficient for now to note that Justin's question is a veiled criticism, the force of which only becomes clear when one understands that the teaching of Christ is the philosophy and truth which takes the prophets as central texts, and that Trypho's interpretation of them is far from true philosophy. These writings frame the dispute. They are the core texts to which both can appeal to make their case and provide "such things as a philosopher needs to know" (*Dial.* 7.1–3).[170] For Justin, Trypho and his teachers have the elements of the true philosophy but not the tools to understand them: "Philosophy is indeed one's greatest possession, and is most precious in the sight of God, to whom it alone leads us and to whom it unites us, and in truth they who have applied themselves to philosophy are holy men. But, many have failed to discover the nature of philosophy, and the reason why it was sent down to men" (*Dial.* 2.1).[171] Recognising the prophets as the legitmate authority is only one part; also necessary are faithful witness and correct interpretation.[172] This is true of philosophical schools in general but sets up the claim of Justin over against the interpretations of Trypho and that of his teachers.

---

170. Ibid., 306.
171. Ἔστι γὰρ τῷ ὄντι φιλοσοφία μέγιστον κτῆμα καὶ τιμιώτατον θεῷ, ᾧ τε προσάγει καὶ συνίστησιν ἡμᾶς μόνη, καὶ ὅσιοι ὡς ἀληθῶς οὗτοί εἰσιν οἱ φιλοσοφίᾳ τὸν νοῦν προσεσχηκότες. Τί ποτε δέ ἐστι φιλοσοφία καὶ οὗ χάριν κατεπέμφθη εἰς τοὺς ἀνθρώπους, τοὺς πολλοὺς λέληθεν.
172. Ibid., 306.

"Philosophy" is the "greatest possession," both something "bestowed" by "holy men" and something that "has been sent down to men," to holy men, something that has come down from "above." In the hands of its practitioners the original seems to have become multiform, and they fail to observe the unity of the truth that was sent down from a single source. This is why it is possible for Platonists, Stoics, Peripatetics, Theoretics, and Pythagoreans to exist as rival claimants, which Justin thinks is problematic:

> I wish to tell you why it has become many-headed. It has happened that those who first handled it [that is, philosophy], and who were therefore esteemed illustrious men, were succeeded by those who made no investigations concerning truth, but only admired the perseverance and self-discipline of the former, as well as the novelty of the doctrines; and each thought that to be true which he learned from his teacher: then, moreover, those latter persons handed down to their successors such things, and others similar to them; and this system was called by the name of him who was styled the father of the doctrine. (*Dial.* 2.2)[173]

Here in these two passages (*Dial.* 2.1-2) Justin is demonstrating his belief that philosophy is the highest and most precious endeavor, not just of humanity, but of humanity in relation to god. It is inherently theological, and although Trypho has seen this, not all have.[174] This kind of debate presupposes a hyperdistinction between faith and philosophy that is anachronistic to Justin.[175] For Justin faith (πίστις) and knowledge (γνῶσις) go together and the piety (εὐσέβεια) is useless

---

173. Οὗ δὲ χάριν πολύκρανος ἐγενήθη, θέλω εἰπεῖν. Συνέβη τοῖς πρώτοις ἀψαμένοις αὐτῆς καὶ διὰ τοῦτο ἐνδόξοις γενομένοις ἀκολουθῆσαι τοὺς ἔπειτα μηδὲν ἐξετάσαντας ἀληθείας πέρι, καταπλαγέντας δὲ μόνον τὴν κατερίαν αὐτῶν καὶ τὴν ἐγκράτειαν καὶ τὸ ξένον τῶν λόγων ταῦτα ἀληθῆ νομίσαι ἅ παρὰ τοῦ διδασκάλου ἕκαστος ἔμαθεν, εἶτα καὶ αὐτούς, τοῖς ἔπειτα παραδόντας τοιαῦτα ἄττα καὶ ἄλλα τούτοις προσεοικότα, τοῦτο κληθῆναι τοὔνομα, ὅπερ ἐκαλεῖτο ὁ πατὴρ τοῦ λόγου.
174. I am not concerned here with discussions as to whether Justin was a genuine philosopher or sought to harmonize philosophy and faith. Such debates frequently miss the subtlety of what Justin is doing. Vladimir de Beer in a recent article has defended this tired argument but for the present task it will only distract and make interpretation of Justin's project more difficult by hardering catergoies unneccearily. See de Beer, "The Patristic Reception of Hellenic Philosophy," *SVTQ* 55 (2012): 373-98.
175. M. O. Young argues convincingly for the anachronistic nature of this distinction in the New Testament and highlights the crossover points with philosophers like Epictetus. The main difference, as with Justin, will ultimately be the traditions, the prophets and the law, which shape this enterprise. See M. O. Young, "Justin, Socrates, and the Middle Platonists," *StPatr* 28 (1989): 161-66.

unless it is rational and reasonable and unless it is demonstrable to others (which is why he was convinced by the *presbutes* when he demonstrated his claims to him). Yet Justin is not content to be an ordinary philosopher and will go on to tell Trypho that philosophy is disordered, that it has become sectarian and self-aggrandizing, and that it has lost its way. While Justin criticizes the philosophies of the Greco-Roman world, he does not do so as a man of faith as opposed to a man of philosophy, but rather as a true philosopher who fights for the one truth over and against failed philosophies or truths. "The existence of many sets of philosophers is contrary to philosophy's nature and purpose, for by nature philosophy is a single ἐπιστήμη—here, as often, 'art.'"[176] Philosophy, for Justin, is an art form of a single and unified nature rather than a factioned discourse of competing schools. This is something on which Justin will rely in making arguments that define who is and who is not a true philosopher, which is a "Christian." More pertinent for now is that philosophy is about truth, not a lofty abstract truth, but philosophy as something eminently practical. Justin's view of philosophy is like that of a universal science, which searches out truth that can be demonstrated and observed. This is illuminated by the Platonic contrast Justin observes between knowledge and opinion (ἐπίσταται καὶ δόξα). It is this contrast which enables him to denounce Crescens in *2 Apol.* 3.5-6 either as a victim of or as acquiescent with irrational opinion:

> And to show that I speak the truth, in the event that these exchanges have not been reported back to you, I am prepared to exchange questions with him again, even in your presence. This too would be a kingly task. But if my questions and his answers were made known to you, then it would be clear to you that he knows nothing. Or, if he does know, but dares not speak for fear of those who would hear, the man is, as I have already said, proved to be a lover not of wisdom but of vainglory who does not honour even the saying of Socrates – which should be held dear: "But a man is not to be honoured in preference to the truth. (*2 Apol.* 3.5-6)[177]

---

176. Ibid., 162.
177. Minns and Parvis relocated this chapter to later in the piece, making it their 8.5-6. καὶ ὅτι ἀληθῆ λέγω, εἰ μὴ ἀνηνέχθησαν ὑμῖν αἱ κοινωνίαι τῶν λόγων, ἕτοιμος καὶ ἐφ' ὑμῶν κοινωνεῖν τῶν ἐρωτήσεων πάλιν· βασιλικὸν δ' ἄν καὶ τοῦτο ἔργον εἴη. εἰ δὲ καὶ ἐγνώσθησαν ὑμῖν αἱ ἐρωτήσεις μου καὶ αἱ ἐκείνου ἀποκρίσεις, φανερὸν ὑμῖν ἐστιν ὅτι οὐδὲν ἐπίσταται. ἢ εἰ καὶ ἐπίσταται, διὰ τοὺς ἀκούοντας δὲ οὐ τολμᾷ

Crescens is a failed candidate for a philosopher by virtue of being a lover of opinion (οὐ φιλόσοφος ἀλλὰ φιλόδοξος) and, knowing that they wish to be seen as wise men, Justin warns the rulers against this frequently.[178] In this way, Justin sees philosophy as a form of critical thinking that distinguishes between knowledge and opinion. It also has a moral shape and requires its exponents to display the courage of their convictions, which Justin presents as lacking in Crescens. One cannot live badly and be a philosopher, and there would be an obvious failure in one's powers to discern and test the truth if that were the case. What this ought to make clear is the gravity of what Justin is claiming for Christ. He is not claiming that following Christ is a helpful option among others, he is claiming that Christ's teachings are the genuine science of the time and anything that does not conform to these is idle and indemonstrable ramblings; it is talk that has a false or confused logic and is impressed more with rhetoric than truth.

This is the operative understanding of philosophy when Justin declares that he is a philosopher: "But my spirit was immediately set on fire, and an affection for the prophets, and for those who are friends of Christ, took hold of me; while pondering on his words, I discovered that his was the only sure and useful philosophy. Thus it is that I am now a philosopher" (*Dial.* 8.1–2).[179]

Here we have Justin's first declaration that he has discovered the true philosophy drawn from the prophets taught by those who love Christ. This reliable and useful philosophy, in contrast to all others, pertains to Christ having the power to "instill fear into those who have wandered from the path of righteousness, whereas they ever remain a great solace to those who heed them" (*Dial.* 8.2).[180] Christ's teaching can change lives and, as such, is something to be practiced. It is a practical and effective way of life, as all philosophy should be. It is at this point

---

λέγειν, ὡς προέφην, οὐ φιλόσοφος ἀλλὰ Φιλόδοξος ἀνὴρ δείκνυται, ὅς γε μηδὲ Τό Σωκρατικον, ἀξιέραστον ὂν τιμᾷ. Ἀλλ᾽ οὔτι γε πρὸ τῆς ἀλητείας τιμητεος ἀνήρ.

178. Ibid., 161.
179. Ἐμοὶ δὲ παραχρῆμα πῦρ ἐν τῇ ψυχῇ ἀνήφθη, καὶ ἔρως ἔχει με τῶν προφητῶν καὶ τῶν ἀνδρῶν ἐκείνων, οἵ εἰσι Χριστοῦ φίλοι· διαλογιζόμενός τε πρὸς ἐμαυτὸν τοὺς λογους αὐτοῦ ταύτην μόνην εὕρισκον φιλοσοφίαν ἀσφαλῆ τε καὶ σύμφορον. Οὕτως δὴ καὶ διὰ ταῦτα φιλόσοφος ἐγώ.
180. δέος γάρ τι ἔχουσιν ἐν ἑαυτοῖς, καὶ ἱκανοὶ δυσωπῆσαι τοὺς ἐκτρεπομένους τῆς ὀρθῆς ὁδοῦ, ἀνάπαυσίς τε ἡδίστη γίνεται τοῖς ἐκμελετῶσιν αὐτούς.

that Trypho and his friends object, having just discovered that Justin is in fact a "Christian" and not the philosopher they expected when they hailed him over. The discussion continues as a detailed Dialogue of who Christ is and his relationship to the prophets, but Justin's philosophical vocation never vanishes from view entirely.

Justin is a philosopher and philosophy is supposed to be the seeking of truth, as is clear by his criticism of the sectarian relativity of the contemporary academy. Given this understanding of philosophy and Justin's claims to be philosopher after Christ, it follows for him that the "Christian" philosophy is true and not opinion. More than this, though, it takes the name of its founder. This may seem elementary but the necessary relationship of philosophies to their founder (and especially Christ's to the "Christian" philosophy) is an important point that Justin is at pains to emphasize:

> Some are called Marcionites, and some Valentinians, and some Basilidians, and some Saturnilians, and others still by other names; each called after the author of the individual method, just as each one of those who consider themselves philosophers, as I said before, claims he must bear the name of the philosophy which he follows, from the name of the father of the particular doctrine. (*Dial.* 35.6)[181]

The above passage confidently asserts that all philosophies are named after their founder. The names mentioned above are not incidental. They will be discussed, chiefly with attention to Marcion below. The salient point here is that all who follow a way, a philosophy, participate in the name of the founder of that particular way. Philosophies take the name of their founder, then. "Christian" is analogous to this inasmuch as it functions as a label for a group of people who follow the teaching of Christ. Of course, Justin would not be content to accept this as a label for one school among others. The analogy serves to show that "Christians" follow a teaching, but Justin sees this teaching as more fundamental and universal than this. It is for this reason that when

---

181. My translation. Καί εἰσιν αὐτῶν οἱ μέν τινες καλούμενοι Μαρκιανοί, οἱ δὲ Οὐαλεντινιανοί, οἱ δὲ Βασιλειδιανοί, οἱ δὲ Σατορνιλιανοί, καὶ ἄλλοι ἄλλῳ ὀνόματι, ἀπὸ τοῦ ἀρχηγέτου τῆς γνώμης ἕκαστος ὀνομαζόμενος, ὃν τρόπον καὶ ἕκαστος τῶν φιλοσοφεῖν νομιζόντων, ὡς ἐν ἀρχῇ προεῖπον, ἀπὸ τοῦ πατρὸς τοῦ λόγου τὸ ὄνομα ἧς φιλοσοφεῖ θιλοσοφίας ἡγεῖται φείρειν.

Justin first speaks about Christ, in *Dial.* 8.2, after having critiqued the multiform philosophy of his age, he simply states "Thus, and for this reason, I am a philosopher" (Οὕτως δὴ καὶ διὰ ταῦτα φιλόσοφος ἐγώ), not "I am a Christian."[182]

> But my spirit was immediately set on fire, and an affection for the prophets, and for those who are friends of Christ, took hold of me; while pondering on his words, I discovered that his was the only sure and useful philosophy. Thus it is that I am now a philosopher. Furthermore, it is my wish that everyone would be of the same sentiments as I, and never fall away from the Saviour's words; for they have in themselves such tremendous majesty that they can instil fear into those who have wandered from the path of righteousness, whereas they ever remain a great solace to those who heed the salvation of your soul, and if you believe in God, you may have the chance, since I know you are no stranger to this matter, of attaining a knowledge of Christ of God, and, after becoming a Christian, of enjoying a happy life. (*Dial.* 8.1–2)[183]

Being taught by Christ and following his teachings thus makes one "a philosopher" rather than the follower of a particular school. There is no sense in which the friends of Christ naturally belong together by any bonds other than his teaching and way of life (which is also his grace and salvation), hence by philosophy. "Christian" philosophy is the sole truth for Justin whereas the pagan philosophical schools are confused amalgamations, bits of truth and irrationality mixed together. It is only later, when Justin points to Psalms and interprets them, especially with regard to the notion of anointment, that Justin makes a strong link between the anointed one, Christ, and the name "Christian": "They further show that the Word of God speaks to those

---

182. Justin stands at the time when the situation is changing however. He does sometimes call himself a "Christian" directly, *2 Apol.* 13.2 is the classic example (Χριστιανὸς εὑρεθῆναι καὶ εὐχόμενος καὶ παμμάχως ἀγωνιζόμενος). But in the *Dial*, speaking to non-pagans his philosophy is presented as primary and not as something extraneous to or outwidth "Judaism."

183. Ἐμοὶ δὲ παραχρῆμα πῦρ ἐν τῇ ψυχῇ ἀνήφθη, καὶ ἔρως ἔχει με τῶν προφητῶν καὶ τῶν ἀνδρῶν ἐκείνων, οἵ εἰσι Χριστοῦ φίλοι· διαλογιζόμενός τε πρὸς ἐμαυτὸν τοὺς λόγους αὐτοῦ ταύτην μόνην εὕρισκον φιλοσοφίαν ἀσφαλῆ τε καὶ σύμφορον. Οὕτως δὴ καὶ διὰ ταῦτα φιλόσοφος ἐγώ. βουλοίμην δ' ἂν καὶ πάντας ἴσον ἐμοὶ θυμὸν ποιησαμένους μὴ ἀφίστασθαι τῶν τοῦ σωτῆρος λόγων· δέος γάρ τι ἔχουσιν ἐν ἑαυτοῖς, καὶ ἱκανοὶ δυσωπῆσαι τοὺς ἐκτρεπομένους τῆς ὀρθῆς ὁδοῦ, ἀνάπαυσίς τε ἡδίστη γίνεται τοῖς ἐκμελετῶσιν αὐτούς. Εἰ οὖν τι καὶ σοὶ περὶ σεαυτοῦ μέλει καὶ ἀντιποιῇ σωτηρίας καὶ ἐπὶ τῷ θεῷ πέποιθας, ἅπερ οὐκ ἀλλοτρίῳ τοῦ καὶ πράγματος, πάρεστιν ἐπιγνόντι σοι τὸν Χριστὸν τοῦ Θεοῦ καὶ τελείῳ γενομένῳ εὐδαίονεῖν.

who believe in him (who are of one soul and one synagogue and one church) as to a daughter, namely, to the church, which has arisen from and participates in his name (for we are all called Christians)" (*Dial.* 63.5).[184]

This is strong language. The word of god speaks to those who believe in him. Those who follow Jesus hear god. He speaks to them as one soul, one synagogue, one church, as to a daughter. Yet, despite such strong language, even in this instance, Justin does not state plainly that it is because "These words also show clearly that the one who made all these things testified that he is to be worshipped as both God and Christ" (*Dial.* 63.5)[185] that people call themselves "Christians," but rather he adds "for we are all called Christians." It appears, then, that the same phenomenon already observed is again present here: "Christians" follow Christ, they are the synagogue and, within that, the gathered ones who hear god through Christ; but others, outsiders, name them as something other, as "Christians" after him.

The greater significance of the link between Christ's name and "Christians" is that in acknowledging it Justin has a tool to differentiate "true Christians" from others. Those who are equally called "Christians" by outsiders, but are not of Justin's understanding of Christ's teaching, have no right to belong to the same flock, either because they have not been instructed the same way, or because these do not display the same way of life. In emphasizing the link between Christ and "Christians," Justin will be able to claim that some of those who are "called Christians" are mis-titled. That being called "Christian" is constituted only by relationship to Christ, who is the teacher, is not incidental to Justin: it is essential. He emphasises it again and again. For example, in *Dial.* 117.3–5 he states the following:

> For only Christians have ventured to give such prayers and thanksgiving for their food, both solid and liquid food, whereby the passion which the Son of God endured for us is commemorated. But your high priests and teachers have caused his name to be profaned and blasphemed throughout the whole world. But those filthy garments, which you have

---

184. See n. 136.
185. See n. 135.

placed upon on all who have become "Christians" by the name of Jesus ... for, first of all, not even now does your nation extend from the rising to the setting of the sun, but there are nations among which none of your race ever dwelt. For there is not one single race of men, whether barbarians, or Greeks, or people addressed by any other name, nomads, or vagrants, or herdsmen living in tents, among whom prayers and thanksgiving are not offered through the name of the crucified Jesus to the Father and Maker of the universe. And the Scripture sets forth that in the time of the prophet Malachi he said, the dispersion of your people over all the earth had not yet come to pass. (*Dial.* 117.3–5)[186]

The close association with the name of Christ is of paramount importance to Justin. His mention of abuse in the form of "filthy garments" which have been placed upon "all who have become Christians by the name of Jesus," risks that modern readers anachronistically read a distorting sense into this quote. For example, Falls translates it thus: "all who have embraced Christianity by the name of Jesus."[187] "All who have embraced Christianity" is quite different from "those who have become Christians," as it prejudices the reader's interpretation, predisposing them to understand the cultural phenomenon of later and present "Christianity" as a defined movement during the time of Justin. Falls's interpretation does not seem justified by the text. Having chosen the word "embraced," Falls has been forced to use "Christianity" rather than "Christians." This provides a reading Justin could not have imagined. The aorist participle γενομένοις is much better understood as simply having become than having more specifically embraced or joined a group. If Justin had meant this he could have said κολλᾶσθαι (to join) or

---

186. My translation. Greek: Ταῦτα γὰρ μόνα καὶ Χριστιανοὶ παρέλαβον ποιεῖν, καὶ ἐπ' ἀναμνήσει δὲ τῆς τροφῆς αὐτῶν ξηρᾶς τε καὶ ὑγρᾶς, ἐν ᾗ καὶ τοῦ πάθους, ὃ πέπονθε δι' αὐτοὺς ὁ υἱὸς τοῦ θεοῦ, μέμνηνται· οὗ τὸ ὄνομα βεβηλωθῆναι κατὰ πᾶσαν τὴν γῆν καὶ βλασφημεῖσθαι οἱ ἀρχιερεῖς τοῦ λαοῦ ὑμῶν καὶ διδάσκαλοι εἰργάσαντο, ἃ ῥυπαρὰ καὶ αὐτὰ ἐνδύματα, περιεθέντα ὑφ' ὑμῶν πᾶσι τοῖς ἀπὸ τοῦ ὀνόματος τοῦ Ἰησοῦ γενομένοις Χριστιανοῖς ... ὅτι πρῶτον μὲν οὐδὲ νῦν ἀπὸ ἀνατολῶν ἡλίου ἕως δυσμῶν ἐστιν ὑμῶν τὸ γένος, ἀλλ' ἔστι τὰ ἔθνη ἐν οἷς οὐδέπω οὐδεὶς ὑμῶν τοῦ γένους ᾤκησεν. Οὐδὲ ἓν γὰρ ὅλως ἐστί τι γένος ἀνθρώπων, εἴτε βαρβάρων εἴτε Ἑλλήνων εἴτε ἁπλῶς ᾡτινιοῦν ὀνόματι προσαγορευομένων, ἢ ἁμαξοβίων ἢ ἀοίκων καλουμένων ἢ ἐν σκηναῖς κτηνοτρόφων οἰκούντων, ἐν οἷς μὴ διὰ τοῦ ὀνόματος τοῦ σταυρωθέντος Ἰησοῦ εὐχαὶ καὶ εὐχαριστίαι τῷ πατρὶ καὶ ποιητῇ τῶν ὅλων γίνωται. Εἶτα δὲ ὅτι κατ' ἐκεῖνο τοῦ καιροῦ, ὅτε ὁ προφήτης Μαλαχίας τοῦτο ἔλεγεν, οὐδέπω ἡ διασπορὰ ὑμῶν ἐν πάσῃ τῇ γῇ, ἐν ὅσῃ νῦν γεγόνατε, ἐγεγένητο, ὡς καὶ ἀπὸ τῶν γραφῶν ἀποδείκνυται.
187. *St. Justin Martyr: Dialogue with Trypho*, ed. Michael Slusser, trans. Thomas B. Falls (Washington, DC: Catholic University of America Press, 2003), 328.

ἀσπαζόμεθα (embrace), which he does indeed use at *1 Apol.* 45.5.[188] In these cases it is Christ's name and teaching which is embraced, not "Christianity." Though these translations may appear tantamount to the same thing, in the context this is not the case as a defined "Christianity/ism" did not yet exist, but is rather still emerging. Philippe Bobichon favors "became Christians" (*sont devenus chrétiens*) and so does the present author because that is what the text seems to demand. Furthermore, the context of persecution in which these people have become "Christians by the name of Jesus" is again suggestive of an external giving of the name. Yet, Justin is trying to accommodate this name, and in *1 Apol.* 45.5 he says they are embracing Christ's name.

At a number of points, Justin emphasizes that people are called "Christians" after the name of Christ, and that this philosophy or teaching is definitively his. In the *Dialogue* there are five instances where Justin emphasises the direct relationship between the title "Christian" and the person of Jesus and two further instances where he draws attention to those who fail to satisfy this connection legitimately.[189] Minns and Parvis noted that Justin often uses λεγόμενος (called) either when he is introducing terminology that the reader might not be familiar with (they cite brethren as a conceptual example) or when he wishes to distance himself from what is implied in the name or title.[190] Examples of the latter include the "sons of Zeus" at *2 Apol.* 54.2, the "stoic philosophers" at *1 Apol.* 20.2, neither of which Justin wants to accept are truly what they are called, and the "Jewish" sects in *Dial.* 80.2 such as Genistae, Meristae, Galileans, Hellenists, Pharisees, and Baptists who are called "Jews" but only pay lip service to god's commands. Interestingly, this pattern reappears when Justin speaks about the naming of "Christians." In the *Dialogue* Justin mentions those "called Christians" five times:[191]

---

188. "The name of Christ, which we everywhere both embrace and teach"—τὸ ὄνομα τοῦ Χριστοῦ, ἡμεῖς πανταχοῦ καὶ ἀσπαζόμεθα καὶ διδάσκομεν. See *1 Apol.* 53.12: "those who embrace the truth"—τἀληθὲς ἀσπαζομένοις; 14.2: "but now embrace only temperance"—νῦν δὲ σωφροσύνην μόνην ἀσπαζόμενοι; *2 Apol.* 3.2: "embrace evil"—φαῦλα ἀσπαζομένοις.
189. *Dial.* 35.1; 63.5; 64.1; 117.3; 35.2; 35.6.
190. Minns and Parvis, *Philosopher*, 131n3.

WHO ARE THE "CHRISTIANS"?

At this point, Trypho interrupted me by saying, "Indeed I know that there are many who profess their faith in Jesus and are considered to be Christians, yet they claim there is no harm in their eating meats sacrificed to idols. "The fact that there are such men," I replied, "who pretend to be Christians and confess the crucified Jesus as their Lord and Christ, yet profess not his doctrines, but those of the spirits of error, only tends to make us adherents of the true and pure Christian doctrine more ardent in our faith and more firm in the hope he announced to us. (*Dial.* 35.1-2)[192]

These words also show clearly that the one who made all these things testified that he is to be worshipped as both God and Christ. They further show that the Word of God speaks to those who believe in him (who are of one soul and one synagogue and one church) as to a daughter, namely, to the church, which has arisen from and participates in His name (for we are all called Christians). That this is the case and that we are taught to forget our ancestral customs is proclaimed in the following words: "Hearken, O daughter, and behold, and incline thine ear; forget thy people and the house of thy father, and the King shall desire thy beauty: because He is thy Lord, and thou shalt worship Him. (*Dial.* 63.5)[193]

Here Trypho said, "Let Him be recognised as Lord and Christ and God, as the Scriptures signify, by you Gentiles, who are all called Christians from his name; but we who serve the God who made him [Christ] are not required to confess or worship Him." (*Dial.* 64.1)[194]

Then I answered, "I am not so despicable, Trypho, as to say one thing and think another. I admitted before that I and many others agreed and believe that such will come to pass. However I signified to you that many who are pure and pious true Christians think otherwise. Moreover, I indicated to you that some who are called Christians, but are godless, impious heretics, teach doctrines that are in every way blasphemous, atheistical, and unwise. But so that you may know that I am not saying this in front of you alone, I shall put together a statement, as best I can, of the debate between us in which I shall document the admission which I have

---

191. 35.1; 63.5; 64.1; 80.3; 80.4.
192. Καὶ ὁ Τρύφων· Καὶ μὴν πολλοὺς τῶν τὸν Ἰησοῦν λεγόντων ὁμολογεῖν καὶ λεγομένων Χριστιανῶν πυνθάνομαι ἐσθίειν τὰ Εἰδωλόθυτα καὶ μηδὲν ἐκ τούτου βλάπτεσθαι λέγειν. Κἀγῶ ἀπεκρινάμην· καὶ ἐκ τοιούτους εἶναι ἄνδρας, ὁμολογοῦντας ἑαυτοὺς εἶναι Χριστιανοὺς καὶ τὸν σταυρωθέντα Ἰησοῦν ὁμολογεῖν καὶ κύριον καὶ Χριστόν, καὶ μὴ τὰ ἐκείνου διδάγματα διδάσκοντας ἀλλὰ τὰ ἀπὸ τῶν τῆς πλάνης πενυμάτων, ἡμεῖς, οἱ τῆς ἀληθινῆς Ἰησοῦ Χριστοῦ καὶ καθαρᾶς διδασκαλίας μαθηταί, πιστότεροι καὶ βεβαιότεροι γινόμεθα ἐν τῇ ἐλπίδι τῇ κατηγγελμένῃ ὑπ' αὐτοῦ.
193. See n. 135.
194. My translation. Greek: Καὶ ὁ Τρύφων· Ἔστω ὑμῶν, τῶν ἐξ ἐθνῶν κύριος καὶ Χριστὸς καὶ θεὸς γνωριζόμενος, ὡς αἱ γραφαὶ σημαίνουσιν, οἵτινες καὶ ἀπὸ τοῦ ὀνόματος αὐτοῦ Χριστιανοὶ καλεῖσθαι πάντες ἐσχήκατε· ἡμεῖς δέ, τοῦ θεοῦ τοῦ καὶ αὐτὸν τοῦτον ποιήσαντος λατρευταὶ ὄντες, οὐ δεόμεθα τῆς ὁμολογίας αὐτοῦ οὐδὲ τῆς προσκυνήσεως.

just made to you. For I do not desire to follow men and their doctrines but desire greatly to follow God and his doctrines. For if you have met any who are called Christians, but who do not confess this truth, but boldly blaspheme the God of Abraham, and the God of Isaac, and the God of Jacob and say there is no resurrection of the dead, and that their souls are taken to heaven when they die; do not understand them to be Christians, just as one, considering rightly, would not confess that the Sadducees, or similar sects of Genistae, Meristae, Galileans, Hellenists, Pharisees, and Baptists, are Jews (do not be offended when I say what I think), but are only called Jews and children of Abraham, paying lip service to God, as God Himself declared, whose hearts are far from Him. But I and others, who are Christians of right mind, know that there will be a resurrection of the dead, and a thousand years in Jerusalem, which will be rebuilt, adorned, and enlarged, as the prophets Ezekiel and Isaiah and others profess. (*Dial.* 80.2–5)[195]

It is not insignificant that two (*Dial.* 35.1; 64.1) of the above statements come from the mouth of Trypho. The first of these is especially interesting because it demonstrates the insecurity of the category of "Christian" that is obvious even to an outsider. Of the five references, three (*Dial.* 35.1; 80.3, 4) employ λεγόμενος and two (*Dial.* 63.5 and 64.1) use καλούμεθα. The former is used when discussing false "Christians."

In *Dial.* 35.1 Trypho mentions having heard of people who "are called Christians" and who eat idolatrous meat and think it will not affect them. Justin adds that these people are not only called "Christians," but are even "confessing themselves to be Christians." However, Justin

---

195. My translation. Κἀγὼ εἶπον· Οὐχ οὕτω τάλας ἐγώ, ὦ Τρύφων, ὡς ἕτερα λέγειν παρ' ἃ φρονῶ. Ὡμολόγησα οὖν σοι καὶ πρότερον ὅτι ἐγὼ μὲν καὶ ἄλλοι πολλοὶ ταῦτα φρονοῦμεν, ὡς καὶ πάντως ἐπίστασθαι τοῦτο γενησόμενον· πολλοὺς δ' αὖ καὶ τῶν τῆς καθαρᾶς καὶ εὐσεβοῦς ὄντων Χριστιανῶν γνώμης τοῦτο μὴ γνωρίζειν ἐσήμανά σοι. Τοὺς γὰρ λεγομένους μὲν Χριστιανούς, ὄντας δὲ ἀθέους καὶ ἀσεβεῖς αἱρειώτας, ὅτι κατὰ πάντα βλάσφημα καὶ ἄθεα καὶ ἀνόητα διδάσκουσιν, ἐδήλωσά σοι. "Ὅτι δ' οὐκ ἐφ' ὑμῶν μόνων τοῦτο λέγειν με ἐπίστασθε, τῶν γεγενημένων ἡμῖν λόγων ἁπάντων, ὡς δύναμές μου, σύνταξιν ποιήσομαι, ἐν οἷς καὶ τοῦτο ὁμολογοῦντά με, ὃ καὶ πρὸς ὑμᾶς ὁμολογῶ, ἐγγράψω. Οὐ γὰρ ἀνθρώποις μᾶλλον ἢ ἀνθρωπίνοις διδάγμασιν αἱροῦμαι ἀκολουθεῖν, ἀλλὰ θεῷ καὶ τοῖς παρ' ἐκείνου διδάγμασιν. Εἰ γὰρ καὶ συνεβάλετε ὑμεῖς τισι λεγομένοις Χριστιανοῖς, καὶ τοῦτο μὴ ὁμολογοῦσι, ἀλλὰ καὶ βλασφημεῖν τολμῶσι τὸν θεὸν Ἀβραὰμ καὶ τὸν θεὸν Ἰσαὰκ καὶ τὸν θεὸν Ἰακώβ, οἵ καὶ λέγουσι μὴ εἶναι νεκρῶν ἀνάστασιν, ἀλλὰ ἅμα τῷ ἀποθνῄσκειν τὰς ψυχὰς αὐτῶν ἀναλαμβάνεσθαι εἰς τὸν οὐρανόν, μὴ ὑπολάβητε αὐτοὺς Χριστιανούς, ὥσπερ οὐδὲ Ἰουδαίους, ἄν τις ὀρθῶς ἐξετάσῃ, ὁμολογήσειεν εἶναι τοὺς Σαδδουκαίους ἢ τὰς ὁμοίας αἱρέσεις Γενιστῶν καὶ Μεριστῶν καὶ Γαλιλαίων καὶ Ἑλληνιανῶν καὶ φαρισαίων βαπτιστῶν (καὶ μὴ ἀηδῶς ἀκούσητέ μου πάντα ἃ φρονῶ λέγοντος), ἀλλὰ λεγομένους μὲν Ἰουδαίους καί τέκνα Ἀβραάμ, καὶ ξείλεσιν ὁμολογοῦντας τὸν θεόν, ὡς αὐτὸς κέκραγεν ὁ θεός, τὴν δὲ καρδίαν πόρρω ἔχειν ἀπ' αὐτοῦ. Ἐγὼ δέ, καὶ εἴ τινες εἰσιν ὀρθογνώμονες κατὰ πάντα Χριστιανοί, καὶ σαρκὸς ἀνάστασιν γενήσεσθαι ἐπιστάμεθα καὶ χίλια ἔτη ἐν Ἱερουσαλὴμ οἰκοδομηθείσῃ καὶ κοσμηθείσῃ καὶ πλατυνθείσῃ, ὡς οἱ προφῆται Ἰεζεκιὴλ καὶ Ἠσαΐας καὶ οἱ ἄλλοι ὁμολογοῦσιν.

distances himself from these people as he believes they are "not teaching His doctrines, but those of the spirits of error." Important for our discussion is that when Justin contrasts himself and his group with these people, he no longer speaks of himself and his group as "Christians," but as "disciples of the true and pure doctrine of Jesus Christ" (*Dial.* 35.2). As noted before, the correct description of Justin's group derives from the school environment, but without a link to the self-descriptor "Christians." On the contrary, the external designation by Trypho and the self-confession of being "Christians" is bundled in a context where Justin distinguishes himself and his people from these. There is subtle distancing from the term "Christian" here. Justin speaks of those who refer to themselves as such as not, and uses descriptions of actions and beliefs, rather than a title, to refer to those who truly are "Christians." The implication is for some the term functions cheifly as a noun of self-designation whereas for true "Christians" it has a more verbal form, where actions are operative to define adherance.

The second text (*Dial.* 63) has already been discussed and mention has been made that "springing from His name" and "partaking of His name (for we are all called Christian)" similarly seem to mean that the name is an external designation, although interpretation of the Psalms can vindicate those so called as "Christians" as being the ones the Scriptures identify as true worshipers. This interpretation is strengthened by the text that follows immediately in *Dial.* 64, where Trypho adds that the gentiles' belief in Jesus "as Lord and Christ and God" does indeed qualify them as "Christians" from his name and as somehow prophesied in the scriptural witness.

The text of *Dial.* 80.3-4 discusses those who only appear to be "Christians" but are "godless, impious heretics" who "teach doctrines that are in every way blasphemous, atheistical, and foolish." As Justin does not want to follow "men or men's doctrines," he feels the need to disassociate himself emphatically from "some who are called Christians" and who do not admit "God and the doctrines [delivered] by Him." Although they are called "Christians," Justin does not believe them to be "Christians." Rather, he believes them to be nothing other than a particular sect, named in the same way as "Jewish" sects such as Genistae, Meristae, Galileans, Hellenists, Pharisees, and Baptists. Contrary to these groups, Justin claims that he and others "are right-minded Christians," the first and sole instance in the *Dialogue* where he applies the name to himself. This use is in parallel to the name "Jew" which in the same context is introduced as another external designation ("called Jews": λεγομένους μὲν Ἰουδαίους). Hence, even if Justin in this instance would have taken the title "Christians" as a positive self-designation. The sequence of evidence underlines that such use by Justin in his *Dialogue* is only in its infancy.

What evidence do his *Apologies* provide? Justin only refers to people "called Christians" twice:[196]

> But someone will say, "Some of those who have already been caught were shown to be criminals." Of course. This often happens, when you examine the lives of those who stand accused. But you do not usually bring in a conviction on account of others who have earlier been shown to be guilty. In general terms, then, we are prepared to admit this. For, just as, among the Greeks, those who taught whatever pleased them are called in every case by the single title "philosopher," even though they contradicted one another in their opinions—so, among the barbarians, an all-embracing common name is given to both those who were wise and those who seemed wise: they are all called Christians. For this reason, when people are related to you, we ask that you always make their actions the subject of your judgement, so that a person who is found guilty might be punished as a wrongdoer, rather than as a Christian; while if anyone is seen to be guiltless he might be acquitted as a Christian who does no wrong. We will not ask you to punish the accusers. For the wickedness that surrounds them and their ignorance of the good is enough for them. (1 Apol. 7)[197]

And there is someone called Marcion, from Pontus, who even now is

---

196. 1 Apol. 7.3 and 26.6.
197. Ἀλλὰ φήσει τις· ἤδη τινὲς ληφθέντες ἠλέγχθησαν κακοῦργοι. καὶ γὰρ πολλοὶ πολλάκις, ὅταν ἑκάστου τῶν κατηγορουμένων τὸν βίον ἐξετάζητε· ἀλλ᾽ οὐ διὰ τοὺς προελεγχθέντας καταδικάζετε. καθόλου μὲν οὖν κἀκεῖνο ὁμολογοῦμεν, ὅτι ὃν τρόπον οἱ ἐν Ἕλλησι τὰ αὑτοῖς ἀρεστὰ δογματίσαντες ἐκ παντὸς τῷ ἑνὶ ὀνόματι φιλοσοφίας προσαγορεύονται, καίπερ τῶν δογμάτων ἐναντίων ὄντων, οὕτως καὶ τῶν ἐν βαρβάροις γενομένων καὶ δοξάντων σοφῶν τὸ ἐπικατηγορούμενον ὄνομα κοινόν ἐστι· Χριστιανοὶ γὰρ πάντες προσαγορεύονται. ὅθεν πάντων τῶν καταγγελλομένων ὑμῖν τὰς πράξεις κρίνεσθαι ἀξιοῦμεν, ἵνα ὁ ἐλεγχθεὶς ὡς ἄδικος κολάζηται, ἀλλὰ μὴ ὡς Χριστιανός, ἐὰν δέ τις ἀνέλεγκτος φαίνηται, ἀπολύηται ὡς Χριστιανὸς οὐδὲν ἀδικῶν. οὐ γὰρ τοὺς κατηγοροῦντας κολάζειν ὑμᾶς ἀξιώσομεν, ἀρκοῦνται γὰρ τῇ προσούσῃ πονηρίᾳ καὶ τῇ τῶν καλῶν ἀγνοίᾳ.

teaching those he can persuade to consider some other, greater than the creator God. And with the help of the demons, he has persuaded many from every race of humankind to utter blasphemies, and he has made them deny God the Maker of this universe and confess some other who is greater, beyond him. And all those springing from them are, as we said, called Christian, just as among the philosophers those who do not share the same doctrines do have the common name of philosophy predicated of them. (1 Apol. 26.5–6)[198]

Both of these occasions concern the manner in which one can distinguish true and false "Christians" among people commonly brought to the Emperor, accused of being "Christians." Justin picks up the aforementioned argument that by a general name alone it cannot be established what somebody teaches or how one lives. Furthermore, in both instances, he draws a comparison with philosophy and the common names (ὄνομα κοινόν) that all philosophers are addressed or called by (προσαγορεύονται καὶ καλοῦνται) regardless of doctrine and may be guilty of the same inattention to truth and detail as the original philosophers. The first text (1 Apol. 7) makes the point that the accusation of being a "Christian" cannot qualify for punishment, and specifically that the Emperor should look into the "deeds of all," and that only the "evil-doer" must be punished, not because he has been called a "Christian" ("as a Christian"), "since by the mere fact of his being a Christian he does no wrong." Similarly to Dial. 80.3–4 discussed above, this statement comes close to accepting the name as a self-designation, although in the context of the passage, which is concerned with contrasting true members of groups from imposters, it still sounds like an external name that is not yet fully adopted but used out of necessity to demonstrate true membership.

The second text (1 Apol. 26) follows on from the previous one and also reminds us of Dial. 35 and 80 where people have been called "Christians" who according to Justin are clearly heretics (followers of

---

198. Μαρκίωνα δέ τινα Ποντικόν, ὃς καὶ νῦν ἔτι ἐστὶ διδάσκων τοὺς πειθομένους, ἄλλον τινὰ νομίζειν μείζονα τοῦ δημιουργοῦ θεοῦ ὃς κατὰ πᾶν γένος ἀνθρώπων διὰ τῆς τῶν δαιμόνων συλλήψεως πολλοὺς πέπεικε βλασφημίας λέγειν καὶ ἀρνεῖσθαι τὸν ποιητὴν τοῦδε τοῦ παντὸς θεόν, ἄλλον δέ τινα, ὡς ὄντα μείζονα, παρὰ τοῦτον ὁμολογεῖν πεποίηκεν. καὶ πάντες οἱ ἀπὸ τούτων ὁρμώμενοι, ὡς ἔφημεν, Χριστιανοὶ καλοῦνται, ὃν τρόπον καὶ οἱ οὐ κοινωνοῦντες τῶν αὐτῶν δογμάτων ἐν τοῖς φιλοσόφοις τὸ ἐπικατηγορύμενον ὄνομα τῆς φιλοσοφίας κοινὸν ἔχουσιν.

their own school or opinion) and one of them, the only one according to Justin who is still alive and teaching, being Marcion, a man of Pontus. As mentioned, Justin uses λεγόμενος for unfamiliar or unwarranted appellations. It is therefore noteworthy that in *Dial.* 35.6 where Justin mentions the followers of "heretical" schools under the names of their founders, which he does only once in that text, he uses καλούμενοι indicating that these are their proper titles.

Justin has been systematically distancing people who might be thought to be "Christians" from the name of Christ, in order to reserve and link the name only to those who truly follow him, who truly spring from his name. In *2 Apol.* 2.16 Lucius admits to being called (προσωνυμίαν) by the name "Christian," reflecting the objective and external nature of the trial narrative in that chapter. At *1 Apol.* 12.9 ἐπονομάζεσθαι, bearing the name, appears as something true "Christians" inherit directly from Christ.[199] The rightful bearers of this name are only those who follow the philosophy of Christ, those who live like him: "For, apart from those who have been persuaded that the unjust will be punished in eternal fire and that the virtuous and those who lived like Christ shall dwell with God in the absence of suffering, apart, that is, from those who have become Christians" (*2 Apol.* 1.2).[200] As with the instances before, the opening of *2 Apology* shows people being persecuted. Mentioning those "who have become Christians" could mean either one of two things. First, it could refer to the persecuted people who "lived like Christ" and 'shall dwell with God" and have become what they have been accused of being, namely Christians. Second, it could be that "Christians" is the self-identity marker of those who have been persecuted. The frequency of the emphasis on the link between the title "Christian" as an external designation and persecution makes it more likely that the former sense also prevails in this passage, although one may see a similar ambiguity as in the two instances before. The name of Jesus Christ does not

---

199. As Paul uses it in Rom 2:17 to describe those who bear for themselves the name "Jew": σὺ Ἰουδαῖος ἐπονομάζῃ.
200. χωρὶς τῶν πεισθέντων τοὺς ἀδίκους καὶ ἀκολάστους ἐν αἰωνίῳ πυρὶ κολασθήσεσθαι, τοὺς δ' ἐναρέτους καὶ ὁμοίως Χριστῷ βιώσαντας ἐν ἀπαθείᾳ συγγενέσθαι τῷ θεῷ (λέγομεν δὲ τῶν γενομένων Χριστιανῶν).

yet instantaneously suggest that Justin's audience positively links "Christians" to Christ, but that the term "Christian" still carries the shaming character as its primary descriptor. The attendant risks of this lack of discernment have already been alluded to and will be discussed further below. Justin's presentation of "Christians" as followers of Christ, the teacher of the philosophical and universal truth, is, of course, part of that challenge and the correction of the shaming name.

Christian Diversity

In his argument for "what" a "Christian" is, which traverses both the *Apologies* and the *Dialogue*, Justin has claimed that Bar Kokhba and the teachers of Trypho are the cause of "Christians" being pushed out of the "Jewish" community and known commonly as shameful people. Contrary to this, Justin has insisted that "Christians" are the true Israelite race in contrast to that other race who only claims to keep god's commandments. Instead, it is only by keeping Christ's doctrines and commandments that one is following the true philosophy. If one does so, one is worthy of Christ's name and god's promises. Yet we have already seen that not all so-called "Christians" do this and in order to demonstrate "what" "Christians" are, Justin must rule out all such false "Christian" impostors in order that his definition of faith can stand.

In *Dial.* 46.1 Trypho asks Justin, "If some even now desire to live in observance of the precepts of the Mosaic Law, and yet believe that the crucified Jesus is the Christ of God and that to him it has been given to judge without exception all men, and that his kingdom is eternal, could they also be saved?"[201] The answers Justin gives reveal the diversity of the "Christian" community and force Justin into a stronger assertion of "what" a "Christian" is. Interestingly, as Trypho has put the question, the issue is not that of the "Christian" relationship to "Judaism," but of "Christians" who want to observe Moses's commandments and those

---

201. Ἐὰν δέ τινες καὶ νῦν ζῆν βούλωνται φυλάσσοντες τὰ διὰ Μωσέως διαταχθέντα καὶ πιστεύσωσιν ἐπὶ τοῦτον τὸν σταυρωθέντα Ἰησοῦν, ἐπιγνόντες ὅτι αὐτός ἐστιν ὁ Χριστὸς τοῦ θεοῦ καὶ αὐτῷ δέδοται τὸ κρῖναι πάντας ἁπλῶς καὶ αὐτοῦ ἐστιν ἡ αἰώνιος βασιλεία, δύνανται καὶ αὐτοὶ σωθῆναι.

"Christians" who do not, but claim that they will be saved. Do the latter, such as Justin, also allow for the former to be saved? Jaroslav Pelikan believes that because "Christians" were increasingly being drawn from pagan backgrounds, "for Jewish Christians, the question of continuity was the question of their relation to their mother; for Gentile Christians, it was the question of their relation to their mother-in-law."[202] Yet we see from Justin's text that "Christians" who "even now" want to observe the laws of Moses not reckoned to belong to a "daughter"-group of "Judaism," but are presented by Justin's Trypho as if they were part of Trypho's own race.

Much contemporary scholarship has, therefore, questioned the binary nature of the relationship between two things, one called "Judaism" and one called "Christianity." Trypho's question prompts Justin to take a position and states (*Dial.* 47.1) that in his opinion Torah observant "Jews" who follow Jesus will be saved: "The logical implication of this exchange might seem to be that, so long as one believes in Jesus Christ, one can continue to follow the customs particular to one's ethnos or genos."[203] Yet this is only true for "Jews," not for non-"Jews," as Justin makes a point of the fact that pagan converts give up the customs of their former lives when they become "Christians" (*Dial.* 121.3). So Justin is forced to admit that the Mosaic Law is peculiarly compatible with the philosophy of Christ, because "Jews" can be "Christians" while still remaining "Jews," making the distinction between "Jewishness" and "Christianness" appears less strong than one might imagine. However, when Trypho pushes him, Justin admits that not all "Christians" share this view and that he disagrees with those who do not (*Dial.* 47.2). This seems to be within tolerable limits, however, since a difference of opinion (Justin thinks—δοκεῖ—and does not state that they will be saved) is not sufficient that those who disagree would not be recognizable to him as "Christians." When Trypho asks the question again (*Dial.* 80.1), Justin responds that there are many "Christians" who do not share his view.

---

202. Jaroslav Pelikan, "De-Judaization and Hellenization: The Ambiguities of Christian Identity," in *The Dynamic in Christian Thought*, ed. Joseph Papin (Philadelphia: Villanova University Press, 1970), 83.
203. Buell, *New Race*, 112.

He calls these pure (καθαρᾶς), pious (εὐσεβοῦς) "Christians" (*Dial.* 80.2). This again makes clear that this group are within tolerable limits for Justin. These are truly "Christians" even if they do not share Justin's view on this.

In the same paragraph, Justin explicitly reintroduces those who ought not to be considered "Christians"; namely, atheistic and impious heretics (Τοὺς γὰρ λεγομέους μὲν Χρστοανούς ὄντας δὲ ἀθέους καὶ ἀσεβεῖς αἱρεσιώτας.). These are in contrast to right-minded (ὀρθογνώμενος) "Christians" like Justin. These "right-minded" "Christians" are not in opposition to other pure, pious, and genuine "Christians" even if they do not agree on all issues. In defining "what" a "Christian" is to Trypho, then, and dispelling ignorant prejudices, Justin has to isolate those whom he considers to bear the name "Christian" illegitimately. These are more than disagreeable or mistaken "Christians," they are failed candidates for being "Christians." To summarize for Justin, the central feature that distinguishes these failed candidates for "Christians" from the true pious "Christians" is that they do not keep "Christian" doctrines; they do not follow Christ's philosophy. In *1 Apol.* 16.8 Justin confidently asserts this: "And whoever are not found living as He taught are not be recognized as Christians, even if they speak the teachings of Christ with their tongues. For he said not those who only speak but those who also do the works will be saved."[204] These failed candidates may be called "Christians" and may confess Christ; they may even, when charged or asked if they are "Christian," admit that they are; but as Justin says in *1 Apol.* 4.1, nothing can be judged by a name alone: simply saying they are "Christians" is not enough to make them "Christians" any more than saying one is a Stoic but following none of the Stoic philosophy makes one a genuine Stoic. Such people might pay lip service to the teachings of Christ (Χριστοῦ διδάγματα), but they cannot be seen to do his works (ἔγρα); they cannot be found to have the shape of life that his philosophy demands. Again Justin says this in *Dial.* 35.2: "'There are such men,' I replied, 'who pretend to be

---

204. οἵ δ' ἂν μὴ εὑρίσκωνται βιοῦντες ὡς ἐδίδαξε γνωριζέσωσαν μὴ ὄντες Χριστιανοὶ κἂν λέγωσιν διὰ γλώττης τὰ τοῦ Χριστοῦ διδάγματα· οὐ γὰρ τοὺς μόνον λέγοντας ἀλλὰ τοὺς καὶ τὰ ἔργα πράττοντας σωθήσεσθαι ἔφη.

Christians and confess the crucified Jesus as their Lord and Christ, yet profess not his doctrines, but those of the spirits of error...."[205]

This distinction is crucial to Justin. Both 1 Apology and the *Dialogue* wrestle with the issue of defining and clarifying "what" and who "Christians" are, and this is because, as the next two chapters will argue, Marcion looms large in Justin's sphere and threatens to define, or confuse what little definition there is of, the identity of followers of Christ, thereby risking imperial suppression as a novel superstition. The following chapters will examine in detail the efforts Justin makes to distinguish his community and theology from that of Marcion and other "heretics." First we will consult the *Dialogue*, especially the eleven introductory chapters which determine the trajectory of the debate in the rest of the piece. The chief concern here will be to note the strategy Justin employs for outlining his own community's beliefs in ways that subtly rule out the foundations of the Marcionite commitments. This is quite a subtle task that involves close attention to the topics under discussion and the significance of Trypho's understanding of who and what "Christians" are. We will also consider the two chapters that seem to have Marcion himself as a more or less direct target (*Dial.* 35; 80). In chapter 3 we will move on to the *Apologies* to consider how Justin, addressing an audience with different cultural commitments and prejudices, advances what "Christians" are in a way that of necessity rules out a theology that could be deemed Marcionite.

So, what is a "Christian" in Justin? As we have seen, this is an internally disputed question. "Christians" are diverse. For Justin diversity is tolerable but there are certain commitments, which center on the teachings and doctrines of Christ, that if broken undermine any sense of a meaningful "Christian" identity. For Justin a "Christian" is not a cultic practitioner, nor a member of a nation with aspirations to power and influence. A "Christian" is simply and only one who follows the teachings and philosophy of Christ. This rules some out, but is something that all should aspire to. There is no such thing for Justin

---

205. ἐκ τοιούτους εἶναι ἄνδρας, ὁμολογοῦντας ἑαυτοὺς εἶναι Χριστιανοὺς καὶ τὸν σταυρωθέντα Ἰησοῦν ὁμολογεῖν καὶ κύριον καὶ Χριστόν, καὶ μὴ τὰ ἐκείνου διδάγματα διδάσκοντας ἀλλὰ τὰ ἀπὸ τῶν τῆς πλάνης πενυμάτων.

as "Christianity" yet, only discipleship and correct living under Christ's direction. This discipleship incorporates one into his name in the same manner as following Plato incorporates one into Plato's name but does not make one a member of specific nation or people. It is a way of life. That some "right-minded" "Christians" disagree with Justin even on the relation to "Jews" suggests that the distinction between "Jews" and "Christians" is becoming mutual, which is contrary to Justin's wishes and description of how "Christians" come to be hated, and that the way of "Christians" is steadily separating from the "Jews" until it becomes a *religion* in its own right.

Justin blames Bar Kokhba and the teachers of Trypho for the persecution of "Christians" by singling them out. He believes Greco-Romans have learned from this. We have seen that there are various reasons why the Greco-Romans had an issue with "Christians" and that Justin sought to get round these by demonstrating that a "Christian" is first and foremost a philosopher, neither a rival nor a new ethnic cultic tradition. Justin has thus made an attempt to clarify what a "Christian" is. This means admitting that not all "Christians" agree on all things. Yet there is further work for him to do as he must outline that not all who are taken to be "Christians" live up to this identity. This is the central feature of Justin's work that the remaining chapters will be dedicated to outlining. Chiefly, Justin is working hard in all of his texts to distinguish himself and his community from that of Marcion.

2

Reading between the Lines: The Conspicuousness of Marcion in the *Dialogue*

Now we shall turn to the *Dialogue* specifically and expound the evidence for an agenda to clarify the "Christian" philosophy which demands distinction from others who are also called "Christians" but, according to Justin, do not merit this name. Yet there is a prior question as to what the *Dialogue* represents as text itself. Andrew Jacobs has characterized the problem as follows:

> The *Dialogue* is a notoriously difficult text to parse—both in historical and literary terms—as a straightforward text of Jewish-Christian differentiation. Despite Justin's frequently rancorous tone throughout the long *Dialogue*, the very dialogic nature of the text hints at ongoing communication and rapprochement: the shared desire to determine what divides Jew from Christian cannot help but gesture at what holds them together. I am not suggesting that, beneath a veneer of discourtesy and acrimony, Justin is trying to get in touch with his "inner Jew"; to the contrary, I think the text lays out for us the ways in which Christians of the second century felt haunted by that "inner Jew," and sought to confront, domesticate, and humble him. Yet at the same time, this early

text illustrates the ways in which such efforts at confrontation and domestication lack clear resolution.[1]

What Jacobs highlights here is the precise relationship of "Christians" to "Jews" in this text, which in this period is a very complicated one and our understanding of it must alter our reading. There have been scholars, like Theodore Stylianopoulos,[2] who think that the *Dialogue* is definitively aimed towards a "Jewish" audience, and others like Jon Nilson[3] who have believed that it is directed towards a pagan audience—albeit Judeophile in outlook. However, both these perspectives, and Jacob's more subtle position, hold to a stable understanding of "Judaism" and "Christianity," not to mention pagan "outsiders." But we cannot rule the question out of court completely, given the complexity of how identity is constructed in the ancient world, as we learn through Buell, Nasrallah, King, Lyman, et al. This means that it is impossible to identify an audience in these terms. Stylianopoulos considers the possibilities that the *Dialogue* could have been directed towards "gnostic" "Christians" or a pagan audience, represented by the addressee Marcus Pompeius, yet each of these is presented with interests distinct from the others. While of course topics of interest vary in importance, we have learned in chapter 1 that "gnostic," "heretical," and "orthodox" "Christianity" are not yet defined enough to be able to identify truly separate and exclusive groups, though it is heading in that direction. They all seem to be called "Christians," as Justin claims. We also know that "Christians," at least some "Christians," are not already completely distinguishable from "Jews," and that the construction of "Jewishness" and "Judaism" is too complicated in itself for us to be able to discuss meaningfully whether the problem of the Law, the central explicit argumentative feature of the text as Stylianopoulos rightly points out, is an intra-"Christian"problem or an inter-"Jewish"-"Christian"problem.[4] Given

---

1. Jacobs, "Dialogical Differences," 299.
2. Theodore G. Stylianopoulos, *Justin Marytr and the Mosaic Law* (SBLDS; Missoula, MT: Scholars Press, 1975), 33-44.
3. Nilson, "Addressed?," 538-46.
4. Stylianopoulos, *Mosaic Law*, 35.

the extent, and different tone, of the handling of scriptural material in the *Dialogue,* in contrast to *1 Apology,* it is reasonable to suppose that the audience of the *Dialogue* is different from that of *1 Apology* and not the rulers directly, as *1 Apology* purports to address. Some variety, or combination, of "Jewish," "Christian," proto-"heretical" audience(s) is most likely. But more important is the question, what was Justin trying to achieve? Justin was trying to define the "Christian" philosophy which was misunderstood and, in his eyes, often misrepresented. Marcionism is the biggest threat to "Christian" identity and that which must be most ruled out by those addressed. Exactly who those people were I do not think the evidence allows us to be clear on, given the complexities of identity we have identified thus far.

Another perennial feature of discussion of the *Dialogue* are complaints about its tangential and repetitious nature. As Skarsaune has noted, the exhaustively detailed exegesis on themes often repeated, which the modern reader finds so tedious, were probably considered by Justin to be among the text's highest virtues. Justin in this regard is a teacher, like Christ and the apostles, and is doing everything he can to ensure that his audience learns the central truth by heart.[5] Often the repetition is due to the unsearchableness of Trypho and his companions, who repeat the same or similar questions, or who retract agreement already given on a certain point prompting Justin to argue it again afresh.[6] None of this structure is accidental or incidental. The fabric of the text in this regard reveals how hard Justin is working to get across "what" the "Christian" philosophy is, what the truths of Jesus Christ are, and for the audience to be left in no doubt. This is frequently an exercise in distinguishing "Christians" from Marcionites, who are created as a group in the process of this clarification. In repeatedly making clear his claims for who Christ is and who his father is, Justin is making out a "Christian" faith that necessarily excludes Marcion.

We will begin analysis of this feature of Justin's work in the *Dialogue*

---

5. Skarsaune, *Proof from Prophecy,* 165–67.
6. Ibid., 165.

first by considering the so called philosophical section which comes at the start of the *Dialogue*. This is very much a part of the wider project of the text and crucially introduces a major thesis that will define and guide what Justin looks for and finds in his exegesis and his claims for who Christ is. After this we will consider where these same themes can be observed later in the text and how they function to exclude Marcion from the stable of the "Christian" philosophy.

The *Dialogue*: Introduction and Commentary

Much scholarly interest has been paid to the opening sections of the *Dialogue*. Many have found these first chapters, which Justin devotes almost entirely to a discussion of philosophy, to be at odds with the rest of the text and perhaps therefore corrupt.[7] Goodenough doubted the veracity of Justin's summary of philosophies:

> This interesting account of Justin's philosophical quest has always been taken literally by his commentators, although the story of his conversion to Christianity which immediately follows it has long been regarded by many scholars as an idealization of Justin's actual experiences. The fact is, however, that the two narratives are one, unbroken by transition.... Justin, in the entire passage, is dramatizing the relations between Christianity and philosophy and has adopted the familiar convention of relating someone's adventures in passing from school to school, and finally in the Christian school, in order to criticise each school by the adventures.[8]

Goodenough also notes the similarity in literary style and convention

---

7. See Niels Hyldahl, *Philosophie Und Christentum. Eine Interpretation der Einleitung zum* Dialog *Justins* (ATDan 9; Copenhagen: Munksgaard, 1966), 22–85; J. C. M. van Winden, *An Early Christian Philosopher: Justin Marty's* Dialogue with Trypho, *Chapters One to Nine: Introduction, Text, and Commentary* (Philosophia Patrum 1; Leiden: Brill, 1971), 1–5; Leslie William Barnard, *Justin Martyr: His Life and Thought* (Cambridge, UK: Cambridge University Press, 1967), 21–27. Tellingly, Barnard, who was influenced by Harnack's view that the text of the *Dialogue* was not sound, especially not the introduction, in his section on the *Dialogue* as one of Justin's texts neglects to even mention chapters one to ten as a section, calling chapters eleven to thirty-one the first part instead. Clearly he did not rate the importance of these chapters in relation to the rest of the work as they receive no mentions in six pages of introductory analysis on the work as whole. The following section, "Background: Greek Philosophy," does briefly mention portions of these chapters but only insofar as they are relevant to ascertaining Justin's understanding of Middle Platonism rather than their function within the *Dialogue* as a work.
8. Erwin R. Goodenough, *The Theology of Justin Martyr* (Amsterdam: Philo, 1968.; repr., Jena: Frommannsche, 1923), 58–59.

to Lucian's *Menippus* where the protagonist travels through many philosophical schools, giving each up on account of mutual contradictions, which undermine their authority in his eyes. Goodenough is not suggesting interdependence, but conventional literary form perhaps, with even wider use in "Jewish" Tannaim also.[9] So for Goodenough this opening section of the *Dialogue* represents an idealized account in order to challenge philosophy over and against "Christianity." Andersen, according to Barnard, thinks Justin's summary reveals leanings towards Middle Platonism.[10] For Andersen the historical data is in the attitude, redolent of Middle Platonism, towards other philosophies that Justin exhibits. Barnard does not doubt the historicity of Justin's account of his philosophical quest, though it does end at an ideal zenith in Christ for him, which took place in a world where eclecticism was typical. He found the truth he was looking for, hence his continuing to wear the philosopher's cloak and invite people into his *school*. It is this, as Lieu puts it, which "authenticates his self-desigation as a philosopher and his wearing of the philosopher's robe."[11] Faith in Christ is a way, a philosophy, the truth, for him. Van Winden, much closer to Goodenough in this regard, has looked more generously at the text and found it to be consistent with the body of the piece, its themes carried on throughout, without contradiction. The reader must approach this introductory section, and the rest of the text, while discarding the knowledge that philosophy does not seem to be the central topic, because the nature of the discussion reveals why so much is devoted to it here.[12] The content here is in many ways consistent with the philosophical situation of the time but more is being outlined than this situation.

In 1975 Stylianopoulos indicated that the *Dialogue* was brimming with anti-Marcionite material but that it was difficult to assess the extent of this because not all of this material was immediately or necessarily indicative of Marcion.[13] Philippe Bobichon, in his recent

---

9. Ibid., 58–59.
10. Barnard, *Justin*, 8–11.
11. Lieu, *Marking of a Heretic*, 299.
12. Van Winden, *Early Christian Philosophy*, 23.

critical edition, has paid much attention to particularly focused contra-Marcionite elements, but even he, however, has not carried this far enough.[14] It is my claim in this chapter that this introductory section (chapters one to eleven) is not only consistent with the rest of the piece, but vital to understanding it. It is an important opening section because it establishes the purpose of the piece which has not been adequately accounted for. This purpose of Justin is to clarify what the "Christian" faith is and what it is not. His biggest challenge, or his fellow traveler who causes the most confusion, is Marcion. Justin's agenda in the *Dialogue* then is to distinguish his theology from that of Marcion, as he states, the only still living and therefore salient "heretic." I focus, therefore, on Marcion to the general exclusion of the other "heretics" for two reasons: (a) because he is the only one presented by Justin as a contemporary teacher; and (b) because Justin provides more information about Marcion than about any of those others like Basilides or Valentinus. In addition, Marcion appears in all of his writings (and we need even to take into account that Justin had written a first text "To Marcion" which unfortunately is lost).

The introductory section of the *Dialogue* has a structure whose intention and historicity has vexed many historians and scholars. The purpose for which it is designed is to outline key theological commitments which separate Justin from Marcion before the interlocutor (or hearer) discovers that Justin is a "Christian." In the previous chapter I showed that "Christianity" is not a uniform enterprise and that there was a great deal of confusion about what a "Christian" is at the time Justin writes. Furthermore the definition of "Christian" was something more in control of outsiders than in the hands of people like Justin. Justin in this section is laying down a series of markers for things which he denies or does not deny. That is, the introductory section is designed to rule out certain key doctrinal commitments, and rule others in, without the dialogue partner being prejudiced by what they already understand "Christians" to be.

---

13. Stylianopoulos, *Justin*, 27–29.
14. More detailed than Bobichon, the contra-Marcionite character is expounded by Vinzent in Vinzent, *Dating of the Gospels*, 15.

The philosophies Justin talks about in his journey are not incidental; they may well represent a real journey of his or an idealized version of his and other popular accounts, but what is most noteworthy are the markers Justin lays down throughout this introduction which he will later draw on more heavily. Goodenough may have been right that the account should not be separated into a "historical" philosophical section and an "idealised" "Christian" section.[15] Andersen may also be right that there are clues in this account linking Justin to genuine Middle Platonism. Neither of these accounts ask anything deeper of this account other than that it be a simple progression from untruth or limited truth to *the* truth in Christ. Justin, however, is much more subtle than this. Rather than telling a simple story, he is laying the groundwork for theology as such, establishing key commitments and ruling out others. He is providing a thematic catalogue as a prelude. The preliminary structure can be observed in the fabric of the text itself.

The key themes and doctrines that are ruled in and out in this section continue throughout the piece and are added to by further commitments. Below we will examine the *Dialogue* introduction in detail, building on the themes of "Christian philosophy" and disputed identity established in the previous chapter. Key themes that provide space for counterpoint between Justin and Marcion, and that recur frequently in the text, are: the oneness of god, his creation of the world, care and providence, his judgment, what it means to live rightly, and the sources of revelation. As the text continues beyond the introductory themes, it will become more sharply focused in relation to Christ, but first it is necessary to establish a general shape for the kind of things possible in Justin's theology (or philosophy as he calls it), the kind of god and revelation he accepts; this is precisely what Justin does in the introductory chapters.

The journey through philosophy in the *Dialogue* introduction is a progression, not a set of conversions. It is intended to show that Justin has reached "philosophical" truth, not a "religious" conversion. He has

---

15. Goodenough, *Theology of Justin*, 58.

not become a "Jew," he has not abandoned his paganism but fulfilled all that was good about it.[16] "Christians" were called atheists, as far as we can tell from Justin, for two potential reasons: (a) because they invent new gods, as Socrates was accused of at *1 Apol.* 5.3, and (b) because they reject the gods of their ancestors and convert into another tradition, which contravened Roman law. The record of Justin's journey through philosophy in the introduction to the *Dialogue* is designed to circumvent both of these reasons. There, Justin travels to the divine philosophy explicitly *through* the Hellenistic philosophical tradition. He reaches its zenith or logical conclusion in "Christianity," and is thus not a convert to another tradition. Secondly, the god he discovers, though it is the god of Adam, Abraham, and Noah, is universal and has all along been the source of all that is good in the philosophical tradition as well as in the Israelite tradition. There is no new god, then, and this god was, in Justin's view, already internal to the Hellenistic tradition.

Before proceeding to detailed analysis of Justin's presentation of the "Christian" philosophy and the ways in which it is subtly distinguished from other forms, particularly Marcionism, it will be useful to provide a brief summary of the opening chapters (*Dial.* 1-8). Justin becomes engaged in a conversation with Trypho, "a Hebrew of the circumcision," who had "escaped from the war lately." Justin is curious, as he thinks that Trypho should be content not with philosophy but with the prophets. Skarsaune summarizes:

> Trypho retorts that philosophy, to his knowledge, is occupied with the very same questions (1:1-3). Yes, says Justin, it ought to be so, but most philosophers have taught these matters in the wrong way, or not at all. Trypho then asks what Justin's own philosophy is (1:4-6). The answer falls into five parts: 1) Praise of the true philosophy as opposed to doctrines of the philosophical schools (2:1). 2) An outline of the history of philosophy (2:2). 3) Justin's philosophical itinerary (2:3-6). 4) The dialogue with the Old Man (3:1-7:3). 5) Justin's conversion to Christianity as the True Philosophy (8: 1-2).[17]

---

16. Nasrallah points out that such a journey was in fact an essential cultural artifact to demonstrate one's true credentials as a philosopher, as one who has the requisite experience to make authoritative claims. Nasrallah, "Mapping the World," 308.

To this I would add that the three chapters up to chapter eleven are transitional chapters where Justin moves the discussion on to the main topic of scriptural interpretation by (a) denying that "Christians" believe baseless tales while the "Jewish" leaders misunderstand the Scriptures (9.1). (b) Trypho raises the question of the non-distinctive and non-observant nature of "Christians" (10.2-4). (c) Justin confidently proclaims and confesses the one true god and his new covenant with all people (11.1-4). From here all the major claims about "what" a "Christian" is have been made and the discussion can continue in detail over the reasonableness of the interpretation of this. We will now take each chapter in turn and take note of Justin's presentation and the work it does.

Dial. 1

Trypho's interest in philosophy launches chapter one. The first noteworthy marker is how Trypho and Justin perceive Justin's identity:

> He answered, "In Argos I was taught by Corinthus, the Socratic philosopher, never to slight or ignore those who wear that gown of yours, but to show them every consideration and to converse with them, since from such a conversation some good might be derived by them or myself. It would be to the advantage of both if either should benefit from this meeting. Accordingly, whenever I see anyone wearing such a gown, I gladly accost him. So, for this same reason, it has been a pleasure to greet you. These friends of mine share my hope of hearing something profitable from you." (*Dial.* 1.2)[18]

From this we learn that Justin dresses as a philosopher so that he is seen as such, and also that this matches his self-understanding. There is nothing about his dress or ethnicity that marks him out as "Christian." The only obvious identification he has is that of a philosopher. Much has been made of this fact in the past. Many have

---

17. Skarsaune, "Conversion," 55.
18. Ὁ δέ· Ἐδιδάχθην ἐν Ἄργει, φησίν, ὑπὸ Κορίνθου τοῦ Σωκρατικοῦ ὅτι οὐ δεῖ καταφρονεῖν οὐδὲ ἀμελεῖν τῶν περοκειμένων τόδε τὸ σχῆμα, ἀλλ' ἐκ παντὸς φιλοφρονεῖσθαι προσομιλεῖν τε αὐτοῖς, εἴ τι ὄφελος ἐκ τῆς συνουσίας γένοιτο ἢ αὐτῷ ἐκείνῳ ἢ ἐμοί. Ἀμφοτέροις δὲ ἀγαθόν ἐστι, κἂν θάτερος ᾖ ὠφελημένος. Τούτου οὖν χάριν, ὅταν ἴδω τινὰ ἐν τοιούτῳ σχήματι, ἀσμένως αὐτῷ προσέρξομαι, σέ τε κατὰ τὰ αὐτὰ ἡδέως νῦν προσεῖπον, οὗτοί τε συνεφέπονταί μοι, προσδοκῶντες καὶ αὐτοὶ ἀκούσεσθαί τι χρηστὸν ἐκ σοῦ.

viewed it as evidence that Justin believes in continuity between Greek philosophy and "Christianity."[19] This, however, is to neglect the nature of his discussion, because as we shall see below his views very much exclude that possibility. But that Justin is a philosopher, as discussed in our first chapter, is the chief marker in this introductionary section is noteworthy because of the nature of the discussion it makes possible. That is, the way it allows various topics to be discussed whilst protecting Justin by initality concealing his "Christian" identity from a prejudicial Hebrew audience.

Justin has laid a subtle but distinct irony here in his presentation. Trypho has said that whenever he sees anyone like him he does not despise them but approaches them with kindness and hopes to converse with them and to learn from them. Trypho is interested in Justin because Trypho has an interest in philosophy and does not see his philosophical education as complete at this point. There is no reason to doubt Trypho's philosophical interest; much of his role in the *Dialogue* is to use logic to dispute Justin's arguments, and he is familiar enough with pagan mythology to suggest that he has enquired into the tradition.[20] In having Trypho enquire of him in this way, however, Justin is anticipating, by concealing his "Christian" identity, *Dial.* 38.1 where Trypho will reveal that the teachers who instructed him admonished him neither to converse with "Christians" nor to have any kind of communication with them. So Trypho has two instructors—Socratics and Hebrews—and while he thinks Justin is a philosopher he can, and indeed pleasures in, addressing him. Had he however known he was "Christian"—or what he thinks a "Christian" is—he would perhaps not have come anywhere near him in the first instance. Justin's words, recorded before this in *1 Apol.* 4.8, on the matter of *bona fide* philosophical identity are instructive here: "some assume the name and appearance of philosophers who behave in no way worthily of their profession." Justin consciously appears to Trypho in this text *as* a philosopher rather than *as* a "Christian," but the

---

19. Van Winden, *Early Christian Philosopher*, 24.
20. Horner, *Listening*, 182.

discussion will reveal that he is in fact one most truly suited to the profession of philosophy—more so than those normally considered philosophers by Trypho—precisely because of his affiliation with Christ.

We also discover that there is nothing that obviously marks Trypho out as a "Jew." Justin has to ask who he is and Trypho strikingly identifies himself as a "Hebrew of circumcision."[21] Such a self-classification is clearly staking a claim. We saw in the previous chapter that "Israel" and "Hebrew" function as internal and disputed identity claims. Trypho is telling Justin not just that he is a "Jew" but that he is a true member of "Israel"—something Justin will deny in the delineation of his philosophy. This exchange demonstrates that Trypho was not easily identifiable, or that his identity was at least disputable as we know from chapter 1, and in this he shares this non-identifiability with those people who by some have been called "Christians." Laura Nasrallah, however, sees a fundamental difference between Trypho's and Justin's characteristics:

> Throughout the *Dialogue* Justin will berate Trypho for his Hebrewness and for circumcision. But even the elements which sound neutral—escaped from the war, an immigrant to Greece—are loaded. The allusion to the Bar Kokhba revolt reminds the audience that while Justin and Trypho look similar—they are from the same part of the world, cosmopolitan, travelling the empire and pursing philosophy—they are not. Jews may be refugees from the effects of the empire they traverse, while Justin and his ilk—those of the "nations" who are Christian—have nothing to do with Judean goings-on. Justin wants to assert to Romans, who may have a hard time distinguishing Christianity from Judaism, that Christians have an identity that is, to use Buell's vocabulary, "fluid" and "universal," compared to Trypho's "fixed" and limited identity.[22]

There is some truth in this. Justin does portray Trypho and his teachers as somehow "fixed" in contrast to the "philosophical" "Christian" tradition that can be picked up by anyone. Moreover, the reference to Bar Kokhba serves as a reminder of the troublesome and rebellious

---

21. Vinzent, *Dating the Gospels*, 63.
22. Laura Nasrallah, "The Rhetoric of Conversion and the Construction of Experience," *StPatr* 40 (2006): 471.

past, which is to be contrasted with the servant nature of "Christians." However, left unqualified, this would be overstated, as Justin does not take all the power for himself in this exchange. He is in the minority in the debate. There is another way of looking at this exchange. Graham Stanton has argued persuasively that Trypho's friends represent proselytes to "Judaism," in as much as "Judaism" exists at this time.[23] As such these pagan proselytes are people from a similar background to Justin, also convinced of the one true god, but who rejected Christ as a route to god. Justin, once Trypho knows he is a "Christian," is of similar status as a pagan interested in Israelite and Hebrew traditions, like one of the friends, albeit errant in his approach. This seems to be what Trypho is implying in *Dial.* 8.4 when he says to Justin, "For I have already considered you a friend,"[24] while chastising him after discovering he is a "Christian." Trypho is warm towards Justin's intentions, his "eagerness to study divine things"—which being truly divine pertain to the one true god rather than any general ontotheology. Though this is speculation, this could be read as though Trypho places Justin in a similar position to that of his other friends, who are not Hebrews born of circumcision as Stanton made clear. Identity is a key issue for both sides, Trypho and Justin, and though Trypho calls Justin a friend he will soon reject his "Christian"claims as blasphemy. The connected topics of philosophy and Trypho's identity are further developed by a subtle but searching question put by Justin in *Dial.* 1.3. Justin asks why Trypho should be interested in philosophy when he has *his own* lawgiver and prophets. That is, what possible interest could Trypho have in Greco-Roman philosophical schools when he already has the materials of the true philosophy? The Law and prophets are thus noteworthy already at this early stage and are identified at this stage as belonging to the Hebrews, setting the scene for Justin to claim them for himself. Justin's question about why a Hebrew should be interested in philosophy also anticipates what the *presbutes* will say about the prophets being the only source of true

---

23. Stanton, "Group Boundaries," 263.
24. φίλον γάρ ἤδη νενόμικα.

knowledge that there is, as well as casting Trypho as one duped by philosophy's teachers and preservers. *Dial.* 2 will reveal that philosophy is erroneous and later Justin will claim that true philosophy comes precisely from the prophets, to whom Trypho does not seem to look for inspiration.

Dial. 1 continues to explore the shape of contemporary philosophy and what its concerns ought to be, and does so in such a way as to determine how Justin will be able to characterize the following of Christ and the true "Israel":

> "Yes, indeed," I said, "we, too, are of the same opinion. But the majority of the philosophers have simply neglected to inquire whether there is one or even several gods, and whether or not a divine providence takes care of us, as if this knowledge were unnecessary to our happiness. Moreover, they try to convince us that God takes care of the universe with its genera and species, but not of me and you and of each individual, for otherwise there would be no need of our praying to him night and day. It is not difficult to see where such reasoning leads them. It imparts a certain immunity and freedom of speech to those who hold these opinions, permitting them to do and say whatever they please, without any fear of punishment or hope of reward from God. How could it be otherwise, when they claim that things will always be as they are now, and that you and I shall live in the next life just as we are now, neither better nor worse. But there are others who think that the soul is immortal and incorporeal, and therefore conclude that they will not be punished even if they are guilty of sin; for, if the soul is incorporeal, it cannot suffer; if it is immortal, it needs nothing further from God. (*Dial.* 1.4–5)[25]

The issue of the number of gods that exist should for Justin be a central issue of philosophy. Van Winden has produced some excellent analysis of this passage which clarifies Justin's thought. He correctly points out that Justin presents two related but distinct statements here.[26]

---

25. Ναί, ἔφην, οὕτω καὶ ἡμεῖς δεδοξάκαμεν. Ἀλλ' οἱ πλεῖστοι οὐδὲ τούτου πεφροντίκασιν, εἴτε εἷς εἴτε καὶ πλείους εἰσὶ θεοί, καὶ εἴτε προνοοῦσιν ἡμῶν ἑκάστου εἴτε καὶ οὔ, ὡς μηδὲν πρὸς εὐδαιμονίαν τῆς γνώσεως ταύτης συντελούσης· ἀλλὰ καὶ ἡμᾶς ἐπιχειροῦσι πείθειν ὡς τοῦ μὲν σύμπαντος καὶ αὐτῶν τῶν γενῶν καὶ εἰδῶν ἐπιμελεῖται θεός, ἐμοῦ δὲ καὶ σοῦ οὐκ ἔτι καὶ τοῦ καθ' ἕκαστα, ἐπεὶ οὐδ' ἂν ηὐχόμεθα αὐτῷ δι' ὅλης νυκτὸς καὶ ἡμέρας. Τοῦτο δὲ ὅπη αὐτοῖς τελευτᾷ οὐ χαλεπὸν συννοῆσαι· ἄδεια γὰρ καὶ ἐλευθερία λέγειν καὶ ἕπεται τοῖς δοξάζουσι ταῦτα, ποιεῖν τε ὅ τι βούλονται καὶ λέγειν, μήτε κόλασιν φοβουμένοις μήτε ἀγαθὸν ἐλπίζουσί τι ἐκ θεοῦ. Πῶς γάρ; Οἵ γε ἀεὶ ταὐτὰ ἔσεσθαι λέγουσι, καὶ ἔτι ἐμὲ καὶ σὲ ἔμπαλιν βιώσεσθαι ὁμοίως, μήτε κρείσσονας μήτε χείρους γεγονότας. Ἄλλοι δέ τινες, ὑποστησάμενοι ἀθάνατον καὶ ἀσώματον τὴν ψυχήν, οὔτε κακόν τι δράσαντες ἡγοῦνται δώσειν δίκην (ἀπαθὲς γὰρ τὸ ἀσώματον), οὔτε, ἀθανάτου αὐτῆς ὑπαρχούσης, δέονταί τι τοῦ θεοῦ ἔτι.

The first is that the problem of god is generally neglected among philosophers. Whether this was actually the case is not all that pressing. Indeed van Kooten has noted that Epictetus sees the aim of philosophy similarly to discern how, if there is a god, his nature may be. As van Kooten notes this program has striking similarity to early "Christian" writing.[27] Why does Justin think it to be an important topic to raise with Trypho? We shall see momentarily. Secondly, there is the existence of a subclass of philosophers who *do not* neglect the problem of god but defend the thesis that his providence is restricted. They take up a special position in connection with the problem of god rather than neglecting it altogether. Still, this is not yet what Justin has in mind at this point. He is trying to express that those defending a restricted providence must also conclude that they have nothing to expect from a god who does not care for them. Hence in daily life they do not take god into account, and in that sense they do not "inquire about the divine."[28] This is different from the first group of philosophers who do not enquire at all. Or they enquire in theory but not in practice, nor in the way they live. The consequence of this neglect is that for the ethical life of the philosophers god is not a relevant factor; there is no punishment and no reward.

Who were these two groups of philosophers? This and related questions have been discussed *ad nauseam.* Hyldahl takes the view that the Stoics are the target but van Winden disagrees, and demurs from the received wisdom by stating that Greek philosophy in general is what Justin has in mind.[29] Most of the time, as we shall see below, Greek philosophy in general does seem to correlate better with what Justin recorded, but there is another layer to the text that I want to bring out. Justin is not primarily talking about any philosophical groups, even though the names and positions of real philosophical groups appear in his reports. He is interested in ways of framing his argument. The question as to whether the number of gods interests

---

26. Van Winden, *Early Christian Philosopher*, 30–31.
27. Van Kooten, "Religion or Philosophy," 397–99.
28. Van Winden, *Early Christian Philosopher*, 32.
29. Hyldahl, *Philosophie,* 99; van Winden, *Early Christian Philosopher*, 32.

philosophers is a worthwhile question to raise with Trypho because it is an important issue for Justin, or rather a central tenet of the true "Christian" philosophy put under threat by Marcion.[30] Justin wants Trypho to recognize that he and his philosophy think this topic to be central whatever others might claim. Furthermore, the second group of philosophers, those who do not neglect the problem of god, but think he does not care, are not a genuine and separate group of philosophers, but another marker that resonates with Marcionite theology. Marcion not only claimed that the god of Israel was not the god of his Christ, he believed this god was an evil god who created and sustained the world but was not loving towards its inhabitants.[31] At the same time his belief in another god, the transcendent god who neither rewarded nor punished, could be read as if this god was indifferent towards humanity. Marcion's belief in the transcendent god as well his acceptance of the reality of the god of Israel, who is the creator of the world and seen as not relevant to "Christians," make him sound a propagator of multiple gods. Furthermore the distinction between Christ and his Father makes him, and Justin who shares this, seem less than monotheistic. Justin of course wants to deny that this makes him less than monotheistic and continually asserts his allegiance to and belief in the one true god, the creator, only. The philosophical discussion then is mainly about establishing positions from which Justin can outline differences in his philosophy, which Trypho has asked to know, and that of Marcion. Trypho soon finds out that Justin is a "Christian" (*Dial.* 8.1). As we know from *Dial.* 38.1, Trypho was not meant to converse or associate with "Christians" in any way, so it becomes clear why Justin hides his identity. Furthermore Trypho's

---

30. On the specific point as to whether god cares for human beings, it should be noted that Basilides may be particularly pertinent as well as Marcion. Bentley Layton characterizes Basilides' system as such: "God does not exert direct and personal providence over human affairs. But God is present in the cosmos by virtue of God's powers or 'angels,' and by the integral operation of a complex structure capable of transmitting and mediating the remote activation of divine reason or logos. In short, God is an absentee manager, reigning as did the Great King of Persia through the agency of his subordinate satraps" (Layton Bentley, "The Significance of Basilides in Ancient Christian Thought," *Representations* 28 [1989]: 142).
31. For Marcion the creator was not only the author of evil in the world, following Isa 45:7, but his essence, which is found in souls, is the cause of it. A world created by him could not have been other; he is a cruel punisher, not one who loves. See Tertullian, *Marc.* 2.9.1.

view of "Christians," as shall become clear, is frequently imbued with a Marcionite character so it is incumbent on Justin to dispel this coloration. Hence Justin uses Trypho to launch into a piece on why "Christians" were different from Marcionites. Given the shame name status of "Christians," Justin has to proceed with subtlety and control the terms of the debate if he is going to be able successfully to differentiate "Christians" from Marcionites and Hebrews from "Israel."

Chapter one ends with Trypho inviting Justin, whom he sees as a wise and learned philosopher on account of his cloak and his insights thus far, to share his own views on god and his own particular philosophy, his way of life. Textually speaking Trypho has taken Justin's bait and the introduction proper now proceeds.

Dial. 2

As we saw in the previous chapter, Justin outlines that philosophy, in his view, does indeed pertain to god, and in fact comes from god, at the beginning of *Dial.* 2.1:

> "I will tell you," I replied, "my personal views on this subject. Philosophy is indeed one's greatest possession, and is most precious in the sight of God, to whom it leads us and to whom it unites us, and in truth they who have applied themselves to philosophy are holy men. But many have failed to discover the nature of philosophy, and the reason why it was sent down to men."[32]

Philosophy is a gift given to men; it has come down to them. We ought not to be misled by the giftedness of philosophy here, however. This is a step in the argument that will allow Justin to claim that the truth of Christ is philosophy without having to reject the category as such. That philosophy's purpose has escaped most of its practitioners is a clue to the central point here: "The point, however, is not the divine nature of philosophy, but the problems engendered by philosophy. Philosophy

---

32. Ἐγώ σοι, ἔφην, ἐρῶ ὅ γέ μοι καταφαίνεται. Ἔστι γὰρ τῷ ὄντι φιλοσοφία μέγιστον κτῆμα καὶ τιμιώτατον θεῷ, ᾧ τε προσάγει καὶ συνίστησιν ἡμᾶς μόνη, καὶ ὅσιοι ὡς ἀληθῶς οὗτοί εἰσιν οἱ φιλοσοφίᾳ τὸν νοῦν προσεσχηκότες. Τί ποτε δέ ἐστι φιλοσοφία καὶ οὗ χάριν κατεπέμφθη εἰς τοὺς ἀνθρώπους, τοὺς πολλοὺς λέληθεν.

for Justin is univocal, but it has become erroneously diverse."[33] This is a central truth on which Justin will rely to differentiate "Christians" from Marcionites and others, and "Jews" from "Israel," by virtue of teaching that demurs from that of god. In detailing this Justin must point out that such diversity belies not just error but membership of a different school, a different philosophy:

> They who first turned to philosophy, and, as a result, were deemed illustrious men were succeeded by men who gave no time to the investigation of truth, but, amazed at the courage and self-control of their teachers as well as with the novelty of their teachings, held that to be truth which each had learned from his own teacher. And they in turn transmitted to their successors such opinions, and others like them, and so they became known by the name of him who was considered the father of the doctrine. (*Dial.* 2.2)[34]

This really is the key passage in this chapter; it establishes the point for what follows in this long introductory section and the wider differentiation project in the whole piece. As we noted in chapter 1 Justin here stresses that philosophies have founders and followers. Amram Tropper, concerning how this system operated in Justin's time, writes:

> A succession, as popularly understood in the classicizing atmosphere of the Second Sophistic (i.e., the cultural renaissance in the Greek-speaking east of the Roman Empire from the mid-first to the mid-third century CE), outlined the transmission of proper doctrine over the course of history. The founder's successors continued his legacy and viewed the interpretation of his writings as the unfolding of his ideas. In a scholastic or intellectual succession list, the central factor was the belief that the founder's heirs transmitted proper doctrine.[35]

Credibility as a member of a school relied upon faithful remembering

---

33. Robert M. Royalty, Jr., "Justin's Conversion and the Rhetoric of Heresy," *StPatr* 40 (2006): 511.
34. Συνέβη τοῖς πρώτοις ἁψαμένοις αὐτῆς καὶ διὰ τοῦτο ἐνδόξοις γενομένοις ἀκολουθῆσαι τοὺς ἔπειτα μηδὲν ἐξετάσαντας ἀληθείας πέρι, καταπλαγέντας δὲ μόνον τὴν καρτερίαν αὐτῶν καὶ τὴν ἐγκράτειαν καὶ τὸ ξένον τῶν λόγων ταῦτα ἀληθῆ νομίσαι ἃ παρὰ τοῦ διδασκάλου ἕκαστος ἔμαθεν, εἶτα καὶ αὐτούς, τοῖς ἔπειτα παραδόντας τοιαῦτα ἄττα καὶ ἄλλα τούτοις προσεοικότα, τοῦτο κληθῆναι τοὔνομα, ὅπερ ἐκαλεῖτο ὁ πατὴρ τοῦ λόγου.
35. Amram Tropper, "Tractate Avot and Early Christian Succession Lists," in *The Ways that Never Parted*, ed. Adam H. Becker and Annette Yoshiko Reed (Tübingen: Mohr Siebeck, 2003), 166.

and representation of the founder of that school's doctrine, then. That is the legacy; without this, the legacy is lost or perverted into something else. Followers follow systems named after founders; that is, they follow the doctrines of men, rather than those of Christ (*Dial.* 48.4). For Justin, however, all schools, barring his own school, were already perverted and taught erroneous doctrines. He will even go as far as to question whether it is worth studying philosophy at all in the face of the critique offered by the *presbutes*. The message he received from the *presbutes* was the philosophy of Christ, given through the prophets. Justin is thus part of a chain of followers of a divine tradition, going back to Christ and passing it on likewise. In this sense, the *presbutes* represents a very particular teacher of Justin's, as Justin saw himself, passing down revelation to his students like Tatian which will then further be received by Irenaeus.[36]

In contrast to his own lineage of tradition, Justin speaks of other schools and their masters as originators of doctrine (πατὴρ τοῦ λόγου) and at *Dial.* 35.6 he calls them ἀρχηγέτου (founder), which is the same word he uses for the leader of the evil demons at *1 Apol.* 28.1[37] and for Simon Bar Kokhba at *1 Apol.* 31.6.[38] Those following and handing on these doctrines only make things worse because these followers usually have lost interest in the truth and are instead starstruck by the patience and self-restraint and novelty of their founders. Justin will go on to discuss a number of contemporary forms of philosophy in the course of making this point. The presentation of these is not unique in his time and may or may not represent his actual experience in Greco-Roman philosophical schools.[39] The point, however, is that this survey of philosophy establishes for him that human wisdom is erroneously equivocal and will allow him to argue below for the true "Christian" philosophy, which is univocal, which will necessarily imply the differentiation of "Christians" from Marcionites, as well as others, but particularly Marcionites given the shape of the discussion Justin

---

36. Skarsaune, "Conversion," 71.
37. ὁ ἀρχηγέτης τῶν κακῶν δαιμόνων.
38. ὁ τῆς Ἰουδαίων ἀποστάσεως ἀρχηγέτης.
39. Royalty, "Justin's Conversion," 510.

has with Trypho. The full illumination of the parallel Justin is drawing with philosophical schools is made by holding it up alongside the argument against "Christian" sectarianism in *Dial.* 35.6 and in *1 Apol.* 26.6. Van Winden includes a diagram to clarify this point:[40]

Philosophy	*Christianity*
One science	One faith
Various schools	Various sects or heresies
Adherents name after the "father of the doctrine"	Adherents named after the "father of the doctrine"
They call themselves philosophers but are not	They call themselves Christians but are not

This journey through the philosophy tale is the foundation for a central analogy of one discipline versus sectarian novelty. Justin believes he follows the true philosophy which comes directly from Christ and that this teaching was predicted and is corroborated by the prophets. This double-source of authority becomes clear once contrasted with Justin's main opponent, Marcion, who had advocated a direct revelation of Christ to Paul and a mediation of it through Paul alone at the expense of all the Prophets (including Moses, John the Baptist, and even contemporary prophets) and their god the creator and god of Israel. I am not suggesting that Marcion is the only target here, but he is the main contestant that Justin had in mind when he elaborates his own line of tradition. And it is in contrast to Marcion that Justin directs his criticism.

Dial. 3

In *Dial.* 3 Justin begins the story of his meeting with the *presbutes* which leads to his conversion. Van Winden wonders whether the παλαιός in Justin's text (which seems tautological beside "elder") might be a corruption of πόλιος,[41] which can commonly be taken to mean gray, or whether old here simply means honorable, respectable or venerable.

---

40. Van Winden, *Early Christian Philosopher*, 43.
41. Ibid., 54.

According to Bruce Chilton, Justin's language of παλαιός τις πρεσβύτης "emphasizes the antiquity and traditional wisdom of his interlocutor more than the English phrase—'a certain old man' does."[42] This would add more to the emphasis on wisdom and antiquity rather than the age of the man. Given that the *presbutes* will present a or rather *the* philosophy through the prophets and Christ, his credentials in wisdom are not irrelevant. Justin has not introduced *a man* but *a wise and experienced man* to present his case. This is especially noteworthy against the view of Hyldahl, who considers the *presbutes* to be a "barbarous stranger" because he asks various questions suggesting he does not know the answers, such as asking Justin if he is merely a lover of words and thus misunderstanding Justin's characterization of himself by φιλολογία, by which Justin means he is a philosopher, and instead takes him to mean he is a lover of words (φιλόσοφος) as opposed to one who is concerned with real life.[43] Van Winden points out that Hyldahl fails to recognise the strategy of the *presbutes* and reads the words too plainly. The *presbutes* is practicing a Socratic method by asking questions to encourage a response following logic, rather than not knowing the answer. This itself shows his wisdom and learning in the respectable ways of this thought world.[44] Furthermore, since the debate is chiefly about Platonism he clearly is not ignorant in such matters according to this method. Rather the question is designed to anticipate the revelation that the "Christian" philosophy is the only way that can truly be considered philosophy and truth. The *presbutes* has lost some of his household and has gone looking for them. I would conjecture, which is it all that one can do with this, that there is an echo of the Good Shepherd here. Given that true identity, the true

---

42. Bruce Chilton, "Justin and Israelite Prophecy," in Parvis and Foster, *Justin Martyr*, 77. Skarsaune said the same in Skarsaune, "Conversion," 70. Also noteworthy is that Justin uses the same word (πρεσβύτεροι) in *Dial*. 84.3 to describe the reliable and wise elders who translated the LXX in contrast to the current teachers of the "Jews" who amend these, suggesting the latter are more recent, novel, and altogether less authentic bearers of the tradition of Israel. See Horner, *Listening*, 132.
43. His ignorance appears confirmed by his questions: "He knows not what is philosophy, but must then ask Justin (*Dial*. 3.4); he has apparently never heard of Greek philosophy" (*Er weiss auch nicht was Philosophie ist, sondern muss Justin danach fragen* [*Dial*. 3,4]; *er hat augenscheinlich niemals von griechischer Philosophie gehort*)" (Hyldahl, *Philosophie*, 168; my translation).
44. Van Winden, *Early Christian Philosopher*, 56.

flock, is a main topic in the *Dialogue* and that Trypho has a group of friends who are probably pagan proselytes, this statement may be considered to cast the *presbutes* as a Christ-type figure looking for his flock who have strayed.[45] Indeed the only other occasion when Justin mentions the *presbutes* is *Dial.* 23.3, where he promises to recount the message he received from that man in order to win those who wish to become proselytes to the philosophy of Christ.[46] This ultimately is only conjecture but it seems to fit.

In the course of this discussion the problem of the nature of philosophy surfaces again and we find a further affirmation of the power of philosophy from Justin: "'Philosophy,' I answered, 'is the knowledge of that which exists, and a clear understanding of the truth; and happiness is the reward of such a knowledge and understanding'" (*Dial.* 3.4).[47] The *presbutes* does not query this, though he will critique the reliability of many philosophical doctrines in the course of their conversation; but as far as Justin is concerned this definition of philosophy always stands and, as he later spells out, its content can only be Christ. Following the above statement the *presbutes* quickly asks Justin what his conception of god is, and he replies: "'God is the Being who always has the same nature in the same manner, and is the cause of existence of all else'" (*Dial.* 3.5).[48] And the *presbutes* was pleased with this answer. That is to say that this answer is a starting point sufficiently close to the "Christian" view that the *presbutes* did not need to challenge it.

Justin is not yet a "Christian," but the answer he has given is not only compatible with the "Christian" philosophy of the *presbutes*, it also shows another typical anti-Marcionite feature. Marcion, by contrast,

---

45. Andrew Hofer had the same intuition regarding the relationship of the *presbutes* to Christ and developed his an account in relation to a number of aspects of the biblical narrative, but chiefly the road to Emmaus story. Andrew Hofer, "The Old Man as Christ in Justin's Dialogue with Trypho," *VC* 57 (2003): 1–21.
46. Skarsaune also takes this second reference as evidence towards the historicity of Justin's meeting with the *presbutes* because at this point in the *Dial.*—after the stylized introduction—there would seem to be little literary merit to reintroducing him in such a causal and matter-of-fact manner with little further consequence. Skarsaune, "Conversion," 70.
47. Φιλοσοφία μέν, ἦν δ' ἐγώ, ἐπιστήμη ἐστὶ τοῦ ὄντος καὶ τοῦ ἀληθοῦς ἐπίγνωσις, εὐδαιμονία δὲ ταύτης τῆς ἐπιστήμης καὶ τῆς σοφίας γέρας.
48. Τὸ κατὰ τὰ αὐτὰ καὶ ὡσαύτως ἀεὶ ἔχον καὶ τοῦ εἶναι πᾶσι τοῖς ἄλλοις αἴτιον, τοῦτο δή ἐστιν ὁ θεός.

would not have been pleased with this statement, because though he would have agreed that the creator is the cause "of existence of all else," he would not think of him as the transcendent (Middle Platonic) divine who "always has the same nature in the same manner." It was precisely this notion of divine consistency which Marcion saw betrayed by the creator of the Old Testament who was described as unreliable, had anthropomorphic characteristics, and changed between love and hate, between promise of salvation and punishment, and acted as a pondering judge.[49] Marcion's alien god, in contrast, was indeed extraneous to the philosophy of both Justin and the *presbutes*. So even in Justin's self-portrait of his pre-"Christian" state he is more "Christian" than Marcion, and creation is for the first time laid down as a distinctive marker of the theological discourse.

The *presbutes* has been pleased that Justin thinks in terms that sound like a singular creator god who is consistent. Naturally at this stage Justin's conception is not meant to sound fully "Christian," even if it is accepted by the *presbutes* to be a correct and reasonable starting point from which to continue the discussion with Justin. The next significant question asked is, how does Justin know this? What is the basis of Justin's knowledge; in what way is it demonstrable? This is the discussion of the nature of science and the possibility of a science of being. The *presbutes*'s intention here is to drive his opponent into a corner in the Socratic manner and prove that there is no science of knowing god, apart from the science revealed by the prophets. When Justin responds to the question as to whether such a science exists, the *presbutes* says: "Well then, is the knowledge of man and God of the same kind as that of music, arithmetic, astronomy, or the like?" (*Dial.* 3.6).[50] Justin admits that the science of knowing god does not proceed in the same way as these other sciences, and so the *presbutes* says that Justin has been wrong to answer that there was a science of knowing

---

49. Stylianopoulos agrees that this is indicative of a clear contra-Marcionism. See Stylianopoulos, *Mosaic Law*, 29–30.
50. Τί οὖν; Ὁμοίως ἐστὶν ἄνθρωπον εἰδέναι καὶ θεόν, ὡς μουσικὴν καὶ ἀριθμητικὴν καὶ ἀστρονομίαν ἤ τι τοιοῦτον.

god, because knowledge proceeds by sight or hearing and this is not possible with god.

What has the point been here? The *presbutes* says: "'Then how,' he reasoned, 'can the philosophers speculate correctly or speak truly of God, when they have no knowledge of him, since they have never seen nor heard him?'" (*Dial.* 3.7).[51] The point is that for the *presbutes* there is one god, maker and sustainer of all, who is consistent and unchanging, but that no one can know him apart from by his own visible and audible revelation. The *presbutes* is trying to rule out the possibility of natural theology, the possibility of any knowing of god that bypasses his revelation in the prophets. Why is this important to him? Because he will later want to demonstrate, at the conclusion of the Socratic dialogue, that the prophets and Christ are the only means of knowledge of god, that only from what god has said through the prophets and done in Christ can we know god. The consequence of this is that any vision of god that does not proceed on this basis is erroneous. Having the *presbutes* outline the only way of knowing god defines the "Christian" philosophy, and it does so to invalidate Marcion's contrary position, which rejected a) the creator god and b) the prophets as mediators of true revelation. It follows then that Marcion's claims to knowledge of god, as a "Christian," qualify as an invalid by the standards of the *presbutes*. And although the text of Justin's introduction is not directly addressing Marcion, Justin prepares the grounds and makes every effort to rule out the principles consistent with typically Marcionite positions (no others, as far as we know, rejected the prophets and the creator).

Dial. 4

In *Dial.* 4.1 the *presbutes* tries to tease out of Justin exactly what in his opinion makes the perception of god possible. The *presbutes* asks: "Will the human mind be capable of seeing god, if not aided by the Holy Spirit?"[52] This is the same spirit who spoke through the prophets.

---

51. Πῶς οὖν ἄν, ἔφη, περὶ θεοῦ ὀρθῶς φρονοῖεν οἱ φιλόσοφοι ἢ λέγοιέν τι ἀληθές, ἐποστήμην αὐτοῦ μὴ ἔχοντες, μηδὲ ἰδόντες ποτὲ ἢ ἀκούσαντες; Ἀλλ' οὐκ ἔστιν ὀφθαλμοῖς, ἦν δ' ἐγώ, αὐτοῖς.

The *presbutes* is asking Justin if it is possible to know god, the one true god, without his spirit guiding. Again this is suggestive of a contra-Marcionite agenda because Marcion rejects what the prophets have said about Christ and thus must have been read as if he rejected the guidance of the god of the prophets. Justin's response is that the human mind can see god unaided, that within the philosophy of Plato the human mind has a sense perception of god, so that a natural theology is still possible. It is not without conditions though. This vision of god comes to those souls who "are well disposed because of their affinity and desire of seeing him" (*Dial.* 4.1).[53] Van Winden details that Justin is here drawing on Plato's theory of the forms: only like knows like, and so "if the human mind is able to know the true reality, it must have some kinship (συγγένεια) with it."[54] This gives the *presbutes* the ammunition he needs to continue to deconstruct the possibility of a natural theology.

The *presbutes* asks in what this affinity consists, and, clarifying his question, he asks if the soul is part of the royal mind itself. As van Winden notes: "His objection against Platonism is obviously: if the human soul is thought to be kindred with god, what is the difference, then, between the two?"[55] The concept of the royal mind is not a clear one in the Middle Platonists of the period. Albinus and Numenius speak of two minds, that of god and a second which is between god and where humans live. The relationship of these to one another is not easy to establish.[56] However the specifics of this need not detain us. The *presbutes* has introduced the concept in order to get Justin to assent to it, which he does, and to elaborate further to a position he can firmly dispute. The *presbutes* now pursues a *reductio ad absurdum* argument concerning the ability of animals to see god according to this Platonic logic. He does this so that he will be able to refute the notion of the transmigration of souls in order to undermine the entire

---

52. Ἡ τὸν θεὸν ἀνθρώπου νοῦς ὄψεταί ποτε μὴ ἁγίῳ πνεύματι κεκοσμημένος.
53. ἐξαίφνης ταῖς εὖ πεφυκυίαις ψυχαῖς ἐγγινόμενον διὰ συγγενὲς καὶ ἔρωτα τοῦ ἰδέσθαι.
54. Van Winden, *Early Christian Philosopher*, 75.
55. Ibid., 75.
56. Ibid., 76.

Platonic doctrine of the nature of the soul.⁵⁷ The important moves for our purposes are that "righteousness" and temperance (σώφρονα) have become new criteria for seeing god in the course of the argument, and the *presbutes* defeats existence of this in the other philosophy by showing that the Platonic doctrine does not have the tools for such righteousness and temperance because the non-righteous would not be treated in a meaningfully different way. As Goodenough put it:

> The Old Man seems to use practical expediency as an adequate philosophical criterion, and from that test alone he has put aside both doctrines. He argues that it is useless to punish people when they do not remember afterwards either the fact or the reason for their having been punished, and concludes that such punishment, because useless, cannot exist.⁵⁸

The *presbutes* rounds off by saying:

> "Therefore," he concluded, "souls do not see God, nor do they transmigrate into other bodies, for they would know that they were being thus punished, and they would be afraid thereafter to commit even the slightest sin. But I do concede that souls can perceive that there is a God, and that justice and piety are admirable." (*Dial.* 4.7)⁵⁹

This is very revealing for the purposes of our argument. Having, insofar as Justin is convinced, debunked the notion of the transmigration of souls, the *presbutes* inserts that there is a grain of truth here, that righteousness and piety (εὐσέβεια) are relevant factors. God exists and can be known, and being righteous is not irrelevant to this, yet they are irrelevant in a system where true punishment does not exist. The implication is that in an otherwise arranged philosophical system this would make sense. This is significant for us because it is precisely the notion of punishment and righteousness that Marcion rejects in god. The *presbutes* is admitting that these are really part of the picture with the true god but only where there is a genuine alternative or

---

57. Ibid., 79.
58. Goodenough, *Theology of Justin*, 67.
59. Οὔτε ὁρῶσι τὸν θεὸν αἱ ψυχαί, οὔτε μεταμείβουσιν εἰς ἕτερα σώματα· ᾔδεσαν γάρ ἂν ὅτι κολάζονται οὕτως, καὶ ἐφοβοῦντο ἂν καὶ τὸ τυχὸν ἐξαμαρτεῖν ὕστερον. Νοεῖν δὲ αὐτὰς δύνασθαι ὅτι ἔστι θεὸς καὶ δικαιοσύνη καὶ εὐσέβεια καλόν, κἀγὼ Συντίθεμαι, ἔφη.

consequences to actions. In Marcion's system this is what is lacking because he deliberately jettisons it. We have already seen in our introduction that it is unlikely that Marcion distinguished between a just and a good god, however he did believe that the creator god was a cruel judge and therefore not just or righteous. Temperance too, as we shall see below, is something Justin claims for "Christians" but says he cannot claim for Marcionites, and that those who are not temperate are those who fall into demon inspired theology like Marcion's (1 Apol. 26.7; Dial. 58.3). The subtext here can be understood thus: if Platonism, that venerable philosophy, cannot see god because the transmigration undermines the necessity of justice, then how much further away is Marcionism, and any kind of "Christianity" which disavows the need to be righteous and temperate before god? Righteousness and temperance have become another marking of the "Christian" philosophy in which all "Christians" must be defined.

Dial. 5

Having dealt with souls, and the lack of expertise philosophers have concerning them, the *presbuts* engineers a shift in the argument towards the nature of the world. He demonstrates that souls are not immortal because if the world is begotten then so must also be souls. Both parties assume the Aristotelian theory in which "unbegotten" and "immortal" are a pair equal and opposite to "begotten" and "perishable."[60] So souls are not free to transmigrate, for the world and everything in it depends on the one true god for its existence and has no life apart from him. The ultimate sovereignty of god in such matters is further demonstrated by what the *presbutes* says next. Having shown that souls and the world are not immortal, he now qualifies his argument by saying, though he has distinguished the perishable from the unperishable logically, that this does not mean that all perishable things die. This is not because they are immortal but because god sustains them. Why so? Because otherwise, according to

---

60. Van Winden, *Early Christian Philosopher*, 87.

this argument, evil doers would get off scot-free. The resulting claim is that god sustains souls; the worthy never to die and the evil in punishment. This is part of the "Christian" doctrine that the *presbutes* is trying to establish and this is why he has had to attack the doctrines of the immortal soul and transmigration. These positions, as far as he is concerned, assume a state of affairs in which the sovereignty of god over ethics and existence is undermined. Of course these Platonic notions are of no serious threat to Justin as he presents the piece. Rather they represent problems that stand against the doctrine of god as understood in relation to Christ and through the prophets with the guidance of the Spirit. They thus challenge Marcion, as indicated above, who in the eyes of Justin must have been seen as undermining the sovereignty of god by neither rewarding righteousness, nor punishing wrongdoing. As above, this is not a direct rebuttal of Marcion but a removal of conditions that make his theology possible, or rather a careful drawing of what sort of arrangements are possible within "Christian" doctrine which necessarily excludes Marcionite tendencies. Since Marcion denied the relevance of punishment, and by extension righteousness, in relation to the one true god, anyone who has heard the *presbutes* could not think Marcion to be a "Christian."

Dial. 6

At the end of the previous section Justin had tried to align the views of the *presbutes* with those of Plato and those of Pythagoras also. Justin is inclined to see the doctrines of the *presbutes* as complimentary to the philosophies he knows as part of the wider discipline of philosophical speculation. To this the *presbutes* angrily retorts: "'I do not care,' he answered, 'if Plato, Pythagoras, or anyone else held such views. What I say is the truth and here is how you may learn it'" (*Dial.* 6.1).[61] Here Plato and Pythagoras are held up in sharp contrast to the truth, which is a marker that we are soon to reach the *presbutes*'s definitive statements about faith. It is not that the statements of these

---

61. Οὐδὲν ἐμοί, ἔφη, μέλει Πλάτωνος οὐδὲ Πυθαγόρου οὐδὲ ἁπλῶς οὐδενὸς ὅλως τοιαῦτα δοξάζοντος. Τὸ γὰρ ἀληθὲς οὕτως ἔχει. μάθοις δ' ἂν ἐντεῦθεν.

philosophers do not have a measure of truth, but they are insignificant in contrast to what the *presbutes* is about to reveal. He next gives a demonstration of the nature of the soul in two parts: first that the soul is not a life force itself but only participates in life, so it is possible for it to come to an end: God is the source of its life; and secondly the means of its coming to an end.[62] Sources for the second part of this argument have been sought by many commentators in contemporary philosophers. As I said above, I am not concerned with the literary sources of the doctrines in this section, chiefly because these are well attested and secondly because they can sometimes prove something of a red herring in demonstrating the force of what Justin is trying to do in this text, namely to rule out and distinguish "Christian" theology from anything that might take a more Marcionite or otherwise non-"Christian"or gnostic shape. Whatever the sources of the *presbutes'* statements are, they are designed to emphasize the sovereignty of god. The uniqueness of god and his power is the central seam of the argument. As van Winden wisely notes:

> More important is that the entire argument of the old man against Platonism is dominated by one idea: "If the Platonic opinion of the soul is true, the soul is not distinguishable from God." Hence the old man's attack on the Platonic theory of a *nous*, which is able from itself to know God; this would mean that the human soul is divine, which, of course, is untrue. Hence also the attack on the immortality of the soul; for "immortal" means "unbegotten" and these are properties of God alone. The unity of this entire argumentation, actually one great deduction ad absurdum, has escaped the commentators.[63]

Van Winden is spot on here, although even he has not noticed that this *deductio ad absurdum* has a relevance in the wider theological landscape of the time, as Bobichon noticed of the later section (*Dial.* 10.1) being a double response to Marcion. Justin, through the speech of the *presbutes*, has been attempting to rule out and separate from "Christian" theology any kind of natural theology so he can assert that the prophets, the prophets who belong to the one true god, are a genuine

---

62. Van Winden, 101.
63. Ibid., 109.

source of revelation. The other part of that argument that will be made is that the prophets speak of Christ, but naturally Justin needs to establish first that they are a genuine source of revelation from the one true god before he can enter into the debate about whether or not the prophets really speak of Christ. These introductory chapters are concerned with the prophets being true revelation of god so that anyone who wants to know god must be conversant with them. The rest of the debate is about why this doesn't make Justin a "Jew." From this point we find ourselves very quickly at the introduction of the prophets.

Dial. 7

From the *presbutes*'s demolition of philosophy, Justin wonders if it is worth perusing at all. Justin asks: "'If these teachers do not know the truth,' I asked, 'then from where might anyone get help?'" (*Dial.* 7.1).[64] He is despairing; perhaps there is no one who can teach truthfully.[65] Just as Justin questioned Trypho in *Dial.* 1 about why he is interested in philosophy and provoked an enquiry into his own philosophy, so Justin has been questioned to the point that he now wants to hear what his opponent's own views are. The *presbutes*'s rejection of affiliation with Plato and Pythagoras is in order that he can introduce the teachers of the truth. Now that Justin has enquired of the *presbutes*, this chapter will introduce the source of revelation, the peak towards which the previous introductory chapters were leading:

> "A long time ago," he replied, "long before the time of those so-called philosophers, there lived blessed men who were just and loved God, men who spoke through the inspiration of the Holy Spirit and predicted events that would take place in the future, which events are now taking place. We call these men the prophets. They alone knew the truth and communicated it to men, whom they neither deferred to nor feared. With no desire for personal glory, they reiterated only what they heard and saw when inspired by a holy spirit. (*Dial.* 7.1)[66]

64. My translation. Τίνι οὖν, φημί, ἔτι τις χρήσαιτο διδασκάλῳ ἢ πόθεν ὠφεληθείη τις, εἰ μηδὲ ἐν τούτοις τὸ ἀληθές ἐστιν.
65. Nasrallah, "Rhetoric of Conversion," 472.
66. Ἐγένοντό τινες πρὸ πολλοῦ χρόνου πάντων τούτων τῶν νομιζομένων φιλοσόφων παλαιότεροι, μακάριοι

And so the prophets enter the scene finally as teachers of those who want to know god in contrast to ordinary human teachers who are charlatans.[67] What these men knew was from god rather than human opinion and they were on good terms with god. The *presbutes*, whose religious/ethnic affiliation is not revealed, is claiming that the prophets are the sole source of truth, and that "their writings are still extant, and whoever consults them will profit greatly concerning knowledge of the beginning and end of things, and all that a philosopher ought to know" (*Dial.* 7.2).[68] This then is the source philosophers should be conversant with, because these prophets are the only ones (Οὗτοι μόνοι τὸ ἀληθὲς καὶ εἶδον καὶ ἐξεῖπον ἀνθρώποις) to have seen the truth. Their teaching is therefore the original teaching, theirs is the primordial philosophy, it is not one among many but the first and only philosophy.[69] Conversely, Barnard thought that Justin regarded Platonism as a preparation.[70] This is actually closer to Trypho's view who sees philosophy as a preparation for something with god. However, for Justin Greek philosophy was not travelling towards god. Instead he sees the "Christian" philosophy as the original and true philosophy, not something he needed to be prepared for in his journey (as the peripatetic advised). His journey is not intended to show an ascent but a meandering until he found the truth. The *presbutes* challenges the best that philosophy can offer, which Justin comes to see is defeated by the prophets.

Though the *presbutes* has appeared somewhat dismissive of his similarities in doctrine with the ancient philosophers, he has not told Justin that he ought not to be a philosopher, but instead a "Christian" (the *presbutes* never uses this label). Rather he has said that philosophers should know and believe the prophets. Justin, in despair,

καὶ δίκαιοι καὶ θεοφιλεῖς, θείῳ πνείματι λαλήσαντες καὶ τὰ μέλλοντα θεσπίσαντες, ἅ δὴ νῦν γίνεται· προφήτας δὲ αὐτοὺς καλοῦσιν. Οὗτοι μόνοι τὸ ἀληθὲς καὶ εἶδον καὶ ἐξεῖπον ἀνθρώποις, μήτ' εὐλαβηθέντες μήτε δυσωπηθέντες τινά, μὴ ἡττημένοι δόξης, ἀλλὰ μόνα ταῦτα εἰπόντες ἃ ἤκουσαν καὶ ἃ εἶδον ἁγίῳ πληρωθέντες πνεύματι.
67. Nasrallah, "Rhetoric of Conversion," 472.
68. My translation. Συγγάμματα δὲ αὐτῶν ἔτι καὶ νῦν διαμένει καὶ ἔστιν ἐντυχόντα τούτοισ πλεῖστον ὠφεληθῆναι καὶ περὶ ἀρχῶν καὶ περὶ τέλους καὶ ὧν χρὴ εἰδέναι τὸν φιλόσοφον.
69. Aurthor J. Droge, "Justin Martyr and the Restoration of Philosophy," *CH* 56 (1987): 319.
70. Barnard, *Justin*, 38.

does not give up on philosophy and replaces it with revelation, as Goodenough understood his acceptance of the prophets. So he embraces philosophy afresh, and all the more as an out-narration of all others, as the true science and demonstrable truth.[71] This is because true knowledge of god comes through direct encounter with god. Though no human mind can see or know god according to Platonic doctrine, the prophets have been filled with god's spirit and were able to speak through it; they had direct experience of god, then. They spoke and wrote the truth down, which the *presbutes* opposed to the teachings of Plato and Pythagoras.[72] The merit of faith in the prophets according to the *presbutes* is the power of the Holy Spirit that filled them.[73] It is not just the words that matter but who and what is said through them. And it requires this Spirit in order to understand the Scriptures, hence Justin's belief that Hebrews like Trypho and their teachers do not understand their Scriptures or their god.[74] Van Winden details Justin's account and emphasis on the nature of the prophet's writings, especially compared with those sophistic works of the philosophers, πιστεύσαντα ἐκείνοις, but one will learn the truth when credence is given to their writings. This very important observation is explained in what follows:

> "For they have not set out their accounts with formal argument, since, superior to all such arguing, they were trustworthy witnesses for the truth; but events past and present compel us to agree with what was spoken by them" [*Dial.* 7.2]. Their writings are not based on logical arguments. On the contrary, since they received the truth through a divine spirit, they are trustworthy witnesses, superior to all logical proofs; past and present prove that what they said is true. Apparently Justin argues here against those who considered the logical argument to be the only valuable one in philosophy.[75]

Who might this be that Justin argues against? Van Winden mentions Galen as a possibility.[76] Quite so, but closer to home is Marcion who

---

71. Nasrallah, "Rhetoric of Conversion," 472.
72. Van Winden, *Early Christian Philosopher*, 113.
73. Chilton, "Justin and Israelite Prophecy," 78.
74. *Dial.* 9.1; 70.4; 29.2; *1 Apol.* 31.5; 36.3.
75. Van Winden, *Early Christian Philosopher*, 114–15.

explicitly rejected the allegorical interpretation of the Scriptures, favoring only and at all times a plain reading of the text which does not allow for the prediction of events in the prophets. On close inspection it is possible that Justin uses the philosophers not only to argue against them, but also Marcion. Van Winden's Galen reference is apposite to reveal this. Galen treated both "Judaism" and "Christianity" as defective philosophies without the means to demonstrate their claims. But his disdain was not reserved for these. He also looked down on members of any philosophical school because they had, as he understood it, privileged allegiance to a teacher or school over demonstration.[77] Galen's objection, then, is just as David Sedley claims in saying: "In the Greco-Roman world, especially during the Hellenistic and Roman periods, what gives philosophical movements their cohesion and identity is less a disinterested quest for the truth than a virtually religious commitment to the authority of a founder figure."[78] Immediately this will appear as an obvious parallel to the argument Justin made in *Dial.* 2.2. Furthermore, Galen also provided a literary account of his journey through philosophical schools, which, though these were not unique of course, is remarkably similar to Justin's in *Dial.* 2.3–5. The key difference is that Galen disavows all sects, whereas Justin chose Plato's before choosing Christ's. However, it should be remembered that Christ's philosophy, though named after him as the founder, is the universal and primordial philosophy; in short, it is not a sect but simply the truth. Justin speaks of it in the manner of a school to make the point he needs about the misapplication of the name "Christian" elsewhere, but fundamentally like Galen he does not choose a school but, as his argument against schools in *Dial.* 2.2 suggests, rejects them in favour of *the truth*. The objection may be

---

76. Ibid.
77. Alexander, "Evidence of Galen," 65–68.
78. Sedley does not deny that, even this being the case, there were original thinkers in the schools of various philosophers, and his argument is not designed to be damning as Justin's is. However, the parallel remains; in Justin's period philosophical schools are characterized by allegiance to an individual beyond a general quest for truth as such, although the philosophical eclecticism of this same period might be thought of as a counterpoint to this. David Sedley, "Philosophical Allegiance in the Graeco-Roman World," in Philosophia Togata: Essays on Philosophy and Roman Society, ed. Miriam Griffin and Jonathan Barnes (Oxford: Clarendon, 1989), 97.

raised that Galen objected to "blind faith" and Justin spoke of the prophets having no proof, which might suggest that he was defending faith of this sort. However the more significant point is that according to Justin, the prophets did not argue for their claims; they were beyond this because these things could not be demonstrated since they had not happened. But in Justin's time they can be seen to have happened, so no one can argue against them. Justin rejects proof no more than Galen. It is perfectly in keeping with this that their writing should be read with *proper faith* (πιστεύαντα) as *Dial.* 7.2 states. This is not a request for blind faith, but for trust and an open-mindedness to see that what the prophets claimed will happen and has in fact happened. In Justin's mind it is an appeal for clarity and sensible thinking.

Concerning the character of the prophets, the *presbutes* says they were just and loved god and did nothing for personal glory but sought only to glorify god,[79] which of course fits the requirement that those who know god must be just and temperate, on which the two interlocutors had agreed already. This ought to be taken as a contrast to those philosophers who love the novelty and fame that Justin has already mentioned in *Dial.* 2.2. In this, Justin criticizes Marcion, who both stressed the idea of novelty and who, by being the founder of a sect, in Justin's eyes reveals himself to be like those philosophers he criticized as seeking fame and personal glory, things enjoyed by Simon and Menander, who appear as Justin Marcion's predecessors in *1 Apol.* 26 and 56. More distinctively against Marcion, Justin maintains that these very prophets "exalted God, the Father and Creator of all things, and made known Christ, his Son, who was sent by him. This the false prophets, who are filled with an erring and unclean spirit, have never done, nor even do now" (*Dial.* 7.3).[80] These are strong words, later on picked up against Marcion by Tertullian.[81] The passage, therefore,

---

79. As Skarsaune notes, this is what distinguishes the true prophets from the false ones. Both may have worked miracles, but the measure of truth is whether they glorify the one true god rather than the spirits of error and demons. Skarsaune, "Conversion," 63.
80. ἐπειδὴ καὶ τὸν ποιητὴν τῶν ὅλων θεὸν καὶ πατέρα ἐδόξαζον καὶ τὸν παρ' αὐτοῦ Χριστὸν υἱὸν αὐτοῦ κατήγγελλον· ὅπερ οἱ ἀπὸ τοῦ πλάνου καὶ ἀκαθάρτου πνεύματος ἐμπιπλάμενοι ψευδοπροφῆται οὔτε ἐποίησαν οὔτε ποιοῦσιν.
81. "With greater honesty and absence of guile the false prophets acted in opposition to the creator by coming in the name of their own god." Tertullian, *Marc.* 3.15.7.

provides further evidence that Marcionite theology is a background canvas against which Justin writes. Marcion would not glorify the maker of all things, the god of Israel, and equate him with the one god, the Father who sent Christ, his Son. Quite the opposite: he would consider such a deity to be a lesser, menial god. Interesting also is the fact that the *presbutes* mentions that the false prophets have been seduced by unclean spirits. This reads as Justin entering another subtle overture about Marcion, as he also says about Marcion in *1 Apol.* 58.3 that the demons have put him forward to do the work which is to "attempt nothing else than to seduce men from god who made them, and from Christ His first-begotten,"[82] clearly resonating with the *presbutes*'s words. The only other time Justin mentions Marcion, he is again in league with devils; it is by their aid (διὰ τῆς τῶν δαιμόνων συλλήψεως) that he is able to achieve his success (*1 Apol.* 26.5).[83]

Finally the *presbutes* rounds off his speech by urging Justin: "Above all, beseech God to open to you the gates of light, for no one can perceive or understand these truths unless he has been enlightened by God and his Christ" (*Dial.* 7.3).[84] This summary is against all the Platonic arguments that propose to lead to god. The *presbutes* insists that only from god and through Christ can this knowledge be given. That the one true god and his son are announced together is also significant. This goes beyond a statement to which Trypho could subscribe. Hence, both Marcion and Trypho are excluded and stand outside the gates of light. And one is reminded of Justin's work πρὸς Μαρκίωνα: "I would not have believed the Lord if he announced another God beside our Creator, Maker and nourisher. But since from the one God who made the world, formed us, and contains and administers all things, the Only-begotten Son came to us. . . ."[85] The god who sends Christ is thus

---

82. οὐ γὰρ ἄλλο τι ἀγωνίζονται οἱ λεγόμενοι δαίμονες ἢ ἀπάγειν τοὺς ἀνθρώπους ἀπὸ τοῦ αὐτοὺς ποιήσαντος θεοῦ καὶ τοῦ πρωτογόνου αὐτοῦ Χριστοῦ.
83. Minns and Parvis note that Justin nowhere uses συλλαμβάνω to mean simply "assist." They argue for a stronger sense, consistent with his use of things achieved through the ἐνέργειαν of the demons (*1 Apol.* 44.12; 54.1; *2 Apol.* 7.3), meaning something like being caught up in the scheme of the demons or working under their power and authority. Minns and Parvis, *Philosopher*, 151n2.
84. Εὔχου δέ σοι πρὸ πάντων φωτὸς ἀνοιχθῆναι πύλας· οὐ γὰρ συνοπτὰ οὐδὲ συννοητὰ πᾶσιν ἐστιν, εἰ μή τῳ θεὸς δῷ συνιέναι καὶ ὁ Χριστὸς αὐτοῦ.
85. *ipsi quoque Domino non credidissem alterum Deum annuntianti praeter Fabricatorem et Factorem et*

the one powerful and creative god who has jurisdiction over all. The revelation of this god is through the prophets and so Marcionite theology is ruled out as non-"Christian" theology. Justin's philosophy will also challenge Trypho, but on the issue of Messianism.

Dial. 8

In *Dial.* 8 Justin records his moment of realization of the truth of divine philosophy. This is the transitional chapter that marks the beginning of the end of the introduction and the start of the discussion proper; the *presbutes* has departed and Justin remerges as the main speaker. This is where Trypho discovers that Justin is a "friend of Christ." From the *presbutes* Justin was filled with a desire and passion for the prophets and all of those who can be counted as *friends of Christ* (οἵ εἰσι Χριστοῦ φίλοι). Being a *friend of Christ* and attending to the prophets are then, for Justin, through the tradition of the *presbutes*, what it means to be "Christian." One cannot follow Christ without reading and believing the prophets, for without them his Christ would be a baseless and a free floating teacher, speaking only his own opinions. There would be no necessary connection to the one true god, the maker of all things, and neither would there be any obvious aim or need for him. Those who are *friends of Christ* here naturally excludes Marcionites, more than any other group, because that which had inspired Justin's heart is necessarily twofold: the writings of the prophets and those who are friends of Christ. Marcionites claim to follow Christ but do not love the prophets, and therefore fail to meet the first criterion. This pairing sets up all the discussion to follow regarding Trypho and the observance of the Law. The love of the prophets in combination with an allegiance

---

Nutritorem nostrum; sed quoniam ab uno Deo, qui et hunc mundum fecit et nos plasmauit et omnia continent et administrat, unigenitus Filius venit ad nos ... (Irenaeus, *Haer.* 4.6.2). A less direct companion statement can be found at *Dial.* 68.1 where Justin says: "'If I undertook,' said I, 'to prove this [that the Christ has been incarnated] by doctrines or arguments of man, you should not bear with me. But if I quote frequently Scriptures, and so many of them, referring to this point, and ask you to comprehend them, you are hard-hearted in the recognition of the mind and will of God.'"
Εἰ τοῦτο, ἔφην, ἐπ' ἀνθρωπείοις διδάγμασιν ἢ ἐπιχειρήμασιν ἐπεβαλόμην ἀποδεικνύναι, ἀναχεισθαι μου οὐκ ἂν ἔδει ὑμᾶς· εἰ δὲ γραφὰς καὶ εἰς τοῦτο εἰρημένας τοσαύτας, πλειστάκις αὐτὰς λέγων, ἀξιῶ ὑμᾶς ἐπιγνῶναι αὐτάς, σκληροκάρδιοι πρὸς τὸ γνῶναι νοῦν καὶ θώλημα τοῦ θεοῦ γίνεσθε.

to Christ and his friends is a sufficient condition of being a true "Christian". Otherwise "Christians" would be Hebrews or Greek proselytes.[86] Also it is noteworthy that the "saviour's words are enough to put to shame or instil fear in those who have strayed from the path [of righteousness]" (*Dial.* 8.2)[87] This sounds very much contrary to the Son of Marcion's good god who does neither judge nor punish, but is characterised by mercy alone. Those who stick by Christ and put his words into practice have nothing to fear accordingly, but those who hear and do not obey are putting themselves at risk. Judgment is strongly part of the Savior's remit in Justin's account of the faith, in stark contrast to Marcion. Naturally, therefore, Marcion and his followers would count among those who have heard his words and do not obey them, given that he espouses a different god than Christ's Father.

Even more intriguing is the fact that Justin wishes that all should desire, like him, "not to fall away (ἀφίστασθαι) from the Saviour's words" (*Dial.* 8.2). As Skarsaune has noted, this is a puzzling thing for Justin to desire for those who have not yet become "Christians."[88] Three explanations present themselves: a) that Trypho's friends, the proselytes, used to be "Christians" and are now seeking to become "Jews," b) that Justin is warning them that by becoming "Jews" they will join an apostate tradition that rejects its true Savior's words, or c) that Justin has Marcionites in mind at this point, and is urging Trypho's friends not to follow their example and join them by rejecting the Christ of god. It seems as though a) is an unlikely explanation because we have no further evidence that would suggest this, and it would be odd for Justin to ask people who have never been "Christians" not to be apostates. Skarsaune favours a version of b).[89] In favour of c) we have our evidence so far, and more to follow, that the topics Justin discusses in defining his "Christian" philosophy are those that most

---

86. I say this cautiously because I understand the risk of sounding as though there was an ordinary "Judaism" and then "Judaism" plus Christ.
87. δέος γάρ τι ἔχουσιν ἐν ἑαυτοῖς, καὶ ἱκανοὶ δυσωπῆσαι τοὺς ἐκτρεπομένους τῆς ὀρθῆς ὁδοῦ.
88. Skarsaune "Conversion," 60.
89. Ibid., 61.

keenly distinguish him from Marcion. Yet Justin is fighting on multiple fronts in all of his texts, and we should be wary of tying too much down to one audience or intention; and, as here, the commonalities between Trypho and Marcion also are obvious. As far as Justin is concerned, both have rejected Christ and neither understand the Scriptures, as was alluded to by the *presbutes* in *Dial.* 7.3 and will be developed further by Justin in relation to grace, so it is possible that he is treating them together here.

Justin urges Trypho and his friends to get to know the Christ of god. The importance of the genitive case (Χριστὸν τοῦ θεοῦ) here should not be overlooked. It would be very easy to gloss over this and think that Justin is encouraging them simply to get to know a Christ or get to know Jesus, or even the Messiah. He says explicitly and specifically that they should know the Christ *of* god, which strongly implies a contrast with any other would-be Christs that they may have heard about. The Christ Justin follows is that of the god of Trypho and there is no space for negotiation or compromise on this. This is an assured contra-Marcionite staking of claim. Justin, then, believes that he has found the singular philosophy, the one which is useful or serviceable. In light of all he has outlined, Justin claims it is for those reasons he is a philosopher. Thus, he has now answered Trypho's request in *Dial.* 1.6 to "tell us what your philosophy is."[90] The philosophy Justin has outlined is the only one that is effective and has the power to change lives. He believes it brings perfection. This philosophy is not just abstract thinking but a way of life; he has found a discipline or rule of faith that is efficacious and comes from Christ with the prophets as its guarantors.

The reaction that comes from Trypho and his friends—who are probably proselytes to "Judaism" as discussed in the previous chapter—is not what Justin would have hoped for. Justin's philosophy is laughable to them. Trypho claims that if Justin had remained a philosopher, a Platonist or some such, then there would have been hope for him: "For, while you adhered to your former school of

---

90. Van Winden, *Early Christian Philosopher*, 119.

philosophy and lived a blameless life, there was hope of a better destiny for you, but, when you have turned away from God and have placed your hope in man, what chance of salvation do you have?" (*Dial.* 8.3).[91] Trypho cannot accept to put one's trust in a man by forsaking god. Compared to such apostasy, philosophy was a blameless life with hope for a better destiny. Trypho clearly sees Justin's new philosophy as different from both the Greco-Roman schools and his own traditions of Israel. It appears to him as some kind of new cult devoted to a human being, not something akin to the god of Israel. Taking into account Justin's view of the pluriform nature of philosophy in *Dial.* 2 and that in *Dial.* 35 an analogy with this is drawn with "heretics" including Marcionites, it is no surprise here that Trypho's words reflect this in seeing the "Christian" philosophy as a novelty founded on man rather than god. Trypho has also claimed that Justin's turn from god to a man was done under the guidance of *men of no reputation or worth* (ἀκολουθῆσαι οὐδενὸς ἀξίοις). Whom does Trypho have in mind (*Dial.* 8.3)? Marcion, or the apostles? The meaning of this charge will become clearer below, where it will be shown to what extent Trypho's view of "Christianity" coincides with Justin's view of the major contemporary heresy he is dealing with. Trypho's view of Justin is now clear. He has admired that Justin is interested in god, unlike many philosophers as previously outlined, and that he has good things to say about the prophets,[92] but he believes Justin has turned away from god, the god of Israel, the maker of all things, in favor of a man. This is not the view Justin has been trying to establish. Justin has worked hard to argue that his Christ is not an alternative to this god, the creator, but that he himself worships him, and, as he goes on to say, is a member of the true Israel.

Trypho outlines things Justin ought to do if he were really interested in god, which amount to keeping the Law. If he does this, he may obtain mercy from god (ἔλεος ἔσται παρὰ θεοῦ) (*Dial.* 8.4). This point is almost

---

91. Μένοντι γάρ σοι ἐν ἐκείνῳ τῷ τῆς φιλοσοφίας τρόπῳ καὶ ζῶντι ἀμέμπτως ἐλπὶς ὑπελείπετο ἀμείνονος μοίρας· καταλιπόντι δὲ τὸν θεὸν καὶ εἰς ἄνθρωπον ἐλπίσαντι ποία ἔτι περιλείπεται σωτηρία;
92. Philippe Bobichon, *Justin Martyr: Dialogue avec Tryphon, édition critique, traduction, commentaire* (Paradosis 47/2; Fribourg: Academic, 2003), 601.

a summary of the whole debate. Trypho and Justin have alternative accounts of how one can obtain mercy from god, and the rest of the piece is a long outworking of the Law versus grace through Christ.[93] Both contestants agree on the presupposition. They both seek mercy from god, from the same god who, both believe, is capable of giving mercy, whereas Marcion would deny that the creator god would be the god of mercy. The contestants' agreement, therefore, seems to be designed to exclude any implicit Marcionism; the very fact that Justin has the audacity to expect mercy from *this* god is a contra-Marcionite statement. The topic of mercy from god will recur frequently in the *Dialogue* as a marker of this distinction and as a mode of talking of god's providential care for all humanity, a key contra-Marcionite topic.[94]

Dial. 9

Justin responds in *Dial.* 9 with the counsel that Trypho does not know what he is saying. Trypho has recommended in the previous chapter that Justin remain a Platonist rather than become somebody who forsakes god. That is, better to be a well-meaning neutral in god's eyes than an apostate. Against Trypho's accusation of Justin having put his confidence in a man and turned away from god by trusting in empty fables, Justin makes an important defence:

> If you will agree to hear our account of him, how we have not been deceived by false teachings, and how we shall not cease to profess our faith in him (even though men thereby persecute us, and the most cruel tyrant tries to force us to deny him), I will prove to you, here and now, that we do not believe in groundless myths nor in teachings without demonstration, but in doctrines that are inspired by the Divine Spirit, abundant with power, and teeming with grace. (*Dial.* 9.1)[95]

The questions arises, then: what is it that Trypho considers to be empty

---

93. Ibid., 600n9.
94. 8.4; 14.5; 18.3; 25.2, 4; 36.4; 43.2; 96.3; 108.3; 118.2; 133.1; 141.2.
95. Εἰ δὲ βούλοιο τούτου πέρι δέξασθαι λόγον, ὡς οὐ πεπλανήμεθα οὐδὲ παυσόμεθα ὁμολογοῦντες τοῦτον, κἂν τὰ ἐξ ἀνθρώπων ἡμῖν ἐπιθέρβνται ὀνείδη, κἂν ὁ δεινότατος ἀπειπεῖν ἀναγκάζῃ τύραννος· παρεστῶτι γὰρ δείξω ὅτι οὐ κενοῖς ἐπιστεύσαμεν μύθοις οὐδὲ ἀναποδείκτοις λόγοις, ἀλλὰ μεστοῖς πνεύματος θείου καὶ δυνάμει βρύουσι καὶ τεθηλόσι χάριτι.

fables which Justin denies? Trypho in the next chapter gives us the explanation, when he states: "But the precepts in your so-called Gospel are so marvellous and great that I don't think anyone could possibly keep them. For I took the trouble to consult them" (*Dial.* 10.2).[96] The dispute, therefore, is revealed to be one of competing sources: "the so-called Gospel," a written text ("I have carefully read it") with its narratives ("empty fables") and its "precepts" ("no one can keep them") in competition with the commandments of the Torah and the narratives of the prophets. As mentioned before, "so-called" (λεγόμενος) is used by Justin, when either the audience is unfamiliar with a concept, or if the concept is something of dubious character. Here, however, Justin makes the case that he himself does not believe "empty fables or words without any foundation," but instead follows "an account of Him" which does neither deceive nor make Justin "cease to confess Him." For Justin, this account is made of "words filled with the Spirit of god, and big with power, and flourishing with grace." This most likely refers to his acceptance of the prophets but we know Justin elsewhere relies on what he calls the *memoirs of the apostles* (Ἀπομνημονεύμασι τῶν ἀποστόλων).[97] Justin is therefore denying that the tradition Trypho refers to as dubious is so, but also that it is the only source, or even the primary source, of witness to Christ.

Justin would recognize Trypho's charge that he believes empty fables, because he thinks "Christians" do not accept the prophetic or Torah traditions, as a charge against Marcionite theology. Trypho is accusing Justin of what he just spent eight chapters denying, and furthermore he blasphemes Christ, the Christ of the one true god, in the process. Thus he responds that Trypho does not understand what he is talking about: "'I excuse and forgive you, my friend,' I said. 'For you know not what you say'" (*Dial.* 9.1).[98] Justin has not turned away from god, the one true god, in favor of a man.

Justin claims that Trypho has been instructed by teachers ignorant

---

96. Ὑμῶν δὲ καὶ τὰ ἐν τῷ λεγομένῳ Εὐαγγελίῳ παραγγέλματα θαυμαστὰ οὕτως καὶ μεγάλα ἐπίσταμαι εἶναι, ὡς ὑπολαμβάνειν μηδένα δύνασθαι φυλάξαι αὐτά·.
97. *Dial.* 100.4; 101.3; 103.6, 8; 104.1; 105.1, 5; 106.1, 3–4; 107.1; 1 *Apol.* 66.3; 67.3.
98. Συγγνώμη σοι, ἔφην, ὦ ἄνθρωπε, καὶ ἀφεθείη σοι· οὐ γὰρ οἶδας ὃ λέγεις.

of the meaning of the Scriptures in forming his views. This refers to prejudiced "Jewish" teachers but it is the same charge that Justin holds against heretics like Marcion. And Justin pleads for Trypho and his friends to hear from him the reasons that "Christians" are not erroneous in their doctrine or life after Christ. This is not a shallow appeal. If Trypho will listen to what Justin's account of Christ is (*Dial.* 9.1),[99] he will hear not just about Christ, but the correct perspective about him. He should be open minded and recognize that his view of "Christianity," based on a misunderstanding that "Christians" reject the Israelite traditions in favor of novel tales, which is rather the Marcionite version of which Justin is trying to rid himself. At risk here is that Trypho may conflate all "Christians" under claims that are more specifically Marcionite from Justin's perspective. The discussion so far, which has centered on one god being the creator, carer, provider, and mercy giver who is just and righteous and who spoke through prophets, evidences that Justin is working hard to dispute this view of a Marcionite "Christianity."

Justin then sets out the aim of the rest of the *Dialogue*: "to prove to you, here and now, that we do not believe in groundless myths nor in teachings without demonstration, but in doctrines inspired by the Divine Spirit, abundant with power, and teeming with grace" (*Dial.* 9.1).[100] These empty fables, of believing in which Justin feels accused, are presumably those gospel narratives which Trypho has read, and Justin has declared his intention to prove that they are true, that Jesus is who "Christians," true "Christians" like him, say he is. In denying he believes empty fables, Justin is not confessing the fiction of the gospel traditions, but denying that they are without foundation, denying that this tradition is separate from the grace and spirit of god, whom both believe is in the prophetic tradition. Horner has pointed out that this is the hook that keeps Trypho involved in the discussion. Having learnt that Justin is a "Christian," he could have, and should have if he aimed to remain obedient to his teachers, conversed with him no more and

---

99. See n. 95.
100. Ibid.

walked away. Trypho, believing "Christians" worship an invented messiah, wants proof of Justin's claims; this request continually recurs and keeps the discussion going, and Justin tries to demonstrate that his belief in Jesus is not groundless.[101]

Justin's declaration of intention is not only a response to Trypho, but is strongly contra-Marcionite. The project to define the "Christian" philosophy as that which follows a Christ who is the "Jewish" Messiah under the one true god, demonstrable through the witness of the prophets, shows Justin's different perspective and clearly rules out Marcionism as a "Christian" enterprise, though not necessarily other "heretical" groups which did neither postulate another god than the god of Israel nor reject the prophets.

This needs to be read in conjunction with the previous chapter, where Trypho has accused "Christians" of following men of no reputation and believing groundless reports. Trypho may well have had in mind the New Testament Scriptures circulating at this time; shortly after this the so-called Gospel (λεγομένῳ Εὐαγγελίῳ) will be mentioned by him (*Dial.* 10.2), or he may mean the apostles, or both. The irony here is that Justin's response refers not only to New Testament texts, but also to the books of the prophets. Marcionites hold only by a New Testament gospel,[102] but Justin's community holds New Testament traditions only as elaborations of the true meaning of what is said in the prophets, as commentaries on the grace revealed in those ancient texts.[103] Justin does not understand the Gospel, the memoirs of the apostles, singular or plural, or reports about Jesus to be stand-alone new revelation. They are necessarily connected with the previous revelation with which Trypho himself has been brought up. Once again Trypho thinks of "Christians" in terms that Justin would apply only to Marcionites. In contrast, Justin is claiming to believe "words filled with the Spirit of God, and great with power, and

---

101. Horner, *Listening*, 155.
102. The question of the origins or shape of this gospel need not detain us here. What is significant is that it is somehow different from that held by other, "orthodox," "Christians" like Justin and that for the latter it is only part of a wider story rather than its own account, as it is for Marcion, which, it appears, is also how Trypho understands its function.
103. Bobichon, *avec Tryphon*, 604.

flourishing with grace," the same texts which Trypho himself accepts.[104] Justin's claim, then, is that Trypho has misunderstood "Christians," that they share a lot, and that he can demonstrate his belief from the same sources that Trypho refers to rather than to something novel and independent.

Grace is the key to this. That which is true for Justin is that which has been imbued with grace. There are numerous examples in the *Dialogue*[105] of grace being the determining factor in understanding; Bobichon has noted that the whole of the *Dialogue* is a demonstration in which grace is the central feature or active agent,[106] but *Dial.* 58.1 is the clearest: "'I intend to quote Scripture to you,' I said, 'without any reliance on mere artistic arrangement of arguments. Indeed, I have no such skill, but this grace alone was given me from God to understand his Scriptures.'"[107] It is grace that intercedes. This grace opens the eyes to see. *Dial.* 92.1 is also strikingly clear in this regard: "If, therefore, one were not endowed with God's great grace to understand the words and deeds of the prophets, it would be quite useless for him to relate their words and actions, when he can give no explanation of them."[108] Ownership of the Scriptures depends on the possession of grace from god. Justin reiterates, this time with reference to the Spirit that speaks through scriptures, and that his interlocutors have no understanding of and no claim upon the Scriptures.[109] In *Dial.* 29.2 he states: "You should be, for they are contained in your Scriptures, or rather not yours, but ours. For we believe and obey them, whereas you, though you read them, do not grasp their spirit."[110] To Justin, Christ speaks in Scriptures when Trypho accuses him of believing only

---

104. Naturally Justin also believes that the words of Christ, which he reports, are equally filled with the Spirit and Grace but the memoirs function mainly as evidence rather than revelation for him.
105. 9.1; 30.1; 32.5; 58.1; 78.10; 92.1; 100.2; 119.1.
106. Bobichon, 604n7.
107. Κἀγὼ εἶπον· Γραφὰς ὑμῖν ἀνιστορεῖν μέλλω, οὐ κατασκευὴν λόγων ἐν μόνῃ τέχνῃ ἐπιδείκνυσθαι σπεύδω· οὐδὲ γὰρ δύναμις ἐμοὶ τοιαύτη τίς ἐστιν, ἀλλὰ χάρις παρὰ θεοῦ μόνη εἰς τὸ συνιέναι τὰς γραφὰς αὐτοῦ ἐδόθη μοι.
108. Εἰ οὖν τις μὴ μετὰ μεγάλης χάριτος τῆς παρὰ θεοῦ λάβοι νοῆσαι τὰ εἰπημένα καὶ γεγενημένα ὑπὸ τῶν προφητῶν, οὐδὲν αὐτὸν ὀνήσει τὸ τὰς ῥήσεις δοκεῖν λέγειν ἢ τὰ γεγενημένα, εἰ μὴ λόγον ἔχει καὶ περὶ αὐτῶν ἀποδιδόναι.
109. Elsewhere, in 1 *Apol.* 31.5, Justin again says that the "Jews" do not understand scripture.
110. ἐν τοῖς ὑμετέροις ἀπόκεινται γράμμασι, μᾶλλον δὲ οὐχ ὑμετέροις ἀλλ' ἡμετέροις· ἡμεῖς γὰρ αὐτοῖς πειθόμεθα, ὑμεῖς δὲ ἀναγινώσκοντες οὐ νοεῖτε τὸν ἐν αὐτοῖς νοῦν.

groundless stories, while, in fact, he is basing his testimony on the same texts Trypho upholds, as well as the memoirs of the apostles as corroboration of the prophecy of these texts. This accusation has importance for distinguishing "Christians" from Marcionites also, because Marcion too does not understand these Scriptures. He reads them at the plainest level, seeing no prophecy of Christ, and setting them in contrast to his new god. Justin's response to him would be just the same as it is to Trypho here: that he has neither the grace to understand the Scriptures nor does he the Spirit, the Spirit of god, who speaks through them. And so Justin's declaration that he can prove (ἀπόδειξις) that he, and the true followers of Christ, believe not in men of no reputation but in words full of grace (τεθηλόσι χάριτι), to which Trypho and his friends find reason to laugh, is tantamount to an early announcement that true "Christians" read the prophetic Scriptures and can demonstrate their claims for Christ from these by grace, thus distinguishing true "Christians" from the followers of Marcion. What is this grace, though; what force or function does it have? Skarsaune cogently explains this by plotting a middle way between Pycke and Joly. Pycke has criticized Joly for seeing Justin's use of grace here as supernatural knowledge and failing to see the rational contents of this knowledge. Skarsaune agrees but considers Pycke's definition, a typological method of interpretation, too general and vague. Rather he points out that where grace is mentioned it is always connected intimately to the apostolic proof from Scripture taught by Christ and passed on to all by the apostles. Without the instruction of the Christ via the apostles the Scriptures cannot be properly understood:

> Justin can talk about the ·grace to understand· and the apostolic instruction in exactly the same terms: (1) Without ·the grace to understand· one cannot understand the Scriptures, Dial. 92:1; 119:1; (2) before Christ revealed the meaning of the prophecies, they could not be understood, Dial. 76:6. This also makes clear the role of rational argument: Once the hidden meaning of the Scriptures has been brought to light by Christ and the apostles, it shows itself to be rational and convincing, and every denial of its validity and cogency is due either to hatred of the truth (Dial. 44:1; 53:2; 68:1; 95:4) or cowardice, Dial. 36:9; 44:1; 112:5.[111]

So for Justin the grace to understand is instruction received from Christ and his true followers. *Dial.* 48.4 repeats this claim quite clearly: "For we have been told by Christ himself not follow the teachings of men, but only those which have been announced by the holy prophets and taught by himself."[112] A "Christian" is someone who believes what Christ taught and what the prophets taught and announced of him who is from their god, the god of Israel, the creator. Without the prophets, "Christian" teaching, as far as Justin is concerned, would be merely human speculation; and without Christ and his apostles this teaching could not be known. This grace, this particular stream of instruction, being a principle seam of the "Christian" philosophy, necessarily rules out the position of Marcion whom Justin believes follows a different Christ and would not be considered a receiver of this, Christ's grace.[113]

Dial. 10

In *Dial.* 10 Justin attempts to define the terms of the debate to follow: "My friends, is there any accusation you have against us other than this, that we do not observe the Law, nor circumcise the flesh as your forefathers did, nor observe the Sabbath as you do?" (*Dial.* 10.1).[114] This is Justin in effect asking Trypho if he has any challenges beyond that which he has already denied, that which is applicable to Marcionites but not to "Christians," and beyond what Justin would admit differentiates his own position from that of Trypho, his non-fleshly understanding of Law observance. In this chapter of the *Dialogue* Justin offers Trypho a series of alternative options for complaint. Like the civil servant manipulating a government minister by offering two solutions, one less than favorable and the other plausible, Justin has prompted Trypho. He asks if Trypho believes "Christians" are immoral and promiscuous or if they charge them with believing untruths.

---

111. Skarsaune, *Proof from Prophecy,* 12.
112. ὑπ' αὐτοῦ Χριστοῦ πείθεσθαι, ἀλλὰ τοῖς διὰ τῶν μακαρίων προφητῶν κηρυχθεῖσι καὶ δι' αὐτοῦ διδαχθεῖσι.
113. Naturally the character of Marcion's relationship to the Paul and his apostolic status complicates this point somewhat; but the overriding dispute is over who god and Christ are, and that can only be known with the proper grace.
114. Μὴ ἄλλο τί ἐστιν ὃ ἐπιμέμφεσθε ἡμᾶς, ἄνδρες φίλοι, ἢ τοῦτο ὅτι οὐ κατὰ τὸν νόμον βιοῦμεν, οὐδὲ ὁμοίως τοῖς προγόνοις ὑμῶν περιτεμνόμεθα τὴν σάρκα, οὐδὲ ὡς ὑμεῖς σαββατίζομεν.

Trypho responds that it is only the latter, as the former is ridiculous, and thus the debate focuses towards why "Christians" hope in a man apart from god and do not keep god's commandments. Since Trypho cannot distinguish "Christians" and Marcionites, because Justin is creating the distinction as he goes, Trypho does not believe in the immorality of "Christians" in general, be they followers of Marcion or otherwise. Bobichon has seen fit to find a connection with Justin's question here and his agnosticism as to whether Marcionites are guilty of such immorality in *1 Apol.* 26.7.[115] There Justin says he does not know if Marcionites are guilty of those things which are said about his own group, but that they are not persecuted according to their doctrines. His refusal to absolve Marcionites as innocent, as he does for his own group, removes them from the class "Christian." Justin's point at *1 Apol.* 26.7 is that all "Christians" are roundly accused of such immorality and that may or may not separate Marcionites from followers of Christ, but certainly their doctrines are different. Bobichon is right to note that this other appearance of very similar accusations comes in the context of discussing those who are followers of Marcion. This is not to say that Marcionites were especially singled out and slandered for this; indeed it is rather Justin's point that they are not. Here in *Dial.* 10.1 Justin is trying to ascertain what Trypho knows about "Christians" and how clearly he understands them before he can outline fully what his own group believes. From his answer Trypho does not distinguish, just as the rulers do not, between "Christians" and others who claim Christ and the accusations made against them all. This information tells Justin what he needs to know, and at the start of his following chapter we will see that he opens immediately with a strongly contra-Marcionite claim.

In *Dial.* 10.4 Trypho gives further details of his understanding of "Christians" by accusing them of not only worshiping a man but failure to be circumcised or to keep god's commandments and rejecting his covenant (basically a repetition of his point from *Dial.* 8.4). This complicates the picture. Justin will deny all these things by claiming

---

115. Bobichon, *avec Tryphon*, 606n2.

spiritual circumcision, eternal decrees, and the new covenant. Yet Trypho accuses "Christians" of these shortcomings while thinking they might still receive favour from god, his god. This suggests Trypho does not simply think "Christians" worship another god, but understands they claim the same god as he. Of course Justin has previously, through the speech of the *presbutes* and his own claim that what "Christians" believed is inspired by the Spirit of god and full of grace, made this claim obvious to Trypho.

Having reached chapter eleven, we have now come to the end of the introduction proper. The transition that began in chapter eight is complete as all the major themes of the rest of the work have now been marked out by Justin. "If, then, you can give a satisfactory reply to these charges and can show us on what you place your hopes, even though you refuse to observe the Law, we will listen to you most willingly, and then we can go on and examine in the same manner our other differences" (*Dial.* 10.4).[116] As Bobichon has noted, this statement of ultimatum from Trypho introduces a whole structural chunk of the *Dialogue.* The introduction has finished, and from chapter eleven to twenty-nine a new section will run which is devoted to the requirements of the Law and the ways in which "Christians" observe the true Law but not the Law of Moses.[117]

Dial. 11

Before moving on, we shall now look at chapter eleven also to see how the other side of this transition looks. In *Dial.* 11 Justin begins his defense that "Christians" do indeed *fear* god, the same god as Trypho worships and no new god as the Marcionites.

> And I answered him, "Trypho, there never will be, nor has there ever been from eternity, any other God except him who created and formed this universe. Furthermore, we do not claim that our God is different from yours, for he is the God who, with a strong hand and outstretched arm, led your forefathers out of the land of Egypt. Nor have we placed our trust in

---

116. Εἰ οὖν ἔχεις πρὸς ταῦτα ἀπολογήσασθαι, καὶ ἐπιδεῖξαι ᾧτινι τρόπῳ ἐλπίζετε ὁτιοῦν, κἂν μὴ φυλάσσοντες τὸν νόμον, τοῦτό σου ἡδέως ἀκούσαιμεν μάλιστα, καὶ τὰ ἄλλα δὲ ὁμοίως συνεξετάσωμεν.
117. Bobichon, *avec Tryphon*, 610n16.

any other (for, indeed, there is no other), but only in him whom you also have trusted, the God of Abraham and of Isaac and of Jacob." (*Dial.* 11.1)[118]

Why would Justin say such a thing? If one has not already recognized the contra-Marcionite stand of Justin in the previous chapters, this statement which rejects "another god" comes, as Stylianopoulos notes, seemingly out of nowhere.[119] Justin has already said that philosophy neglects the question of the number of gods and the relevance of this for human life, but he has not suggested that "Christians" believe in any other god. Why would Justin still then begin his defense that "Christians" fear the same god as Trypho does by denying they serve any other god? Of course this could be in keeping with the tradition of "Jewish" monotheism, simply a statement against idolatry. This is possible but ignores what we have seen so far, that Marcion's theological claims are being subtly and continuously ruled out by Justin. Justin's blunt statement here makes much more sense if he believes Trypho is confused on this point or at least might harbor an unarticulated suspicion that Justin believes in another god in some fashion, despite his protestations so far. It is hard to imagine a passage that more succinctly and deliberately distinguishes the faith of Justin from that of Marcion.

Stylianopoulos made this point with regard to the intended audience: "These statements [the above and those which accuse heretics of blasphemy of the creator, *Dial.* 35.5; 80.4; *1 Apol.* 58.1] in no way have their *Sitz in Leben* in the Jewish-Christian debate, but in the controversies of ancient Christianity against Marcion."[120] Indeed, this rejection of another god makes most sense against the threat of Marcion to Justin and the "Christian" philosophy. After being asked to prove that he fears god—the god of Trypho—in the space of a few sentences Justin has said that "Christians" do not consider themselves

---

118. Οὔτε ἔσται ποτὲ ἄγλλος θεός, ὦ Τρύφων, οὔτε ἦν ἀπ' αἰῶνος, ἐγὼ οὕτως πρὸς αὐτόν, πλὴν τοῦ ποιήσαντος καὶ διατάξαντος τόδε τὸ πᾶν. Οὐδὲ ἄλλον μὲν ἡμῶν, ἄλλον δὲ ὑμῶν ἡγούμεθα θεόν, ἀλλ' αὐτὸν ἐκεῖνον τὸν ἐξαγαγόντα τοὺς πατέρας ὑμῶν ἐκ γῆς Αἰγύπτου ἐν χειρὶ κραταιᾷ καὶ βραξίονι ὑψηλῷ· οὐδ' εἰς ἄλλον τινὰ ἠλπίκαμεν, οὐ γὰρ ἔστιν, ἀλλ' εἰς ὃν καὶ ὑμεῖς, τὸν θεὸν τοῦ Ἀβραὰμ καὶ Ἰσαὰκ καὶ Ἰακώβ.
119. Stylianopoulos, *Mosaic Law*, 25.
120. Ibid., 26.

to have one god of their own and Trypho to have another, which is about as close as one could come to saying "we are not Marcionites" to someone who does not know what a Marcionite is. Justin is making it as plain as possible that he believes in only one true god, the creator. That this is for him a direct response to the challenge to show that he does neither scorn the covenant nor spurn the commandments shows he sees the challenge as not to be seen as a Marcionite, as he goes straight on to deny the central feature of Marcion's theology; two gods, one evil creator and one good, transcendent god.

In saying this Justin also affirms the traditions of the prophetic Scriptures and strengthens the link between his god and the history of the covenant and commandments. The god in whom "Christians" believe is not just a creator, he is not just a demiurge. He also is the very same god who called the Israelites out of slavery. He is a just deliverer and he is the god of Trypho's forefathers Abraham, Isaac, and Jacob. There is to be no doubt whatsoever that "Christians" believe, and believe exclusively, in the one god who begot the Israelites. Any doubt on this score would leave Justin open to appearing as a Marcionite, and that is exactly what Justin wants to rule out. Justin willingness to say the law at Horeb is obsolete, "out of date" is perhaps a better translation:[121]

> Now, I have read, Trypho, that there will be a final law and a covenant above of all, which now binds all men to observe who seek the inheritance of God. For the law promulgated on Horeb is now old, and was given to yourselves alone; but this law is for all. Now, a newer law put against the older cancels the older and a covenant coming afterwards terminates the older one. An eternal and final law—namely, Christ himself—has been given to us, and the covenant is trustworthy, after which there shall be no further law, no commandment nor decree. (*Dial.* 11.2)[122]

---

121. Murray J. Harris, *The Second Epistle to the Corinthians* (Grand Rapids: Eerdmans, 2005), 302—Justin here uses παλαιός to mean lacking relevance, as Paul does at 2 Corinthians 3:14, though Paul is not consistent with his adjectives for the Old Covenant.
122. My translation. Greek: Νυνὶ δὲ ἀνέγνων γάρ, ὦ Τρύφων, ὅτι ἔσοιτο καὶ τελευταῖος νόμος καὶ διαθήκη κυριωτάτη πασῶν, ἣν νῦν δέον φυλάσσειν πάντας ἀνθρώπους, ὅσοι τῆς τοῦ θεοῦ κληρονομίας ἀντιποιοῦνται. Ὁ γὰρ ἐν Χωρὴβ παλαιὸς ἤδη νόμος καὶ ὑμῶν μόνων, ὁ δὲ πάντων ἁπλῶς· νόμος δὲ κατὰ νόμου τεθεὶς τὸν πρὸ αὐτοῦ ἔπαυσε, καὶ διαθήκη μετέπειτα γενομένη τὴν προτέραν ὁμοίως ἔστησεν. Αἰώνιός τε ἡμῖν νόμος καὶ τελευταῖος ὁ Χριστὸς ἐδόθη καὶ ἡ διαθήκν πιστή, μεθ' ἣν οὐ νόμος, οὐ πρόστιγμα, οὐκ ἐντολή.

Justin is walking a fine line here because he is in partial agreement with Marcion on the point of the covenant, and so Trypho's lack of distinction may seem justified. Marcion thinks Christ brought a new revelation from a different god. This was the antithesis of the law of the lower god.[123] Justin, in talking of the old law in contrast to the new law in Christ, then, is at risk of appearing Marcionite, taking a radical Pauline stance, Marcion's favoured apostle no less. At this point Justin looks most like he could have been influenced by Marcion's system, and so has to be extremely careful. Justin talks about a last law or covenant (τελευταῖος νόμος καὶ διαθήκη) which is hierarchically the foremost ("chiefest of all"), universal and for all who seek the inheritance of god (τοῦ θεοῦ κληρονομίας). He and Marcion agree that the law promulgated on Horeb is somehow contrasted with the gospel and that the former does not apply to "Christians," but only to his interlocutors, and that the law "which comes after in like manner" "has abrogated that which is before it . . . has put an end to the previous one." However, he calls the last law "an eternal and final law" (νόμον αἰώνιον)[124] which will not be replaced "after which there shall be no further law, no commandment nor decree." This eternal law has continuity with the law at Herob which immediatley demonstrates that Justin is not in the same camp as Marcion. Although the law and gospel, the old and new covenants, are contrasted, they are from the same god. His proof for this position again marks his contra-Marcionite agenda because it is evidenced by the prophets rather than a new direct revelation:

> Have you not read these words of Isaiah: "Hear me, listen to me, my people; and give ear to me, you kings: for a law shall go forth from me, and my judgement shall be a light to the nations. My justice approaches swiftly, and my salvation shall go forth, and nations shall have hope in my arm?" And concerning this new covenant, God spoke through Jeremiah

---

123. Marcion did not operate a system that opposed the old to the new. He did not offer a replacement but an alternative to the Law and what his Christ brought was not a new Law. He opposed the Old Testament but only because it represented an alternative, and a cruel one at that, to the gospel of his Christ and god. See Moll, *Arch-Heretic*, 150.
124. It is interesting to note that Justin actually only directly calls the law old three times, *Dial.* 11.2; 67.9, 10 (covenant and law here); 122.5, in comparison to eight mentions of the new covenant and five of the new law.

thus: "Behold, the days shall come, said the Lord, and I will make a new covenant with the house of Israel, and with the house of Judah: it will not be like the covenant which I made with their fathers, in the day that I took them by the hand to lead them out of the land of Egypt.'" (*Dial.* 11.3)[125]

In quoting these passages from the prophets Isaiah and Jeremiah, Justin takes evidence from the prophets that god has predicted a new covenant, the one Justin claims to serve, and Christ the savior who brings it to all nations; and yet it is a "covenant with the house of Israel and with the house of Judah." Hence, Justin has to interpret these sayings by pointing to a spiritual Israel:

> If, therefore, God predicated that he would make a new covenant, and this for a light to the nations, and we see and are convinced that, through the name of the crucified Jesus Christ, men have turned to God, leaving behind them idolatry and other sinful practices, and have kept the faith and have practiced piety even unto death, then everyone can clearly see from these deeds and the accompanying powerful miracles that he is indeed the New Law, the new covenant, and the expectation of those who, from every nation, have awaited the blessings of God. We have been led to God through this crucified Christ, and we are the true spiritual Israel, and the descendants of Judah, Jacob, Isaac, and Abraham, who, though uncircumcised, was approved and blessed by God because of his faith and was called the father of many nations. All this shall be proved as we proceed with our discussion. (*Dial.* 11.4-5)[126]

This reference to the prophets distinguishes Justin from Marcion, although he makes use of the the "new covenant" which Paul demonstrated from Jeremiah 31:31-32, which appears to emphasize

---

125. Ἢ σὺ ταῦτα οὐκ ἀνέγνως ἅ φησιν Ἡσαΐας; Ἀκούσατέ μου, ἀκούσατέ μου, λαός μου, καὶ οἱ βασιλεῖς πρός με ἐνωτίζεσθε, ὅτι νόμος παρ' ἐμοῦ ἐξελεύσεται καὶ ἡ κρίσις μου εἰς φῶς ἐθνῶν. Ἐγγίζει ταχὺ ἡ δικαιοσύνη μου, καὶ ἐξελεύσεται τὸ σωτήριόν μου, καὶ εἰς τὸν βραχίονά μου ἔθνη ἐλπιοῦσι. Καὶ διὰ Ἰερεμίου περὶ ταύτης αὐτῆς τῆς καινῆς διαθήκης οὕτω φησίν· Ἰδοὺ ἡμέραι ἔρχονται, λέγει κύριος, καὶ διαθήσομαι τῷ οἴκῳ Ἰσραὴλ καὶ τῷ οἴκῳ Ἰούδα διαθήκην καινήν, οὐχ ἣν διεθέμην τοῖς πατράσιν αὐτῶν, ἐν ἡμέρᾳ ᾗ ἐπελαβόμην τῆς χειρὸς ἐξαγαγεῖν αὐτοὺς ἐκ γῆς Αἰγύπτου.
126. Εἰ οὖν ὁ θεὸς διαθήκην καινὴν ἐκήρυξε μέλλουσαν διαταχθήσεσθαι καὶ ταύτην εἰς φῶς ἐθνῶν, ὁρῶμεν δὲ καὶ πεπείσμεθα διὰ τοῦ ὀνόματος αὐτοῦ τοῦ σταυρωθέντος Ἰησοῦ Χριστοῦ ἀπὸ τῶν εἰδώλων καὶ τῆς ἄλλης ἀδικίας προσελθόντας τῷ θεῷ καὶ μέχρι θανάτου ὑπομένοντας τὴν ὁμολογίαν καὶ εὐσέβειαν ποιεῖσθαι, καὶ ἐκ τῶν ἔργων καὶ ἐκ τῆς παρακολουθούσης δυάμεως συνιέναι πᾶσι δυνατὸν ὅτι ?τι οὗτός ἐστιν ὁ καινὸς νόμος καὶ ἡ καινὴ διαθήκη, καὶ ἡ προσδοκία τῶν ἀπὸ πάντων τῶν ἐθνῶν ἀναμενόντων τὰ παρὰ τοῦ θεοῦ ἀγαθά. Ἰσραηλιτικὸν γὰρ τὸ ἀληθινόν, πνευματικόν, καὶ Ἰούδα γένος καὶ Ἰακὼβ καὶ Ἰσαὰκ καὶ Ἀβραάμ, τοῦ ἐν ἀκροβυστίᾳ ἐπὶ τῇ πίστει μαρτυρηθέντος ὑπὸ τοῦ θεοῦ καὶ εὐλογηθέντος καὶ πατρὸς πολλῶν ἐθνῶν κληθέντος, ἡμεῖς ἐσμεν, οἱ διὰ τούτου τοῦ σταυρωθέντος Χριστοῦ τῷ θεῷ προσαχθέντες, ὡς καὶ προκοπτόντων ἡμῖν τῶν λόγων ἀποδειχήσεται.

novelty, like Marcion's theology. Justin identifies Jesus Christ with the "new law" and the "new covenant" and sees his own people ("we") as "the true spiritual Israel" and "descendants of Judah, Jacob, Isaac, and Abraham" (Ἰσραηλιτικὸν γὰρ τὸ ἀληθινόν, πνευματικόν). Because Justin wants to defend his belief in the same god as the one Trypho trusts, he adds that it was this god who had approved of Abraham "in uncircumcision." Justin is firmly claiming Trypho's heritage while not wishing to live according to the commandments of Moses and the Law, while Marcionites may have seemed more credible to Trypho since they would neither wish to live according to the Law nor, consequently, claim the "Jewish" heritage.

Justin ends the chapter by saying that he will proceed to prove all this in the course of his discussion with Trypho. And so we are at the end of the introduction which summaries what Justin intends in the beginning of his long and elaborate proof of it.[127] If anyone wants to know the subject of the *Dialogue* then they just need read these first eleven chapters. The central topic is an apology for what true "Christian" faith is that separates clearly from Maricionism. Having covered chapter eleven we have now reached the end of the introduction proper. The transition that began in chapter eight is complete as all the major themes of the rest of the work have now been marked out by Justin. From chapter twelve to twenty-nine Justin will devote his attention to dealing with the requirements of the Law in detail. After this the bulk of the piece considers how the prophecies foretell Christ; and the final section, from around chapter 109, considers the relationship between "Jews" and "Christians."

Summary

This introductory section has introduced the main themes. The first of these is the question of how many gods there are and what character they/this god has. This is a major topic in chapters one and three. Chapters five and six emphasis the themes of god's sovereignty,

---

127. Skarsaune, *Proof from Prophecy*, 168.

responsibility, and care for his creation, as well as his righteousness and judgment, while chapter seven introduces the prophets as the agents of revelation of this the true god. Chapters eight, nine, ten, and eleven move the debate on to the matter of a scriptural debate over which party is truly a child of this god. That is, the themes given in the previous chapters are assumed as definitions of the character of god and the debate concerns who knows him. These characteristics of god, as we have seen, are naturally contra-Marcionite. That the one single god is creator, both cares for and judges all human beings, and speaks through prophets was rejected by Marcion. Trypho's complaint that those who follow Christ forsake god is unfounded as far as Justin is concerned, and Justin shows himself to start from the same understanding of god as Trypho. From this premise, however, Justin wants to show that Jesus Christ is the crucified one in whom Trypho should trust, from this very same god. However, as evidenced by recurance of similar material further on in the *Dialogue*, Trypho's questions about the god "Christians" believe in were not settled once and for all.

Repetition of Themes in the Dialogue

The Number of Gods

The issue of the number of gods Justin believes in as a "Christian" continually arises in the *Dialogue*. On no less than four occasions[128] Trypho directly asks Justin to justify his belief in *another* god, and on eight occasions Justin declares directly his belief in the one true god.[129] Clearly the number of gods followers of Christ believe in and Christ's relationship to the Father is at issue. Given that Marcion truly professed *another* god, greater than the creator and another Christ from this greater god, as Justin says in *1 Apol.* 26.5 and 58.1, Trypho's repeated requests and Justin's assertions are a convenient means of clarification. Every time Trypho claims to be unconvinced by Justin's

---

128. 50.1; 55.1; 56.12; 68.4.
129. 11.1 (twice); 56.4; 56.11; 60.5; 74.3; 93.2; 115.4.

arguments for Christ, Justin is afforded the opportunity to clarify what he means, though he does not always do so immediately, and uses scripture to do so. Bobichon has noticed and commented on this theme:

> Justin carefully distinguishes the term ἄλλος θεός and ἕτερος θεός. The first of these two formulas, which comes most often from Trypho, refers to gnostic polytheism or theses (11.1, 5; 50.1; 56.3, 4, 9, 11, 14, 15; 60.5; 68.3, 4; cf. 61.2; 65.7; 93.2). The second, usually used by Justin, is the word «numerically (ἀριθμῷ) distinct» from the father (55.1; 56.4, 11; 62.2; cf. 65.1, 5; 128.4; 129.4). The distinction is clearly underlined in 56.4, 11, where the two expressions appear. We find, however, ἄλλος where ἕτερος would be better, at 56.1, 14 and 61*.2*. Cf. *I Apol.* 58.1 in reference to Marcion's views: ἄλλον δέ, τινα καταγγέλλει παρὰ τὸν δημιουργὸν τὸν πάντων θεὸν καὶ ὁμοίως ἕτερον υἱόν. The issue addressed here will be remembered in 50.1* (intervention from Trypho) and treated from 56.1 (citing Gen 18:1-3; 19:27-28; recall the question by fellow Trypho, two findings in 60.5 and 68.3-4). But in the meantime it has resulted in a double development with regard to the Law (Chs. 11-29), and the theophanies (Chapter 56). The dual response Justin offers here is a simultaneous refutation of the theses of Marcion (cf. *I Apol.* 26.5; 58.1).[130]

Justin consistently uses ἄλλος in *1 Apology* when describing Maricon's belief in *another* god and ἕτερος when speaking of his own belief in Christ as *another* god but not a different deity from the one true god. Bobichon provides a full list of references for this (quoted above). *Dial.* 56.3 is a good example of this pattern. There Trypho says that Justin has not proved there is *another* god using ἄλλος: "Οἱ δὲ ἔφασαν νενοηκέναι μέν, μηδὲν δὲ ἔχειν εἰς ἀπόδειξιν τοὺς λελγμένους λόγους ὅτι

---

130. Bobichon, *avec Tryphon*, 610. "Justin distingue soigneusement les expression allos theos et eteros theos. La premiere de ces deux formules, qui émane le plus souvent de Tryphon, fait référence au polythéisme ou aux theses gnostiques (11,1.5; 50,1; 56,3.4.9.11.14.15; 60,5; 68,3.4; cf. 61,2; 65,7; 93,2). La seconde, généralement utilisée par Justin, désigne le Verbe, «numériquement (ἀριθμῷ) distinct» du Pére (55,1; 56,4.11; 62,2; cf. 65,1.5; 128,4; 129,4). La distinction est clairement soulignée en 56,4.11, ou apparaissent les deux expressions. On trouve cependant allos la ou eteros conviendrait mieux, en 56,1*.14 et 61,2*. Cp. *I Apol.* 58,1, a propos des théories de Marcion: ἄλλον δέ τινα καταγγέλλει παρὰ τὸν δημιουργὸν τὸν πάντων θεὸν καὶ ὁμοίως ἕτερον υἱόν. La question abordée ici sera rappelée en 50,1* (intervention de Tryphon) et traitée a partir de 56,1 (citation de Gen 18,1-3; 19,27-28; rappel de la question par les compagnons de Tryphon, avec deux conclusions en 60,5 et 68,3-4). Mais elle aura donné lieu entre temps a un double développement consacré a la Law (chap. 11-29), puis aux théophanies (chap. 56). La double réponse que Justin offre ici constitue une réfutation simultanée des theses de Marcion (cf. *I Apol.* 26,5; 58,1)."

θεὸς ἢ κύριος ἄλλος τίς ἐστιν ἢ λέλεκται ὑπὸ τοῦ ἁγίου πενύματος παρὰ τὸν ποιητὴν τῶν ὅλων)" Justin's reply conversely uses ἕτερος: "ὅτι εστὶ καὶ λέγεται θεός καὶ κύριος ἕτερος ὑπο τὸν ποιητὴν τῶν ὅλων." Positively Justin has used ἕτερος, to refer to the *other* god he believes in (numerically distinct but the logos of the one god) and in the same passage uses ἄλλος negatively to deny that there is a separate god with a different Christ: "the Maker of all things, above whom there is no other God."[131] At the end of this same chapter (*Dial.* 56.11) Justin uses ἕτερος in precisely the same way as before when speaking of Christ as *another* but not separate god. That this is the case suggests that Justin is trying, in the manner described by Bobichon, to distinguish himself from Marcion's theology since Trypho's use appears to presume something approximate to a Marcionite position. The careful but subtle differentiation from the Marcionite position is absolutely necessary because otherwise Justin might appear to be or think the same as Marcion, or might even be thought to have be influenced by Marcion on this particular point. That would be fatal to Justin's project, so he has to outline that his understanding of the *second god* is unique. Furthermore, that Justin needs to work hard to establish his belief in the one true god, the creator of all things, quite firmly flags this topic as a clue to a deeper background, a Marcionite threat in the context.

Providence

Trypho does not accuse Justin of not believing in god's providence and care. In the introduction Justin raises the issue that some deny that god cares for humanity, beyond indifferently sustaining the material existence of the world (*Dial.* 1.4). Without this care for humanity there are no proper standards, no fear of judgment or hope for reward; in short, no righteousness, which is the measure of god's mercy for both Justin and Trypho. We know that Marcion did not believe that the creator, the god of Moses, cared for all of humanity, but nor did he think him indifferent. Rather Marcion thought this god to be the

---

131. ὁ τῶν ὅλων ποιητής, ὑπὲρ ὅν ἄλλος θεὸς οὐκ ἔστι (*Dial.* 56.4).

creator and sustainer of material existence but also a cruel judge who manipulated his people, the "Jews." Justin unites himself and Trypho as those who believe that god does indeed care for humanity. However, Trypho is puzzled as to how Justin thinks he, and "Christians," can have a share in god's providence and mercy while not doing as He commands. For Trypho god cares for all but all have to live according to his commandments. Ultimately Trypho and Justin's position is similar then; both believe god cares for all, but they have different mechanisms for receiving his care. The topic of god's care and relevance to human beings runs through the entire *Dialogue*.

In *Dial.* 23.2 Justin says: "Therefore, we must confess that He, who is unchanging, has commanded these similar things to be performed because of sinful men, and we must profess Him to be benevolent, foreknowing, without need of anything, righteous, and good."[132] God is, according to Justin, benevolent or kindhearted (Φιλάνθρωπον) and in need of nothing (ἀνενδεῆ). Woven in with this is god's foreknowledge, consistency, and righteousness, which will be dealt with below. Another example of the theme of god's providence is evident in *Dial.* 106.1: "The rest of the psalm shows that he knew that his Father would grant him everything, and would raise him from the dead. It also shows that he urged all of every race who fear God to praise him because of his mercy, through the mystery of the crucified one."[133] Something similar is said shortly after at *Dial.* 108.3: "we pray that even now you may mend your ways and find mercy from God the Father of all, who is most benign and compassionate."[134] This god, the one true god, is a god who has mercy and compassion (ἐλέους, πολυελέου) upon those who seek him by faith (πίστει), who also become god's children, no less than on descendants of Judah, Jacob, Isaac and Abraham. Both these quotations present a vision of the creator god that is very different

---

132. Δι' αἰτίαν δὲ τὴν τῶν ἁμαρτωλῶν ἀνθρώπων, τὸν αὐτὸν ὄντα ἀεὶ ταῦτα καὶ τὰ τοιαῦτα ἐντετάλθαι ὁμολογεῖν, καὶ φιλάνθρωπον καὶ προγνώστην καὶ ἀνενδεῆ καὶ δίκαιον καὶ ἀγαθὸν ἀποφαίνειν ἔστιν.

133. My translation. Greek: Καὶ ὅτι ἠπίστατο τὸν πατέρα αὐτοῦ πάντα παρέχειν αὐτῷ, ὡς ἠξίου, καὶ ἀνεγερεῖν αὐτὸν ἐκ τῶν νεκρῶν, καὶ πάντας τοὺς φοβουμένους τὸν θεὸν προέτρεπεν αἰνεῖν τὸν θεὸν διὰ τὸ ἐλεῆσαι καὶ διὰ τοῦ μυστηρίου, τοῦ σταυρωθέντος τούτου πᾶν γένος τῶν πιστευόντων ἀνθρώπων ... τὰ λείποντα τοῦ ψαλμοῦ ἐδήλωσεν.

134. ἀλλ' εὐχόμεθα κἂν νῦν μετανοήσαντας πάντας ἐλέους τυχεῖν παρὰ τοῦ εὐσπλάγχνου καὶ πολυελέου πατρὸς τῶν ὅλων θεοῦ.

from that of Marcion. He is not the angry and distant god Marcion believes him to be, but a benevolent and merciful god; and he is available to all, not just the "Jews" as Marcion believes. Bobichon notes that the mercy of god is one of the topics that Justin and Trypho hold in common and that is raised repeatedly.[135] Seven times, and a further five in scriptural quotation,[136] Justin mentions mercy as something that comes from god as an expectation or something to be hoped for. Trypho of course concurs that god is merciful and compassionate but he thinks this is towards him and his people. Marcion, however, held the god of the "Jews," the creator, to be a cruel and petulant judge, not a kind and merciful father. Even if Marcion could envisage mercy from this god, his view would be the same as Trypho's, that it belongs only to the "Jews," only to those who live according to the Law. Yet it is Justin's claim that through Christ the mercy of god is given. Not only then does this god give mercy to all nations, but he does so through Christ his Son. And yet, Justin and Trypho both think that mercy is linked to justice, and justice involves threat and punishment, both of which are rejected by Marcion. In *Dial.* 8.4 Trypho urges Justin to observe the Sabbath, circumcision and all the written law so that he may then receive mercy from god. These are the means of becoming righteous before god in Trypho's tradition. In *Dial.* 47 Justin quotes Isaiah 55:3–13 which echoes this sentiment. If the unrighteous changes his ways and returns to the Lord he will receive god's mercy. It is he who turns away and repents from the former ways that receives the mercy of this god. Who turns from idolatry and other sins and lives the life of god will receive god's compassion. The debate between Justin and Trypho is not about whether mercy exists, then; both parties assume that god not only created this world but has vision and care for human life. The debate is about how it is that "Christians" might gain or expect to gain this mercy from god while not living according to this commandments; in short how can "Christians" be righteous before this god? This in itself is a contra-Marcionite framing of the issue.

---

135. Bobichon, *avec Tryphon*, 600n9.
136. 18.2; 43.2; 96.3; 106.1; 108.4; 133.1; 141.2; in Scripture: 14.5; 25.2, 4; 36.4; 118.2.

Justice and Righteousness

Righteousness (δικαιοσύνη) and Justice (δίκαιος or judgment as κρίσιν) are major issues in the *Dialogue*. They determine how one is seen and accepted by god. However, they are very much Justin's terms. Justin sets up righteousness as a prerequisite while speaking as a Platonist in discussion with the *presbutes* in *Dial.* 4.3, and the *presbutes* accepts this as congruent with the "Christian"philosophy. Trypho never speaks of being righteous or just before god explicitly. That said, many of the appearances of these terms and concepts occur in the context of scriptural quotations which Trypho accepts; righteousness comes up most commonly with reference to the righteousness of god, Christ, the prophets and patriarchs, the eternal will and decrees of god, and those who follow Christ and are saved and just with reference to god. In *Dial.* 92.5 Justin quotes Deuteronomy 32:4: "God is true and righteous, and all His ways are judgments, and there is no unrighteousness in him."[137] This is a statement of what Justin believes and of what Trypho must already believe. That god is righteous and just is something Trypho and Justin agree on. Yet it is another matter in which Justin's "Christian" philosophy distinguishes itself from who Marcion believes this god to be. Trypho takes the righteousness and justice of god as read but questions them with reference to Christ. According to Trypho one needs to be just and righteous before god, and assumes that such righteousness only happens to a life lived in accordance with the Law. Justin has to work incredibly hard to establish that "Christians" do not reject (like Marcion) the Law itself, but that, although he is stating that the Law belongs to Trypho, and that "Christians" do not need to follow its commandments, they are still living under the grace of this god because Christ's commandments are consistent with the eternal law which is part of Trypho's Law, and as the creator's agent Christ will judge the righteous according to this.

The first step in establishing that "Christians" can be righteous before god is that they have a righteous example. Ultimately this will

---

137. Ἀληθὴς ὁ θεὸς καὶ δίκαιος καὶ πᾶσαι αἱ ὁδοὶ αὐτοῦ κρίσεις, καὶ οὐκ ἔστιν ἀδικία ἐν αὐτῷ.

be Christ but it begins with the prophets. The *presbutes,* in *Dial.* 7.1, established that these were righteous men who listened to god and Trypho would not want to demur from this. "Christians" listen to god's messengers, though Justin believes that only "Christians" understand them correctly. For Justin the prophets and patriarchs are righteous on account of their faith rather than the Law or ancestry. "Christians" are saved according to Justin by their righteousness, which means their faith. "Whereas, the Gentiles who believe in Christ and are sorry for their sins shall receive the inheritance, along with the patriarchs, the prophets, and every just descendant of Jacob, even though they neither practice circumcision nor observe the Sabbaths and feasts" (*Dial.* 26.1).[138] Justin has similar reasons for arguing so strenuously for circumcision being given as a sign rather than for righteousness; righteousness becomes the bridge here by which Justin can connect the past and present under the same god.[139] The promises made to Israel are applicable to gentiles under righteousness; thus righteousness is a characteristic of the universal "Israel." Naturally this is just the sort of connection that Marcion would have found completely unacceptable. That the prophets and patriarchs may have been righteous men he would have had no need to question, provided they remained righteous men without relevance or import to "Christians." That they might have been made right by the god of Israel, the creator, because of something they share with "Christians" would be wholly unacceptable to Marcion. Marcion would not accept that the prophets and patriarchs lived according to faith rather than the Law. This is a link he would not acknowledge, demarcating them as part of the "Jewish" god and his people and not part of a "Christian" dispensation. Furthermore, according to Justin, this god, the one true god who is righteous and just, not only accepts those who do have faith in him, but wishes all to have faith in him and has made eternal decrees in keeping with his righteousness and justice that are relevant for all people: "But

---

138. τὰ δὲ ἔθνη τὰ πιστεύσαντα εἰς αὐτὸν καὶ μετανοήσαντα ἐφ' οἷς ἥμαρτον, αὐτοὶ κληρονομήσουσι μετὰ τῶν πατριαρχῶν καὶ τῶν προφητῶν καὶ τῶν δικαίων ὅσοι ἀπὸ Ἰακὼβ γεγέννηνται. εἰ καὶ μὴ σαββατίζουσι μηδὲ περιτέμνονται μηδὲ τὰς ἑορτὰς φυλάσσουσι.
139. Jospeh B. Tyson, "Anti-Judaism in Marcion," *SCJR* 1 (2005–2006): 204.

the fact that God can be falsely accused by the unintelligent of not having always taught the same truthful doctrines to all, you can blame on your own sinfulness" (*Dial.* 30.1).[140] Justin further mentions god's eternal righteous decrees twice, as well as his acts of righteousness which are the same for all.[141] This gives Trypho and those like him a share in god's vision, albeit with conditions, but it is also strongly contra-Marcionite. It is tantamount to declaring again and again that the god of Israel is the only and universal god; what he designs is good and true and ordained for all. There is no space for another god with his own decrees for Justin. "Christians" as far as Justin is concerned fulfill the commandments and will of the one true god, by faith. Righteousness as a pan-human quality afforded by trust in the god of the "Jews" is not something Marcion could ever count as "Christian," and so in arguing for "Christians'" place among the dispensation of Israel, as the true Israel according to faith, Justin again demarcates the true "Christian" philosophy from a Marcionite one.

For Justin, the god of Israel is judge, already a major stumbling block to Marcion, but even more so, as he also believes that he judges through Christ Jesus. In *Dial.* 46.1 Trypho asks: "'But,' inquired Trypho, 'if some even now desire to live in observance of the precepts of the Mosaic Law, and yet believe that the crucified Jesus is the Christ of God and that to him it has been given to judge without exception all men, and that his kingdom is eternal, could they also be saved?'"[142] Justin's eventual answer to this is basically yes. The significant points are the acknowledgment that Christ is the Christ of god, of the one true god, so that "Christians" can be both non-Law observing, but also obedient to the Law. Christ has an ultimate role to be the judge of *all* people eternally. This is not an isolated point. Justin repeats it often. Indeed no less than nine times is Christ explicitly referred to as a judge and numerous Old Testament quotations imply this view.[143] Bobichon

---

140. Ἀλλὰ τῇ αὐτῶν κακίᾳ ἐγκαλεῖτε, ὅτι καὶ συκοφαντεῖσθαι δυνατός ἐστιν ὁ θεὸς ὑπὸ τῶν νοῦν μὴ ἐχόντων, ὡς τὰ αὐτὰ δίκαια μὴ πάντας ἀεὶ διδάξας.
141. *Dial.* 28.4, 46.2, 47.2, 92.5, 93.1.
142. Ἐὰν δέ τινες καὶ νῦν ζῆν βούλωνται φυλάσσοντες τὰ διὰ Μωσέως διαταχθέντα καὶ πιστεύσωσιν ἐπὶ τοῦτον τὸν σταυρωθέντα Ἰησοῦν, ἐπιγνόντες ὅτι αὐτός ἐστιν ὁ Χριστὸς τοῦ θεοῦ καὶ αὐτῷ δέδοται τὸ κρῖναι πάντας ἁπλῶς καὶ αὐτοῦ ἐστιν ἡ αἰώνιος βασιλεία, δύνανται καὶ αὐτοὶ σωθῆναι; ἐπυνθάνετό μου.

notes that this belief is omnipresent in the *Dialogue* and is completely inseparable, in Justin's theology, from the second coming of Christ.[144] As if to drive home his point again towards the end of his text, Justin says: "I have also shown that the prophecy of Isaiah, 'his burial has been taken away from the midst,' referred to Christ, who was to be buried and to rise again. I have stated already on many occasions that this same Christ will be the Judge of both the living and the dead" (*Dial.* 118.1).[145] This would have been a view completely unpalatable to Marcion, and strongly distinguishes Justin's theology from his.

That Prophecies Predict Christ

The question of whether the Messiah has come and can be shown to be Jesus Christ is the central question of the *Dialogue*. It is a belief that Trypho rejects at *Dial.* 8.4: "But if the Messiah has been born and exists anywhere, he is not known, nor is he conscious of his own existence, nor has he any power until Elijah comes to anoint him and to make him manifest to all. But you have believed this foolish rumour, and you have invented yourselves a Christ for whom you blindly give up your lives."[146]

Trypho does not think it plausible that the Messiah of whom Justin speaks has come, and so Justin expends most of his words on exegesis designed to demonstrate that this Christ, his Christ, the Son of the one true god, was predicted by the prophets. Indeed, even past the halfway point of the piece Trypho is still asking Justin to justify his claims:

> "Prove to us," interrupted Trypho, "that this man who you claim was crucified and ascended into heaven is the Christ of God. It has indeed been proved sufficiently by your Scriptural quotations that it was predicted in the Scriptures that Christ should suffer, and that he should come again

---

143. *Dial.* 35.8; 36.1; 46.1; 47.5; 49.2; 96.2; 118.1; 132.1; 141.1.
144. Bobichon, *avec Tryphon*, 680.
145. Καὶ ὅτι περὶ τοῦ θάπτεσθαι μέλλοντος καὶ ἀνίστασθαι Χριστοῦ ἦν ἡ προφητεία τοῦ Ἡσαΐου, φήσαντος· Ἡ ταφὴ αὐτοῦ ἦρται ἐκ τοῦ μέσου, προεῖπον. Καὶ ὅτι κριτὴς ζώντων καὶ νεκρῶν ἁπάντων αὐτὸς οὗτος ὁ Χριστός, εἶπον ἐν πολλοῖς.
146. Χριστὸς δέ, εἰ καὶ γεγένηται καὶ ἔστι που, ἄγνωστός ἐστι καὶ οὐδὲ αὐτός πω ἑαυτὸν ἐπίσταται οὐδὲ ἔχει δύναμίν τινα, μέχρις ἂν ἔλθῃ Ἠλίας χρίσῃ αὐτὸν καὶ φανερὸν πᾶσι ποιήσῃ· ὑμεῖς δέ, ματαίαν ἀκοὴν παραδεξάμενοι, Χριστὸν ἑαυτοῖς τινα ἀναπλάσσετε καὶ αὐτοῦ χάριν τὰ νῦν ἀσκόπως ἀπόλλυσθε.

in glory to accept the eternal kingdom over all nations, and that every kingdom should be made subject to him. But what we want you to prove is that Jesus is the Messiah spoken of in the Scriptures." (*Dial.* 39.7)[147]

The heart of this central debate was established at the very beginning of the piece in *Dial.* 1.3, where Justin asks his new acquaintance why he is interested in philosophy when he has his own prophets. What was unknown but revealed to the reader in *Dial.* 7.1, and throughout, is that the prophets and not the gospel which Trypho claimed to have read and admired are the measure of everything for Justin. They are god's messengers who spoke with his Holy Spirit and predicted Christ. That he can demonstrate who Christ is by their words is essential because through this he can demonstrate that god foreknew (προγνώστην) and ordained that this Christ would come. That is, the god of Israel, the creator, has provided this Christ and he therefore cannot be associated with any other god new or old. Marcion could not possibly accept this, and so in attempting to convince Trypho that this is so, Justin hopes not only to enlighten his dialogue partner, but to distance himself from Marcionite understandings of the "Christian" philosophy. That these "Jewish" prophets predicted Christ is Justin's strongest defense because it demonstrates that Christ does not come from a new hitherto unknown god and establishes a continuity between the Old Testament and New Testament which the literalism of Marcion challenged.[148] For these reasons Justin is relentless in his insistence upon Christ's prediction in the prophets to Trypho: "in Christ, the Son of God, who was proclaimed as the future Eternal law and new covenant for the whole world (as the above-quoted prophecies clearly show)" (*Dial.* 43.1).[149] Again he says: "Isaiah, indeed, foretold that Christ would come

---

147. Καὶ ὁ Τρύφων· Ἤδη οὖν τὸν λόγον ἀπόδος ἡμῖν, ὅτι οὗτος, ὃν φῇς ἐσταυρῶσθαι καὶ ἀνεληλυθέναι εἰς τὸν οὐρανόν, ἐστίν ὁ Χριστὸς τοῦ θεοῦ. Ὅτι γὰρ καὶ παθητὸς ὁ Χριστὸς διὰ τῶν γραφῶν κηρύσσεται, καὶ μετὰ δόξης πάλιν παραγίνεσθαι, καὶ αἰώνιον τὴν βασιλείαν πάντων τῶν ἐθνῶν λήψεσθαι, πάσης βασιλείας αὐτῷ ὑποτασσομένης, ἱκανῶς διὰ τῶν προανιστορημένων ὑπὸ σοῦ γραφῶν ἀποδέδεικται· ὅτι δὲ οὗτός ἐστιν, ἀπόδειξον ἡμῖν.
148. Tyson, "Anti-Judaism in Marcion," 206.
149. υἱὸν τοῦ θεοῦ Χριστόν, ὅστις καὶ αἰώνιος νόμος, καὶ καινὴ διαθήκη τῷ παντὶ κόσμῳ ἐκηρύσσετο προελευσόμενος, ὡς αἱ προλελεγμέναι προφητεῖαι σημαίνουσι.

forth as a rod from the root of Jesse" (*Dial.* 86.4).¹⁵⁰ A denser and bolder declaration is found at *Dial.* 100.2, 4:

> He revealed, then, to us by his grace all that we have learned from the Scriptures, so that we know him as the first-begotten of God before all creatures, and as the Son of the patriarchs since he became incarnate by a virgin of their race, and condescended to become a man without comeliness or honour, and subject to suffering . . . and since we call him by the same title [Son of God], we have understood that this is really he and that he proceeded before all creatures from the Father by his power and will (for in the prophetic writings he is called Wisdom, and Day, and the East, and Sword, Stone, Rod, Jacob, and Israel, in one respect or another); and that he became incarnate of the Virgin, in order that the disobedience caused by the serpent might be destroyed in the same manner in which it had originated.¹⁵¹

A cluster of important themes are presented together here. First, as was alluded to in *Dial.* 7.1, 3; 58.1, Justin perceives what he understands about Christ from the Scriptures by grace. This is in contrast to the many occasions where Justin counsels Trypho against teachers who do not understand what is written and cannot see Christ predicted. This is usually explicitly aimed at rabbis but surely, as discussed with reference to the men of no reputation in *Dial.* 8.3, it has a wider context in Marcion's lack of appreciation of Christ in the prophets. For Justin, grace, the gift of the one true god, is required to understand what the Scriptures are saying. As we saw above, grace as the determining agent of understanding is an important theme in the piece, and the main topic of *Dial.* 58 and 92. In Justin's understanding Trypho's predecessors have failed to grasp that the Christ has come because of their hard hearts (σκληροκάρδιος) and inept teachers, both of which obscure the true proclamation of the kingdom: "For he who is ignorant of him is likewise ignorant of God's will; and he who scorns and hates him

---

150. Ῥάβδον ἐκ ῥίζης Ἰεσσαὶ γενήσεσθαι τὸν Χριστὸν Ἡσαΐας προεφήτευσε.
151. Ἀπεκάλυψεν οὖν ἡμῖν πάντα ὅσα καὶ ἀπὸ τῶν γραφῶν διὰ τῆς χάριτος αὐτοῦ νενοήκαμεν, γνόντες αὐτὸν πρωτότοκον μὲν τοῦ θεοῦ καὶ πρὸ πάντων τῶν κτισμάτων, καὶ τῶν πατριαρχῶν υἱόν, ἐπειδὴ διὰ τῆς ἀπὸ γένους αὐτῶν παρθένου σαρκοποιηθείς, καὶ ἄνθρωπος ἀειδὴς, ἄτιμος καὶ παθητὸς ὑπέμεινε γενέσθαι . . . υἱὸν αὐτὸν λέγοντες νενοήκαμεν ὄντα καὶ Πρὸ πάντων ποιημάτων ἀπὸ τοῦ πατρὸς δυνάμει αὐτοῦ καὶ βουλῇ προελθόντα, ὃς καὶ σοφία καὶ ἡμέρα καὶ ἀνατολὴ καὶ μάχαιρα καὶ λίθος καὶ ῥάβδος καὶ Ἰακὼβ καὶ Ἰσραὴλ κατ᾽ ἄλλον καὶ ἄλλον τρόπον ἐν τοῖς τῶν προφητῶν λόγοις προσηγόρευται, καὶ διὰ τῆς παρθένου ἄνθρωπον γεγονέναι, ἵνα καὶ δι᾽ ἧς ὁδοῦ καὶ κατάλυσιν λάβῃ.

clearly hates and scorns him also who sent him; and he who has no faith in him does not believe the words of the prophets, who preached his Gospel and proclaimed him to all men" (*Dial.* 136.3).[152] By their rejection of Christ, Israel proved that they have not understood the prophets. But the reverse is also true for Justin. Whoever hates the prophets cannot know who Christ truly is and does not know who god truly is. A double critique is found here then; Christ, god, and the prophets go together, so Marcion is as much in error as the Trypho, even more so the former, however, since Marcion believes himself to be a "Christian." By this then Justin again establishes what is and is not "Christian" and firmly puts Marcion outside of this definition. Other "heretical" or "gnostic" groups may be isolated for other reasons, but none, as far as we know, rejected the prophets and the god of Israel so directly, which is definition of the "Christian" philosophy for Justin. The passage from *Dial.* 100 also presents a Christ to have taken flesh and been born of a virgin, which is a further distinction between Justin's and Marcion's beliefs.[153] This is not just any virgin but a virgin of the family of the patriarchs. Justin has drawn a line from Abraham to Christ via Mary.[154] Justin and Trypho variously discuss the issue of the virgin birth; it is frequently peppered throughout the text,[155]

---

152. Ὁ γὰρ τοῦτον ἀγνοῶν ἀγνοεῖ καὶ τὴν βουλὴν τοῦ θεοῦ, καὶ ὁ τοῦτον ὑβρίζων καὶ μισῶν καὶ τὸν πέμψαντα δηλονότι καὶ μισεῖ καὶ ὑβρίζει · καὶ εἰ οὐ πιστεύει τις εἰς αὐτόν, οὐ πιστεύει τοῖς τῶν προφητῶν κηρύγμασι τοῖς αὐτὸν εὐαγγελισαμέοις καὶ κηρύξασιν εἰς πάντας.
153. Two key features of Marcion's theology conspire to form his denial of the virgin birth. First, Christ's appearance was sudden and unheralded, he having descended straight from heaven fully formed. The second is that he was not of genuine human flesh as one born, but a phantasm. The former point is detailed by Tertullian over and over again, as in *Marc.* 1.19.2; 4.7.2. It perhaps is most clearly expressed by Tertullian, however in 4.21.11, where he says: "No question thereafter of his wallowing in uncleanness in a mother's lap, of his nuzzling at her breasts, of a long infancy, a tardy boyhood, of waiting for manhood: no, he was brought to birth out of heaven, at once full-grown, at once complete, Christ with no delay, spirit and power and god—and nothing more." This is backed up by Epiphanius, who dedicates *Pan.* 3.4.1 to the point: "And he says that Christ has descended from on high, from the invisible Father who cannot be named, for the salvation of souls, and to confound the God of the Jews, the Law, the prophets, and anything of the kind." The other constituent of Marcion's denial, Christ's lack of flesh, is best attested by Tertullian, *Carn. Chr.* 1.10: "Marcion, with the purpose of denying Christ's flesh, also denied his nativity: or else, with intent to deny his nativity, denied his flesh. Evidently his intention was that nativity and flesh should not give mutual testimony each to the other, inasmuch as there can be neither nativity without flesh nor flesh without nativity."
154. Bobichon, *avec Tryphon*, 829.
155. 23.3; 43.1, 5, 7, 8; 45.4; 48.2; 50.1; 57.3; 63.1; 66.1, 2, 4; 67.1, 2; 68.6; 70.4; 71.3; 75.4; 84.1, 2; 85.2; 100.2, 3, 5; 101.1; 105.1; 113.4; 120.1; 127.4.

which points to how much Justin wants to emphasize his allegiance to this doctrine. Also, as Bobichon notes, this is the first time in the "Christian" tradition that an explicit link between Mary and Eve is made, which will be carried on by Irenaeus and Tertullian. In making this link Justin again places Christ firmly in the context of god's providence in the Old Testament Scriptures.[156] This is a firm marker of Justin's contra-Marcionite theology. Marcion could not and would not accept the virgin birth and so Justin's holding firmly by it strongly distinguishes him from Marcion and establishes Christ as part of the history of the people of "Israel."

There is a further key element that prophets predict which necessarily separates the "Christian" philosophy from Marcionism. This is the new covenant (καινῆς διαθήκης). The prophets have not only announced Christ. They have also announced his new covenant, a central aspect of Marcion's theology. The new covenant is an obvious point of dispute between Trypho and Justin, though Trypho comes to accept that the old law was given in response to the hardness of heart of the "Jews"; but the place of this new covenant in the old is one of the greatest differentiations Justin could offer between himself and Marcion. This had to be the case because it is one of the issues on which they are closest together and may even speak to the influence of Marcion upon Justin at an earlier stage in his career.

> Now, I have read, Trypho, that there will be a final law, and a covenant, above all others, which now binds all men to observe who seek the inheritance of God. For the law promulgated on Horeb is now old, and was given to yourselves alone; but this law is universally for all. Now, a later law put against the older abrogates the older; just so, a covenant coming terminates the older one. An eternal and final law—namely, Christ himself—has been given to us, and the covenant is trustworthy, after which there shall be no further law, no commandment, no decree. (*Dial.* 11.2)[157]

Following this, Justin gives further evidence from Scripture in the form of Isaiah 51:4-5, Jeremiah 31:31, and Isaiah 55:3, in order to

---

156. Bobichon, *avec Tryphon*, 830.
157. See n. 122.

demonstrate that not only is this his claim, but it is a scriptural and prophetic claim. This is absolutely necessary for Justin because Marcion believed that there was no continuity between the gospel of Christ, from the higher god, and the covenant made with the "Jews," by the lower god, and that his *Antithesis* exposed the differences between these two deities. It is no surprise, then, that this claim, followed immediately by scriptural exegesis, occurs very early on the in *Dialogue*, right at the point that Justin is launching into his detailed definition of what the "Christian" philosophy is, once Trypho knows he is a "Christian"and has made his accusations. This is about the strongest move Justin can make to connect the newness of Christ firmly to the continuity of the one true god, which he also attempts to do when speaking of god's eternal decrees (αἰώνια δικαιώματα, αἰωνίους καὶ φύσει δικαιοπαξίας)[158] for all people. Christ is a radical change, but he is of god, the one true god, the creator; his newness is a renewal movement in eternal righteousness rather than a novel creation or discovery of a world without sin and consequences.

Prophecies take up the bulk of the *Dialogue*, which is traditionally understood as Justin's rebuttal of Trypho and the "Jewish" position. Be that as it may, these Scriptures are more than this, and Skarsaune's contribution in detailing the depth and sources of Justin's understanding of them is invaluable.[159] Their presence as part of the "Christian"tradition is itself a contra-Marcionite move. In claiming the prophets, Justin isolates Marcionites who see the prophetic tradition as only for the "Jews" and stakes the claim again that "Christians" are indeed the true "Israel." Furthermore, that the prophets predict Christ and the new covenant demonstrates most powerfully that Marcion is mistaken by the standards of the "Christian" philosophy and has not, as Israel has not, the grace from god to understand the Scriptures. Israel may be errant and mistaken in this, but Marion is simply something else by his rejection of the prophets; he is not an errant "Christian" but a failed candidate for a "Christian"; his view is a new

---

158. 46.2; 47.2; 67.10.
159. Skarsaune, *Proof from Prophecy*.

and radical superstition with no antiquity, merely the doctrine and opinion of one man.

Philosophies and "Christians"

So far we have seen Justin present his theology via themes which would distinguish his "Christian" philosophy from Marcionism. This has been quite a subtle enterprise. However, there is a section in the *Dialogue* where Marcion, (or rather Marcionites on this occasion), than appear directly. Marcionites are not the only group to be mentioned, though Marcion is the only contemporary, and many of the themes we have observed with reference to him in the rest of the text can be seen to concentrate in this section as well as in subsequent sections where Marcion is not named but strongly implied.

After this long and important introductory section where the shape of truth and the error of philosophical diversity is established, Trypho and Justin move on from the topic of philosophy for twenty-four chapters in order to discuss the core of the *Dialogue*, the correct interpretation of the Hebrew Scriptures in light of Justin's "Christian" claims. The of philosophy reappears significantly at *Dial.* 35. "This long silence strengthens the argument that the discussion of the philosophical schools in the *Dialogue* has more to do with the rhetoric of heresy than with Justin's actual experience of philosophical theology."[160] Royalty is right here: the introductory section, as discussion above, has little to do with the philosophies of the time, despite the considerable energy devoted to ascertaining what of Justin's philosophical background can be discerned in these pages, and has a great deal to do with clarification of who and "what" genuine "Christians" are. Others must be ruled out, most pressingly given the topics discussed and his contemporary threat, Marcionites. Lack of uniformity is evidence of lack of rational investigation into truth, so anything being given or claiming the name "Christian" which does not fit what Jesus taught, at least in the manner Justin understands this,

---

160. Royalty, "Justin's Conversion," 512.

cannot and must not be considered "Christian," and Marcion above all. *Dial.* 35, as pointed out by Royalty, comes on the back of two chapters where Justin has exposed his interlocutor's error and misinterpretation, the proclivity to be led by bad human teachers which causes Trypho to question how some "Christians" can disagree.[161] This is a serious charge given that diversity means failure, and so it sets Justin up to show that this is not in actual fact the case because those who misinterpret are, at least in serious matters, not "Christians" at all.

At this point is worthwhile quoting in full the sections of Dialogue which seem not only to have Marcionite topics at the fore but more directly feature the problem of Marcionism and other gnostic groups. I will now quote both of these chapters in full because they are the most explicit portions in this text of Justin's problem of distinguishing "Christians" from Marcionites and others.

> At this point, Trypho interrupted me by saying, "I know that there are many who profess their faith in Jesus and are considered to be Christians, yet they claim there is no harm in their eating meats sacrificed to idols." "The fact that there are such men," I replied, "who pretend to be Christians and admit the crucified Jesus as their Lord and Christ, yet profess not His doctrines, but those of the spirits of error, only tends to make us adherents of the true and pure Christian doctrine more ardent in our faith and more firm in the hope He announced to us. As we look about us, we see events actually taking place which He predicted would happen in His name. Indeed, He foretold: 'Many will come in My name, clothed outwardly in sheep's clothing, but inwardly they are ravening wolves.' And: 'There will be schisms and heresies.' And: 'Beware of false prophets, who come to you in clothing of sheep, but inwardly they are ravening wolves.' And: 'There will arise many false Christs and false Apostles, and they will deceive many of the faithful.' My friends, there were, and still are, many men who, in the name of Jesus, come and teach others atheistic and blasphemous doctrines and actions; we call them by the name of the originator of each false doctrine. (For each has his own peculiar method of teaching how to blaspheme the Creator of the universe, and Christ, whose Advent was foretold by Him, and the God of Abraham, and of Isaac, and of Jacob. They are all outside of our communion, for we know them for what they are, impious atheists and wicked sinners, men who profess Jesus with their lips, but do not worship Him in their hearts. These men call themselves Christians in much the same way as some Gentiles engrave

---

161. Ibid.

the name of God upon their statues, and then indulge in every kind of wicked and atheistic rite.) Some of these heretics are called Marcionites, some Valentinians, some Basilidians, and some Saturnilians, and others by still other names, each designated by the name of the founder of the system, just as each person who deems himself a philosopher, as I stated at the beginning of this discussion, claims that he must bear the name of the philosophy he favors from the founder of that particular school of philosophy. Not only from these events do we conclude, as I said, that Jesus possessed foreknowledge of what would happen to Him, but also from the many other happenings which He predicted would befall those who believe and profess that He is the Messiah. He even foretold all the suffering we would have to bear when those of our own household put us to death. Consequently, we can find no fault with either His words or actions. For this reason, too, we pray for you and for everyone else who hates us, that you may repent with us, and refrain from blaspheming Jesus Christ, who is proved to be totally without blame and reproach by His own deeds and by the miracles which even now are wrought in His name by the words of His teaching and the prophecies concerning Him. We pray, also, that you may believe in Jesus Christ, and thus at His second triumphant coming you will be saved and not be condemned by Him to the fire of hell." (Dial. 35)[162]

162. Καὶ ὁ Τρύφων· Καὶ μὴν πολλοὺς τῶν τὸν Ἰησοῦν λεγόντων ὁμολογεῖν καὶ λεγομένων Χριστιανῶν πυνθάνομαι ἐσθίειν τὰ εἰδωλόθυτα καὶ μηδὲν ἐκ τούτου βλάπτεσθαι λέγειν. Κἀγὼ ἀπεκρινάμην· καὶ ἐκ τοῦ τοιούτους εἶναι ἄνδρας, ὁμολογοῦντας ἑαυτοὺς εἶναι Χριστιανοὺς καὶ τὸν σταυρωθέντα Ἰησοῦν ὁμολογεῖν καὶ κύριον καὶ Χριστόν, καὶ μὴ τὰ ἐκείνου διδάγματα διδάσκοντας ἀλλὰ τὰ ἀπὸ τῶν τῆς πλάνης πνευμάτων, ἡμεῖς, οἱ τῆς ἀληθινῆς Ἰησοῦ Χριστοῦ καὶ καθαρᾶς διδασκαλίας μαθηταί, πιστότεροι καὶ βεβαιότεροι γινόμεθα ἐν τῇ ἐλπίδι τῇ κατηγγελμένῃ ὑπ᾽ αὐτοῦ. Ἃ γὰρ προλαβὼν μέκκειν γίνεσθαι ἐν ὀνόματι αὐτοῦ ἔπι, ταῦτα ὄψει καὶ ἐνεργείᾳ ὁρῶμεν τελούμενα. Εἶπε γάρ· Πολλοὶ ἐλεύσονται ἐπὶ τῷ ὀνόματί μου, ἔξωθεν ἐνδεδυμένοι δέρματα προβάτων, ἔσωθεν δέ εἰσι λύκοι ἅρπαγες. Καί· Προσέχετε ἀπὸ τῶν ψευδοποφητῶν, οἵτινες ἐλεύσονται πρὸς ὑμᾶς, ἔξωθεν ἐνδεδυμένοι δέματα προβάτων, ἔσωθεν δέ εἰσι λύκοι ἅρπαγες. Καί· Ἀναστήσονται πολλοὶ ψευδόχριστοι καὶ ψευδοαπόστολοι, καὶ πολλοὺς τῶν πιστῶν πλανήσουσιν. Εἰσὶν οὖν καὶ ἐγένοντο, ὦ φίλοι ἄνδρες, πολλοὶ οἳ ἄθεα καὶ βλάσφημα λέγειν καὶ πράττειν ἐδίδαξαν ἐν ὀνόματι τοῦ Ἰησοῦ προσελθόντες· καὶ καλούμενοί εἰσιν ὑφ᾽ ἡμῶν ἀπὸ τῆς προσθυνυμίας τῶν ἀνδρῶν, ἐξ οὗπερ ἑκάστη διδαχὴ καὶ γνώμη ἤρξατο. Ἄλλοι γὰρ κατ᾽ ἄλλον τρόπον βλασφημεῖν τὸν ποιητὴν τῶν ὅλων καὶ τὸν ὑπ᾽ αὐτοῦ προφητευόμενον ἐλεύσεσθαι Χριστὸν καὶ τὸν θεὸν Ἀβραὰμ καὶ Ἰσαὰκ καὶ Ἰακὼβ διδάσκουσιν· ὧν οὐδενὶ κοινωνοῦμεν, οἱ γνωρίζοντες ἀθέους καὶ ἀσεβεῖς καὶ ἀδίκους καὶ ἀνόμους αὐτοὺς ὑπάρχοντας, καὶ ἀντὶ τοῦ τὸν Ἰησοῦν σέβειν ὀνόματι μόνον ὁμολογεῖν. Καὶ Χριστιανοὺς ἑαυτοὺς λέγουσιν, ὃν τρόπον οἱ ἐν τοῖς ἔθνεσι τὸ ὄνομα τοῦ θεοῦ ἐπιγράφουσι τοῖς χειροποιήτοις, καὶ ἀνόμοις καὶ ἀθέοις τελεταῖς κοινωνοῦσι. Καί εἰσιν αὐτῶν οἱ μέν τινες καλούμενοι Μαρκιανοί, οἱ δὲ Οὐαλεντινιανοί, οἱ δὲ Βασιλειδιανοί, οἱ δὲ Σατορνιλιανοί, καὶ ἄλλοι ἄλλῳ ὀνόματι, ἀπὸ τοῦ ἀρχηγέτου τῆς γνώμης ἕκαστος ὀνομαζόμενος, ὃν πρόπον καὶ ἕκαστος τῶν φιλοσοφεῖν νομιζόντων, ὡς ἐν ἀρχῇ προεῖπον, ἀπὸ τοῦ πατρὸς τοῦ λόγου τὸ ὄνομα ἧς φιλοσοφεῖ φιλοσοφίας ἡγεῖται φέρειν. Ὥστε καὶ Ἐκ τούτων ἡμεῖς, ὡς ἔφην, τὸν Ἰησοῦν καὶ τῶν μετ᾽ αὐτὸν γενησομένων προγνώστην ἐπιστάμεθα, καὶ ἐξ ἄλλων δὲ πολλῶν ὧν προεῖπε γενήσεσθαι τοῖς πιστεύουσι καὶ ὁμολογοῦσιν αὐτὸν Χριστόν. Καὶ γὰρ ἃ πάσχομεν πάντα, ἀναιρούμενοι ὑπὸ τῶν οἰκείων, προεῖπεν ἡμῖν μέλλειν γενέθαι, ὡς κατὰ μηδένα τρόπον ἐπιλήψιμον αὐτοῦ λόγον ἢ πρᾶξιν φαίνεσθαι. Διὸ καὶ ὑπὲρ ὑμῶν καὶ ὑπὲρ τῶν ἄλλων ἁπάντων ἀνθρώπων τῶν ἐχθραινόντων ἡμῖν εὐχόμεθα, ἵνα μετανοοῦντες σὺν ἡμῖν μὴ βλασφημῆτε τὸν διά τε τῶν ἔργων καὶ τῶν ἀπὸ τοῦ ὀνόματος αὐτοῦ καὶ νῦν γινομένων δυνάμεων καὶ ἀπὸ τῶν τῆς διδαχῆς λόγων καὶ ἀπὸ τῶν προφητευθεισῶν εἰς

If Justin is to be taken literally here, this reads as though those with whom Justin is concerned here positively designated themselves as "Christians" (Χριστιανοὺς ἑαυτοὺς λέγουσιν). It seems Justin does indeed say they "called themselves" "Christians," which is the first claim of its kind in "Christian" literature. The first group mentioned here to have done this is the Marcionites, though it seems perhaps all use the term, and by now perhaps Justin's group is adopting it too since Justin attempts to give them more appropriate alternative names formed from the name of their respective founders. This passage comes in response to Trypho's question about "Christian"diversity where Justin outlines the failed candidates for "Christians," those who are "outside of our communion" (οὐδενὶ κοινωνοῦμεν). In this passage we find false prophets and false Christs who would teach blasphemously towards the creator and Christ and unholy doctrines in Christ's name, and will be inspired by devils (τῆς πλάνης πενυμάτων, ἡμεῖς).

Justin says something similar in *Dial.* 82.3: "Many have disseminated atheistic, blasphemous, and perverse doctrines, falsely branding them with his name, and they have taught, and still do, whatever that unclean spirit of the Devil has suggested to their minds."[163] These claims are remarkably similar to what Justin has to say about Marcion in *1 Apol.* 26.5–6. There too blasphemies are taught in the name of the "Christians" in association with devils. Even stronger, in *1 Apol.* 58.2 Marcion is even described as being a wolf, which directly parallels the image quoted here where the wolf steals lambs. The false "Christians" in this passage teach their own atheistic doctrines rather than those of Christ, just as is said of Marcion in the two passages mentioned from *1 Apology*. So these people reject the god of Israel as their own and pay only lip service to Christ. And despite this they have the audacity to call themselves "Christians." If Justin is right, then Marcion was not only the first who, as one can read in Tertullian, conceptualized "Christianity" in antithesis to "Judaism," he may also have been the

---

αὐτὸν προφητειῶν ἄμωμον καὶ ἀνέγκλητον κατὰ πάντα Χριστὸν Ἰησοῦν, ἀλλὰ πιστεύσαντες εἰς αὐτὸν ἐν τῇ πάλιν γενησομένῃ ἐνδόξῳ αὐτοῦ παρουσίᾳ σωθῆτε καὶ μὴ καταδικασθῆτε εἰς τὸ πῦρ ὑπ' αὐτοῦ.

163. Πολλοὶ γὰρ ἄθεα καὶ βλάσφημα καὶ ἄθικα ἐν ὀνόματι αὐτοῦ παραχαράσσοντες ἐδίδαξαν, καὶ τὰ ἀπὸ τοῦ ἀκαθάρτου πνεύματος διαβόλου ἐμβαλλόμενα ταῖς διανοίαις αὐτῶν ἐδίδαξαν καὶ διδάσκουσι μέχρι νῦν·

first, or one of the first, to adopt the name "Christian" for his group and bring about questions of identity that Justin is trying to lay to rest.[164] True, others are mentioned also, but these did not reject the god of Israel and the prophets as Marcion did. Furthermore, Marcion (or Marcionites) is the only name that keeps coming up in both of Justin's major texts. It is accompanied by others, but these differ from place to place; only Marcion is consistently the dangerous threat, it seems.

Marcion is not the only, but he is the chief propagator, the false prophet that Justin has in mind. He, Justin, contrasts him with the true prophets of the one true god who profess the one and only true Christ. Trust in the prophets of the Scriptures and in their Christ automatically divorces him from Marcion.

Justin rounds this section off by again announcing that Christ was prophesied and that blasphemy against him ought to cease for fear of judgement from him. As Bobichon notes, this is the first explicit mention Justin makes of the eternal and universal judgement in relation to Christ. A very long list of references and proof texts (both Old and New Testaments)[165] appears in both of Justin's major works on this theme. Bobichon goes as far as to call this theme omnipresent and an obsession for Justin.[166] Why is this such a concern for Justin? That Christ was prophesied and that he will pronounce eternal judgement represents a direct contradiction of Marcion. Leaning heavily on this theme strongly distinguishes Justin's theology from that of Marcion. Again we have no reason to suppose that Valentinus or Basilides had any objection to god's or Christ's judgment, so we have here a whole chapter where not only are Marcionite themes the key topics, but Marcion himself, and his followers, are a central, if not the only, target of Justin. This is particularly striking when we take on board Robert Royalty's point about the unique heresiological structure of this passage:

> The formal difference in *Dial.* 35 and these other heresiological passages

---

164. Tertullian, *Marc.* 4.6.3.
165. Bobichon, *avec Tryphon*, 680n29.
166. Ibid.

[*Dial.* 80; *1 Apol.* 26; 56; 58] is the specification of groups rather than the taxonomy of the founders of this group. *Dial.* 35 is heresiological, but not doxographical. Justin notes the ἄλλον τρόπον of these teachers, but he makes no attempt to describe their teachings or connect them genealogically or taxonomically at this point or in this text.[167]

As we have already noted, Justin does here allude, as he has done throughout the text, to the teachings of Marcion. Indeed that has been rather the whole point, to escape these teachings, not by naming them explicitly but by articulating an alternative that rules them out necessarily. Justin does not perform a taxonomy of Marcion at all in this text because, as we have noted, it would not be helpful to do so in front of Trypho. Rather he rules him out implicitly. The appearance of Marcionites here then is something of a smuggled truth. It appears there is no taxonomy and these names are simply equivalent and expedient examples, but the passage and the themes of the text reveal that Marcionism is indeed the teaching that is being detailed negatively.

A companion passage to *Dial.* 35 can be found at *Dial.* 80 and also provides clues that Marcionism is the present threat that Justin is trying to rule out and exclude from the shape of the "Christian" philosophy in this piece:

> Moreover, I indicated to you that some who are called Christians, but are godless, impious heretics, teach doctrines that are in every way blasphemous, atheistical, and unwise. But that you may know that I am not saying this in front of you alone, I shall put together a statement, as best I can, of the debate between us; in which I shall document the admission which I have just made to you. For I do not desire to follow men and their doctrines but greatly to follow but God and his doctrines. For if you have met any who are called Christians, but who do not confess this truth, but boldly blaspheme the God of Abraham, and the God of Isaac, and the God of Jacob; and say there is no resurrection of the dead, and that their souls are taken to heaven when they die; do not understand them to be Christians, just as one considering rightly, would not confess that the Sadducees, or similar sects of Genistae, Meristae, Gelilaeans, Hellenists, Pharisees, Baptists, are Jews (do not be offended when I say what I think), but are only called Jews and children of Abraham, paying lip service

---

167. Royalty, "Justin's Conversion," 513–14.

to God, as God Himself declared, whose hearts are far from Him. But I and others, who Christians of right mind, know that there will be a resurrection of the dead, and a thousand years in Jerusalem, which will be rebuilt, adorned, and enlarged, as the prophets Ezekiel and Isaiah and others profess. (*Dial.* 80.3–5)[168]

Although Justin is not saying that he "and others, who are right-minded Christians" will be better "Jews" and children of Abraham, he insinuates it by reassuring Trypho that he holds strongly to that which the prophets have announced, which Trypho ought also to accept. Right-minded "Christians" are no blasphemers or atheists, but are in relation with the god of Abraham and Isaac. The Marcionite profile of this is known by now, as Bobichon also has noted.[169] And although Basilides and Valentinus could well be part of Justin's criticism, the fact that Marcion and Marcionites appear consistently, whereas the others do not, and that Justin wrote to Marcion makes him seem to be the more pressing target also here. Indeed, Marcion rejected the resurrection of the bodies, and only taught an eternal life of the soul.[170] In addition, the passage is reminiscent of *1 Apol.* 26.6 where Justin outlines that the followers of Marcion may be called "Christians," just as all philosophers are called philosophers, but really should not be.

Conclusion

We have seen in this chapter that Justin in his *Dialogue with Trypho* sets out a number of key themes to define "Christian" philosophy, and that these are particularly notable because they speak to areas of disagreement between Justin's "Christian" philosophy and the

---

168. See chapter 1 n. 195.
169. Bobichon, *avec Tryphon*, 787n8.
170. On this point Epiphanius is clear. At *Pan.* 3.3.5. and 3.4.5 he develops it by saying: "As I indicated, Marcion says resurrection is not of bodies but of souls, and he assigns salvation to these and not to bodies. And he similarly claims that there are reincarnations of souls, and transmigrations from body to body." In the early tradition Tertullian also alludes to Marcion's denial here in *Res.* 2.10: "Consequently, forced to assign Christ also to a different dispensation lest he be considered to belong to the Creator, they have first gone astray in respect of his flesh, maintaining either, according to Marcion and Basilides, that it had no true existence, or, according to the successors of Valentinus, with Apelles, that it was of a quality of its own. And thus it follows that they shut the door against the salvation of that substance of which they deny that Christ is partaker: for they are aware that it is equipped with the strongest precedent of resurrection if already in Christ the flesh has risen again."

doctrines of Marcion. The introductory section, frequently viewed as odd or out of sorts with the rest of the piece, in this examination presents a succinct distillation of the key themes which define the "Christian" philosophy through the speech of Trypho, Justin, and the *presbutes*. The purpose and truth of philosophy, in contrast to the doctrines of men, is asserted along with a single god who is creator but also providential carer for all in the world. Furthermore, this god is just and righteous and wishes to reward rather than to punish. Finally this god spoke through the prophets and is therefore the god of Israel; Trypho's god. This god is the father of Christ and for all people. These points define the shape of the "Christian" philosophy which Justin seeks to demonstrate to Trypho, and by saying so he distances himself from having founded his belief on empty fables. Fundamentally such an exposition rules out a theology that sees Christ as a new phenomenon from a new god, not predicated in the prophets or of any antiquity at all. It denies that the god of Israel, the creator, is cruel and manipulative, and believes that he is rather merciful and compassionate to all people and demonstrably so by the revelation he has given rather than by the opinions of men, men like Marcion. The following chapter will turn attention to Justin's *Apologies* and consider what evidence can be found for a deeper relevance or influence of Marcion there as something or someone from whom Justin seeks to distinguish himself.

3

Case by Case

Introduction

This chapter will argue that chief among Justin's purposes in *1 Apology* is an act of differentiation: against other "Christians," Justin must distinguish himself from those others, restrict the category of "Christians" to only true "Christians," and claim that all others and only those others can and should be charged of atheism by the Emperor.

The argument will proceed in six main parts. First the nature of the Roman understanding of "Christians", first discussed in chapter 1 will be reconsidered as background to the charges brought and their context. After this, Justin's case for "Christians" not being atheists, which subtly exposes Marcionites as fitting of charge, will be examined. Following this, the argumentative framework that Justin builds around the demons will be introduced to show the distinction between all that is "Christian" and all that is not, which should naturally lead the rulers to favor "Christian" truth over any other; this naturally establishes Marcionism as *other* and not to be trusted. Fourthly the case will be made that Justin relies heavily on asserting the "Christian's" relationship with the creator of the universe, the god of the "Jews," and the concept of this god's judgment as guarantors for the truthfulness of followers. This exposes that Marcionites do not follow this god, marking Marcionism out as a new superstition, so the rulers have no guarantees that they are not liars who will say anything to curry favor. Next we will consider how Justin claims "Christ" for the creator and relies on his teaching, suggesting that Marcionites must rely on another god because Christ is inseparable from the creator, the god of the "Jews." Finally, we will examine the manner in which Marcion is presented by Justin as a tool of the demons, which ought to lead the rulers to persecute him and his followers only while finding favour towards "Christians."

Politics

Justin begins the apology by appealing to the rulers' sense of justice and fairness and asking for investigation on a case-by-case basis rather than on a general classification basis (the class being "Christian"). This is important for Justin, especially because there are those who are called "Christian" who should not be, and so the only way to know who should be punished is to investigate on a case-by-case basis. We should not move on without noticing the strangeness of Justin's request, however. "Christians" are seemingly noticeable enough, whatever degree of understanding those who try them had, to warrant trial. Seemingly they are no longer simply part of the "Jewish" tradition but stand out to some degree. Justin, despite arguing against persecution, is implicitly accepting of this and is actually requesting a further or deeper judicial process. He does not ask that the trials stop, but that they be more probing.

There is a political dimension to this address, in that the situation for "Christians" has changed. Up until relatively recently, "Christians" were tolerated under the protections afforded to "Judaism." Such protections included privileges like the right to observe the Sabbath and other festivals, tax raising powers to send to the temple, exemptions from military service and from sacrifices of the imperial cult. As Zetterholm's analysis has shown, these privileges constituted a strong self-identity with considerable regulatory power. In Antioch, at least, this constituted almost a state within a state, a devolved parliament and judicial system if you will. In other words, they were considered one of the *collegia* established and protected by ancient tradition.[1] Indeed, going back as far as Julius Caesar, when action was taken against *collegia*, synagogues and "Judaism" were exempted.[2] With their status as "Jews" seemingly less obvious, it is incumbent on Justin, as it was in the *Dialogue*, to present a "Christianity" that demonstrates its "Jewish" roots and so avoids the appearance of atheism.

Marcion of course represents a clear and present danger to this. Politically speaking, the problem is the loss of protection or freedom of practice afforded to a "Jewish" sect, once, as with Marcion, a self-distinction is introduced between "Judaism" and "Christianity." By setting up a god for "Christians" distinct from the god of the "Jews" and rejecting the care and will of that god for them, pushes "Christians" towards the appearsnce of atheism. Furthermore, this would leave gentile "Christians," according to Justin by this time the majority,[3] guilty of conversion to a non-native tradition or superstition:[4] this was against Roman law.

Justin's response is not, and cannot be, simply that "Christians" are in actual fact a sect of the "Jews," hence to revert to a pre-Marcion stage of "Christianity," but in accepting the new situation of "Christians" being separate from "Jews," he advocates that "Christians" are the "true Israel." The "Christian" philosophy, as in the *Dialogue*, has ancient "Jewish" antecedents but cannot be limited to the "Jews" alone. The "Jews" knew god's law, which for Justin can be split into what was given to them alone and what is universal. The

---

1. Magnus Zetterholm, *The Formation of Christianity in Antioch: A social-scientific approach to the separation between Judaism and Christianity* (London: Routledge, 2003), 37.
2. Ibid., 32.
3. *1 Apol.* 53.4–5 states that though the "Jews" and Samaritans are called by the prophetic spirit of the house of Israel, it was prophesied and came to pass that believers in god from the nations (pagans) would be more numerous than the "Jews" and the Samaritans.
4. This (*superstitionem*) is how Pliny, Suetonius (*Nero.* 16.2), and Tacitus (*Ann.* 15.44) describe "Christian" beliefs.

universal portion of the law is applicable to all and many pagans have demonstrated participation in this. The universal theology Justin puts forward has the consequence of claiming "Jewish" privileges for the worship of the one true god and not losing the protection given by Roman law. These are the very real political realities which are more than incidental to Justin's rejection of Marcion's theology. Not only has Marcion created a new god over against the one true god, but by doing so he imperils all true believers because they all share the one name "Christian." In order to counter the political Marcionite threat, then, Justin has not only to accept judicial persecution but turn it to his advantage. He has to ask for more litigation, not less, and of a more probing nature. By this acquiescence it might be possible to weed out the Marcionites and expose them for the atheists they are while affording "Christians" tolerance.

In order to make clear the change represented in what Justin asks for from the rulers, a bit more background into the legal status of "Christians" and their interactions with the Roman authorities will be helpful. I take Pliny the Younger's epistle to Trajan concerning the Christians as the best available source of information here. Prior to this, although "Christians" are mentioned and come up for punishment under Nero and Domitian, it is not at all clear that they are being punished as "Christians" *qua* "Christian" rather than as an element of "Jewish" fanaticism with no firmly established boundary between the "Jewish" and Christian sects.[5] With Pliny, however, we meet a new era in "Christian"–state relations on a general and judicial level.

Pliny's Case Law

In Pliny's letter to Trajan concerning "Christians" it is clear that "Christians" represent something new to him:

> Pliny seems to be under the impression that there have been *cognitiones de Christianis*, somewhere, sometime, somehow, in his adult lifetime. Some such impression must be implied by his note that he has not been present

---

5. Pliny the Younger, *C. Plinii Caecilii Secundi Epistulae ad Traianum imperatorem cum eiusdem responsis*, ed. E. G. Hardy (London: Macmillan, 1889), 240–43.

at any. But in gaining the impression that some such cases have occurred he seems to have picked up no information as to how, with no hints to guide him, and no likely sources of information to follow up before troubling the emperor Trajan. At least, he claims none.[6]

This is interesting because it is so unlikely for a man such as Pliny. Pliny had been a successful advocate in the *centumviral court*, acting as judge and assessor,[7] as well holding the positions of *Tribune, Praetor, Consul,* and finally Governor of Bithynia where he would have been sole judge across the province. This is clearly a man of vast legal and political experience. Furthermore, Pliny was a contentious and thorough scholar of law. That there is no precedent is reasonably clear from the fact that Pliny always mentions what he follows elsewhere even if he is unsure of its status, and where he does not act, he tries to show the effort he has gone to in order to find precedent. He is only silent on this in this one letter which concerns "Christians," and it is by far his longest to Trajan. Clearly he is genuinely unaware of any precedent for how to proceed.[8] Downing is even bolder:

> There have been no cases of Christians being brought to the courts in his province—ever. He does not simply fail to refer to them—there are none, none for him in Bythinia and Pontus, but also none in Trajan's archives, and none in any other context that he or Trajan might think relevant, no sign "x is what has been done", and it seems sensible; nor "x, y, and z are what have been done, and z seems preferable." There has been no action in the courts against Christians for their allegiance in Pontus or Bythinia, and none in the provinces around for his local advisers to bring to his attention.[9]

If this is the case, and the evidence of Pliny's unique collection of letters suggests that it is, then this experienced Roman official is genuinely encountering something new, or being able to distinguish for the first time something that had blended in before. There may have been occasions where "Christians" were involved in disputes, but

---

6. Gerald F. Downing, "Pliny's Prosecutions of Christians: Revelation and 1 Peter," *JSNT* 34 (1988): 107.
7. Pliny the Younger, *Pliny the Younger: Complete Letters*, trans. P. G. Walsh (Oxford: Oxford University Press, 2009), xvi.
8. Downing, "Pliny's Prosecutions of Christians," 110.
9. Ibid., 112–13.

that Pliny cannot refer to them is very surprising. Hardy speculates that such occasions may have been local tribunals brought by "Jews" where the offence was not focused on Christianity as such.[10] Up until this point "Christians," though occasionally named in persecutions, were under the radar as part of the "Jewish" tradition.[11] Something is changing in Bythinia. It may not be incidental that Bythinia is the location. Bythinia had a large "Jewish" population, although Pliny never mentions "Jews" in his letters. In Rome such communities would be diluted by the general populace and blend in, but where they formed a large proportional body they would be more obvious. This being the case, any unrest within that community would be more likely to be problematic for the authorities. The Romans were wary of the "Jews" following the first war, and tensions had been growing steadily for some time; the *Fiscus Iudaicus* was a fresh and humiliating attack by the Romans on all "Jews"[12] and the Kitos war is imminent. As growing numbers of people are anonymously accused of being "Christian," unrest which cannot be ignored is clearly present. It is possible, and perhaps likely, that fellow "Jews" are those who accuse "Christians" of being "Christians," because they are either unhappy with the position

---

10. Hardy, *C. Plinii Caecilii Secundi Epistulae*, 60.
11. Ibid., 239.
12. The extent to which "Christians" suffered under and participated in the *Fiscus Iudaicus* and whether Nerva's reform of it constitutes a wholesale redefinition of "Judaism" to the exclusion of "Christians" is an extremely complicated question. Goodman and Heemstra favor this view; Jossa also understands the *Fiscus Iudaicus* as indicative of a strong split between "Judaism" and "Christianity"; but other scholars, such as Schafer and Feldman, avoid this link. There can be little doubt that Suetonius's record of the targets as those who conceal their Jewish origin and those who practice a Jewish life in secret may have included "Christians" in both groups, and that Nerva's reform restricting the tax to those who practiced the ancestral customs must have had significant effect. However we know that the question of identity for "Jew," "Christian," and "Israel" is extremely complicated and socially negotiated. Furthermore, it does not seem immediately clear why "Christians" as a body would seek to avoid the tax. Simply to avoid paying is a possible reason, but it seems a lot to ask to expect "Christians" to have taken a stand as "Israel" and isolated themselves as atheists. It does not seem reasonable to claim that "Christians" were firmly distinguished in this legal reform, but it surely has significance for the beginning of an answer to the question of whether "Christians" were outside the boundary of "Israel." See Marius Heemstra, *The Fiscus Judaicus and the Parting of the Ways* (Tübingen: Mohr Siebeck, 2010); Martin Goodman, "Diaspora Reactions to the Destruction of the Temple," in *Jews and Christians: The Parting of the Ways A.D. 70 to 135*, ed. James Dunn (Tübingen: Mohr Siebeck, 1992), 27–38; Giorgio Jossa, *Jews or Christians? The Followers of Jesus in Search of their own Identity* (Tübingen: Mohr Siebeck, 2006), 140–41; Peter Schäfer, *Judeophobia: Attitudes Toward the Jews in the Ancient World* (Cambridge, MA: Harvard University Press, 1997), 113–16; Louis H. Feldman, *Jew and Gentile in the Ancient World* (Princeton, NJ: Princeton University Press,1993), 99–100.

of "Christians" towards the ancestral customs or wary that "Christian" worship of a man risks provoking the Romans to clamp down on the community perceived to have a messianic leader.

Beyond the fact that Pliny cannot cite precedents or suggestions for procedure is the fact that he, being the conscientious investigator that he was, embarks on a fact finding mission to discover just what it is that these people believe and practice. Up until this point it had been unknown to him. As the charges spread Pliny felt the need to ascertain what exactly he was dealing with. He questions those named by an informer and the results were inconclusive. Various understandings of "Christian" practice and blame or innocence were brought before him such that he found it necessary to take further steps at investigation. Beyond those charged and brought to him, Pliny tortures[13] two slave women who were deaconesses with the express intention of getting to the bottom of the issue. Pliny's report on what he discovers, on the more reliable evidence given under torture, is that "Christianity" only amounts to superstition, though a very influential one that has, as he has discovered, spread far and wide and that threatens traditional Roman worship. Clearly something new, or differently understood, is being discovered in Bythinia and the scale of this threat to the Roman cult causes Pliny to inform the emperor and seek advice.

What is even more interesting for our purposes is the practice that Pliny innovates and its endorsement by Trajan. The procedure that Pliny institutes is the well-known sacrificial test. First he inquires of the accused if they are indeed "Christians," for, as Pliny proceeds, the name itself functionally serves as the crime: if they confess this, they are taken off to be executed. Such as these are not a problem for Pliny: the fact that they will not deny their faith even though they know this brings death is enough to convict them as perverse and vile. Rather it is the other group that presents a challenge.[14] Those who

---

13. The significance of this is perhaps that Pliny would not be convinced of testimony given without torture but it was prohibited to torture witnesses who were free persons. However, evidence provided by slaves was inadmissible except obtained under torture. So Pliny in seeking out these slave women is searching for a stronger, more reliable, test case. See Pliny the Younger, *Correspondence with Trajan from Bithynia (Epistles X)*, trans. Wynne Williams (A&P; Warminster: Aris and Phillips, 1990), 143.

deny the charge and prove it by calling upon the Roman gods and making sacrifice to them, as well as cursing Christ. Pliny's somewhat anxious instinct is to acquit and set these free and Trajan endorses this procedure provided it is executed *ad hoc* rather than systematically. What is most interesting here is the sacrificial test which firmly marks the "Christians" out as a new tradition.

Though the "Jews" were atheists, the Romans as a rule tolerated this. It would appear that a sacrificial test was not necessary to ascertain whether the "Jews" rejected the gods, but Ste. Croix does note an earlier example of the sacrificial test being applied to "Jews" in 67 CE in order to ascertain who was "Jewish." This example is recorded by the reliable "Jewish" source Josephus in his account of the "Jewish" war, and since it may have significant implications for the practice Pliny employs, I will quote much of what Josephus says directly:

> The Jewish race, densely interspersed among the native populations of every portion of the world, is particularly numerous in Syria, where intermingling is due to the proximity of the two countries. But it was at Antioch that they specially congregated, partly owing to the greatness of that city, but mainly because the successors of King Antiochus had enabled them to live there securely. For, although Antiochus surnamed Epiphanes sacked Jerusalem and plundered the temple, his successors on the throne restored to the Jews of Antioch all such votive offerings as were made of brass, to be laid up in their synagogue, and, moreover, granted them citizen rights on an equality with Greeks. Continuing to receive similar treatment from later monarchs, the Jewish colony grew in numbers, and their richly designed and costly offerings formed a splendid ornament to the temple. Moreover, they were constantly attracting to their religious ceremonies multitudes of Greeks and these they had in some measure incorporated with themselves. Now just at the time when war had been declared and Vespasian had recently landed in Syria, and when hatred of the Jews was everywhere at its height, a certain Antiochus, one of their own number and highly respected for the sake of his father, who was chief magistrate of the Jews in Antioch, entered the theatre during an assembly of the people and denounced his own father and the other Jews, accusing them of a design to burn the whole city to the ground one night; he also delivered up some foreign Jews as accomplices to the plot. On hearing this, the people, in uncontrollable fury, ordered the men who had been delivered up to be instantly consigned to the flames,

---

14. Perkins, *The Suffering Self*, 18.

and all were forthwith burnt to death in the theatre. They then rushed for the Jewish masses, believing the salvation of their native place to be dependent on prompt chastisement. Antiochus further inflamed their fury; for, thinking to furnish proof of his conversion and of his detestation of Jewish customs by sacrificing after the manner of the Greeks, he recommended that the rest should be compelled to do the same, as the conspirators would thus be exposed by their refusal. This test being applied by the Antiochenes, a few submitted and the recalcitrant were massacred. Antiochus, having next procured the aid of troops from the Roman general, domineered with severity over his Jewish fellow-citizens, not permitting them repose on the seventh day, but compelling them do everything exactly as on other days, and so strictly did he enforce obedience that not only at Antioch was the weekly day of rest abolished, but the example having been started there spread for a short time to other cities as well.[15]

The important difference to note between this and Pliny's account is that here the test is a popular movement, not a state procedure, and importantly a recommendation of the "Jewish" agitator rather than a state policy designed by a Roman official such as Pliny.[16] The aid of Roman troops given to Antiochus does however suggest Roman support for this process (no real surprise given the recent rise in hostilities between "Jews" and Romans in Judaea). Despite the differences, the evidence here of a test applied to ascertain whether the accused will sacrifice to the gods and renounce their past represents a possible precedent. Pliny usually cites precedent, which makes it unusual that he does not mention this, but if he was indeed aware of it, perhaps it was more commonplace at the time since so that it would not need to be referenced. The truly noteworthy point here is that this test is being used in order to establish who is "Jewish" in a society where the "Jewish" population is large, as much as ten percent according to Zetterholm, and has diluted the pagan population.[17] A demonstration of loyalty among the popular consciousness is being demanded. The rioting of the "Jews" in other places may have been understood to be a clear and present threat at this time and in this

---

15. Josephus, *B.J.* 7.3.3.
16. Zetterholm, *Christianity in Antioch*, 118.
17. Ibid., 118.

place. Indeed, as Zetterholm notes, some of the Antiochenes may even have seen action in the war in Palestine, as the Romans are known to have supplemented their legions with auxiliary forces that were often chiefly constituted of those from Syria.[18] Compared with the Antiochene case, it is less surprising if in both cases the accusations were coming from within and also in Pliny's case we are still dealing with an inner-"Jewish" debate. At least in Antioch, it was not the pagans who were upset, but the "Jews" themselves, though tensions are high as Josephus intimates; in Pliny's case, it was not the Roman authorities who instigated the process, but the people who provoked the authorities to act. Provocation from within the community was a necessary accelerator for the Roman authorities to get involved.

What, then, is the relationship between this and Pliny's circumstance? An obvious difference is that the test is not suggested as coming from the accusers in Pliny's case, or at least not reported as such. And while the accuser in Josephus was clearly a traditional "Jew," it is unclear who the accusers in Pliny's case were. We do not know. But it is within the realm of possibilities that these accusers were "Jews" as in Antioch, who had reason to despise "Christians" as a sect that, by its appeal to Christ, potentially seems to have threatened the "Jewish" customs (Sabbath observance, Torah interpretation, circumcision) and by extension the social order of the province by exposing the "Jewish" population to the possibility of losing their political protections.

Although a speculation, it is a plausible one. If this view were to be taken seriously, then it would become possible to suggest that Pliny is not so much innovating a new test as applying a loosely established practice of determining who counts as a "Jew," or atheist, and using it for "Christians" because he, admitting to not knowing what they are, does not see them as a strictly non-"Jewish" entity. The fact that he does not juxtapose them with "Jews" is also suggestive of this. Such a juxtaposition could establish a former, loose link between "Christians" and "Jews," but the lack of it could also suggest that it did not occur to Pliny that these people were beyond "Judaism." Another point that

---

18. Ibid., 118–19.

might push the evidence in this direction is to ask why Pliny sees fit to test whether "Christians" will sacrifice to the gods. Why does he think "Christians" exclude the gods from their worship or do not sacrifice? Have his interrogations revealed this, his policy as instituted before he widens the scope of his investigation, or is it because he makes a natural connection between these people accused of being "Christians" and "Jews"? This cannot be answered firmly but it is a plausible account of the evidence. Given that this cannot decide the issue we must consider the alternative, that Pliny marks the beginning, or a beginning in a particular location, of starting to see "Christians" as outside of "Jewishness," however subtly to begin with.

The Romans knew the "Jews" were atheists but respected and protected their traditions. The "Jews" were, so to speak, licensed atheists.[19] Schäfer sums up the complexity of the "Jewish" association with this term quite well:

> The charge of "Atheism" (*atheotēs* or *asebeia, impietas*) was raised by many pagan authors against the "Jews," who did not participate in pagan cults. It did not have legal consequences, however, because—according to established Roman legislation—the "Jews" were exempted "from participation in state cults, including that of the Emperor." When Domitian used the charge of "atheism," that is, treason (*maiestas*), in order to eliminate people he deemed dangerous to his reign or wanted to get rid of for other reasons, he most certainly did not abolish ancient privileges. But privileges were vulnerable and could be disregarded.[20]

Even though this was the case and the "Jews" were often hated, there would be no reason to put "Christians" to death for confessing to being "Christians" if they were understood as being "Jews", even if they were seen as strangers or foreigners. Though even in this case the social unrest being caused by great numbers of "Christians," who are being accused by at least some anonymous people, suggests that a threat to Roman social order in the neglect of the state cults was being perceived by fellow "Jews." Though it is possible that Pliny assumes a "Jewishness" of "Christians," there isn't enough evidence to be

---

19. See Ste. Croix, "Persecuted?," 135.
20. Schäfer, *Judeophobia*, 116.

confident in this claim. What is clear is that Pliny is using the term "Christian" as a shame name, whether of "Jewish" origin or not, and that over time this distinction will eventually lead to two separate *religions*, though the completion of this process is far from Pliny's or even Justin's time.

It seems, then, that Pliny and Trajan are taking the first official steps in opening the courts to hear cases brought against "Christians" *qua* "Christians." "Christians" have clearly already got a bad reputation, since Pliny thinks them punishable in the first instance even if then he does not have any information about what they believe or how they live. Yet, they are becoming more distinguishable from "Jews," who still have privileges, however limited these may have been in various locations and at various times following unrest. "Christians are vulnerable to local enemies when a governor arrives who is intent on imposing order and law. It is very likely appropriate to describe the informers as 'trying it on' with the new governor; but this is the first occasion for such a 'try-on' or, at least, the first successful attempt."[21] This demonstrates the political reality that Justin faced in another part of the empire fifty years later, and after the Bar Kokhba revolt. "Christians" are being informed on in a similar manner, it seems, and are no longer protected under "Jewish" toleration laws, but stand alone.

If "Christians" no longer had an acceptable stake in the toleration afforded to "Judaism," and were seen as at least plausibly distinct, then it is important, from Justin's perspective, that the rulers understand who they are dealing with. If they are a new thing, they at least ought to be well and fairly defended. There is however a further dimension here, Hardy said, "The toleration hitherto enjoyed by the Christians must for the future, if granted at all, be granted independently of any supposed connection with the Jews."[22] This is not quite what Justin attempts to do. Marcion might have made a plausible contemporary attempt at this, though there is no evidence of an apology from him;

---

21. Downing, "Pliny's Prosecutions of Christians," 113.
22. Hardy, *C. Plinii Caecilii Secundi Epistulae*, 56.

but Justin seeks to demonstrate a legitimate "Jewish" connection with theological and political consequences.

It is not open to Justin to claim that his community are in fact "Jews," and his theological convictions rule this possibility out also. However, in his claim to be the true spiritual Israel, Justin is making the case against atheism in "Christians." In his claim for the universality of "Christianity," his counter-assertion is that "Christians" are not the illegal converts, but that the pagans are. This is made all the more pressing by the fact of Marcion's theological project, which deepens and solidifies the separation of "Christian" and "Jew." The more successful Marcion's mission, the less chance "Christians" had of staying within the law and not being executed; though Justin claims they are not afraid of death if it comes, they still do not court it, for that would be contrary to god's law as Justin argues in *2 Apol.* 4.3. Marcionism is then a very direct political, as well as theological, threat to the following of Christ as Justin understands it.

This helps to establish, and make more intelligible, Justin's project in *1 Apology*. Justin is not claiming that the trial of "Christians" is ill-founded or denying their legitimacy or that of their authorities in any way. Despite the probable futility of doing so, he might still have made a protest on these grounds. Rather he not only accepts this procedure but looks to extend it. Justin appeals for more investigation on the part of the rulers. The reason he wishes for thorough investigation is that, on the strengths of his presentation of "Christian" truth, the theology of Marcion can be exposed as counter-"Christian" and the political threat that it represents can be expurgated. The key line in *1 Apology* is: "But we do know that they [Marcionites and potentially other heresies] are neither persecuted nor put to death by you, at least on account of their doctrines" (*1 Apol.* 26.7).[23] This will be discussed in detail below, but it reveals that the rulers are not distinguishing between "Christians" who are Marcionites, or others Justin would not consider "Christian," and are treating all together while Justin believes not all "Christians" are created equal or even share the same category.

---

23. My translation. ἀλλ' ὅτι μὴ διώκονται μηδὲ φονεύονται ὑφ' ὑμῶν—κἂν διὰ τὰ δόγματα—ἐπιστάμεθα.

By deepening his investigations, which go beyond the mere name applied to them and consider doctrines and lifestyle, Justin hopes to make the distinction clear. If this were successful, which it clearly was not since Justin himself was martyred, it would afford "Christians" a share in the toleration given to the "Jews" without them having to be, by their own standards, "Jews," keepers of the ancestral practices of the covenant, but instead the philosophers who know the truth.[24] Having considered the novel and unexpected nature of Justin's proposal for case-by-case judgments against the background of the pattern begun, if not universally established, by Pliny, we are now in a position to look in further detail at the specifics of how Justin presents the need for this case and its intended aims.

Being understood as being outside of "Judaism," to whatever degree, can "Christians" be seen as anything other than atheists? If they are not "Jews," they are a new cult, and what they worship is unclear. As Pliny understood, they are a superstitious bunch. Though the "Jews" were considered atheists by the Romans,[25] they were generally accepted. Cut off from this exceptional status, Justin has to defend freshly the non-atheistic beliefs of "Christians," without adopting the Roman cult of gods, hence his need to define what true "Christianity" means. Reclaiming the god of the "Jews" as truly "Christian" is the central element of this defense, which is qualified by alerting the rulers to the role of the demons who cause misconceptions of the truth. Each of these points isolates Marcion's theology in contrast to true "Christianity," which can enjoy the same toleration as "Judaism," even possibly at its expense, identifying Marcionism as a positive example of anti-"Christian"/anti-truth propaganda.

---

24. But we know this is precisely the working definition of "Jewishness" that Nerva seemed to put in place with his reform of the *Fiscus Iudaicus*, so Justin is fighting a losing battle.
25. It is known that Flavius Clemens and Flavia Domitilla were put to death in Domitian's reign on the charge of atheism for their sympathies with the "Jewish" people and, in effect, for denying the traditional state gods. William R. Schoedel, "Christian 'Atheism' and the Peace of the Roman Empire," *CH* 42 (1973): 310. Josephus also refers to the "Jews" being accused of atheism in *Ag. Ap.* 2.148.

Who Are the Atheists?

In his attempt to explain that not all "Christians" are truly "Christian" and worthy of protection, or that not all are criminal as some may be, Justin points out that some of the poets and philosophers were atheistic and yet are loved and lauded by the rulers (*1 Apol.* 4.9). Thus, it seems like a contradiction when "Christians" are charged with what sound like similar charges and hated on account of them. From Justin's point of view this is unfair but not surprising. Socrates is an example of a similar scenario (*1 Apol.* 5.3) from within the Greco-Roman tradition. He was hated and given the same charge (of inventing new divinities) when he exposed the demons. This also is the particular form of atheistic charge all "Christians" encounter: they are thought to be atheists chiefly because they are thought to invent new divinities. In Justin's view and presentation, it is the Marcionites who are to be distinguished from "Christians" as those who invent new divinities. True "Christians," by contrast, are worshippers of the one true god, the god of the "Jews" and the universal god of all. Justin alludes to the disjunction between "Christians" and Marcionites (*1 Apol.* 7.3) by pointing out that just as there are many who are called by the title *philosopher* and not all are worthy of the title (just as he has already said in *1 Apol.* 4.8), there likewise are those who seem or might be thought to be "Christians" and yet are not worthy to be called such. This is the background of every claim Justin makes for the faith, because not all who claim the name "Christian" are really so. The denial of atheism for Justin, then, is strictly limited to "Christians" and excludes any pretenders to this school.

Justin makes a further salient connection between "Christians" and Socrates, however: both Socrates and "Christians" are falsely accused, and this is because they both expose the demons (which the poets and philosophers do not do even in their most speculative and vulgar moments). In short, both are accused because both speak the truth. Hence Justin does not agree that "Christians" are atheists, because they speak the truth, reveal the demons for what they are, and worship the only true god (6.1). As we shall see below, Marcion is in league with these very same demons, so any contrast between "Christian" truth and demonology ensures that Marcion cannot be counted as belonging to the "Christian" side. Justin admits that "Christians" can be considered atheists in the sense that they do not offer worship to that which the rulers call gods.[26] "Christians," those who truly follow Christ's doctrines, worship only the one true god and his Son in connection with the prophetic Spirit. This puts them in the same position towards the Roman traditions as the "Jews," who also are atheists, but tolerated ones, in that they refuse to offer sacrifice because they are bound by the one true god.[27] In their investigations, then, the rulers must judge carefully on a case-by-case basis who is "Christian" and who is atheist, rather than who is "Christian" and therefore atheist. In Justin's presentation, "Christians" cannot by definition be guilty of atheism, and are unlikely to be guilty of anything else owing to their good character before god. If someone fails the test of being a "Christian," as Justin defines it, and they are not a "Jew" or a pagan, then they are guilty of atheism.

Justin's next move, after establishing the possibility of hypocrisy, diversity, and failed candidates in all traditions as much as among "Christians," is to set out the major tenet of the "Christian" life, that which if absent guarantees the exponent is not "Christian" whatever they claim and virtually assures all that they are atheists: "And we confess that we are atheists, so far as gods of this sort are concerned, but not in regard to the most true God, the Father of righteousness and temperance and the other virtues, who is unalloyed with evil" (1 Apol. 6.1).[28] "Christians" then may appear atheists but once under

---

26. In this regard "Christians" resemble the manner in which the Romans considered "Jews," as we have already seen, to be atheistic, because of their strict monotheism and refusal to acknowledge the gods. That said, "Jews" were as Ste. Croix puts it, "licensed atheists" who were at least willing to pay lip service to the Roman cult via their own god. See Ste. Croix, "Persecuted?," 135. Of course "Christians" appearing to put their trust in a man rather than a god, as Trypho accuses Justin in Dial. 10.3, makes them appear purer and stranger atheists.
27. The mechanics of how "Christians" share in this "Jewish" inheritance is largely left to the Dialogue, where concepts such as the spiritual Israel and the circumcision of the heart are discussed at length. 1 Apology deals with the failure of the "Jews" to recognize Christ, but does not detail the specifics of how "Christians" inherit the god of Israel.

investigation this cannot be sustained because they worship an ancient and venerable god. He is not only pure and temperate, qualities which the rulers should appreciate and expect to see echoed in his followers, but as Justin will frequently mention he is also the maker and father of all and thus all are already in relationship to him, as he is the god of the universe. Justin calls God creator or maker, and once begetter of all, nine times in *1 Apology* in total. It is clear enough, as in the *Dialogue*, that he has the god of the "Jews" in mind, the one whom Marcion also calls the Creator but who he does not think is the god of "Christians" and the Father of Jesus Christ. That the creator god is the god of the "Jews" is taken as witnessed by the Old Testament. In 8.2 Justin says: "For we desire the eternal, pure life, and we seek after communion with God the Father and maker of all, and we are eager to confess we are Christians." Justin here is plainly and closely associating a pure life, communion with this god and life under Christ. These necessarily go together in the definition of "Christianity" as it is emerging. There can be no confusion then as to the identity of the god in question. Osborn has drawn attention to the Platonic phrase from Timaeus 28c as Justin was using Platonic doctrine against Marcion specifically.[29] Widdicombe has criticized this reading of the text but the fact remains, as Widdicombe agrees, that Justin's pattern of usage of the Father reflects a biblical picture and that he sees the creator and this father as one and the same entity; this in itself is a denial of the Marcionite position.[30]

Both parties believe this god is the maker of the universe and sustains it. They differ as to how, Marcion thinking his care fickle, weak, and not for all, while Justin thinks it universal care; but there

---

28. My translation. καὶ ὁμολογοῦμεν τῶμ τοιούτων νομιζομένων θεῶν ἄθεοι εἶναι, ἀλλ᾽ οὐχὶ τοῦ ἀληθεστάτου καὶ πατρὸς δικαιοσύνης καὶ σωφροσύνης καὶ τῶν ἄλλων ἀρετῶν ἀνεπιμίκτου τε κακίας θεοῦ.
29. Eric F. Osborn, *Justin Martyr* (Tübingen: Mohr Siebeck, 1973), 20.
30. Peter Widdicombe, "Irenaeus and the Knowledge of God as Father," in *Irenaeus: Life, Scripture, Legacy*, ed. Sara Parvis and Paul Foster (Minneapolis: Fortress, 2012), 117–18. Widdicombe raises some strong textual points; however, his note that Justin does not refer to god as Father in "any of the anti-Marcionite instances" unnecessarily restricts Justin's distinction from Marcion to *1 Apol.* 26 and 58, which fails to appreciate the function of those passages as part of a wider project. Furthermore, at 58.1 Justin speaks of "Christ his Son" (υἱὸν αὐτοῦ /) which strongly implies fatherhood.

can be no question that the same god is at issue. Marcion's other, transcendent god would not have created this world in the first place, but wants to rescue its citizens from the cruelty of the creator god who did make it. For Justin, however, the maker of the world offers good things; indeed Justin twice claims that god cares for this world.[31] This parallels *Dial.* 1.4, where Trypho poses the question as to whether or not all philosophy concerns god and his providence, and Justin replies that there are some who attempt to teach that god does not care for humanity. In *1 Apol.* 28.4, in the context of explaining how evil can exist and why god has not extinguished it, Justin asserts that to deny that god cares for humanity is to deny he exists or to suggest that he delights in evil, the latter of which being precisely the charge that Marcion brought against the god of the "Jews." Returning to *1 Apol.* 8.2, Justin has expressed that those who believe in this god are eager to be known as "Christians," which is to say: those who are "Christians" by definition believe in this god. All other candidates should be treated as something other than "Christian" from his perspective.

The reasons for Marcion's rejection of this god have been much debated and naturally centre on Marcion's understanding of materiality and the presence of evil in the world:

> That the God described in the Old Testament is the Creator of the world is his foremost feature, and it is at the same time the feature which more than anything else makes Marcion detest him. Besides Marcion's Biblicism, the only real premise of his theology is the fact that he had nothing but disgust and hatred for the world and for life itself, hatred so huge that he even refused to promote the continuation of mankind.... This irrational hatred apparently was the one unifying thought of all Marcionites throughout the centuries. As much as the scholars' wish to find an explanation for this hostility to the world is understandable, it is simply beyond explanation. It is not for us to look into a man's soul. What we can do is to comprehend Marcion's logic starting from this point of view, a logic we have already discovered above. Having realized that the world is a terrible place, Marcion needed to blame someone for this status, and there could be no doubt that it was the Creator's fault, a God who even admitted himself: "It is I who create evil."[32]

---

31. *1 Apol.* 28.4; 44.11.
32. Moll, *Arch-Heretic*, 59.

The last quote comes from Isaiah 45:7, and Tertullian attributed it special significance with regard to Marcion.[33] This very same god, the god of the Old Testament, is accepted by Justin as the only god and certainly the only god of those who are understood to be "Christians": not the author of evil but the source of righteousness and truth. Service to this one ancient god is the first marker of the "Christian" life and defense against atheism.

In stating that "Christians" follow this god, Justin takes steps to make it clear that this god exists in contrast to man-made deities: "But neither do we use a multitude of sacrifices and garlands of to honor those whom human beings formed and set up in temples and called gods, since we know that such things are dead and lifeless and do not possess the form of God" (*1 Apol.* 9.1). The principle related above, and in the rest of that chapter, about the unreality of idol worship is not simply inserted so as to castigate paganism but to set up the contrast between invented deities and the ineffable one true god of the "Christians." This is done as a way of reinforcing the non-negotiable tenet that the god of the "Jews," known to the Romans from ancient times, is the only god "Christians" worship. Anything man-made cannot be god; anything that takes a form other than that of the one true god is an idol, is atheism. This tenet of worship of the one true god for "Christians" is the foundation for Justin's exclusion of Marcion's theological and political threat.

"Christians" not only worship the one true god but do so rightly. Justin contrasts the sober worship of "Christians" with irrational and superstitious tendencies of the rulers (the rulers are said not to judge well but with senseless passion—οὐ κρίσει ἐξετάζετε ἀλλὰ ἀλόγῳ πάθει—at *1 Apol.* 5.1, whereas the "Christians" honour god with *reason and truth*—λόγῳ καὶ ἀληθείᾳ—at *1 Apol.* 6.2 and worship rationally —λόγου τιμῶμεν—at *1 Apol.* 13.3). "Christians" do not indulge in libations and other trappings of idol worship because this is "religious" superstition, nor do they follow the opinions of men. Rather they follow the teachings of the teacher who is the Son of god, creator of all,

---

33. Tertullian, *Marc.* 1.2.2, 7.

the teacher of the universal divine philosophy (this is sober, plain, and true *teaching* rather than superstition, δεισιδαιμόνων).

Later, in *1 Apol.* 58.3, Justin will explicitly contrast sobriety and purity with Marcionite doctrine and the irrationality of demon-influenced tradition. Christian virtue, too, has a political dimension. Vice, intemperance, and corruption go hand in hand with idol worship and the creation, as Justin sees it, of false deities (*1 Apol.* 9). "Christians" are not taken in by these but live in gratitude and holiness, which lead them away from human or evil concerns. They live in ways they have been taught, and they are reliable: modelling always temperance, justice and kindness. Justin is using the rulers' own fears and justifications against them. New superstitions were perceived as threats to the Roman order. Justin is repeating this back to them, ensuring that when Marcion is recognized as such his group will be under threat, but also turning it against them by suggesting that their gods are the new deities in contrast with the one true god. And yet the rulers see "Christians" as the political threat, believing they seek an alternative human kingdom, as that would stand as a threat to Rome:

> But you, when you heard that we were awaiting a kingdom, rashly supposed that we were talking about one that was human, though we were talking about the one that is with God. This is apparent also from our confessing, when we are examined by you, that we are Christians, though we know that the penalty appointed for a confessor is death. For if we were awaiting a human kingdom we would have denied, in order to avoid being killed, and we would have tried to escape detection, in order to obtain what we were waiting for. But since our hopes are not for this present time, killers have not been of concern to us. In any case, all are obliged to die. (*1 Apol.* 11.1–2)[34]

We must not forget the background here. As in Pliny's time, there had been a recent and bloody war involving the "Jews" which led to

---

34. Καὶ ὑμεῖς ἀκούσαντες βασιλείαν προσδοκῶντας ἡμᾶς ἀκρίτως ἀνθρώπινον λέγειν ἡμᾶς ὑπειλήφατε, ἡμῶν τὴν μετὰ θεοῦ λεγόντων, ὡς καὶ ἐκ τοῦ ἀνεταζομένους ὑφ' ὑμῶν ὁμολογεῖν εἶναι Χριστιανούς, γινώσκοντες τῷ ὁμολογοῦντι θάνατον τὴν ζημίαν κεῖσθαι, φαίνεται. εἰ γὰρ ἀνθρώπινον βασιλείαν προσεδοκῶμεν, κἂν ἠρνούμεθα ὅπως μὴ ἀναιρώμεθα καὶ λανθάνειν ἐπειρώμεθα ὅπως τῶν προσδοκωμένων τύχωμεν. ἀλλ' ἐπεὶ οὐκ εἰς τὸ νῦν τὰς ἐλπίδας ἔχομεν, ἀναιρούντων οὐ πεφροντίκαμεν τοῦ πάντως ἀποθανεῖν ὀφειλομένου.

a change of relations with the Romans. "Jews" were still tolerated but the patience of the Romans had been challenged. As Hardy suggested, the state religion would be more consciously asserted at this time and any new or questionable superstition could expect to be viewed with the highest suspicion. It is quite natural then that the rulers might think "Christians" an imminent threat. Indeed Janssen has pointed out that "Christian" eschatological beliefs about the end of empire and the eternal reign of peace bore a striking resemblance to the beliefs of the Gauls and other peoples the Romans considered a dangerous *superstitio* on account of sounding as if they wish to over throw Rome.[35] Justin not only denies their threat, but also the basis for it, by denying the threatening novelty of "Christians" in asserting that they are part of the ancient and venerable, or at least accepted, worship of the god of the "Jews."[36] That the Romans are a superstitious bunch in contrast to "Christians" is part of the argument, but the subtler and more incisive point is that if "Christians" are not this political threat on account of their worship of the god of the "Jews," then anybody who claims to be "Christian" but does not worship this god is not only a failed candidate for being a "Christian" but poses precisely the threat that the rulers consider "Christians" to pose. In short Marcionites are not "Christians" but a new superstition with a newly invented deity and with all the attendant risks.

Demonology

It is impossible to discuss atheism in *1 Apology* without discussing the demons which are the conceptual frame that drive the entire argument. The demons feature in the *Dialogue* and in *2 Apology*, but the argument of *1 Apology* relies on an understanding of their practices to vindicate "Christians" and expose imposters. By building the argument around the demons, Justin is able to expose Marcion as an anti-"Christian." in fact, as I will argue below, it may be possible that Justin

---

35. L. F. Janssen, "'Superstitio'" and the Persecution of the Christians," *VC* 33 (1979): 153–54.
36. Indeed Justin will demonstrate implicitly that "Christians" are even less of a threat than the volatile "Jews" in his discussion of the judgment of god and what it means for "Christians."

is presenting Marcion even more strongly as actually being one of the demons himself, rather than merely a failed candidate for a "Christian." This also suggests that the rulers are truly atheists themselves; this may be why they cannot clearly see the true non-atheists when they are presented with them. Demonology is central to the whole enterprise; without it the politics of atheism remains unclear and an insurmountable challenge to Justin.

Minns and Parvis provide a succinct summary of the role of the demons in *1 Apology* that I shall quote in full:

> Especially in view of Justin's claim to be a philosopher, the modern reader cannot fail to be struck by the frequency with which he makes reference to the "wicked demons" (δαίμονες φαῦλοι). Paradoxically, it is precisely because he is a philosopher that he does this. The demons are brought in to explain how it is that things go wrong in a world designed by a good and rational creator. They cause human beings to prefer what is irrational to what is rational, good people to be persecuted, and lifeless gods to be worshipped. They spread lies about Christian behavior, provoke Christians to heresy, and seek to deflect people from understanding the truth of the prophecies by inventing myths about the pagan gods that have superficial similarities to Christian doctrines and practices. They are the result of sexual union between women and angels to whom God assigned the providential care of human beings and "things beneath the firmament." The origin of this seems to be Jewish speculation based upon Gen 6:1-4. Justin's views about the demons might not be universally scorned by pagan contemporaries. According to Plutarch (*De Stoicorum Repugnantiis* 1051C = *SVF* II.1178), Chrysippus had also considered the possibility that it was because of wicked demons (δαιμονία φαῦλα) that evil befell good human beings.[37]

Even in this presentation there is obvious counter-Marcionite subcontent. Not only is there an apologetic function for evil in a world created by a good creator, but more incisively the idea that the myths created are superficial imitations of "Christian" doctrine and practice. This is precisely what Justin is trying to show of Marcion, contextualizing Marcion within the demonology that highlights his charlatanism. Though pagan contemporaries might not have despised such a framework, Minns and Parvis are correct in highlighting its

---

37. Minns and Parvis, *Philosopher*, 69.

Jewish origin.[38] Vinzent has spelled this out further with reference to Justin's claims in the *Dialogue*:

> Demons are objects of worship of false prophets in the ancient times [D7], are equated with "wicked men," Jews, who are said to persecute the Christians for not observing "fleshly circumcision, and the Sabbaths" [D18, *1 Apol.* 57]. Jews, the ones "of old time served" the demons [D30], and are accused to even have sacrificed their children "to demons" [D19, 73]. In addition, the "gods of the nations" are called "idols of demons" [D55, 73]. Thus, Justin's demonology is not part of pagan mythology, but is based on Jewish thinking, and yet turned against them. Jewish belief has become the foundation of pagan mythology. Especially magicians are held captive by demons [D78], and Christians will be misled and persecuted by them. In our passage on Marcion [*1 Apol.* 26], Justin does not hint at pagan mythology, but at Jewish demonology.[39]

So the demons prey upon and encourage the irrationality that prevents the rulers, and anyone else, from seeing the sober truth, setting up imitations of god, just as idol worship took the Israelites away from god (*1 Apol.* 57.1; 58.2).[40] Those who live without reason, who cannot assert their passionless and rational power, are taken under the power of the demons. It is sensible to see that "Christians" are not atheists (*1 Apol.* 13.1) because they are the ones who worship the god that is real, but this sense is only accessible to those not duped by the demons. To those under the spell of the demons this appears as illogical rather than sensible, and thus Justin issues a warning to the rulers to be on their guard against the demons. "Christians" flee from the influence of the demons by relying on Christ who is the very word of the unbegotten god (*1 Apol.* 14.2) rather than being the son of another god. The demons, and those under their influence, are tricksters:

---

38. For a detailed account of the "Jewish" origins of Justin's demonology, particularly his reliance on the *Book of Enoch*, see Reed, "Demonic Mimesis," 141–71.
39. Vinzent, *Dating of the Gospels*, 43.
40. Skarsaune has made a similar point very clearly: "Justin's demonology is not to be explained against the background of Greek philosophical demonology (the most relevant being that of the Platonic tradition). To Platonists, e.g. Xenocrates and Plutarch, the demons have a mainly positive function, filling the gap between god and man. They are never thought of as rivals or imitators of god, or leading men away from god. This idea is not Greek in origin, but originates from 'Jewish' and 'Christian' sources. Its main sources are to be found in the apocalyptic literature of Judaism (e.g. 1 Enoch and Test. XII Patr. and the LXX)" (Skarsaune, "Conversion," 65).

But in order that we might not appear to be tricking you we thought it worthwhile, before the demonstration, to make mention of a few of the teachings of Christ himself, and let it be for you, as powerful kings, to examine whether we have been taught and do ourselves teach these things truthfully. And his words are brief and concise, for he was not a sophist, but his speech was the Power of God.[41] (*1 Apol.* 14.4–5)

Below we will examine the specific teaching of Christ that Justin thereafter elaborates, noticing some strong contra-Marcionite presentation. Immediately, however, it is pertinent to note how Justin has framed the debate. The demons are charlatans leading people away from god by pale imitation, but "Christians" are truth-tellers because they know the true god and rely on his son's teaching. Furthermore the rulers will get to judge this for themselves, openly and honestly presented before them as a case rather than being manipulated unawares by demons and their servants.

Plausibility, or recognition, is an important part of this thesis. In order to show that the demons and their followers imitate and distort godly "Christian" doctrine, he needs to be able to show there is a plausible similarity between them. If Justin could not show this then Marcion's part in this as the present and most threatening imitator of "Christian" doctrine would be hollow and would fail to expose him as an anti-"Christian." Consequently, the political threat that Marcionism posed would remain dangerous, as Marcionites would still be confused with "Christians," making "Christianity" seem like a new and illegal superstition.

Justin then asks the rulers to reflect upon the claims "Christians" make: are they really any less plausible than the things the poets and philosophers of their own tradition say? Justin is quite subtle in his purposes here: "On the one hand, Justin highlights the affinities between pagans and 'Christians' in order to question why the latter are singled out for persecution. On the other hand, these commonalities lay the groundwork for his subsequent explanation of 'Christianity,'

---

41. ἵνα δὲ μὴ σοφίζεσθαι ὑμᾶς δόξωμεν, ὀλίγων τινῶν τῶν παρ' αὐτοῦ τοῦ Χριστοῦ διδαγμάτων ἐπιμνησθῆναι καλῶς ἔχειν πρὸ τῆς ἀποδείξεως ἡγησάμεθα, καὶ ὑμέτερον ἔστω ὡς δυνατῶν βασιλέων ἐξετάσαι εἰ ἀληθῶς ταῦτα δεδιδάγμεθα καὶ διδάσκομεν. βραχεῖς δὲ καὶ σύντομοι παρ' αὐτοῦ λόγοι γεγόνασιν, οὐ γὰρ σοφιστὴς ὑπῆρχεν, ἀλλὰ δύναμις θεοῦ ὁ λόγος αὐτοῦ ἦν.

fostering sympathy among non-'Christian' readers by suggesting that 'Christian' doctrines are not as bizarre as they may have been misled to believe."[42] So some of the things "Christians" say sound as if they are very similar to the beliefs of the poets and philosophers (*Dial.* 20; 21; 22 list many such similarities). Yet these might not seem so bizarre upon reflection, as they believe, but in many ways the things "Christians" say seem less incredible (ἀπιστότερον) than some of those of the poets and philosophers (*Dial.* 18; 19). Plato is particularly noted as similar to "Christian" ideas. Justin again points out the inconsistency of persecuting "Christians" if their doctrines are not, as it seems, abhorrent to Greco-Roman culture.

> ... and the teachings of writers, Empedocles and Pythagoras, Plato and Xenocrates, and those who say the same sort of things. Receive us, at least like these, since we believe in God not less, but rather more, than they do. ...[43] If therefore we say some things similarly to the poets and philosophers whom you respect, and some things that exceed them and are divine, and for which we alone offer proof, why are we unjustly hated more than all?[44] ... And when we say that the Logos, which is the first offspring of God, was born without sexual intercourse as Jesus Christ our teacher, and that after his crucifixion, death, and resurrection he went up to heaven, we introduce nothing stranger than those you call the sons of Zeus.[45] ... But if in fact we say that, in a special manner, and not in the manner of an ordinary birth, he was born from God, as we said before, as Logos of God, consider this the same as your calling Hermes the logos who announces the things that come from god.[46]

"Christian" teachings are not without resonance in the pagan world, then, and Justin offers other examples beyond these. Some of the things "Christians" say may even be strikingly similar to things said in

---

42. See Reed, "Demonic Mimesis," 164.
43. 1 *Apol.* 18.5–6. καὶ τὰ τῶν συγγραφέων διδάγματα, Ἐμπεδοκλέους καὶ Πυθαγόρου Πλάτωνός τε καὶ Ξενοκράτους καὶ τῶν τὰ αὐτὰ τούτοις εἰπόντων· οἷς κἂν ὁμοίως ἡμᾶς ἀποδέξασθε, οὐκ ἧττον ἐκείνων θεῷ πιστεύοντας ἀλλὰ μᾶλλον.
44. 1 *Apol.* 20.3. εἰ οὖν καὶ ὁμοίως τινὰ τοῖς παρ' ὑμῖν τιμωμένοις ποιηταῖς καὶ φιλοσόφοις λέγομεν ἔνια δὲ καὶ μειζόνως καὶ θείως καὶ μόνοι μετὰ ἀποδείμξεως, τί παρὰ πάντας ἀδίκως μισούμεθα.
45. 1 *Apol.* 21.1. Τῷ δὲ καὶ τὸν λόγων ὅ ἐστι πρῶτον γέννημα τοῦ θεοῦ ἄνευ ἐπιμιξίας φάσκειν ἡμᾶς γεγεννῆσθαι Ἰησοῦν Χριστὸν τὸν διδάσκαλον ἡμῶν καὶ τοῦτον σταυρωθέντα καὶ ἀποθανόντα καὶ ἀναστάντα ἀνεληλυθέναι εἰς τὸν οὐρανόν, οὐ παρὰ τοὺς παρ' ὑμῖν λεγομένους υἱοὺς τῷ Διῒ καινόν τι φέρομεν.
46. 1 *Apol.* 22.2. εἰ δὲ καὶ ἰδίως παρὰ τὴν κοινὴν γένεσιν γεγεννῆσθαι αὐτὸν ἐκ θεοῦ λέγομεν λόγον θεοῦ, ὡς προέφημεν, κοινὸν τοῦτο ἔστω ὑμῖν τοῖς τὸν Ἑρμῆν λόγον τῶν παρὰ θεοῦ ἀγγελτικὸν λέγουσιν.

pagan myths. A key part of Justin's argument is that the "Christian" beliefs are demonstrable by the prophets, in contrast to the pagan myths, but prior to this is the point that the pagan mythology is itself a work of the demons:

> But what was foretold by these evil demons, myth-making through the poets, spoke of as having happened. In the same way they brought about the allegation of infamous and impious deeds against us, of which there is neither witness nor demonstration, and of this we shall make proof (1 Apol. 23.3).... But those who hand down the myths invented by the poets supply no demonstration at all for the youths who learn them by heart. These things we demonstrate to have been said by the working of the evil demon for the deception and misdirection of the human race. For when they heard through the prophets that the future coming of Christ was proclaimed and that the impious among human beings were going to be punished by fire, they threw many so-called sons of Zeus into the discussion, considering they would be able to bring it about that human beings would consider the things said about Christ to be marvellous fable, and similar to things said by the poets. (1 Apol. 54.1–2)[47]

Greco-Roman culture, then, is built on a deception which Justin is exposing as Socrates did within this very tradition. This provokes the ire of the demons and causes a redoubling of their efforts, which we shall see below is the context into which Justin directly places Marcion. At 1 Apol. 21.4 he speaks of the myths about Zeus being written to *persuade to corruption* those who are being taught; those who get the privilege of education, and thus power, in the Greco-Roman world. The first time the demons are mentioned by Justin, they appear as apparitions, which was the standard term of the manifestations of the gods in Greco-Roman religion,[48] and is followed by the naming of the demons, unknowingly, by humanity as the gods of that very culture.[49] Minns and Parvis point out that "Tatian accused the Greeks

---

47. τὰ δὲ διὰ τούτων προειρημένα οἱ κακοὶ δαίμονες διὰ τῶν ποιητῶν ὡς γενόμενα εἶπον μυθοποιήσαντες· ὃν τρόπον καὶ τὰ καθ' ἡμῶν λεγόμενα δύσφημα καὶ ἀσεβῆ ἔργα ἐνήργησαν, ὧν οὐδεὶς μάρτυς οὐδὲ ἀπόδειξίς ἐστι, καὶ τούτου ἔλεγχον ποιησόμεθα.... Οἱ δὲ παραδιδόντες τὰ μυθοποιηθέντα ὑπὸ τῶν ποιητῶν οὐδεμίαν ἀπόδειξιν φέρουσι τοῖς ἐκμανθάνουσι νέοις, ἃ ἐπὶ ἀπάτῃ καὶ ἀπαγωγῇ τοῦ ἀνθρωπείου γένους εἰρῆσθαι ἀποδείκνυμεν κατ' ἐνέργειαν τῶν φαύλων δαιμόνων. ἀκούσαντες γὰρ διὰ τῶν προφητῶν κηρυσσόμενον παραγενησόμενον τὸν Χριστὸν καὶ κολασθησομένους διὰ πυρὸς τοὺς ἀσεβεῖς τῶν ἀνθρώπων, προεβάλλοντο πολλοὺς λεχθῆναι λεγομένους υἱοὺς τῷ Διΐ, νομίζοντες δυνήσεσθαι ἐνεργῆσαι τερατολογίαν ἡγήσασθαι τοὺς ἀνθρώπους τὰ περὶ τὸν Χριστὸν καὶ ὅμοια τοῖς ὑπὸ τῶν ποιητῶν λεχθεῖσι.
48. Minns and Parvis, *Philosopher*, 91n1.

of having established poetry 'only in order to describe battles and the amours of the gods and spiritual corruption.'"[50] This is again to say that the works of Greco-Roman culture are deceptive by nature. In Justin's view, things said by the poets are counter-versions of the prophetic witness which lack demonstration. These poetic and philosophical narratives constitute Greco-Roman culture itself, though as a parody of the revelation of god through the prophets and Christ. By this line of argument Justin hopes to persuade the rulers to throw off deception, not only so that they may follow Christ, but also so that they can clearly see what is truly of god, and what is not. This would enable them to see clearly the imitations of "Christian" doctrine and practice contemporaneous in Marcion and recognize in this a new superstition separate from "Christianity," which worships the same god as the "Jews" and does so legitimately. Below we will discuss the significant way in which Marcion is presented explicitly as a tool of the demons. At present it is sufficient to know that Justin considers this to be the case, and that this creates a juxtaposition between truth, from god, and deception; imitation and invention of new deities. The case-by-case judgment for which Justin is appealing, then, is between legitimate worship of the god of the "Jews," the one true god, and the illegitimate worship of an invented deity in the name of Christ by Marcionites.

Evidence of True Worship

The opposite of demonology is true worship of god. That is, the opposite of deception is truth, and the opposite of deception is reliability and trustworthiness. Just as the distinction Justin made of "Christians" seeking a heavenly kingdom rather than an alternative earthly kingdom" (*1 Apol.* 11) drew attention to the good citizenship of true "Christians," Justin draws out that it is their relationship to the true god that guarantees "Christians" are not a political threat to the Roman rulers. Implicitly anything that does not show itself to be the truth, to be of god, is potentially a new and suspect superstition

---

49. A slightly fuller account of this naming (culture making) is given at *2 Apol.* 4(5).5–6.
50. Minns and Parvis, *Philosopher*, 135n2.

whose intentions are unknown. Moreover, Justin makes this argument in terms loaded with particular contra-Marcionite distinctions.

"Christians" do not wish to live by lying because purity of life, that which god commands, is their goal. They do not fear death, but do fear losing their righteousness before god, so their trustworthiness is a logical corollary of their worship of god (the one true god who is judge of all). Right away it should be clear that Marcion fails as a candidate for a "Christian" on this score because he does not expect anything from this god at all, let alone worship him. Indeed in *1 Apol.* 8.2 Justin suggests that "Christians" have to convince god as much as man that they are "Christian": "For we who have been persuaded and believe that these things [eternal and pure lives] can be obtained by those who have persuaded God through their actions that they were his followers."[51] The means of persuading (πείσαντας) god is through one's actions, the shape of one's life. As the *Dialogue* made clear, doctrines and behavior are not separate enterprises. Philosophy for Justin *was* a way of life; the divine philosophy is the life lived in the way Jesus taught, just as a Platonist lived a life after the shape of Plato's doctrines or Stoic philosophical practitioners lived in certain ways as predicated by their doctrines. They stand, like Marcion, as an alternative position to his. The doctrines Marcionites follow do not issue from the ancient god of the "Jews" and cannot be said to aim at righteousness before him. The purity of life and trustworthiness of these doctrines cannot be said to be theirs either, and they ought to be seen as a new and suspect superstition.

Further evidence of such a distinction can be seen by the "Christian" motivation to serve god. This motivation does not come from a desire to conform to doctrines as such, but of seeking to do so because this is what god wills. Building on *1 Apol.* 8.2 and 10.1, Justin suggests that god only allows into his presence those who imitate his good attributes, and in *1 Apol.* 21.6 he says that "Christians" "have been taught that only those who live holy and virtuous lives *close* to god (ἐγγύς θεῷ)

---

51. οἱ πεπεισμένοι καὶ πιστεύοντες τυχεῖν τούτων δύνασθαι τοὺς τὸν θεὸν δι' ἔργων πείσαντας ὅτι αὐτῷ εἴποντο.

are made divine." Naturally, Platonists thought they would attain the ability to see god (as Justin testifies in *Dial.* 4.1) through their life lived according to Plato's doctrines, but it is not clear that they would come to know god (*Dial.* 10.4 θεὸν δὲ γινώσκουσιν, *Dial.* 141.2) or be *close to* him or made divine as Justin and Trypho understand what it is to be in relation to god. Justin believes god himself has clearly laid out the shape of the life he desires for humanity, and that it is his authority that determines their life, along with knowing the truth. "Christians" need to persuade god that they embody this truth rather than merely paying lip service to it, which brings them *close to him* and makes them divine.[52] That which has come from god is true; the doctrines of the "Christians," then, are the divine philosophy. Persuading god that one is "Christian" is intimately tied to following his ways (doctrine, teaching, shape of life) which are Christ's ways: this is precisely what Justin disputes with Marcion and what, if it can be demonstrated to the rulers, extinguishes Marcion's political threat by isolating his community from the trustworthy and venerable "Christian" community.

The desire to please god is why "Christians" should be thought trustworthy. Furthermore, they should not be thought flatterers, because their trustworthiness is not predicated on flattery or pretension, but on the nature of their relationship with god. Justin twice claims that his appeal should not be misunderstood as flattery (*1 Apol.* 2.3; 8.1):

> For it was not to flatter you with this document nor to win your favour by our speech that we appeared before you. It was rather to demand that you give judgement in accordance with careful and exacting reason, instead of being held fast by preconception or the desire to please superstitious men and, prompted by irrational impulse and long-entrenched ill-repute ... (*1 Apol.* 2.3)[53]

---

52. It is still somewhat early in the patristic period for confident notions of theosis, so it is more likely that Justin means perfection or immortality here than anything we can recognize as divinization in the later tradition.
53. Οὐ γὰρ κολακεύσοντες ὑμᾶς διὰ τῶνδε τῶν γραμμάτων, οὐδὲ πρὸς χάριν ὁμιλήσοντες, ἀλλ᾽ ἀπαιτήσοντες κατὰ τὸν ἀκριβῆ καὶ ἐξεταστικὸν λόγον τὴν κρίσιν ποιήσαθαι προσεληλύθειμεν, μὴ προλήψει μηδ᾽ ἀνθρωπαρεσκείᾳ τῇ δεισιδαιμόνων κατεχομένους, ἢ ἀλόγῳ ὁρμῇ καὶ χρονίᾳ προκατεσχηκυίᾳ.

The close association here of the irrational impulse with superstition alludes to the work of the demons and contrasts "Christian" claims with demonically inspired ones that, it seems, flatter to deceive, saying anything to take people further away from the truth. And this is exactly the claim that is made of Marcion in *1 Apol.* 58.2: that he leads away the irrational just as demons do. "Christian" claims are to be opposed to these because Justin gives his appeal for the rulers rather than for their own sakes. The advantage is to them to be corrected, and there is no advantage to the "Christian" in deception. God only allows the righteous into his presence, so "Christians" must be righteous. "But we do not wish to avoid death by telling lies, for we desire the eternal, pure life, and we seek after communion with God the Father and maker of all" (*1 Apol.* 8.2).[54] "Christians" have no desire to lie, and seek to give the truth only because the truth reveals god. If "Christians" lie they imperil themselves, so it is to be assumed that they tell the truth, having no excuse before god, just as the rulers do not if they follow superstition over the truth having heard it (*1 Apol.* 3.5). This is why no one can harm "Christians" by death or insult unless they can genuinely convict them of any wrong (*1 Apol.* 2.4). For "Christians" are innocent before god: to them that is all that matters. Conversely, anyone who cannot appeal to this god, who is the motivation and cause of their trustworthiness, appears by contrast a flatterer: such people are associated with irrationality which is a clue to their servility to the demons.

The contrast, then, between "Christians" and others with whom the rulers may come into contact is that "Christians" are good citizens, rational and not politically threatening. The necessary condition of this is worship of the true god, and those without this condition, of whom Marcion is the only one to propose an alternative, cannot be "Christians" nor can they enjoy the benefits and virtue Justin claims for "Christians." As Alasdair MacIntyre said when recounting the nature of virtues, "We cannot be genuinely courageous or truthful

---

54. ἀλλ' οὐ βουλόμεθα ζῆν ψευδολογοῦντες, τοῦ γὰρ αἰωνίου καὶ καθαροῦ βίου ἐπιθυμοῦντε τῆς μετὰ θεοῦ τοῦ πάντων πατρὸς καὶ δημιουργοῦ διαγωγῆς ἀντιποιούμεθα.

and be so only on occasion."[55] It is because of their relationship to god that "Christians" are always truthful. They are truthful without regard to consequences, even when this may cause death, because the immediate circumstances are secondary to the will and judgement of god. "Christians" have no reason to cheat or lie because they are held to a universal standard.[56] Marcionites, however, cannot be said to have a reason not to lie or cheat and so cannot be trusted. All others, which naturally includes Marcion, should not enjoy the presumption of innocence until proven guilty. "Christians" will never be found guilty on the basis of the truth of their doctrines, which come from god who will decide if they are genuinely observed or wrongfully imitated.

That the Judgment of a Loving God Acts as a Guarantee

The trustworthiness of "Christians" which is predicated on the condition of the worship of the one true god undermines any notion of a political threat they may pose by depicting them as rational and compulsive truth-tellers. There is a further stage to this: it presupposes that this god is a judge, and specifically a universal judge, which immediately brings to mind the contrast between Justin and Marcion on this very point:

> Yet we more than all people are your allies and fellow soldiers for peace, since we think that it is impossible for one who does evil, or is grasping, or a schemer, to escape God's notice and that each goes to eternal punishment or salvation just as his actions deserve. For if all people knew this no one would choose evil even for a little, knowing that he is going to be condemned to eternal fire, but he would restrain himself in every way and adorn himself with virtue so that he might obtain good things from God and be saved from the regions of punishment. For those who seek to escape notice when they do evil, because of the laws and punishments imposed by you, do evil knowing that it is possible to escape your notice because you are human beings. But if they were to learn and were to be persuaded that it is not possible for anything to escape notice, not only anything done, but even anything planned—they would be decent in

---

55. Alasdair MacIntyre, *After Virtue* (London: Duckworth, 1985), 198.
56. MacIntyre, *After Virtue*, 198.

every way at least because of the laws and punishments imposed, as you yourselves will agree. (*1 Apol.* 12.1-3)[57]

Nothing can escape the notice of god. The rulers may charge and try suspects, who of course do their best to conceal their actions. For god, however, there are no suspects by definition of who god is. He knows always the guilty from the innocent; no trials are required. Thus the provisional and limited nature of the rulers' authority and judicial power is brought into relief against god's.[58] Justin says that if all knew this there would be no wickedness. All who know that god sees them act rightly; those who do not, or who reject this, are thus the only possible candidates for criminal or other evil actions. Because Marcion rejects that the judgment of this god is pertinent to "Christians" and reserved only for the "Jews," he and his followers are made suspicious by not being able to claim this knowledge that naturally causes "Christians" to be trustworthy. The rulers cannot necessarily discern flatterers and liars who seek to evade them, but they cannot fool god. Any dishonest group could potentially conceal their true identity from the rulers, which in this context suggests the possible subtext that this is precisely what Marcionites do or could be understood to be doing, but their true identity cannot be hidden from god. There is a positive element to god's omniscience also. Punishment comes of evil, but a life lived well, according to god's ways and doctrines, results in blessings. This god is not simply an angry tyrant, but a god who gives good gifts.

In highlighting that god sees all things, Justin is attempting to inspire the rulers to be thorough in their investigations so that they are not deceived by the irrational and superstitious as they are presently

---

57. Ἀρωγοὶ δ' ὑμῖν καὶ σύμμαχοι πρὸς εἰρήνην ἐσμὲν πάντων μᾶλλον ἀνθρώπων, οἳ ταῦτα δοξάζομεν, ὡς λαθεῖν θεὸν κακοεργὸν ἢ πλεονέκτην ἢ ἐπίβουλον ἀδύνατον εἶναι καὶ ἕκαστον ἐπ' αἰωνίαν κόλασιν ἢ σωτηρίαν κατ' ἀξίαν τῶν πράξεων πορεύεσθαι. εἰ γὰρ οἱ πάντες ἄνθρωποι ταῦτα ἐγίνωσκον, οὐκ ἄν τις τὴν κακίαν πρὸς ὀλίγον ᾑρεῖτο, γινώσκων πορεύεσθαι ἐπ' αἰωνίαν διὰ πυρὸς καταδίκην, ἀλλ' ἐκ παντὸς τρόπου ἑαυτὸν συνεῖχε καὶ ἐκόσμει ἀρετῇ ὅπως τῶν παρὰ τοῦ θεοῦ τύχοι ἀγαθῶν καὶ τῶν κολαστηρίων ἀπηλλαγμένος εἴη. οἳ γὰρ διὰ τοὺς ὑφ' ὑμῶν κειμένους νόμους καὶ κολάσεις πειρῶνται λανθάνειν ἀδικοῦντες, ἀνθρώπους ὄντας λανθάνειν ὑμᾶς δυνατὸν ἐπιστάμενοι ἀδικοῦσιν, εἰ δ' ἔμαθον καὶ ἐπείσθησαν ἀδύνατον εἶναι λαθεῖν τι, οὐ μόνον πραττόμενον ἀλλὰ καὶ βουλευόμενον, κἂν διὰ τὰ ἐπικείμενα ἐκ παντὸς τρόπου κόσμιοι ἦσαν, ὡς καὶ ὑμεῖς συμφήσετε.
58. Costica Bradatan, "Faith and Persuasion in Berkeley's Alciphron," *HeyJ* 47 (2006): 558.

vulnerable to being. God sees the shape of the whole life, all actions and moods of the heart, which the rulers cannot possibly see—but they could at least look beyond the charge, the name, brought against the individual at that moment. They ought, as Justin has said in *1 Apol.* 4.1, to examine actions, and how they live, as well as whether they will make an offering to the Roman gods. Judgment along these lines is fair and ought to reveal that "Christians" are trustworthy. Whether Marcionites are shown to be untrustworthy, though Justin does not rule this out, is not necessarily the point. The main point is that there is a necessary condition of "Christian" life, the worship of the one true god, which guarantees that true "Christians" are trustworthy because they want to please god and gain his blessing rather than punishment. It is sufficient to realize that Marcionites do not share this necessary condition because Marcion thinks of god as a cruel judge. Furthermore, he rejects the pertinence of jurisdiction to "Christians" —as Marcion thought of himself being, which Justin is disputing. Thus, though some Marcionites may be trustworthy, they cannot necessarily be considered so as "Christians," or as part of an ancient and venerable tradition—they must be considered as belonging to a fundamentally novel superstition.

God as Merciful Judge

The function of this god, the true god, as judge is something Justin emphasises greatly. *1 Apol.* 6.1 also alludes to god's function as judge by calling him the "Father of Justice" (πατρὸς δικαιοσύνης). It is not simply that he is a judge, or a just judge, that Justin wants to emphasize, however. At *1 Apol.* 10.1 this god's justice is also combined with god's "lovingkindness" (φιλανθρωπίαν) to highlight that he is not a cruel judge—cruelty is not a feature of the judge if the justice is truthful. For the sake of clarity, it is worth recalling how Marcion thought of this god. As was discussed in chapter 1, Löhr and Moll have both argued it is unlikely that Marcion himself made a distinction between a just and a good god. Rather he thought of the god of the "Jews," the creator and maker of all, as a judge, which Justin concurs with, but as a particularly cruel, limited and petulant one. The contrast between "Christians" and Marcionites here then is not whether this god is a judge but whether "Christians" are subject to his judgment and what character this has. There is a disjunction between the two as to the character of this god: this is the route which leads to Marcion's dissent from him and Justin's following of him. As we saw above, this god, for Justin, not only cares for the world by sustaining it but cares for all who are in it universally and consistently, in contrast to Marcion's view of him as weak and fickle, and as opposed to his other god who seeks to rescue humanity from this god. Not only this, but Justin cannot conceive of this god as cruel judge but only as a merciful one who delays his judgment in order that more may have the chance to repent and come round to his path for human flourishing (*1 Apol.* 28.2).

Not only is this god just and merciful and caring, which Marcion would consider oxymoronic where the god of the "Jews" is concerned. He is also "*unalloyed with evil*" (*1 Apol.* 6.1)—ἀνεπιμίκτου τε κακίας (unmixed-up with evil)—which is a strikingly contra-Marcionite phrase, since Marcion believed that the god of the "Jews" was the author and explanation of evil in the world and rejects him because of it. Justin's phrase here makes most sense as a response to and denial of that very notion. Also at *1 Apol.* 6.1 (quoted above) Justin issues a declaration of what "Christians" reject and what they do not reject. The one true god, as detailed here, is the Father of all good things (all virtues), just and temperate as well as having nothing to do with evil. As Minns and Parvis note, justice and temperance are the two cardinal virtues for Justin, though the latter usually means chastity in Justin's usage.[59] Marcion could not think of a god who in the Old Testament required sacrifices and libations as temperate; but Justin of course has a different reading of the Old Testament, and does not understand the commands for such things as part of this god's universal decree but rather as limiting and as containment exercises for the sinfulness of the "Jews." Temperance (or chastity) is also one of the virtues that Justin cannot defend on behalf of pseudo-"Christians." In *1 Apol.* 26.7,

---

59. Minns and Parvis, *Philosopher*, 91n8.

directly after Marcion is mentioned, Justin says he does not know if the accusations of intemperance made of "Christians" are true of those just mentioned. This is because he cannot speak for them, as they are not part of his group (and he immediately announces in *1 Apol.* 26.8 his *Syntagma* where the rulers can learn more about Marcion and others if they wish).[60] This god is merciful also. The mercy of god is an agreed-upon topic in the *Dialogue*, where the question concerns who receives it rather than whether it exists, appearing ten times from both protagonists and from Scripture. Explicitly it is mentioned only once in *1 Apology*, but it carries a lot of weight because it comes from the words of Christ himself: "And: 'Be kind and merciful just as your Father is kind and merciful, and causes the sun to rise on the sinful and unjust and evil'" (*1 Apol.* 15.13).[61] Christ himself here has declared *his* Father, the god of the "Jews" for Justin, to be kind and merciful, which as we know is a stark contrast with the view of Marcion of this god and of the sonship of his Christ.

Though mercy itself is mentioned once directly in *1 Apology*, its corollary repentance appears more frequently. The god of the "Christians," the Father of all, creator and god of the "Jews," is a god who forgives and seeks a good relationship with his creatures. At *1 Apol.* 40.7 Justin asserts that god the Father calls everyone to repentance before the day of judgment. At *1 Apol.* 61 he says:

> All those who are persuaded and believe that these things which we teach and say are true, and who give an undertaking that they are able so to live, are taught to pray and ask with fasting for forgiveness from God for their past sins, and we pray and fast for them. Then they are led by us to where there is water and they are reborn in the kind of rebirth in which we ourselves were also reborn ... and [in order that they] should attain the forgiveness of sins, that is, those committed previously, there is pronounced, in water, over the one choosing to be reborn and who

---

60. This of course takes the *Syntagma* to be a text which includes further detail about Marcion beyond what is found in *1 Apology* and πρὸς Μαρκίωνα. It is possible, however, that γεγενημένων is intended to exclude Marcion from this text, which is written about past heresies, and consequently draw attention to him as the present subject and threat under discussion.
61. Bellinzoni demonstrates that in this instance Justin's debt is demonstrably to Luke 16:18 rather than Matt 5:32; 19:9 or Mark 10:12. See A. J. Bellinzoni, *The Sayings of Jesus in the Writings of Justin Martyr* (Leiden: Brill, 1967), 70.

repents of sins committed, the name of the Father of all and the Lord God. (1 Apol. 61.2, 3, 10)[62]

So this god accepts those who repent and ask to be forgiven. He allows them to be reborn as his children. God's mercy here is contrary to the theology of Marcion, who did not believe this god to be a forgiving god nor find a place for repentance in his theology, where the higher other god rescued those unfairly under the judgment and punishment of the creator god.[63] Justin's most striking rebuttal of this comes in the form of the very words of Christ: "For Christ did not call the just or the chaste to repentance, but the irreligious, and licentious, and unjust. And he spoke thus: 'I did not come to call the just but sinners to repentance, for the heavenly Father desires the repentance of the sinner rather than his punishment'" (1 Apol. 15.7, 8).[64] Here Christ himself defends the Father who desires repentance, which Marcion's god does not, and does not wish punishment upon people, contrary to the beliefs of Marcion. Furthermore Justin believes Christ has a part in the judging endeavor of this god. He is part of the very same god, the Father of all. 1 Apol. 8.4 states: "In similar fashion, Plato said that Rhadamanthus and Minis would punish the unrighteous who came into their presence. We say that the same thing will happen, but that it will be done by Christ and to their bodies; they will be punished everlastingly, not just for a period of a thousand years, as he said."[65]

---

62. ὅσοι ἂν πεισθῶσι καὶ πιστεύωσιν ἀληθῆ ταῦτα τὰ ὑφ' ἡμῶν διδασκόμενα καὶ λεγόμενα εἶναι, καὶ βιοῦν οὕτως δύνασθαι ὑπισχνῶνται, εὔχεσθαί τε καὶ αἰτεῖν νηστεύοντας παρὰ τοῦ θεοῦ τῶν προημαρτημένων ἄφεσιν διδάσκονται ἡμῶν συνευχομένων καὶ συννηστευόντων αὐτοῖς. ἔπειτα ἄγονται ὑφ' ἡμῶν ἔνθα ὕδωρ ἐστί, καὶ τρόπον ἀναγεννήσεως ὃν καὶ ἡμεῖς αὐτοὶ ἀνεγεννήθημεν ἀναγεννῶνται ... ἀφέσεώς τε ἁμαρτιῶν ὑπὲρ ὧν προημάρτομεν τύχωμεν, ἐν τῷ ὕδατι ἐπονομάζεται τῷ ἑλομένῳ ἀναγεννηθῆναι καὶ μετανοήσαντι ἐπὶ τοῖς ἡμαρτημένοις τὸ τοῦ πατρὸς τῶν ὅλων καὶ δεσπότου θεοῦ ὄνομα.
63. Marcion of course believed his own higher god was the merciful god. This god according to him loves freely: "without any obligation of kinship it [perfect goodness] is willingly and liberally expended upon strangers" (Sine ullo debito familiaritatis in extraneos voluntaria et libera effunditur; Tertullian, Marc. 1.23.3). In this regard Justin shares a somewhat similar view, at risk of being seen as influenced by Marcion, since he also believes that Christ freely brings mercy and acceptance to the gentiles. This is one of the reasons why maintaining the nationhood of Israel, as well as judgment and repentance, are so important to Justin in order to show that the mercy to which he appeals is the same that Trypho thinks of, not that which Marcion thinks of.
64. See Mat. 9:13; Mark 2:17; Luke 5:32; and Ezek 18:23; 33:11. Bellinzoni notes that here Justin offers a harmonized version of Jesus' saying. It is taken almost exclusively from Matt 9:13 and Mark 2:17 but includes εἰς μετάνοιαν (into repentance) from Luke 5:32. He also notes that numerous patristic writers given exactly the same rendering as Justin of this saying. Bellinzoni, Sayings, 76.
65. Πλάτων δ' ὁμοίως ἔφη 'Ραδάμανθυν καὶ Μίνω κολάσειν τοὺς ἀδίκους παρ' αὐτοὺς ἐλθόντας· ἡμεῖς δὲ

Justin's reporting of Plato's account from *Phaedrus* 249a may be loose but the point that matters here is that Christ is not separate or independent from the god who judges, the god of the "Jews." Christ is a part of the naming of unrighteousness and the unwillingness to let it stand. Marcion could not abide this by any means. His Christ and higher god have nothing to do with judgment, he only sweeps in to save people from the judgment of the creator god.

The notion that Jesus Christ could be part of the same judging endeavour as this god would be anathema to Marcion. Of course Marcion's image of the creator is for Justin highly unsatisfactory and blasphemous. For Justin, god is a god, the only true god, who is righteous and merciful. The identification of Christ as part of the judgment process, and therefore part of and a witness to his mercy also, is then a quite fundamental difference between Justin and Marcion. If "Christians" follow the teachings of Christ, which come from the one true god and are the truth, then Marcion differs fundamentally from this and his doctrines cannot be considered "Christian." Consequently they are not from the one true god; they must be atheist and thus the work of the demons and untrue. Justin has presented a "Christian" theology that may seem obvious and natural, but most significantly it is one to which Marcion could not possibly assent at a time when "Christians" are ill-defined. If this is what "Christianity" is, then Marcionism by virtue of rejecting it must be an atheistic superstition and thus not subject to the protection due to "Christians" who worship the ancient and venerable true god, and do so rightly, unlike the "Jews" who cause so much trouble for the Romans.

Different Teacher, Different Confession

Presenting Christ as in league with the creator and part of his judgment would have been completely unacceptable to Marcion and so this "Christianity" that Justin presents can have no room for Marcionites.

τὸ αὐτὸ πρᾶγμά φαμεν γενήσεσθαι, ἀλλ' ὑπὸ τοῦ Χριστοῦ καὶ τοῖς αὐτῶν σώμασι, αἰωνίαν κόλασιν κολασθησουμένων ἀλλ' οὐχὶ χιλιονταετῇ περίοδον, ὡς ἐκεῖνος ἔφη, μόνον.

This claim is essential to Justin; his entire political plea relies on "Christians" being legitimate worshippers of the one true god and thus trustworthy. But they are not "Jews," but are *called* "Christians." Justin must repeatedly emphasize then that their route to this god is through Christ and that Christ and his teaching is necessarily bound up with this god, which of course casts Marcion out of the "Christian" circle. The teaching of the "Christians" must be demonstrably that of the creator god, rather than a superstition invented by human ingenuity, and likely hidden agenda, coming not via the law but via Christ. Furthermore it must be made clear to the rulers that Justin's group is the only one that springs or originates from Christ, and that has a right to his name: any others who are commonly referred to by, or use, his name are in actual fact part of a completely different school or "religion."

In *1 Apol.* 8.2 Justin uses the phrase "persuaded and believe" (πεπεισμένοι καὶ πιστεύοντες). Minns and Parvis point out that this is a doublet of which Justin is quite fond. It occurs five times in *1 Apology*,[66] and emphasizes that the way of life Justin and others practice is not something they have created, not something novel, but is rather something passed on: passed on from a singular source, the Father himself through the prophets (of the Spirit) and Christ. The making of this point is not limited to this favored doublet, however, *1 Apol.* 10.1 repeats the above phrase as well as saying they have been taught (δεδιδάγμεθα). *1 Apol.* 10.2 continues the point by outlining what it is that "Christians" have been taught (δεδιδάγμεθα), and *1 Apol.* 10.4 claims that "Christians" are persuaded and led into faith by Christ (πείθει τε καὶ εἰς πίστιν). In *1 Apol.* 4.7 Justin speaks of people having learned or received from Christ. The word Justin uses (παραλαβόντες) is the same word Paul uses for the reception of teaching in 1 Corinthians 15:33 and Philippians 4:9 (*1 Apol.* 13.1 uses this as well as 10.1, 2 already noted).[67] Justin has in mind that his way of life, the "Christian" life, has been

---

66. See 10.1; 17.4; 18.2; 61.2.
67. Minns and Parvis, *Philosopher*, 89n1.

passed on to him; it is, so to speak, *received* wisdom. *1 Apol.* 12.9 and 6.2 both make a similar point:

> That all these things would happen, our teacher, I say, foretold. He is Jesus Christ, who is the Son and apostle of the Father of all and Lord God, and from him it is that we have the name Christians; This God we do venerate and worship, and also the Son who came from him and taught us these things, and the company of the other good angels who follow him and are like him, and also the prophetic Spirit. (*1 Apol.* 12.9; 6.2)[68]

In both of these passages[69] Justin is leaving no room at all for error as to the source of what he has learned. His way of life is received, but it is not received from any men of old or teachers *whose opinions are of no value* (*1 Apol.* 2.1). The provenance of his teaching is clear: there is one source, and one source alone, of this way of life, and that is from the Father via Christ, and the prophetic Spirit (the angel is admittedly confusing here but this is one of the names of Christ listed in *Dial.* 61.1; 127.4, and does not necessarily rank Christ among the angels, as Minns and Parvis note).[70]

The Son and the Spirit here are singled out for worship too and tied as closely as they can be to the Father, the most true god; there can therefore be no confusion for Justin as to whose Christ provides the teaching of the "Christians." We know that the prophetic Spirit, about whom Justin will surprisingly fill most of the pages of *1 Apology* despite its ostensible concern for pagan mythology, demonstrates for Justin the action and word of god throughout history from eternity and necessitates that Christ and all he speaks is bound up inseparably with the one true god (the god of Abraham and Isaac), the kind, merciful and caring judge. The prophetic Spirit, here tied to Christ and the Father, demonstrates the consistency of the work of this god now and forever. In *1 Apol.* 8.3 Justin outlines what "Christians" have learned from Christ, which they now pass on and teach themselves.[71] He is arguing for a

---

68. γενήσεσθαι ταῦτα πάντα προεῖπε, φημί, ὁ ἡμέτερος διδάσκαλος καὶ τοῦ πατρὸς πάντων καὶ δεσπότου θεοῦ υἱὸς καὶ ἀπόστολος ὢν Ἰησοῦς Χριστός, ἀφ' οὗ καὶ τὸ Χριστιανοὶ ἐπονομάζεσθαι ἐσχήκαμεν· ἀλλ' ἐκεῖνόν τε καὶ τὸν παρ' αὐτοῦ υἱὸν ἐλθόντα καὶ διδάξαντα ἡμᾶς ταῦτα, καὶ τὸν τῶν ἄλλων ἑπομένων καὶ ἐξομοιουμένων ἀγαθῶν ἀγγέλων στρατόν, πνεῦμά τε τὸ προφητικόν.
69. *1 Apol.* 12.10 also makes a point similar to these.
70. Minns and Parvis, *Philosopher*, 93n2.

single unbroken line of revelation, definitive truth, which is first and foremost a way of life rather than cosmic speculation, a sort of proto-apostolic succession that includes the prophets.

In denying the maker of all and Christ's sonship in him, Marcion designates himself as part of something else entirely. Justin says directly at *1 Apol.* 26.6: "All who spring from them are, as we said, called Christians, just as among the philosophers those who do not share the same doctrines do have the common name of philosophy predicated of them."[72] The point made here, that those grouped under a common category are very often not the same thing at all, has been previously made by Justin in *1 Apology* also. At *1 Apol.* 4.8 he says: "For, indeed, some assume the name and appearance of philosophers who behave in no way worthily of their profession. And you know that among the men of ancient times those who contradicted one another in their thought and teaching are nevertheless called by one name of philosopher."[73] The purpose here is not to legitimize the diversity of the category "Christian" but to draw attention to its inadequacy as a tool for judgment. This is very clearly the case in *1 Apol.* 7.2 where Justin is prepared to admit in general terms that it may be possible for some "Christians" to be found guilty of crimes and that this should legitimize summary judgments on the basis of the name alone.[74] The justification Justin gives for his general admission of the possibility of

---

71. Indeed at 14.4, immediately before the chapters that introduce Christ's own teaching, Justin says that it is for the rulers to decide if they, "Christians," indeed teach and perform these teachings truthfully. Clearly he is asking them, indirectly but clearly, to discern who is truly "Christian" by virtue of Christ's teaching and who are charlatans.
72. καὶ πάντες οἱ ἀπὸ τούτων ὁρμώμενοι, ὡς ἔφημεν, Χριστιανοὶ καλοῦνται, ὃν τρόπον καὶ οἱ κοινωνοῦντες τῶν αὐτῶν δογμάτων ἐν τοῖς φιλοσόφοις τὸ ἐπικατηγορούμενον ὄνομα τῆς φιλοσοφίας κοινὸν ἔχουσιν.
73. καὶ γάρ τοι φιλοσοφίας ὄνομα καὶ σχῆμα ἐπιγράφονταί τινες οἳ οὐδὲν ἄξιον τῆς ὑποσχέσεως πράττουσι. γινώσκετε δ' ὅτι καὶ οἱ τὰ ἐναντία δοξάσαντεσ καὶ δογματίσαντες τῶν παλαιῶν τῷ ἑνὶ ὀνόματι προσαγορεύονται φιλόσοφοι.
74. Minns and Parvis consider Justin's admonition of guilt on behalf of "Christians" inconsistent and potential evidence of corruption in the text. See Minns and Parvis, *Philosopher*, 93n3. Also, if Justin were to be read as saying "Christians" have been found guilty, he would not be undermining his appeal against the presumption of guilt in name because it should be read as implicit that he would be referring to pseudo-"Christians," as a genuine "Christian" would not be found guilty of any crime because they fear god more than human authority. This is supported by his immediate appeal that some are only *called* "Christians" in the same passage; these are those who have been found guilty but they are not "Christians." Admittedly the claim that conviction follows genuine investigation seems to run counter to Justin's claim, and perhaps corruption is in evidence here, but the sense that guilt is on the part of imposter "Christians" is plain.

guilt among "Christians" is that philosophers can teach whatever they please and contradict one another seemingly without risk to the title or category of philosophy.[75] The same may well be true of those who go under the title "Christian" but this is followed by an immediate appeal for the rules necessary to investigate beyond the name and see who really follows the doctrines of Christ. Clearly the guilty "Christians" could only be heretics for Justin here; true "Christians" fear and love the one true god too much to be criminal in any sense.

The category of "Christian" itself is highlighted by Justin, then, as somewhat useless to the rulers in making judgments. The only way to know who has been persuaded by and follows the Christ of the one true god is by attention to how they live and whether they keep his doctrines. It is apt, then, that he details the teaching of Christ directly in chapters fifteen, sixteen, and seventeen to distinguish "Christians" from Marcionites and relieve "Christians" of any political threat:

> But in order that we might not appear to be tricking you we thought it worthwhile, before the demonstration, to make mention of some few of the teachings of Christ himself, and let it be for you, as powerful kings, to examine whether we have been taught and do ourselves teach these things truthfully. And his words are brief and concise, for he was not a sophist, but his speech was the Power of God. (1 Apol. 14.4–5)[76]

The teaching of "Christians" is the doctrines of Christ. As chapter 2 showed, Justin specifies Christ most commonly as a teacher, something which was also true for Marcion,[77] in order to distinguish his doctrines from those who take the names of other men.[78] This final portion of 1 Apol. 14 introduces three chapters' worth of quotations from Jesus dedicated to detailing some of his directly given teaching in order to support his claims, previously made, for the trustworthiness and nonthreatening nature of "Christian" lives. This teaching is reliable

---

75. And we can tell that this is something of a ruse since precisely this point is used to deny the veracity of philosophy in the pagan world in the *Dialogue*.
76. See n. 41.
77. See Matthias Klinghardt, *Das älteste Evangelium und die Entstehung der kanonischen Evangelien* (2 vols.; Tübingen: Francke, 2015).
78. As we saw in the previous chapter, *Dial.* 35.6 details that those who claim Christ but follow the doctrines of other men are known by the names of these other men, by the founders of *their* specific, non-"Christian" by definition, doctrines.

because a) Christ is no sophist like those under the power of the demons trying to trick them; and b) to reiterate the point, what he says has the power of god (δύναμις θεοῦ ὁ λόγος αὐτοῦ ἦν), in that he is closely connected with god, the creator. In each of the three following chapters Christ demonstrates the ethical shape of "Christian" life which should be admirable and nonthreatening to the rulers, and ties it necessarily to the Father of all. The question put to the rulers here is to ascertain whether Justin's community, the "Christians," teaches these same things and thus can be considered "Christians," and implicitly that any group who can be seen not to be in line with these sayings must not be "Christians" and therefore not subject to the defense of "Christian" morality and civility made by Justin in the opening chapters.

Christ taught temperance (1 Apol. 15.1), tying him to a virtue of the Father found in 1 Apol. 6.1. Jesus speaks of his own mission in a way necessarily related to that of the Father. We have already noted that Jesus claimed (1 Apol. 15.8) that the Father prefers repentance of the sinner: following naturally from this is what he uses in countering Marcion's claim that the father of all is a merciless tyrant. Justin can be understood to be asserting the different provenance of his teaching from Christ from that of Marcion in a very subtle way, by utilizing the words of Christ speaking directly to establish his true teaching and his true followers. Again at 1 Apol. 16.2 Justin quotes Jesus's words from Matt 5:16,[79] saying: "Let your good works shine before people, so that seeing them they may honor your Father in heaven." Once more he has successfully demonstrated to the rulers that Christ's teaching is ethical and honorable (good works) and that it is naturally and essentially related to the Father of all, the one true god. The latter part of 1 Apol. 16 is particularly illuminating as to the provenance of genuine "Christian" teaching. There Justin quotes a collection of Jesus' sayings about who his followers are:

---

79. Bellinzoni notes that 1 Apol. 16.2 combines various parts of Matthew's gospel, but the portion quoted above parallels 1 Apol. 15.16 with a number of differences that are echoed by Clement, Eusebius, Tertullian, and Origen, suggesting a fixed post-Matthean textual variant. See Bellinzoni, *Sayings*, 94.

And when someone approached him and said, "Good teacher," he replied: "No one is good except God alone, who made all things." And whoever are not found living as he taught are not to be recognized as Christians, even if they speak the teachings of Christ with their tongues. For he said that not those who only speak but those who also do the works will be saved. For he said this: "Not everyone who says to me 'Lord, Lord,' will enter into the Kingdom of Heaven, but the one who does the will of my Father who is in Heaven. For he who hears me and does what I say hears the one who sent me. And many will say to me, 'Lord, Lord, did we not eat and drink and work miracles in your name?' and then I will say to them, 'Depart from me, workers of wickedness.' Then there will be weeping and gnashing of teeth, while the just shine like the sun, and the unjust are sent to the eternal fire. For many will come in my name outwardly clothed in the skins of sheep but inwardly being ravenous wolves; from their works you will know them. And every tree which does not produce fruit is cut down and thrown into the fire." And we request that those who do not live according to his teaching, and are only called Christians, be punished by you as well. (1 Apol. 16.7–14)[80]

This is a particularly clever and subtle set of quotations that reflect the synoptic tradition Justin presents here.[81] Justin gets so much into this. Jesus again emphasizes the connection between himself and the Father of all. Jesus says that only god is good, where Justin adds the words "maker of all things" (ὁ ποιήσας τὰ πάντα) to the synoptic quotation in order to make absolutely clear who this god is, that he is the god of Jesus, the one true god, and not just a god of the "Jews" but father of the entire creation.[82] Justin points out again that there exist those who appear to pay reverence to Christ but do not truly hold to what

---

80. καὶ προσελθόντες αὐτῷ τινος καὶ εἰπόντος 'Διδάσκαλε ἀγαθέ,' ἀπεκρίνατο λέγων· 'Οὐδεὶς ἀγαθὸς εἰ μὴ μόνος ὁ θεός, ὁ ποιήσας τὰ πάντα.' ἅ δ' ἂν μὴ εὑρίσκωνται βιοῦντες ὡς ἐδίδαξε γνωριζέσθωσαν μὴ ὄντες Χριστιανοὶ κἂν λέγωσιν διὰ γλώττης τὰ τοῦ Χριστοῦ διδάγματα· οὐ γὰρ τοὺς μόνον λέγοντας ἀλλὰ τοὺς καὶ τὰ ἔργα πράττοντας σωθήσεσθαι ἔφη. εἶπε γὰρ οὕτως· 'Οὐχὶ πᾶς ὁ λέγων μοι Κύριε κύριε εἰσελεύσεται εἰς τὴν βασιλείαν τῶν οὐρανῶν ἀλλ' ὁ ποιῶν τὸ θέλημα τοῦ πατρός μου τοῦ ἐν τοῖς οὐρανοῖς. ὃς γὰρ ἀκούει μου καὶ ποιεῖ ἃ λέγω ἀκούει τοῦ ἀποστείλαντός με. πολλοὶ δὲ ἐροῦσί μοι Κύριε κύριε οὐ τῷ σῷ ὀνόματι ἐφάγομεν καὶ ἐπίομεν καὶ δυνάμεις ἐποιήσαμεν; καὶ τότε ἐρῶ αὐτοῖς Ἀποχωρεῖτε ἀπ' ἐμοῦ, ἐργάται τῆς ἀνομίας. τότε κλαυθμὸς ἔσται καὶ βρυγμὸς τῶν ὀδόντων ὅταν οἱ μὲν δίκαιοι λάμψωσιν ὡς ὁ ἥλιος, οἱ δὲ ἄδικοι πέμπωνται εἰς τὸ αἰώνιον πῦρ. Πολλοὶ γὰρ ἥξουσιν ἐπὶ τῷ ὀνόματί μου ἔξωθεν μὲν ἐνδεδυμένοι δέρματα προβάτων, ἔσωθεν δὲ ὄντες λύκοι ἅρπαγες· ἐκ τῶν ἔργων αὐτῶν ἐπιγνώσεσθε αὐτούς. πᾶν δὲ δένδρον μὴ ποιοῦν καρπὸν ἐκκόπτεται καὶ εἰς πῦρ βάλλεται.' κολάζεσθαι δὲ τοὺς οὐκ ἀκολούθως τοῖς διδάγμασιν αὐτοῦ βιοῦντας λεγομένους δὲ μόνον Χριστιανοὺς καὶ ὑφ' ὑμῶν ἀξιοῦμεν.
81. 1 Apol. 16.7–14: Mat. 19:16; 10:17; Luke 18:18; Mark 10:18; Luke 18:19; Matt 19:17; 7:21; Luke 10:16; Matt 7:24; 7:22; Luke 13:26; Matt 7.23; Luke 13:27.
82. Minns and Parvis, *Philosopher*, 119n10.

Christ taught, those who do not live according to his teaching, and are only called "Christians" (λεγομένους δὲ μόνον Χριστιανούς), those who appear to follow his doctrines but do not, whose teaching does not come from Christ in the final analysis and who therefore are not trustworthy and are guilty of being imposters. Of course Justin does not rule out that such as these might speak some of the genuine teachings of Christ, even if they speak the teachings of Christ with their tongues. He is outlining these people as imposters; such imposters could not be plausible, judged as they are by the confusion which abounds as to who and what is "Christian," if they did not successfully imitate some of the form of the real thing, as Justin understood it.

Somewhat like the demons hearing what was said of Christ by the prophets (1 Apol. 54.4) and imitating them without understanding, so these imposters may speak some of Christ's words but show by their actions that they do not understand them, that they are not "Christians." Any who appear to be followers of Christ but whose actions betray them are, in the words of Jesus, workers of wickedness. Following this, Justin has Jesus introduce the imposters in his name as not only false candidates for "Christians" but as scheming and dangerous tricksters. Those who are not truly "Christian" are therefore wicked and duplicitous. Here in particular we find an obvious allusion to Marcion, who is described as a wolf and his followers like lambs led away from the truth: "Many, believing him [Marcion] as if he alone knew the truth, laugh at us, though they have no demonstration for the things they say, but, being irrational, they are snatched away, like lambs by a wolf, and become fodder for godless doctrines and demons" (1 Apol. 58.2).[83] The demons prey on the irrational; through Marcion, many have come under their spell. He has come forward in the name of Christ (those who spring from him are called "Christians"; 1 Apol. 26.6) and has snatched sheep as a wolf does, just as Justin records Christ warning. Justin then requests that those who do not live according to the teachings of Christ but are merely called "Christians," just as those

---

83. ᾧ πολλοὶ πεισθέντες ὡς μόνῳ τἀληθῆ ἐπισταμένῳ ἡμῶν καταγελῶσιν, ἀπόδειξιν μηδεμίαν περὶ ὧν λέγουσιν ἔχοντες, ἀλλὰ ἀλόγως ὡς ὑπὸ λύκου ἄρνες συνηρπασμίαν, βορὰ τῶν ἀθέων δογμάτων καὶ δαιμόνων γίνονται.

who spring from Marcion are called "Christians," be punished, that is, that they be singled out for punishment as guilty non-"Christians." At *1 Apol.* 3.1 and 7.4 Justin had requested proper judgment of actions by the rulers where criminality can be exposed for what it is rather than confused with "Christianity": "so that a person who is found guilty might be punished as a wrongdoer, rather than as a Christian; while if anyone is seen to be guiltless he might be acquitted as a Christian who does no wrong" (*1 Apol.* 7.4). Justin is therefore requesting that these people, who are seemingly Marcionites by the allusion to sheep and wolves repeated at *1 Apol.* 58.2, where Marcion is the main topic, be punished as wicked deceivers attempting to mislead the rulers in contrast to the reliable "Christians" who follow Christ and his universal Father of all whom they seek to please.

Another Confession

Apart from the Marcionite denial of the source of the teaching of Christ, Justin has another way of isolating Marcionites from the true Christ. This is that, though they may confess Christ by the standards of their own belief, this cannot be counted as a genuine "Christian" confession but as something which means something very different in their minds. At *1 Apol.* 26.5 Justin says that Marcion has made those he has persuaded to "deny God the Maker of this universe and confess some other who is greater, beyond him."[84] At face value it seems that Justin is simply declaring that Marcion believes in a different god than that of "Christians," but the language used here is more suggestive than that. Naturally Justin does not say Marcion has persuaded these many people to deny Christ, since Marcion believes in Christ. Rather he has persuaded them to deny the maker of all, who for Justin is the Father of Christ and for Marcion the lower creator god. This denial for Justin is tantamount to denying Christ because in denying the Father Marcion is denying that Christ is from this god. Crucially, this means that at trial the difference between "Christians" and Marcionites would

---

84. καὶ ἀρνεῖσθαι τὸν ποιητὴν τοῦδε τοῦ παντὸς θεόν, ἄλλον δέ τινα, ὡς ὄντα μείζονα, παρὰ τοῦτον ὁμολογεῖν πεποίηκεν.

be far from obvious if the only test was to deny Christ, since both claim Christ. The essential point is that though Marcionites are called "Christians" they worship another Christ, the son of another god, which Justin declares explicitly at *1 Apol.* 58.1.

Minns and Parvis have pointed out that Justin uses highly charged judicial language of *confession* (ὁμολογία) and *denying* (ἀρνέομαι), where "denier" seems to have become something of a technical term to describe an apostate.[85] *1 Apol.* 26.5 is again pertinent: "... and he has made them [those he has persuaded] deny God the maker of this universe and confess some other who is greater, beyond him."[86] This brings to mind Justin's use of such judicial language when discussing the rulers' practice of convicting *confessors* of Christ and freeing *deniers* without investigation, at *1 Apol.* 4.6.[87] There Justin asks that all should be investigated for how they behave, this being indicative of what they really believe, rather than what they claim. More than the name should be taken into account; both Pliny, in his letter to Trajan,[88] and Urbicus in *2 Apol.* 2 failed to do this. Justin's use of the language of *confessing* and *denying* (which is in the process of becoming technical "religious" language beyond its primary judicial origin) is designed here to evoke just this association and to demonstrate that Marcionites, by denying the Father, deny that they are "Christians" and confess something else, another son. Even then, if they confess Christ at trial before the rulers, they should be counted among those who are freed for denying him, though they should be punished as liars and atheists who follow the demons perpetuating the deception that rules over the whole pagan world. At *1 Apol.* 4.6 Justin requested careful judicial investigation into the lives of defendants because what people say is not sufficient testimony to secure a reliable judgment on what they believe. In short, actions speak louder than words.

That Marcionites did not deny Christ at trial is attested by Eusebius

---

85. Minns and Parvis, *Philosopher*, 87n3.
86. See n. 83.
87. Minns and Parvis, *Philosopher*, 151n5.
88. Of course we know Pliny did at least try to investigate what "Christians" believed but was unable to ascertain a consistent answer so gave up and asked Trajan, who did not seem terribly interested in what they believed so long as they ceased to be "Christians" or were punished for not recanting.

citing an anonymous writer: "For some of the other heresies have innumerable martyrs, but I do not suppose that we shall accept them for that reason, nor admit that they have the truth. In the first place, indeed, the so-called Marcianists of the heresy of Marcion say that they have innumerable martyrs to Christ...."[89] Of course, this is later than the current period; secondly, the claim for many martyrs is one made by Marcionites themselves rather than given as a direct external report. Still the author does not seem to doubt it; rather, he argues that martyrdom is no security for the truth. Had he wanted to deny it presumably he would have done so. Yet he goes on to say: "but nevertheless Christ himself they do not confess according to truth."[90] That is, there may well be many martyrs for the Marcionite heresy but they do not *confess* Christ in spirit and truth, they do not mean it the way "Christians" do. So Marcionites may well confess Christ before the rulers and be killed for it, but Justin's argument has been trying to say what the anonymous writer said, that they do not actually confess the same thing as "Christians." They do not confess the same Christ. Eusebius also records that three Christians were martyred in Caesarea under the persecution of Valerian for their conspicuous confession of Christ, and that a woman in the same city was martyred but that she was a Marcionite.[91] He actually does not say she was martyred but that she endured to the end, so as to deny her the title of martyr. He is clearly making a similar distinction between "Christians" and Marcionites while not denying that Marcionites have been killed for their beliefs, or (more likely and accurately) taken for "Christians" and executed accordingly.

Indeed, that Marcionites are killed as "Christians," but should not be, seems to be precisely the force of what Justin is trying to say in *1 Apol.* 26.7. There he says: "But that they are not persecuted nor killed by you, at least because of their doctrines, we are sure."[92] This comes after he

---

89. Eusebius, *Hist. eccl.* 5.16.21: καὶ γὰρ τῶν ἄλλων αἱρέσεών τινες πλείστους ὅσους ἔχουσι μάρτυρας, καὶ οὐ παρὰ τοῦτο δήπου συγκαταθησόμεθα, οὐδὲ ἀλήθειαν ἔχειν αὐτοὺς ὁμολογήσομεν. καὶ πρῶτοί γε οἱ ἀπὸ τῆς Μαρκίωνος αἱρέσεως Μαρκιανισταὶ καλούμενοι πλείστους ὅσους ἔχειν Χριστοῦ μάρτυρας λέγουσιν....
90. Eusebius, *Hist. eccl.* 5.16.21: ἀλλὰ τόν γε Χριστὸν αὐτὸν κατ' ἀλήθειαν οὐχ ὁμολογοῦσιν.
91. Eusebius, *Hist. eccl.* 7.12.
92. ἀλλ' ὅτι μὴ διώκονται μηδὲ φονεύονται ὑφ' ὑμῶν—κἂν διὰ τὰ δόγματα—ἐπιστάμεθα.

says that he does not know if they are guilty of the infamous deeds that he himself has denied "Christians" perform, another clue that they ought to be counted as a separate group, because Justin does not feel it appropriate to allow his defense to apply to them also. Clearly the rulers do not know either, since they punish without the proper investigation for which Justin has been appealing. The fact that these "Christians" are not killed by the rulers *on account of their doctrines* is fundamental to Justin's case for theological and political distinction from them. Yet Minns and Parvis find this point puzzling in quite a vital and illuminating way. They believe Justin risks undermining his case with this point:

> This is a strange argument if part of an apology intended for the emperors. Justin seems to be prepared to admit that the heretics are killed, but not for their doctrines. The implication would have to be that the authorities discriminated amongst persons accused of being Christians, and prosecuted some for reasons other than their beliefs, perhaps because of the suspicion of *flagitia*. But it is a large part of his own case that orthodox Christians are unjustly suspected of *flagitia*, and therefore, presumably, it could be claimed that they are not persecuted for their beliefs either.[93]

Minns and Parvis go on to suggest that this passage may therefore be explained as a later addition to *1 Apology* by established orthodox Christians looking for resources against heretics. This does not seem necessary, however. In fact it seems that Minns and Parvis have read the passage correctly but come to the wrong conclusion. It is indeed Justin's implication that the rulers are prosecuting "Christians" for some reason other than their doctrines. This has been his argument all along: that they do not examine their way of life, which comes from the teaching of Christ. For Justin the doctrine, the philosophy, and the life lived ought to be inseparable. This being the case any conviction of "Christians" that assumes *flagitia* of them does not convict according to their doctrines but according to the *valueless and irrational opinions of superstitious men,* which Justin is arguing they are not. Exactly the same is true of Marcionites who are punished according to the name

---

93. Minns and Parvis, *Philosopher*, 153n1.

of Christ rather than that of Marcion; this is the point which Justin is trying to address. The rulers are not discriminating among persons being accused of being "Christians" and prosecuting for some other reason, as Minns and Parvis suggest. Rather they are not discriminating in any way; they do not pay attention to doctrines but simply note the name and persecute all indiscriminately: this is what Justin's whole appeal has been trying to change. This claim is absolutely central, then, because not killing Marcionites on account of their doctrines means they are classed alongside Justin as "Christians," when, in his view, they ought not to be because the provenance of their teaching is different. It comes from Marcion, not from the Christ of the one true god: this the rulers would appreciate if they practiced genuine case-by-case investigation instead of summary convictions simply on the basis of the misapplied title "Christian." If this were understood by the rulers, Marcionites would be punished as the atheists and political dissidents that they are, and "Christians" would be tolerated as the loyal, traditional, and truthful people that they are before the one true god.

In summary, by presenting Christ as bound up, and necessarily so, with the creator as a teacher of his doctrines, Justin shifts the ground available to Marcion to claim Christ for his god. According to Justin, Marcionites have not only another god but another son, one who is not the "Jewish" Messiah and who preaches different doctrines than those of the creator. "Christians" are those who are persuaded by and follow the doctrines of Christ, which are the doctrines of the one true god, who is the ancient and venerable god of the "Jews," who always was and is in fact universal. This naturally isolates Marcionites as a politically novel sect with an invented deity and a teacher who preaches new doctrines; this in turn should of course make Marcionism appear as an illegal superstition to the Romans. "Christians" are martyred for confessing Christ; they are prepared to die for his doctrines because, as we have seen, their relationship with god, which does not cease at death, is guaranteed by them. Marcionites might too be prepared to die for what they believe (indeed there are reports of

Marcionite martyrs), but as far Justin is concerned, they are not and should not be considered "Christian" martyrs. They may well confess Christ's name at trial, but the name means something very different to them because they do not believe he is the son of the one true god; he is a different Christ than the "Jewish" Messiah. So though they die for what they believe, that which they believe is something other than "Christian," and they die in vain rather than as "Christian" martyrs. This knowledge should reveal to the rulers that they are far more dangerous. "Christians" seek no earthly kingdom and always tell the truth because of their love and fear of god. Marcionites, however, have an invented god and so are deceivers who do not love or fear god and thus have no relevant check on their behavio;, they have no incentive not to lie in their theology. For Justin any guilty "Christian" is in fact no "Christian" at all. "Christians" are trustworthy because of their relationship with god: anyone who claims to be "Christian" but does not worship god threatens the case Justin is making in order to end persecution. The particularity of the doctrines, the content of the truth, this is what matters. It simply is not negotiable. The only teaching and confession that can absolve "Christians" of being atheists or illegal converts is the teaching of Christ from the one true ancient and universal god. Marcion must then be exposed as alien to this because he and his followers worship a different and invented new god while still calling on the name of Christ.

Marcion: Tool of the Demons or One of the Demons?

The strongest manner in which Justin excludes Marcionites from the fold of the politically non-threatening "Christians" is where he does so explicitly, by twice presenting Marcion as a cog in the demonic machine. Presenting him thus, as a tool of the demons, is intended to emphasize strongly that this group is not "Christian." We have seen that this is not the sole allusion to Marcionism in *1 Apology*, but it is the high point where the argument for differentiation cannot be mistaken.

Justin says, at *1 Apol.* 26 and 58, that the demons have been *putting forward* certain men (προεβάλλοντο, produce, bring forward, present) who include Simon, Menander, and Marcion. All three of these represent heresies (if *1 Apol.* 26.8 can be taken as subsuming all), though it is well established that care with that term is need when dealing with second-century material. Are all three the same? What kind of company is Justin being described as keeping? Simon and Menander are described as Samaritans, a people and place Justin knew intimately, and sorcerers. Being sorcerers, they fit one of the marks of the action of the demons which Justin relates in *2 Apol.* 5.4. There the demons, who are the progeny of fallen angels, mislead humanity by magical changes,[94] fear of punishment, and the teaching of improper worship, libations, and sacrifices.[95] All of these are tactics are designed to deceive. Beyond this the demons were taken by humanity to be gods, the pagan gods of the nations, which Justin denies at *1 Apol.* 5.4 by saying that "Christians" not only deny that these gods are gods at all, but assert that they are unholy demons.

While Simon was taken to be a god by his followers, and according to Justin by the Senate and Roman people, Marcion is not described as a magician or one who takes divinity upon himself. So is he out of place here? Difference need not be tantamount to inequality. Minns and Parvis, also puzzled by Marcion's bedfellows here, have recently argued that Marcion seems out of place in this passage because he does not seem to fit Justin's purposes of exposing those who have pretended to be gods. This is said of Simon and can be presumed of Menander, who was his disciple, but we do not know this of Marcion. Minns and Parvis believe that material on Marcion may have migrated into its present position from the *Syntagma*, this triggered by Justin's mention of the previous "heretics."[96] This is possible but I don't think it is necessary. Sebastian Moll has a simpler and more compelling explanation. Moll points out that Harnack found this juxtaposition

---

94. The manuscript attests writings, but here we follow Minns and Parvis and Thrilby in interpreting a reference to demons being able to take different shapes, in line with *1 Apol.* 14.1, which refers to the demons' power to deceive humanity in different guises.
95. Reed notes echoes of 1 Enoch in regard to these concepts in Justin's text. See Reed, "Demonic Mimesis," 149.
96. Minns and Parvis, *Philosopher*, 149n9.

most distasteful and that this, given Harnack's prejudices, is illuminating for Justin's purposes:

> "The juxtaposition of Marcion with the founders of sects who posed as gods is completely inappropriate and particularly spiteful, but it does show how dangerous Marcion appeared to Justin ... and in what great esteem Marcion was held in his church." We can leave it open as to whether his grouping of these people is indeed malicious and unfounded; in Justin's view it certainly was not. Nevertheless, it seems confusing at first that he would mention his contemporary Marcion, with his apparently large number of followers, in connection with other heretics who must have been dead for decades.... Therefore Harnack's statement gives us a good hint at the reasons for Justin's choice. He is not after a particular heretical system or movement; he is after the "big names" in heresy, after those men who are worshipped by their followers and who claim alone to know the truth.[97]

For Moll, then, Marcion appears not accidently in a general stream of "heretics," but rather deliberately in a stream of specific "heretics"; the reader is given a clue as to how to understand Marcion. That is, he is contextualized by the company with whom he is presented. Each of those presented were, in Justin's view at least, people who attracted acclaim to themselves. They are after all for Justin alternative *founders* (ἀρχηγέτης) to Christ, thereby denigrating the uniqueness and universality of Christ and the divine "Christian" philosophy. This is, chiefly, what Marcion has in common with Simon and Menander, whether he called himself divine or not, and whether or not he performed magical deeds.

Secondly, his commonality with Simon and Menander is a direct result of his collusion with the demons rather than only a coincidence of drawing attention to themselves. *1 Apol.* 58.1 says that the demons put Marcion forward much in the same way as they inspire the misdirection of the worship of god in idols named after them.[98] Justin says of Menander that he was worked on by the demons, which was

---

97. Moll, "Justin and the Pontic Wolf," 148.
98. See *1 Apol.* 9.1. Justin does not, strictly speaking, say here that the demons created the idols, but rather that they are the inspiration for them. However, given that we know that demons actively imitate and deceive in other ways for Justin, it seems that we should take it as implicit that they are not merely passive muses in this operation as far as Justin is concerned.

usually understood to imply demonic possession. 26.5, however, says that Marcion works *with the help* or assistance of the demons, which strongly links Marcion with the work of the demons, perhaps even as a willing participant. Caution is advisable here, however, since, as Minns and Parvis note, συλλαμβάνω is not used by Justin in this sense elsewhere, and his speech at *1 Apol.* 44.12; 54.1; *2 Apol.* 6(7).3, where he speaks of ἐνέργειαν of the demons, more readily suggests being caught up or ensnared in the demons' activity.[99] Whichever sense is preferred, Marcion is being presented as a dangerous individual on account of his association with the demons, whether it be as ally or as instrument. In this regard at least, he is in the company of Simon and Menander. Indeed, Justin's point in 57.1 (following further discussion of Simon and Menander), that the demons were still not able to persuade all by their schemes but only able to effect the persecution of "Christians," is followed immediately with the reintroduction of Marcion: this reads as a new and redoubled effort by the demons in the present time to dissuade humanity from the worship of the one true god using him as a tool. This is all the more pertinent if it is accepted that the *Syntagma* seems in the text to refer to past heresies rather than the present Marcionite one, which is their successor and the present danger. This being the case, Marcion is not out of place alongside Simon and Menander, but rather yet another attempt by the demons to deceive humanity.

In the knowledge of this the rulers should see matters clearly. If Marcion is under the power of, or collaborating with, the demons, the same demons who have been attempting to lead humanity away from the truth and placate them with false gods all along, then Marcion and his followers must be atheists because they are part of the enterprise designed to conceal the one true universal god that Justin has been presenting. At the very least the rulers ought to see that such people cannot be "Christian" if they are under the power of those dedicated to concealing the true god of the "Christians." This should lead them to recognize Marcionites as not only as unreliable "Christian" witnesses

---

99. Minns and Parvis, *Philosopher*, 151n2.

or benignly mistitled "Christians." Not only are they not "Christians," which is sufficient to cast them as a novel superstitious threat, but they are positively anti-"Christian," and by extension anti-truth, by virtue of their association with and possession by the demons. As Rebecca Lyman said when discussing the principle of multiplicity proving falsity: "Just as the pagan sacrifices were demonic counterfeits of the sacraments, so hairesis was the demonic counterfeit of the truth, characterized by innovation, human ingenuity, and multiplicity."[100] They are dangerous as a new thing in their own right, but they ought to be even more dangerous and hated because they are active and deliberate deceivers who must have a hidden and pernicious agenda.[101] Justin's task has been to outline who and what true "Christians" are and to isolate Marcionites from this in order to secure the legal protections he is arguing for "Christians." Presenting Marcion and his followers as demoniacs is the high point of this enterprise, so important he does it twice for emphasis, which ought to leave the rulers in no doubt as to their independent and untrustworthy status.

Conclusion

Marcion is more than a fringe figure in Justin's texts. The above analysis has shown that his influence exceeds the two references to him in *1 Apology* and to Marcionites in the *Dialogue*. These are only the surface; the obvious clues to the threat he posed to Justin's "Christian" community are revealed by deeper analysis of the text, which gives further evidence of his specter in Justin's project.

In chapter 1 it was demonstrated that Justin wrote in a period when what it meant to be a "Christian" was far from decided internally, and when it also was not immediately obvious to the Romans who

---

100. Lyman, "The Politics of Passing," 46.
101. It is interesting to note, as le Boulluec does, that Justin does not hold philosophy responsible for the creation of "heretical" schools, onto which they map analogically, but strictly demonology. In this regard Justin differs from the tradition that follows him, from Tatian and Tertullian (le Boulluec, *La Notion d'hérésie*, 91). Justin maintains a positive view of philosophy and insists that the true philosophy is that of Christ. This is because he never departs from the idea that an evidential model for philosophy is the gold standard. Everything must be demonstrable or else it is the opinion of men.

or what "Christians" were. It was shown that the extent to which "Christians" were a separate community from "Jews" is a complicated question with an unclear answer. The answer depends on how one defines "Jews," which recent scholarship has demonstrated is just as complicated as defining "Christians" in this period. Justin's writing in the *Dialogue* firmly situates "Christians" within a "Jewish" milieu, but separated from it. His desire is to demonstrate the critical nature of their rootedness within this tradition. Aside from the story he tells about the persecution at the hands of Trypho's teachers, the obvious unstated threat is that of Marcion, who actively wanted to remove "Christians" from the "Jewish" community and deny that their god and prophets had any relevance for "Christians."

Chapter 1 then went on to demonstrate that Justin's chief task in all of his work is to clarify "what" a "Christian" is and to do so in a way that secures their heritage as part of "Israel." In executing this task Justin sets out that his faith is a philosophy under Christ who is consistent with the witness of the prophets. This needs to be understood in contrast to philosophers, or any kind of school, who follow a leader who puts forward his own opinions rather than the "truth," the prophetic words of god; Justin notes that there are many who are *called* or seem to be "Christians" but who fail to live by the words of god through Christ, who in fact follow a different philosophy. The strongest possible way to pay lip service to Christ but to betray him simultaneously would be to deny his Father, to blaspheme against the one who sent him. Even if other "heretical" groups can be considered threatening to Justin also, which I do not deny, Marcion, the one he calls a contemporary, is the most prominent of these and the only one to whom he dedicated an entire piece in itself, the now-lost πρὸς Μαρκίωνα.

Chapter 2 considered the evidence from the *Dialogue* for Marcion's significance to Justin. This proceeded in a thematic manner demonstrating that the topics Justin discussed and the way he discussed them were frequently suggestive of a contra-Marcionite agenda; that the things he affirmed were more than coincidentally things which Marcion, and sometimes only Marcion among "heretics," would most strongly want to deny. This began with the sometimes-overlooked introductory section to the *Dialogue*, which deals with the concept of philosophy and introduces the prophets. In this section we saw that, in addition to establishing the notion of novel and vain human teaching in contrast to true inspired and demonstrable philosophy, Justin introduced major themes, themes which are resonantly contra-Marcionite, evidenced throughout the text. These themes include the number of gods there are, the creator, the god of the "Jews" as the one true god, the providence, mercy, and compassion of this god towards humankind, his justice and righteousness, and the prophets who predicted that Christ would come forward from *this* god. These themes are established in the introduction, and define the rest of the work, outlining a vision of the "Christian" philosophy that strongly contradicts the Marcionite vision. This contra-Marcionite agenda is confirmed by the extended attention Justin gives to "heretical" "Christians" in *Dial.* 35 and 80, both of which overlap considerably with things said explicitly of Marcion, most notably the words of Jesus himself that there will be deceivers who are wolves in sheep's clothing (in *Dial.* 35.3 and *1 Apol.* 16.13): this resonates with Justin's description of Marcion at *1 Apol.* 58.2 as a wolf who deceives and carries away the lambs who are Christ's followers and does so with the help of devils. Therefore, despite only mentioning Marcionites once, the form of the *Dialogue* itself as well its specific descriptions of those who should not be considered "Christians" is strongly suggestive of an implicit contra-Marcionite agenda.

Chapter 3 turned our attention to *1 Apology* and the political dimension of Justin's trying to distinguish the followers of Christ from Marcion before the Roman rulers. Further examination of the rulers' understanding of "Christians" here confirmed what had been raised in chapter 1, that the rulers did not have a clear or focused understanding of "what" "Christians" were, nor necessarily distinguished them completely from "Jews" in this period. This of course made Justin's case of distinction from Marcionites more pressing because Marcion's vision of following Christ surrendered the heritage of Israel due to "Christians," and therefore presented them to the Romans as following a novel superstition worshipping an unknown or invented god, thereby running the risk of being seen as an atheistic, secretive, and political threat to the Roman order. Added to this, these people would be seen as converts from their native traditions to this new superstition, which would also have been to the distaste of the Roman authorities. Only the universality of Justin's basic and true philosophy can avoid this latter suspicion and maintain links with Israel in an at least potentially legitimate way for the Romans.

In this chapter we saw Justin's efforts to convince the rulers that "Christians" are not atheists, and thus his implicit condemnation of Marcionites as atheists. This was because the non-atheistic status of "Christians" is predicated only on the worship of the one true god which Marcion, and no other heretic, denies is part of the "Christian" faith. Carrying his case forward, it was shown how Justin presented the work and role of the demons in this world to frustrate and conceal the work and love of the one true god, the god of Israel. This was the reason the rulers had failed to recognize the fundamental and universal philosophy which comes from god. The crucial point for our purposes, however, is that on both occasions where Justin mentions Marcion by name in *1 Apology* he is presented as working with or under the influence of the demons. This being the case, he could not possibly be a "Christian" because his life and work is to frustrate the work of the one true god and keep others away from the truth. The strong implication, then, is that any who deny the creator as god and claim to be "Christians" are agents of the demons and ought to be punished, or at least avoided, as demoniacs not "Christians."

Marcionites may well confess Christ at trial, but it is Justin's contention that they confess *another* Christ and *another* god different from those of the "Christians." In a different way than the *Dialogue*, but no less significantly, *1 Apology* establishes the worship of the one true god, the god of Israel, as the central and minimum tenet of being a follower of Christ. These texts together argue strongly for this in order to define this philosophy so that it can be distinguished from the novel and politically suspect Marcionite philosophy. Justin may well only mention Marcion and his followers on a few occasions, but his agenda is so focused on asserting what Marcion denied and what his community threatened to undermine that the specter of Marcion in these texts has to be recognized as greater than the few direct references Justin gives. It is very unfortunate that πρὸς Μαρκίωνα, known to Justin's successors, is unavailable to us in order to see what detail Justin went into and what additional claims he might have made in making this agenda more explicit. Despite this, however, there is more than enough evidence in the *Dialogue* and the *Apologies* to discern how and why Justin sought to clarify and define what it is to follow Christ, and to do so in a way that clearly separates "Christians" from Marcionites in much the same way that Marcion wanted to distinguish "Christians" from "Jews."

Bibliography

Ancient Texts

Dio, Cassius. *Dio's Roman History*. Translated by E. Cary and H. B. Foster. London: Heinemann; Cambridge, MA: Harvard University Press, 1925.

Diognetus. *The Epistle to Diognetus (with the Fragment of Quadratus)*. Edited by C. N. Jefford. Oxford: Oxford University Press, 2013.

Epiphanes. *The Panarion of St. Epiphanius, Bishop of Salamis*. Translated by P. R. Amidon. New York: Oxford University Press, 1990.

Eusebius. *Chronicorum Canonum*, vol. 2. Edited by A. Schoene. Berlin: Weidemann.

———. *The Ecclesiastical History*, vols. 1 & 2. Translated by K. Lake. London: Heinemann, 1949.

Irenaeus of Lyon. *Against the Heresies book II*. Translated by D.J. Unger. New York: Paulist, 2012.

———. *Contre Les Hérésies*. Translated by A. Rousseau. Paris: Cerf, 1965.

———. *On the Apostolic Preaching*. Translated by John Behr. PPS. Crestwood, NY: St. Vladimir's Seminary Press, 1997.

Josephus, Flavius. *The Jewish War, Books IV-VII*. Translated by H. St. J. Thackeray. London: Heinemann; Cambridge, MA: Harvard University Press, 1928.

———. *The Life and Against Apion*. Translated by H. St. J. Thackery. London: Heinemann; Cambridge, MA: Harvard University Press, 1926.

Justin Martyr. *Apologies*. Pages 80-323 in *Justin, Philosopher and Martyr: Apologies*. Translated by Denis Minns and Paul Parvis. Oxford: Oxford University Press, 2009.

_____. *Dialogue avec Tryphon*. Translated by Philippe Bobichon. Fribourg: Academic Press Fribourg, 2003.

_____. *Dialogue with Trypho*. Edited by Michael Slusser. Translated by Thomas B. Falls. Washington, DC: Catholic University of America Press, 2003.

_____. *The Dialogue with Trypho*. Translated by L. Williams. London: SPCK, 1930.

Pliny the Younger. *C. Plinii Caecilii Secundi Epistulae ad Traianum imperatorem cum eiusdem responsis*. Edited by E. G. Hardy. London: Macmillan, 1889.

_____. *Complete Letters*. Translated by P. G. Walsh. Oxford: Oxford University Press, 2009.

_____. *Correspondence with Trajan from Bithynia (Epistles X)*. Translated by Wynne Williams. Warminster: Aris & Philips, 1990.

Severus, Sulpicius. *Libri qui supersunt*. Edited by Karl Halm. Vienna: Geroldi, 1866.

Suetonius. *The Twelve Caesars*. Translated by R. Graves and Michael Grant. Harmondsworth, UK: Penguin, 1989.

Tacitus, Cornelius. *Annals*. Translated by R. Mellor. Oxford: Oxford University Press, 2011.

_____. *Annals of Tacitus, vol. II: Books XI-XVI*. Translated by H. Furneaux. Oxford: Clarendon, 1907.

Tertullian. *Adversus Marcionem*. Translated by E. Evans. Oxford: Oxford University Press, 1972.

_____. *Apologeticus*. Edited by J. E. B. Mayor. Translated by A. Souter. Cambridge, UK: Cambridge University Press, 1971.

Modern Texts

Abusch, Ra'anan. "Negotiating Difference: Genital Mutilation in Roman Slave Law and the History of the Bar Kokhba Revolt." Pages 71-91 in *The Bar Kokhba War Reconsidered*. Edited by Peter Schäfer. Tübingen: Mohr Siebeck, 2003.

Alexander, Loveday. "Paul and the Hellenistic Schools: The Evidence of Galen." Pages 60-83 in *Paul in his Hellenistic Context*. Edited by Troels Engberg-Pedersen. Edinburgh: T&T Clark, 1994.

Aveling, J. C. H. *The Jesuits*. London: Blond & Briggs, 1981.

Barnard, Leslie William. *Justin Martyr: His Life and Thought*. Cambridge, UK: Cambridge University Press, 1967.

Bauckham, Richard. "The Two Fig Tree Parables in the Apocalypse of Peter." *JBL* 104 (1985): 269–87.

Beard, Mary, North, John and Price, Simon, ed. *Religions of Rome*: 1 vol. *A History*. Cambridge, UK: Cambridge University Press, 1998.

Beer, Vladimir de. "The Patristic Reception of Hellenic Philosophy." *SVTQ* 55 (2012): 373–98.

Bellinzoni, A. J. *The Sayings of Jesus in the Writings of Justin Martyr*. Leiden: Brill, 1967.

Blanchetière, François. "The Threefold Christian Anti-Judaism." Pages 185–210 in *Tolerance and Intolerance in Early Judaism and Christianity*. Edited by Graham Stanton and Guy B. Stroumsa. Cambridge, UK: Cambridge University Press, 1998.

Boulluec, Alain le. *La Notion d'hérésie dans la littérature grecque IIe-IIe siècles*. Paris: Etudes Augustiniennes, 1985.

Boyarin, Daniel. *Border Lines: The Partition of Judaeo-Christianity*. Philadelphia: University of Pennsylvania Press, 2007.

———. "Justin Martyr Invents Judaism." *CH* 70 (2001): 427–61.

———. "Rethinking Jewish Christianity: An Argument for Dismantling a Dubious Category (to which is Appended a Correction of my *Border Lines*)." *JQR* 99 (2009): 7–36.

———. "Semantic Differences; or, 'Judaism'/Christianity." Pages 65–86 in *The Ways that Never Parted*. Edited by Adam H. Becker and Annette Y. Reed. Tübingen: Mohr Siebeck, 2003.

Bradatan, Costica. "Faith and Persuasion in Berkeley's Alciphron." *HeyJ* 47 (2006): 545–61.

Buck, Lorraine. "Justin Martyr's Apologies: Their Number, Destination and Form." *JTS* 54 (2003): 45–59.

Buell, Denise Kimber. "God's Own People: Spectres of Race, Ethnicity, and Gender in Early Christian Studies." Pages 159–90 in *Prejudice and Christian Beginnings: Investigating Race, Gender, and Ethnicity in Early Christian Studies*. Edited by Laura Nasrallah and Elisabeth Schussler Fiorenza. Minneapolis: Fortress, 2009.

———. "Race and Universalism in Early Christianity." *JECS* 10 (2002): 429–68.

———. "Rethinking the Relevance of Race for Early Christian Self-Identity." *HThR* 94 (2001): 449–76.

———. *Why This New Race: Ethnic Reasoning in Early Christianity.* New York: Colombia University Press, 2005.

Calciu-Hanga, Rodica. "Semantic change in the age of corpus Linguistics." *JHSS* 1 (2012): 45–58.

Chilton, Bruce. "Justin and Israelite Prophecy." Pages 77–87 in *Justin Martyr and His Worlds.* Edited by Sara Parvis and Paul Foster. Minneapolis: Fortress, 2007.

Cotton, Hannah M. "The Bar Kokhba Revolt and the Documents from the Judaean Desert: Nabataean Participation in the Revolt (*P. Yadin* 52)." Pages 133–52 in *The Bar Kokhba War Reconsidered.* Edited by Peter Schäfer. Tübingen: Mohr Siebeck, 2003.

Croix, G.E.M. de Ste. "Why were the Early Christians Persecuted?" Pages 105–52 in *Christian, Persecution, Martyrdom, and Orthodoxy.* Edited by Michael Whitby and Joseph Streeter. Oxford: Oxford University Press, 2006.

Davies, Jason P. "Justin Martyr and the Restoration of Philosophy." *CH* 56 (1987): 303–19.

———. *Rome's Religious History: Livy, Tacitus and Ammianuns on their Gods.* Cambridge, UK: Cambridge University Press, 2004.

Downing, F. Gerald. "Pliny's Prosecutions of Christians: Revelation and 1 Peter." *JSNT* 34 (1988): 105–23.

Drijvers, Han. "Syrian Christianity and Judaism." Pages 124–47 in *The Jews Among Pagans and Christians: In the Roman Empire.* Edited by Judith Lieu, John North, and Tessa Rajak. London: Routledge, 1992.

Droge, Arthur J. *Homer or Moses? Early Christian Interpretations of the History of Culture.* Tübingen: Mohr Siebeck, 1989.

Feldman, Louis H. *Jew and Gentile in the Ancient World.* Princeton: Princeton University Press, 1993.

Fredriksen, Paula. "What 'Parting of the Ways?'" Pages 36–63 in *The Ways that Never Parted.* Edited by Adam H. Becker and Annette Y. Reed. Tübingen: Mohr Siebeck, 2003.

Gibbon, Edward. *The History of the Decline and Fall of the Roman Empire, Vol. II.* London: Dent, 1966.

Grant, Robert M. *The Greek Apologists of the Second Century.* London: SCM, 1988.

———. "A Woman of Rome: The Matron in Justin, *2 Apology* 2.1-9." *CH* 54 (1985): 461-72.

Goodenough, Erwin R. *The Theology of Justin Martyr.* Amsterdam: Philo, 1968; repr., Jena: Frommannsche Buchhandlung, 1923.

Goodman, Martin. "Diaspora Reactions to the Destruction of the Temple." Pages 27-38 in *Jews and Christians: The Parting of the Ways A.D. 70 to 135.* Edited by James Dunn. Tübingen: Mohr Siebeck, 1992.

Gordon, Richard. "Superstitio, Superstition and Religious Repression in the Late Roman Republic and Principate (100 BCE-300 CE)." *Past Present* 199 (2008): 72-94.

Hadot, Pierre. *Philosophy as a Way of Life: Spiritual Exercises from Socrates to Foucault.* Oxford: Blackwell, 1995.

Haley, Shelly P. "Be Not Afraid of the Dark: Critical Race Theory and Classical Studies." Pages 27-49 in *Prejudice and Christian Beginnings: Investigating Race, Gender, and Ethnicity in Early Christian Studies.* Edited by Laura Nasrallah and Elisabeth Schussler Fiorenza. Minneapolis: Fortress, 2009.

Harris, Murray J. *The Second Epistle to the Corinthians.* Grand Rapids: Eerdmans, 2005.

Harnack, Adolf. *History of Dogma*, vol. 1. Translated by Neil Buchcanan. Boston: Roberts, 1895.

———. *Marcion: The Gospel of the Alien God.* Translated by J. E. Steely and L. D. Bierma. Durham, NC: Labyrinth, 1990.

Heemstra, Marius. *The Fiscus Judaicus and the Parting of the Ways.* WUNT 277. Tübingen: Mohr Siebeck, 2010.

Hill, Charles E. *From the Lost Teaching of Polycarp: Identifying Irenaeus' Apostolic Presbyter and the Author of* Ad Diognetum. WUNT 186. Tübingen: Mohr Siebeck, 2006.

Hofer, Andrew. "The Old Man as Christ in Justin's Dialogue with Trypho." *VC* 57 (2003): 1-21.

Horbury, William. *Jews and Christian in Contact and Controversy.* Edinburgh: T&T Clark, 1998.

Horner, Timothy J. *Listening to Trypho: Justin Martyr's Dialogue Reconsidered.* Leuven: Peeters, 2001.

Hyldahl, Niels. *Philosophie Und Christentum: Eine Interpretation der Einleitung zum Dialog Justins.* AtDan 9. Kopenhagen: Munksgaard, 1966.

Isaac, Benjamin. "Roman Religious Policy and the Bar Kokhba War." Pages 37–54 in *The Bar Kokhba War Reconsidered.* Edited by Peter Schäfer. Tübingen: Mohr Siebeck, 2003.

Jacobs, Andrew S. "Dialogical Differences: (De-)Judaizing Jesus' Circumcision." *JECS* 15 (2007): 291–335.

Janssen, L. F. "'Superstitio' and the Persecution of the Christians." *VC* 33 (1979): 131–59.

Jossa, Giorgio. *Jews or Christians? The Followers of Jesus in Search of their own Identity.* Tübingen: Mohr Siebeck, 2006.

Katz, Steven T. "The Rabbinic Response to Christianity." Pages 259–98 in *The Cambridge History of Judaism: Volume Four the Late Roman-Rabbinic Period.* Edited by Steven T. Katz. Cambridge, UK: Cambridge University Press, 2006.

Kimelman, Reuven. "Rabbinic Prayer in Late Antiquity." Pages 573–611 in *The Cambridge History of Judaism, Vol. 4: the Late Roman-Rabbinic Period.* Edited by Steven T. Katz. Cambridge, UK: Cambridge University Press, 2006.

Klinghardt, Matthias. *Das älteste Evangelium und die Entstehung der kanonischen Evangelien.* 2 vols. Tübingen: Francke, 2015.

Kooten, George H. van. "Is Early Christianity a Religion or a Philosophy?" Pages 393–408 in *Myths, Martyrs and Modernity: Studies in the History of Religions in Honour of Jan N. Bremmer.* Edited by Jitse Dijkstra, Justin Kroesen, and Yme Kuiper. Leiden: Brill, 2010.

Lampe, Peter. *From Paul to Valentinus.* Minneapolis: Fortress, 2003.

Layton, Bentley. "Accusations of Jewish persecution in early Christian sources, with particular reference to Justin Martyr and the Martyrdom of Polycarp." Pages 279–95 in *Tolerance and Intolerance in Early Judaism and Christianity.* Edited by Graham Stanton and Guy B. Stroumsa. Cambridge, UK: Cambridge University Press, 1998.

Lieu, Judith. *Christian Identity in the Jewish and Graeco-Roman World.* Oxford: Oxford University Press, 2004.

———. *Image and Reality: The Jews in the World of the Christians in the Second Century.* Edinburgh: T&T Clark, 1996.

———. *Marcion and the Marking of a Heretic: God and Scripture in the Second Century.* Cambridge, UK: Cambridge University Press, 2015.

———. *Neither Jew nor Greek.* Edinburgh: T&T Clark, 2003.

———. "The Significance of Basilides in Ancient Christian Thought." *Representations* 28 (1989): 135–51.

Livesey, Nina E. "Theological Identity Making: Justin's Use of Circumcision to Create Jews and Christians." *JECS* 18 (2010): 51–79.

Löhr, Winrich. "Did Marcion distinguish between a just god and a good god?" Pages 131–46 in *Marcion und seine kirchengeschichtliche Wirkung: Marcion and His Impact on Church History.* Edited by Gerhard May, Katharina Greschat, and Martin Meiser. TU 150. Berlin: de Gruyter, 2002.

Lyman, Rebecca. "The Politics of Passing: Justin Martyr's Conversion as a Problem of 'Hellenization.'" Pages in 36–50 in *Conversion in Late Antiquity and the Early Middle Ages: Seeing and Believing.* Edited by Kenneth Mills and Anthony Grafton. Rochester, NY: University of Rochester Press, 2003.

Nasrallah, Laura S. "Mapping the World: Justin, Tatian, Lucian, and the Second Sophistic." *HThR* 98 (2005): 283–314.

———. "The Rhetoric of Conversion and the Construction of Experience." *StPatr* 40 (2006): 467–74.

Nilson, Jon. "To Whom is Justin's *Dialogue with Trypho* Addressed?" *TS* 38 (1977): 538–46.

Norelli, Enrico. "Marcion: ein chrstlicher Philosoph oder ein Christ gegen die Philosophie?" Pages 113–30 in *Marcion und seine kirchengeschichtliche Wirkung: Marcion and His Impact on Church History.* Edited by Gerhard May, Katharina Greschat, and Martin Meiser. TU 150. Berlin: de Gruyter, 2002.

MacIntyre, Alasdair. *After Virtue.* London: Duckworth, 1985.

Malkin, Irad. "Greek Ambiguities: 'Ancient Hellas' and 'Barbarian Epirus.'" Pages 187–212 in *Ancient Perceptions of Greek Ethnicity.* Edited by Irad Malkin. Washington, DC: Centre for Hellenic Studies; Cambridge: Harvard University Press, 2001.

———. "Introduction." Pages 1–28 in *Ancient Perceptions of Greek Ethnicity.* Edited by Irad Malkin. Washington, DC: Centre for Hellenic Studies; Cambridge, MA: Harvard University Press, 2001.

Moll, Sebastian. *The Arch-Heretic Marcion.* Tübingen: Mohr Siebeck, 2010.

_____. "Justin and the Pontic Wolf." Pages 145–51 in *Justin Martyr and His Worlds.* Edited by Sara Parvis and Paul Foster. Minneapolis: Fortress, 2007.

Osborn, Eric F. *Justin Martyr.* Tübingen: Mohr Siebeck, 1973.

Parvis, Paul. "Justin, Philosopher and Martyr." Pages 22–38 in *Justin Martyr and His Worlds.* Edited by Sara Parvis and Paul Foster. Minneapolis: Fortress, 2007.

Parvis, Sara. "Justin Martyr and the Apologetic Tradition." Pages 115–28 in *Justin Martyr and His Worlds.* Edited by Sara Parvis and Paul Foster. Minneapolis: Fortress, 2007.

Parvis, Sara, and Paul Foster. "Introduction: Justin Martyr and His Worlds." Pages 1–10 in *Justin Martyr and His Worlds.* Edited by Sara Parvis and Paul Foster. Minneapolis: Fortress, 2007.

Pelikan, Jaroslav. "De-Judaization and Hellenization: The Ambiguities of Christian Identity." Pages 81–124 in *The Dynamic in Christian Thought.* Edited by Joseph Papin. Philadelphia: Villanova University Press, 1970.

Perkins, Judith. *The Suffering Self: Pain and narrative representation in early Christianity.* London: Routledge, 1995.

Raisanen, Heikki. *Marcion, Muhammad and the Mahatma: Exegetical Perspectives on the Encounter of Cultures and Faiths.* London: SCM, 1997.

Reed, Annette Yoshiko. "The Trickery of the Fallen Angels and Demonic Mimesis of the Divine: Aetiology, Demonology, and Polemics in the Writings of Justin Martyr." *JECS* 12 (2004): 141–71.

Rengstorf, K.H. Χριστιανός (Christianos), Christian." Page 343 in *The New International Dictionary of New Testament Theology,* vol. 2. Edited by Colin Brown. Grand Rapids: Zondervan; Exeter, UK: Paternoster, 1975.

Rives, James B. *Religion in the Roman Empire.* Oxford: Wiley-Blackwell, 2007.

Robinson, Armitage J. "On a Quotation from Justin Martyr in Irenaeus." *JTS* 31 (1930): 373–78.

Roth, Dieter T. "Marcion and Marcionites." In *The Encyclopedia of Ancient History.* Edited by Roger S. Bagnall et al. Oxford: Wiley-Blackwell, 2012. Online:

http://onlinelibrary.wiley.com/doi/10.1002/9781444338386.wbeah05110/pdf.

———. "Marcion's Gospel: Relevance, Contested Issues, Reconstruction." *ExpTim* 121 (2010), 287–94.

———. "Marcion's Gospel and Luke: The History of Research in Current Debate." *JBL* 27 (2008): 513–27.

———. *The Text of Marcion's Gospel.* Leiden: Brill, 2015.

Royalty, Robert M., Jr. "Justin's Conversion and the Rhetoric of Heresy." *StPatr* 40 (2006): 509–14.

Schäfer, Peter. "Bar Kokhba and the Rabbis." Pages 1–22 in *The Bar Kokhba War Reconsidered.* Edited by Peter Schäfer. Tübingen: Mohr Siebeck, 2003.

———. *Judeophobia: Attitudes Toward the Jews in the Ancient World.* Cambridge, MA: Harvard University Press, 1997.

Schoedel, William R. "Christian "Atheism" and the Peace of the Roman Empire." *CH* 42 (1973): 309–19.

Sedley, David. "Philosophical Allegiance in the Graeco-Roman World." Pages 97–119 in *Philosophia Togata.* Edited by Miriam Griffin and Jonathan Barnes. Oxford: Clarendon, 1989.

Skarsaune, Oskar. "The Conversion of Justin Martyr." *ST* 30 (1976): 53–73.

———. "Justin and the Apologists." Pages 121–36 in *The Routledge Companion to Early Christian Thought.* Edited by Jeffrey D. Bingham. London: Routledge, 2010.

———. *The Proof from Prophecy.* Leiden: Brill, 1987.

Slusser, Michael. "How Much Did Irenaeus Learn from Justin?" *StPatr* 40 (2006): 515–20.

———. "Justin Scholarship: Trends and Trajectories." Pages 13–21 in *Justin Martyr and His Worlds.* Edited by Sara Parvis and Paul Foster. Minneapolis: Fortress, 2007.

Smith, James K.A. *Letters to a Young Calvinist.* Grand Rapids: Brazos, 2010.

Stanton, Graham. "Justin Martyr's *Dialogue with Trypho*: Group Boundaries, 'Proselytes' and 'God-fearers.'" Pages 279–95 in *Tolerance and Intolerance in Early Judaism and Christianity.* Edited by Graham Stanton and Guy B. Stroumsa. Cambridge, UK: Cambridge University Press, 1998.

Stroumsa, Guy B. *The End of Sacrifice: Religious Transformations in Late Antiquity.* Chicago: Univeristy of Chicago Press, 2012.

Stylianopoulos, Theodore. *Justin Martyr and the Mosaic Law.* SBLDS. Missoula, MT: Scholars Press, 1975.

Thorsteinsson, Runar M. "The Literary Genre and Purpose of Justin's *Second Apology*: A Critical Review with Insights Ancient Epistolography." *HThR* 105 (2012): 91–114.

Tomson, Peter J. *If This Be from Heaven: Jesus and the New Testament Authors in their Relationship to Judaism.* Sheffield: Shefflied Academic, 2001.

———. "The Names Israel and Jew in Ancient Judaism and in the New Testament." *Bijdr* 47 (1986): 120–40.

Tropper, Amram. "Tractate Avot and Early Christian Succession Lists." Pages 159–88 in *The Ways that Never Parted.* Edited by Adam H. Becker and Annette Y. Reed. Tübingen: Mohr Siebeck, 2003.

Tyson, Joseph B. "Anti-Judaism in Marcion and His Opponents." *SCJR* 1 (2005–2006): 196–208.

Vinzent, Markus. *Christ's Resurrection in Early Christianity and the Making of the New Testament.* Franham: Ashgate, 2011.

———. "Give and Take amongst Second Century Authors: The Ascension of Isaiah, the Epistle of the Apostles and Marcion of Sinope." *StPatr* 50 (2011): 105–29.

———. *Marcion and the Dating of the Synoptic Gospels.* StPatr Supplements 2. Leuven: Peeters, 2014.

———. "Marcion the Jew." *JAAJ* 1 (2013): 159–201.

Walzer, Richard. *Galen on Jews and Christians.* Oxford: Oxford University Press, 1949.

Weis, P. R. "Some Samaritanisms of Justin Martyr." *JTS* 45 (1944): 199–205.

Widdicombe, Peter. "Irenaeus and the Knowledge of God as Father." Pages 141–50 in *Irenaeus: Life, Scripture, Legacy.* Edited by Sara Parvis and Paul Foster. Minneapolis: Fortress, 2012.

———. "Justin Martyr and the Fatherhood of God." *Laval théologique et philosophique* 54 (1998): 109–26.

Williams, Margaret H. *Jews in a Graeco-Roman Environment.* Tübingen: Mohr Siebeck, 2013.

Winden, J. C. M. van. *An Early Christian Philosopher: Justin Martyr's* Dialogue with Trypho, *Chapters One to Nine: Introduction, Text, and Commentary.* Leiden: Brill, 1971.

Wischmeyer, Wolfgang. "A Christian? What's That? On the Difficulty of Managing Christian Diversity in Late Antiquity." *StPatr* 34 (2001): 270–81.

Young, M. O. "Justin, Socrates, and the Middle Platonists." *StPatr* 28 (1989): 161–65.

Zetterholm, Magnus. *The Formation of Christianity in Antioch: A Sociological Approach to the Separation between Judaism and Christianity.* London: Routledge, 2003.

Ancient Literature Index

Cassius Dio,
Romom History
69.13.2......19

Diognetus
The Epistle to Diognetus
4.6–5.4......27, 29

Epiphanius
Panarion
33.3.2......xxvii
3.4.1......152
3.3.5......161
3.4.5......161

Eusebius
Chronicorum Canonum
660, 18......17

Ecclesiastical History
5.16.21......209

Irenaeus
Against the Heresies
1.27.2......xxvi–xxvii, xxxiv
3.12.12......xxvii
3.25.2......xxvi
3.25.3......xxvi
4.6.2......123
4.34.1......xxxiii
4.35.15......xxxiii

Josephus
The Jewish War
7.3.3......171

Against Apion
2.148......176

Origen
On First Principles
2.5.2......xxxii

Pliny the Younger
Ep. Tra.
10.96.3......42

10.96.8......43

Sulpicius Severus
Chron.
2.30.7......41

Suetonius
Nero
16.2......165

Tacitus
Ann. 15.44.4......9, 41

Tertullian
Adversus Marcionem
1.2.2......180
1.2.3......xxxiii, 198
1.2.7......180
1.9.2......xxxiii
1.25.2......xxvi

2.9.1......103
2.11.1......xxvi
2.21.2......xxxii
3.5:4......xxxii
3.6.2......xxxii
3.7.1......xxxii
3.12.1......xxvii
3.15.7......122
4.6.3......159
4.33.4......xxiv

De carne Christi
1.10......152

De Resurrectione Carnis
2.10......161

Apologeticus
18.4......49

Author Index

Bauckham, Richard, 18
Barnard, Leslie William, 92, 93, 118
Bellinzoni, A. J., 197-98, 204
Bobichon, Philippe, 94, 116, 126,
    130-31, 134-35, 142-43, 145, 149,
    152-53, 159, 161
Boyarin, Daniel, 3, 8, 9, 13, 14, 26,
    38, 65, 66
Buell, Denise Kimber, 3, 6, 7, 9, 26,
    28, 29, 33, 39, 43, 49, 84, 90, 99

de Ste Croix, G. E. M., 45, 48, 170,
    173, 179

Foster, Paul, xi, 1

Grant, Robert M., 2
Goodenough, Erwin R., 92-93, 95,
    113, 119

Horner, Timothy J., 10-11, 23-25,
    98, 108, 129-30
Hyldahl, Niels, 92, 102, 108

Isaac, Benjamin, 41

Jacobs, Andrew S, 14-15, 25, 89-90

Katz, Steven T, 23, 47

Lieu, Judith, xix, xxii, xxiii, xxvi,
    xxv, 6, 9, 10, 13, 17, 36, 37, 93,
    142
Livesey, Nina E, 14, 34
Löhr, Winrich, xxvi-xxx, 195
Lyman, Rebecca, 6, 60, 90, 216

Minns, Denis, xvii, 70, 76, 122, 184,
    188-89, 196, 200-202, 206, 208,
    210-11, 213-15
Moll, Sebastian, xix-xxxii, 6, 138,
    180, 195, 214

Nasrallah, Laura S., 6, 27, 28, 29, 30,
    90, 96, 99, 117, 118, 119
Nilson, Jon, xi, xiii, 90
Norelli, Enrico, xxx-xxxi

Parvis, Paul, xvii, 70, 76, 122, 184, 188–89, 196, 200–202, 206, 208, 210–11, 213–15

Reed, Annette Y., xii, 34, 106, 185, 187, 213
Roth, Dieter T., xix, xx, xxv

Sara Parvis, xi, 1
Schäfer, Peter, 17, 19, 41, 50, 168, 173
Skarsaune, Oskar, 18, 31, 45, 60, 66, 91, 97, 106, 108, 109, 121, 124, 132, 133, 140, 154, 185
Slusser, Michael, xxv
Stanton, Graham, vii, 14, 36, 50, 100
Stroumsa, Guy B., 14, 36, 45, 47, 50

Stylianopoulos, Theodore, 90, 93–94, 110, 136

Thorsteinsson, Runar M., xvii, 55
Tomson, Peter J., 7–8, 10, 30

van Kooten, George H., 67, 102
Von Harnack, Adolf, xix, xx, xxii–xxviii, xxxii–xxxvi, 2, 92, 214

Van Winden, J. C. M, xv, 92–93, 98, 102, 107–8, 112, 114, 116, 119–20, 125